For Rabbi Weissberg
with warm regards (and
gratitude!) from the Mumbles
author.

    Hillel Kieval
    June 1995

The Making of Czech Jewry

STUDIES IN JEWISH HISTORY
Jehuda Reinharz, General Editor

MOSHE ZIMMERMAN
Wilhelm Marr:
The Patriarch of Antisemitism

JEHUDA REINHARZ
Chaim Weizmann:
The Making of a Zionist Leader, paperback edition

JACK WERTHEIMER
Unwelcome Strangers:
East European Jews in Imperial Germany

JACQUES ADLER
The Jews of Paris and the Final Solution:
Communal Response and Internal Conflicts, 1940–1944

BEN HALPERN
A Clash of Heroes:
Brandeis, Weizmann, and American Zionism

HILLEL J. KIEVAL
The Making of Czech Jewry:
National Conflict and Jewish Society in Bohemia, 1870–1918

OTHER VOLUMES ARE IN PREPARATION

THE MAKING OF CZECH JEWRY

National Conflict and Jewish Society in Bohemia, 1870–1918

Hillel J. Kieval

New York   Oxford
OXFORD UNIVERSITY PRESS
1988

Oxford University Press

Oxford   New York   Toronto
Delhi   Bombay   Calcutta   Madras   Karachi
Petaling Jaya   Singapore   Hong Kong   Tokyo
Nairobi   Dar es Salaam   Cape Town
Melbourne   Auckland

and associated companies in
Berlin   Ibadan

Published by Oxford University Press, Inc.,
200 Madison Avenue, New York, New York 10016

Oxford is a registered trademark of Oxford University Press

Library of Congress Cataloging-in-Publication Data

Kieval, Hillel J.
The making of Czech Jewry.

(Studies in Jewish history)
Bibliography: p.
Includes index.
1. Jews—Czechoslovakia—Bohemia—Cultural assimila-
tion. 2. Zionism—Czechoslovakia—Prague. 3. Bohemia
(Czechoslovakia)—Ethnic relations. I. Title.
II. Series.
DS135.C96B638   1988   305.8′924′04371   87-1597
ISBN 0-19-504057-0 (alk. paper)

2 4 6 8 9 7 5 3 1

Printed in the United States of America
on acid-free paper

To Patti, Michael, and Shira.

Marrying, founding a family, accepting all the children that come, supporting them in this insecure world and perhaps even guiding them a little, is, I am convinced, the utmost a human being can succeed in doing at all.

Franz Kafka, *Letter to His Father.*

Acknowledgments

My research on the formation of modern Czech Jewry has taken me to many libraries and archival collections in the United States, Czechoslovakia, and Israel. I would like to take this opportunity to express my thanks to those institutions that so generously made their materials available to me: Widener Library at Harvard University (special thanks here go to Charles Berlin, head of the Judaica Collection, and to Zuzana Nagy of the Slavic Division); the Jewish National and University Library in Jerusalem; the Leo Baeck Institute in New York (Fred Grubel, Secretary); Goldfarb Library at Brandeis University (and in particular to Charles Cutter and James Rosenbloom of the Judaica Division); the Univerzitní Knihovna, the Národní Muzeum, and the Památník Národního Písemnictví, all in Prague.

To the administrators and research personnel of a number of specialized archives worldwide, I owe special thanks. These individuals include Mordechai Nadav, Director of the Archives at the Jewish National and University Library in Jerusalem, and his colleagues, Margot Cohn, Director of the Martin Buber and the Hugo Bergmann archives, and Reuven Klingsberg, Director of the Felix Weltsch and the Avigdor Dagan collections; Michael Heymann and I. Philipp of the Central Zionist Archives in Jerusalem; Sybil Milton and Michael Riff of the Archives and Library of the Leo Baeck Institute in New York; Josef David and the staff of the Archives of the Memorial for National Literature (Památník Národního Písemnictví) in Prague; and Jan Havránek of the Archiv Univerzity Karlovy in Prague. I extend particular gratitude to the scientific staff of the State Jewish Museum (Státní Židovské Muzeum) in Prague, to Vladimír Sadek, Head of Research, Bedřich Nosek, Head of Collections, and Miroslav Jaroš, former Director—all of whom not only welcomed my steady company for several months but also took pains to encourage my work and to offer help wherever possible.

For providing financial support during this long project, my thanks go to the International Research and Exchanges Board (IREX); the Graduate School Research Fund at the University of Washington; and the Tauber Institute for the Study of European Jewry at Brandeis University. I owe a tremendous debt of gratitude to the Society of Fellows at Harvard University, and to its Chairman Burton Dreben, who provided me with an intellectual home for three years and with the freedom to pursue my interests wherever they might lead.

I wish to acknowledge the many individuals at Oxford University Press who have worked hard to see this book through to completion: Nancy Lane, senior editor; Jehuda Reinharz, general editor of the series Studies in Jewish History; Marion Osmun; and Adrienne Mayor.

I also would like to thank the following presses for permitting me to reprint selections from several of my articles that have previously been published: The Johns Hopkins University Press, for permission to incorporate parts of "In the Image of Hus: Refashioning Czech Judaism in Post-Emancipatory Prague," *Modern Judaism* 5 (1985), in Chapters 2 and 3; and Oxford University Press, for permission to use parts of "Education and National Conflict in Bohemia: Germans, Czechs, and Jews," in Ezra Mendelsohn, ed., *Studies in Contemporary Jewry,* vol. 3 (New York, 1987), in Chapter 2. In Chapter 3, parts of "Nationalism and Antisemitism: The Czech-Jewish Response" have been republished from *Living With Antisemitism: Modern Jewish Responses,* edited by Jehuda Reinharz, by permission of University Press of New England. Copyright © 1987 by Trustees of Brandeis University.

To my teachers Franklin L. Ford and Yosef Hayim Yerushalmi, who have followed this project since its earliest stages, I offer thanks for their patience, their guidance, and their ultimate confidence in my abilities as a historian. The clarity of their thought and expression has long served as an inspiration for my own work.

Many individuals have read and commented on parts of this book in manuscript form over the years. I would like to mention in this regard Todd M. Endelman, William O. McCagg, Jehuda Reinharz, Stephen Schuker, Bernard Wasserstein, Eugene Black, Daniel Chirot, Joel S. Migdal, John Toews, Peter Sugar, and the other members of the History Research Group at the University of Washington, James D. Wilkinson, Milena Chelli, David Stern, Michael Silber, Michael Stanislawski, Peter Jelavich, Lois Dubin, Keith Pickus, and Philip Kieval. My thanks to all; I trust that I have been able to incorporate some of their very helpful suggestions. Whatever errors of fact and interpretation that remain are, of course, my own.

Lastly, it is to my wife Patti and to my children Michael Yaakov and Shira Deborah that this book is dedicated. They have sustained me throughout with love, understanding, and—at times inexplicable—good cheer.

Contents

The Making of Czech Jewry

Introduction

This book sets out to capture the dimensions of a society and culture in transition. Over the last third of the nineteenth century and the first decades of the twentieth, Bohemian Jewry underwent a number of transformations—demographic, occupational, political, and linguistic—changes which in my view altered Jewish society and culture in the Czech lands definitively. On one level, my goals are to identify both the agents and the circumstances of these changes, to examine the content of new ideological and cultural formulations, to assess the effects of these developments on Bohemian Jewry, as well as to place them in the larger context of East Central Europe.

My principal aims, however, lie in the areas of interpretation and explanation. In contrast to the prevailing picture of Prague and Bohemian Jewry as bastions of German culture and political liberalism in the middle of a hostile Slavic world—a world which, for all intents, lay far removed from Jewish culture—I shall be emphasizing the multiethnic character of the region, the linguistic dexterity and cultural ambiguity of its Jewish population, and the decisive impact of national conflict on the creation of Jewish attitudes and behavior in the twentieth century.[1]

Emblematic of this period of transition in Bohemian Jewish life were two large-scale, cultural experiments: the promotion of Jewish assimilation to the Czech nation and to its linguistic culture (which I shall refer to, in its institutional context, as the "Czech-Jewish movement"); and the elaboration of a specifically Jewish national program, an alternative to both German and Czech assimilation ("Prague Zionism"). The book pays special attention to these two poles of Jewish cultural *engagement.* Not only do they highlight the extent of Jewish disenchantment with the Austrian-German consensus of the emancipatory period (1780–1870), but they also serve as guideposts for the potential directions that Jewish attitudes and behavior would take down to the outbreak of the Second World War. In following the careers of these

3

cultural bellwethers until the start of the Czechoslovak Republic, I hope to be able to reveal their major strengths and weaknesses, contrast their basic concerns as well as their solutions to national conflict, and assess their respective prospects for the leadership of Czech Jewry under the new political order after 1918.

Prague Zionism and the Czech-Jewish movement offer variations on the single theme of cultural transformation. True, participants in the Czech-Jewish movement saw themselves as agents of cultural and national assimilation, while the Zionists were obsessed with the limits of the assimilatory process and with the elaboration of an independent cultural position. But the two movements grew out of a common historical context, developed interpretations of Jewish experience that shared crucial features, and even managed to arrive at a mutual appreciation of the other's role in the overall redirection of Jewish life in both the Habsburg state and its successor. Both the "Czech Jews" and the Zionists deliberately distanced themselves from the liberal German consensus of the mid-nineteenth century, seeking instead to create a modern Jewish culture more attuned to the multinational realities of East Central Europe.

In this sense in particular, modern Czech Jewry must be seen as having encompassed more than the narrowly assimilationist wing of the Jewish community. Rather, it was all that grew out of the transformation of "Bohemian" Jewry: the Czech national Jews; the discoverers of Jewish nationality; the bilingual, but nationally indifferent, mass of rural and smalltown Jews; the bridgebuilders between German and Czech culture; and the ever-dwindling number of defenders of the German cultural ideal. All of these tendencies are present in the modern Czech-Jewish community.

One important distinction between the Jewries of Central and Eastern Europe and those of the West is the fact that the former underwent two "modernizations" between the late Enlightenment and the end of the First World War, two distinct processes of prolonged, sociocultural change and adaptation. This study concentrates on the second stage of the modernization process in the Czech lands, to which I have applied the label "secondary acculturation."[2] The first stage of sustained cultural contact and adaptation stretched from about 1780 to 1870. It was this first modernization that witnessed the breakdown of the self-governing Jewish community; the establishment of a secular, Jewish school system; the entry of Jews into the secondary schools, the universities, and the professions; and the gradual restructuring of Jewish occupational and economic activities. This was the age of "Jewish emancipation," marked on one end by the absolutist reforms of Joseph II (coregent with Maria Theresa 1765–80, sole ruler 1780–90) and on the other by the recognition of full political equality in the Constitution of 1867.[3]

Joseph's accession to the Habsburg throne in 1780 ushered in an era of direct government interference in the affairs of the Jewish community and the institution of wide-ranging social, economic, and cultural reforms. The first salvo in a decade-long volley of proclamations and laws was also the most dramatic. The Edict of Toleration (*Toleranzpatent*), issued for Bohemia in October 1781, and for Moravia the following February, affirmed the principle of religious toleration (for Protestants and Orthodox Christians as well as for Jews), but, more important, it aimed at restructuring Jewish economic life and reorienting Jewish culture.[4] Joseph's expressed purpose in introducing the edict was neither to encourage Jewish settlement in his lands nor to remove the demographic restrictions under which Jews had long been living, but simply to render the Jews already living in Austria "more useful" to the state. To this end he opened all forms of trade and commerce to Jewish participation, encouraged Jews to establish factories, and urged them to engage more fully in artisanal production and agriculture. Unwilling, however, to challenge the status quo in the shop or the countryside, Joseph's order continued to bar Jews from attaining the degree of mastership or citizenship as well as from owning the plots of land that they were to farm.[5]

The most far-reaching changes occasioned by the Toleranzpatent took place not in the area of economic activity but rather in the cultural and educational realm. The government was in the process of redesigning the entire elementary school system in the country and, toward this end, invited all of the Jewish communities that were large enough to set up government-supervised schools of their own to instruct students in mathematics, geography, German language, and morality. Parents who lived in communities that could not afford to construct their own schools could send their children to Gentile establishments. Meanwhile the doors of the universities and institutions of higher education were declared open for Jewish enrollment.[6]

The Toleranzpatent erased in one stroke the use of Hebrew and Yiddish in business records. Subsequent edicts went on to bolster the cultural provisions of the Josephine reform and further transformed the social and legal character of the community. The juridical autonomy of the Jewish community in civil and criminal matters was suspended in 1784. An ordinance of 1786 made the granting of marriage certificates to Jews dependent on the parties' ability to demonstrate that they had attended a *Normalschule* (modern elementary school). Legislation the following year made the adoption of German personal and family names mandatory. In 1788 Jews were required to serve in the Austrian army. Finally, in 1797—in a law that was never completely enforced—the state required that all rabbis and cantors appointed by the Jewish community be able to produce a degree in philosophy from one of the monarchy's universities.[7]

Formal political emancipation for the Jews never entered into the thinking of Joseph II or his successor Leopold II. And, with the onset of political reaction following Leopold's death in 1792, even the processes of social and cultural integration began to slow down. A systematic review of recent Jewish legislation in 1797 (the so-called *Judensystemalpatent*) both acknowl-

edged and affirmed the extent to which the Jews of Austria had been incorporated into the state and society. But there was to be little additional legislation on the Jews until the revolutionary months of 1848–49.[8] From 1848 to
1867 a series of laws and constitutional decrees gradually removed all of the
remaining restrictions on Jewish life. The legal validity of the ghetto was
formally abolished in 1848, and Jews were permitted to reside in all areas of
Bohemia and Moravia. Emperor Franz Josef's Constitutional Edict of 1849
granted Jews equality with Christians under law. After 1859 the last barriers
to free economic activity and association were torn down, and the government also confirmed the right of Jews to own land. Finally, with the creation
of the Dual Monarchy (Austria-Hungary) in 1867, the state proclaimed the
full political emancipation of the Jews.[9]

One cannot overly stress the role that the German-Jewish Normalschule
played in redirecting Jewish culture both in Prague and in the Bohemian
countryside. It was in the area of educational policy, after all, that government interference in Jewish affairs and the ideology of the Jewish Enlightenment (*Haskalah*) most neatly coincided. The promise of directing the scope
and content of Jewish education for generations to come, of being able to
mold attitudes and behavior, loyalties and beliefs, captured the imaginations
of both Jewish illuminati and the Gentile authorities. The *maskilim* (Jewish
enlighteners) recognized in Joseph II's call for the establishment of the
German-Jewish school an invitation not only to alter the world view of
traditional Judaism, but also to create a new kind of Jewish individual,
educated in Western science and languages, committed to the use of reason
in determining questions of truth and value, loyal to king and to country,
and loving of his fellow citizen.[10]

Despite deep-seated suspicions on the part of Prague's rabbinical leadership of both the motives and the effects of Haskalah, figures such as Ezekiel
Landau (1713–93) and Elazar Fleckeles (1754–1826) ultimately gave their
approval to the educational reforms. Between 1790 and 1831, years during
which formal attendance records were kept, some 17,800 children received a
Western-style education at the Prague school. This figure represented a
yearly average of 424 students, approximately 40 percent of those who
would have been eligible to attend.[11] The surrounding communities of Bohemia proved to be at least as willing as Prague Jewry to support the government's educational program. A report for the year 1787, five years after the
project was begun, claimed that 559 students were attending twenty-five
rural Jewish schools; another 278 Jewish children had enrolled in Christian
schools in more than fifty different localities.[12] For the first several decades,
then, the majority of Prague's Jewish children did not attend the community
school. On the other hand, neither did the vast majority of those in places
such as Berlin or Frankfurt. Throughout this period wealthier families preferred to hire private tutors to teach in their homes; public education remained largely the domain of the poor and dispossessed. Over the next half-

century, however, German-Jewish acculturation progressed rapidly, affecting nearly all segments of Bohemian and Moravian Jewish society.

The acculturation of Bohemian Jewry which took place during the period of emancipation was predicated on the assumption that the German language and culture were to be the principal vehicles of social advancement and national integration. Already by the turn of the nineteenth century, however, new demographic and political realities would call such assumptions into question. Advances in universal education, together with the beginnings of urbanization and industrialization, began to produce an articulate, Czech-speaking middle class engaged in a full-fledged cultural and linguistic revival of its own. Virtually at the precise moment that the Jews of Bohemia could be found assiduously adopting the German language and assimilating German cultural patterns, an increasingly vociferous and influential group within Czech society was challenging the very position of German in the balance of political and cultural forces.

This is not to say that the Jews were oblivious to the changes that were going on about them. Although the majority of Jews, together with a great many Czechs, were content to reap the rewards of a German education and take advantage of the general flowering of German culture, a small number of intellectuals associated with the Young Bohemia literary movement thought differently. Writers and journalists such as Isidor Heller, Moritz Hartmann, Rudolf Glaser, and Siegfried Kapper advocated in the years preceding 1848 a program of political democracy based on a rapprochement between Slavs and Jews.[13] Hartmann, in his book of poems *Kelch und Schwert* (Chalice and sword, 1845), evoked the memory of the Czech reformer Jan Hus (c.1374–1415), and went so far as to liken the political plight of the Czech nation to the Jewish condition:

> You, martyr of the nations, / When will you rise
> up again? / For indeed, like Palestine's child, /
> Though not dispersed to the South and the
> North, / Your children have become homeless and
> strangers / in their own land.[14]

In 1844 David Kuh published a long essay in the *Allgemeine Zeitung des Judentums* entitled "A Word to Jews and Slavs," in which he argued that German culture's dominance in Austria had much to do with its ability to assimilate and combine a variety of cultural stimuli. He urged Czech leaders to look to the as-yet unassimilated mass of Bohemian Jews as a valuable reservoir of talent on which to draw in the creation of their own *Bildungsnation* (cultural nation).[15] Meanwhile, Siegfried Kapper (1821–79), the physician-poet, created some excitement in Czech literary circles in 1846 when his second volume of poetry, *České listy* (Czech leaves), appeared. It was the first work by a modern Jewish author to be written in Czech. In one poem he appealed directly to the Czech people not to exclude him from its national awakening:

> Only a non-Czech call me not, I pray, / For I too
> am a son of Czech domains! / The way your heart
> beats for your native land, / Thus fervently mine
> courses through the veins.
>
> What if my tribe once dwelt near Jordan's
> shores, / This need not break my brotherhood with
> thine! / Or is there a law to hinder my resolve./
> To place my heart and soul upon my country's
> shrine?[16]

Tentative efforts such as these at a Czech-Jewish alignment by and large went either unnoticed or unappreciated. Czech nationalism had not yet fully matured into a political movement for cultural autonomy, and, in any event, its leaders did not put a very high value on the prospects of Jewish cooperation. The popular Czech journalist Karel Havlíček-Borovský (1821–56) flatly rejected Kapper's appeal. Attacking the notion of Czech-Jewish assimilation, Havlíček insisted that the Jews be seen as a distinct nation:

> It cannot be asserted that the Jews living in Bohemia or Moravia are Czechs of
> Mosaic faith . . . we must regard them as a separate—Semitic—nation which
> lives only incidentally in our midst and sometimes understands or speaks our
> language . . . and this bond which ties them together is stronger by far than the
> bond to the country in which they live.[17]

The Jews, for their part, felt no compulsion to alter a course of cultural assimilation which was still less than a century old, and which continued to hold out the promise of social and political integration. Moreover, workers' demonstrations in Prague in 1844 and in 1848—during the course of which much violence and anger was directed at Jewish businesses and property— reinforced the view in the minds of Jewish notables that the Czech population was fundamentally antisemitic.[18] On the whole, the middle decades of the nineteenth century (1830–70) had the effect of solidifying the German-Jewish cultural synthesis. Particularly in the cities and towns of Bohemia, Jews remained committed devotees of German language and education, loyal servants of the Habsburg king, and ardent supporters of the (German) Progressive party.

Not until the 1870s and 1880s did the combined effects of rural population growth, migration to the cities, the creation of a Czech national school system, and growing political pressure, lead toward a second (and ultimately more definitive) modernization of Bohemian Jewish life. The book examines this transformation from a number of perspectives. Chapter 1 seeks to understand the demographic and social roots of the Czech-Jewish phenomenon. Chapter 2 looks at the early struggles within the Jewish community for linguistic, religious, and educational restructuring. Chapter 3 examines the troubled political relationship between the Czech-Jewish movement and Czech nationalism in the 1890s; it closes with an analysis of the crucial realignment in both Czech-Jewish thought and politics at the turn of the twentieth century. Chapter 4 considers the origins and early development of Jewish nationalism in Prague and Bohemia. Chapter 5 focuses on the particularly fruitful collaboration between the young Zionist intellectuals of Prague and the philosopher Martin Buber. Chapter 6 examines the fate of both Prague Zionism and the Czech-Jewish movement over the course of the First World War. And the final chapter looks briefly at the alignment of Jewish cultural and political forces on the eve of the First Czechoslovak Republic.

In closing, I wish to remark that this is a work in social and cultural history. The scope of its investigation deals primarily with the elaboration of new attitudes, behavioral patterns, and values. But my approach incorporates three levels of analysis. It consists first of all in systematically reconstructing the demographic, social, and political contexts in which cultural activity takes place. Intellectual and cultural developments themselves are then examined from the perspectives of form, content, and the meanings attached to them by participants. The final step reintroduces the cultural event to its political and social context in order to examine the question of the effects of such change. It is essentially a "contextual" methodology, painstaking at times, but necessary if one is to hope to arrive at satisfying answers to the twin questions of genesis and impact.

1

Prague Besieged:
Population Movement
and Cultural Discontinuity

The Demographic Revolution: Prague and the Villages

The history of Bohemian Jewry from the beginning of the eighteenth to the first half of the twentieth century revolves to a large extent around the changing relationship between town and countryside, center and periphery. At the dawn of enlightened absolutist rule in Central Europe, Prague stood out as the only large city with the exception of Frankfurt am Main not to have expelled its Jewish population.[1] Jews had been removed from the larger Moravian towns in the middle of the fifteenth century and from the Royal Cities of Bohemia in the 1540s. Jews continued to populate small market towns and villages, however, and in Prague they created what by 1700 had become one of the largest Jewish communities in the world.[2]

The survival of Prague as a Jewish center in an era in which Jews were normally excluded from urban life gave Bohemian Jewry a unique demographic configuration. Unlike Germany, which possessed only scattered Jewish settlements of relatively small size; unlike Moravia and Poland, where Jews lived for the most part in compact settlements in medium-sized towns (as well as in some villages); and unlike Hungary, where down to the end of the eighteenth century the vast majority of Jews were *Dorfjuden* (village Jews), more than a third of the Jewish population of Bohemia lived in a dense concentration at the center. The rest were dispersed in the small towns and villages of the surrounding Czech countryside.

In such patterns of center and periphery, it is the core that enjoys the position of preeminence. Until the end of the Thirty Years' War the scattered Jewish communities of Bohemia were viewed as mere extensions of Prague, whose chief rabbi enjoyed jurisdiction over the entire province. This state of affairs changed in 1659 when the rural communities challenged Prague's authority in matters of taxation and succeeded in establishing an independent *Landesjudenschaft* (association of Jewish communities).[3] However, even this institutional division of Bohemian Jewry into two camps could not guarantee the independence of the rural communities. The *Landesrabbinat* (Chief Rabbinate of Bohemia), established in 1679, remained a distinct institution for less than forty years. By 1715 the powerful chief rabbi of Prague, David Oppenheim (1664–1736), had acquired the additional title of *Landesrabbiner*. Thereafter, the office remained attached to the Prague rabbinate until the middle of the eighteenth century, by which time the position was simply eliminated.[4]

The balance of power between Prague and the Jewish countryside began to shift in favor of the countryside over the course of the eighteenth century. The reasons for this change lay in a combination of political and demographic factors which sometimes produced paradoxical results. During the 1720s, for example, Habsburg officials set out to limit the size of Bohemian Jewry by instituting restrictions on the right to marry and on legal areas of settlement. The *Familiantengesetze* (Familiants Laws) of 1726–27 established a ceiling on the number of Jewish families allowed to reside in Bohemia and Moravia, granted permission to marry to only the eldest son in a household, and decreed that further Jewish expansion into areas that had not been allowed in 1724 was illegal.[5] The government took these measures largely in response to what was correctly perceived to have been a rapid growth in the Jewish population. However, the new law managed only to delay and, at best, deflect this population burst.

While it is true that the legislation played havoc with Jewish family life until the middle of the nineteenth century, forcing the younger members of Jewish households to emigrate—usually to Hungary or to southern Poland—many Jews discovered ingenious ways to circumvent its effects. Some Jews, particularly in Prague, established "households within households" by entering into illegal, or "garret" marriages. Others sought to evade the watchful eye of the authorities by leaving the cities and towns, where burgher town councils tried zealously to uphold all restrictions against Jews, and settling in villages and market towns under the protection of the nobility, whose interests in such matters tended to be at odds with those of the cities and the central government.[6] Then, between 1745 and 1748 the Jews of Prague—but not those of rural Bohemia—suffered a temporary expulsion. In the intervening years Prague Jews were allowed to tarry in Bohemian villages to tidy up their business affairs. An undetermined number stayed in the countryside when the expulsion order was rescinded in 1748, although most did in fact return to the capital city. Over the short term, the combination of restrictive legislation and temporary expulsion simply held the Jewish population at a steady level.[7] But the long-term effects worked in favor of the Jews in the countryside and, in the end, failed to put a stop to the growth of the Jewish population.

The original government census of 1724 had indicated that the Jews of

Bohemia were scattered among 800 localities. Most of these contained only small pockets of Jews. One hundred could be considered towns with Jewish quarters; another 100 contained at least a synagogue; but as many as 600 of these localities consisted of small villages with only a handful of Jews and no official institutions.[8] Over the course of next 125 years, the centrifugal pattern of Jewish settlement increased while the population expanded. In 1849 instead of 800 localities with Jewish populations there were now 1,921. Only 207 of these formed actual communities of more than ten families with a formal synagogue; 148 managed to assemble a *Betstube* (prayer room) on Sabbaths and holidays by drawing on the resources of neighboring villages. Meanwhile the population had grown as well, from some 30,000 or 40,000 in the middle of the eighteenth century to 75,459 by 1850.[9]

In the course of this expansion the relative importance of the Prague community declined. Population statistics before the mid-nineteenth century are generally unreliable. Nevertheless, one can safely say that the Jewish population of the city did not surpass its high mark of 1702 until after 1850; the number of Jews may even have declined over the course of the eighteenth and early nineteenth century.[10] Jewish vitality, measured in terms of growth, was a feature of the countryside. Whatever the prestige of the cultural institutions of Jewish Prague, whatever leadership it had taken in providing for the social and educational transformation of Bohemian Jewry, ultimately it was the nonurban Jewish population of the mid-nineteenth century—and its descendants—which had the power of numbers to determine the nature of Jewish life in the Czech lands. And it was this small-town and village population that would take the lead in the 1860s and 1870s in a postassimilatory cultural transformation of great import.

With the repeal of the Familiantengesetze and the granting of *Freizügigkeit* (freedom of movement) in 1849, and with the opening of all areas of economic life to full Jewish participation at the end of the following decade, members of this burgeoning Jewish population found new and unprecedented opportunities open to them.[11] At the same time, the rationale for ever-deepening penetration into the countryside had disappeared, and from this point on the centuries-long pattern of Jewish settlement in Bohemia reversed itself. Small village communities gave way to larger concentrations in adjoining towns; this movement was followed by further migration to the large administrative and industrial centers of the country. Eventually thousands were to take the additional step of emigrating to more economically advanced areas of Europe and overseas.[12] By 1880 almost half of Bohemian Jewry lived in towns with more than 5,000 inhabitants. In 1921, 69 percent resided in towns of more than 10,000 people, and the number of Jews who continued to live in localities with less than 2,000 inhabitants dropped to 14.5 percent of the total.[13] Meanwhile the Jewish population of Bohemia continued to climb, although at a lower rate than that of the population at large. It

Table 1. Jewish Population of Bohemia

Year	No. of Jews	Percent of Total Population
1850	75,459	1.72
1869	89,933	1.80
1880	94,449	1.70
1890	94,479	1.62
1900	92,746	1.47
1910	85,826	1.27
1921	79,777	1.19

Derived from: Jan Heřman, "The Development of Bohemian and Moravian Jewry, 1918–1938," in U. O. Schmelz, P. Glikson, and S.Della Pergola, eds., *Papers in Jewish Demography, 1969* (Jerusalem, 1973); Jan Heřman, "The Evolution of the Jewish Population in Bohemia and Moravia, 1754–1953," in U. O. Schmelz, P. Glikson, and S. Della Pergola, eds., *Papers in Jewish Demography, 1973* (Jerusalem, 1977).

reached its peak of 94,479 in 1890, but in the intervening forty years the percentage of Jews in the Bohemian population had fallen from 1.72 to 1.62 percent (see Table 1).[14]

With the *Landflucht* (flight from the countryside) of the second half of the nineteenth century, the Prague Jewish community began to recapture the strength that it previously had lost to the provincial communities. Each census, beginning with that of 1869, showed not only a steady rise in the Jewish population but also that an ever-increasing percentage of the country's Jews were living in the capital city. In 1880 greater Prague had a Jewish population of 20,508—21.7 percent of the Bohemian Jewish community. In 1900 the Jewish population of the capital had exceeded 27,000 individuals, comprising nearly 30 percent of Bohemian Jewry. By 1921 fully 39.8 percent of all Czech Jews lived in Prague, which had a Jewish population of close to 32,000.[15] While the Jewish population of Prague more than doubled between 1869 and 1921, this growth did not keep pace with the expansion of the city as a whole. In 1869 the Jews constituted 6.3 percent of the population of greater Prague and managed until 1900 actually to increase their percentage to 7.9. Thereafter they fell steadily behind, dropping to 6.3 percent in 1910 and to 4.7 percent by 1921 (see Table 2).[16]

As Jan Heřman has shown, Prague owed the steady growth in its Jewish population both to natural increase (the preponderance of births over deaths) and to a positive migration balance (greater in-migration than emigration). By far the lion's share of the increase, however, belonged to in-migration. Over 69 percent of the expansion of the Prague Jewish community between 1869 and 1910 resulted from this factor alone.[17] As of 1921, 60

Table 2. Jewish Population of Prague and the Inner Suburbs

Year	No. of Jews	Percent of Total Population	Percent Jews of Bohemia
1869	15,214	6.3	16.9
1880	20,508	7.5	21.7
1890	23,473	7.8	24.8
1900	27,289	7.9	29.4
1910	29,107	6.3	33.9
1921	31,751	4.7	39.8
1930	35,425	4.2	46.4

Derived from: Jan Heřman, "The Evolution of the Jewish Population in Prague, 1869–1939," in U. O. Schmelz, P. Glikson, and S. Della Pergola, eds., *Papers in Jewish Demography, 1977* (Jerusalem, 1980). For a definition of the classification "Prague and the inner suburbs," see note 15, Chapter 1.

percent of all Prague Jews had been born outside of the city. Eight out of ten of these people had come from the surrounding Czech-speaking countryside, the other two from a German-speaking region of Bohemia.[18]

Demographic trends within the country at large mirrored in many respects the revolution that was occurring within the Jewish population of Bohemia, yet in certain key areas the patterns diverged. The general population of Bohemia also expanded greatly over the course of the nineteenth century, and waves of immigrants from the Czech-speaking countryside literally overwhelmed Prague and other industrial centers after 1850. Prague's population grew steadily during the 1840s, 1850s, and 1860s, even though the annual birth rate for the city and the inner suburbs did not begin to exceed the death rate until the 1870s. Indeed, between 1881 and 1890 Prague could boast a natural rate of increase of only 3.1 percent, yet the total population of the city grew by 25 percent.[19] As was the case with the Jewish community, the overwhelming majority of these migrants came to Prague from the Czech-speaking regions of central and eastern Bohemia. In 1900 immigrants made up almost 60 percent of the "citizen residents" of the city and the inner suburbs; fully 85 percent of these people had originated in the predominantly Czech-speaking parts of Bohemia.[20]

For both the city of Prague and its Jewish community, the political and cultural implications of this kind of population movement were enormous. If, as Gary Cohen has argued, the demands of the Czech-speaking lower and middle classes in Prague in the 1840s and 1850s for linguistic equality and economic and political opportunity spurred the German-speaking professional and commercial classes openly to assert their own German ethnic identity, the Czech political victories of the following decades must have created much discouragement among these same German elites. In the municipal elections of 1861 the Czechs captured seventy-five of the ninety seats on the Town Council. By 1882 the number of German councillors had fallen to four, all of whom resigned their positions before the end of the year in protest to Mayor Tomáš Černý's reference to the city as "golden and Slavonic Prague."

One can measure the decline of German influence in Prague in other ways as well. Street signs in the 1840s bore Czech names alongside the German. In 1861 the order of names was reversed so that the Czech designation appeared above the German. By 1893 the Town Council had decided to eliminate the German names from street signs altogether.[21] A more direct indication of the growth of Czech political power in Prague emerges from statistical information on declared national loyalties or, according to the designation preferred by Habsburg officials, "language of daily use." Official government censuses began to record the linguistic preferences of the population only in 1880. Nevertheless, one can observe an impressive shrinkage in the size of the self-consciously German community in Prague even beginning with this late date. Close to 42,000 residents of Prague declared their language of daily use to be German in 1880 (this figure equaled 15.5 percent of the city's population). Over the course of the next decade, the number declined slightly in absolute terms (to 41,385), but as a percentage of the whole it slipped to 12 percent. Even greater shrinkage occurred during the turbulent decade of the 1890s— the heyday of Young Czech political influence. In 1900 only 33,776 Prague residents openly affirmed their German nationality, a mere 7.5 percent of the total population; meanwhile, nearly 415,000 residents—92.3 percent of the total—proclaimed the Czech nationality.[22]

The decline of German national culture in Prague is brought into starkest relief when one remembers that throughout the nineteenth century, the ratio of Czechs to Germans in all of Bohemia remained fairly constant. Even after 1880, Germans continued to represent a steady 37 percent of the total population of Bohemia.[23] However, the German-speaking areas along the northern, western, and southern borders of Bohemia did not send many immigrants to Prague. Vienna, with nearly five times the population of Prague in 1910, the seat of the imperial government, center of great economic opportunity, and, above all, an unambiguously German capital, attracted the vast majority of Bohemia's ethnic Germans. That it did not prove to be as attractive a magnet to Czech-speaking Bohemians also owed a great deal to the importance of national sentiment in the second half of the nineteenth century. Places like Prague and Plzeň in Bohemia, Olomouc and Brno in Moravia, could provide the panoply of social, economic, and educational advantages that accrued to one in an industrialized society and at the same time guarantee the full measure of Czech national self-expression. Migration to Vienna ultimately entailed assimilation to German culture, although this fact did not prevent many thousands of Czechs from moving to the imperial capital.

The migratory movement of Jews in the Czech lands diverged from that of the general population in several important respects. Moravian Jewry, long in the habit of eastward migration (during the period of restrictive social legislation, the younger members of Moravian Jewish families tended to settle in Hungary), and more susceptible to Viennese cultural domination than their Bohemian coreligionists, migrated much more frequently to Vienna than to Prague. Bohemian Jews tended to prefer Prague, but they also settled the newly industrializing towns of northern and western Bohemia, which often had a German cultural makeup.

The most important variation, however, concerned the nature of Jewish acculturation in the various centers of in-migration. When Czech workers, peasants, and even middle-class professionals settled in cities such as Prague, they did not affiliate—either through choice or through exclusion—with the cultural, educational, and social institutions of the German-speaking community. Czech cultural loyalties found continued expression in urban society through avenues such as schools, the church, civic and patriotic societies, social clubs, and literary circles. Jewish migrants faced a more complicated situation. They naturally sought to become integrated into the existing Jewish community. This process included affiliating with officially recognized religious institutions and representations, but it also involved associating with groups that one might call "implicitly Jewish"—not publicly designated as such, but whose social composition and shared culture were recognized by outsiders and insiders alike as being Jewish. One would include in this category those social and civic organizations and schools which a large percentage of Prague Jews frequented.

All such institutions down to the end of the nineteenth century functioned in the German language and propagated German culture in a broad sense. Yet most in-migrating Czech Jews saw no apparent difficulty or cultural contradiction in affiliating with such bodies. Some may have been oblivious to the raging national controversy between Czechs and Germans at this time, although this hardly seems likely. More to the point were the effects of a century or more of historical conditioning. The entire process of Jewish cultural modernization and social mobility that had been set in motion in the 1780s had been predicated on the use of German as a linguistic vehicle, on loyalty to the central government, and on faith in the ameliorative powers of political liberalism.[24] The eventual implementation of Jewish emancipation in 1867 appeared to have corroborated each of these elements. From the Jewish point of view, the use of German in one's daily activities did not necessarily indicate a position on the nationality controversy. Rather it demonstrated allegiance to the goal of integration into Austrian state and society as well as to the means of attaining that goal. Hence, the willingness of Czech Jewish migrants to enter German-Jewish institutional life in Prague may have signaled nothing more than an implicit vote of confidence in the efficacy of the integration process.

Having said this, one must nevertheless add that the Bohemian Jewish population possessed a marked ability to break out of expected patterns of allegiance and association. Special attention to the linguistic declarations of Prague Jews between 1890 and 1910 will be given in the following chapter. For the moment it will suffice to point out that, of the approximately 106,000 residents of Prague proper (districts I–VII) in 1900 who came from the Czech-speaking regions of Bohemia, only 5,100 declared German to be their every-day language. It is safe to conclude that most of the people in this second category were Jewish.[25] On the other hand, these 5,000 or so individuals composed a distinct minority within the group of recently arrived Czech Jews.[26] Moreover, a good deal of Czech cultural assimilation took effect among Jews who had arrived from the German-speaking parts of Bohemia as well. We have noted that Jews from the so-called Sudeten territories demonstrated a greater willingness than non-Jews to settle in Prague. Once the Jews did move to the Czech capital, many proclaimed Czech to be their language of daily use. The figures for 1900 indicate that half of the residents in Prague I–VII who had originated in Bohemia's German-speaking parts had abandoned that language (for official purposes at least) in favor of Czech. Unfortunately, one cannot know exactly how many of these "Sudeten Czechs" were Jews.[27]

Nevertheless, one can say with certainty that by the last quarter of the nineteenth century the social and demographic characteristics of the Prague Jewish community had been completely transformed. The size of the community was in the process of doubling, and, in the midst of this process, the traditional social strata were overwhelmed by "new Jews." Virtually all of its growth came from village and small-town Jews whose own numbers had been swelling for more than a century and who came to the city in search of economic opportunity and social advancement. Moreover, if Prague Jewry traditionally had been German out of cultural conviction and devotion to the Habsburg House, rural Bohemian Jewry tended to be bilingual through the combined forces of circumstance and cultural habit.

No simple model of urban adaptation or cultural assimilation could predict the direction that Jewish culture, politics, and group identity would take over the next half century. For one thing, a larger set of variables—including, among other things, the flexibility or rigidity of existing Jewish institutions, the impact of Czech national politics on the Jewish community, and the rise or decline of antisemitism—must be brought to bear. Nevertheless, it is clear that the demographic revolution that was occurring both within and outside of Bohemian Jewry was working to create an unstable situation in which further social, cultural, and political change of considerable magnitude was likely to ensue.

Cultural Politics and Popular Protest: Prague in the 1860s and 1870s

The earliest Jewish expressions of dissatisfaction with the community's generally pro-German orientation coincided with the first waves of Czech-Jewish immigration to Prague. Yet it appears to have been constitutional politics, rather than demography, which lay behind this development. The October Diploma of 1860 and the February Patent of the following year introduced genuine parliamentary life for the first time at both the national and the regional level and served as an impetus for all types of political activity. The Austrian population enjoyed freedom of the press and assembly to a degree unheard of since the revolutionary days of 1848 and 1849. New elections were held at the municipal, provincial, and national levels; political and patriotic societies emerged; newspapers were founded; pamphlet literature accumulated in bookstalls and on street corners. All of these activities provided people with new opportunities to promote the claims of favored national groups and social classes and to denigrate the positions of rivals.

The year 1861 also saw the first popular disturbances directed against the Jews of Prague since 1848. Public relations between Czech and Jewish notables had become strained to the point of open enmity during the closing years of the 1850s, when David Kuh's newspaper, *Tagesbote aus Böhmen,* a mouthpiece of German-Jewish commercial interests, denounced the so-called Králové Dvůr and Zelená Hora manuscripts (purportedly discovered by the Czech romantic poet Václav Hánka, in 1819) as forgeries.[28] Subsequent Czech nationalist agitation, though aimed ostensibly at reducing or removing German influence in municipal bodies, such as the Town Council and the quasi-parliamentary Chamber of Commerce, had the indirect effect of encouraging violence against the homes and business establishments of German-speaking Jews. The disturbances of August 1861 in Prague ended only with the massive intervention of both the police and the military and only after some 1,300 windowpanes in Jewish neighborhoods had been shattered.[29]

Two years later a hotly contested *Landtag* (Bohemian Diet) election elicited a minor pamphlet war among the Jews of Bohemia. Markus Teller (1814–75), a former activist in the Young Bohemia literary movement who had become disenchanted with Czech intolerance toward Jews, inaugurated the campaign with his tract *Die Juden in Böhmen: Ihre Stellung in der Gegenwart.*[30] Teller put forward a position that was fast becoming a Bohemian Jewish orthodoxy. While declaring neutrality on the overall nationality controversy, he nevertheless polemicized against Czech popular excesses and argued that Jewish interests could only be served by supporting the central government in Vienna (the only authority to come to the aid of the Prague Jews in 1861) and the liberal German establishment at home.

Teller's polemic drew an anonymous response which claimed to represent the position of Bohemian Jews living outside of Prague. Written in German, like much of the early literature of the Czech national revival, the pamphlet *Die Juden und die Nationalen* articulated for the first time cultural and political convictions that dissented from those of the Prague Jewish mainstream.[31] Like the Czech nationalists who two years earlier had established the newspaper *Národní listy* (National press), the author of *Die Juden und die Nationalen* also drew upon the Czech Revolution of 1848 for inspiration. Liberal freedoms and the equality of nations formed the watchwords of his manifesto, which ultimately displayed complete indebtedness to the ideology of liberal Czech nationalism.

Die Juden und die Nationalen argued that the Jews of Bohemia, particularly those of the towns and villages outside of Prague, were not naturally allied to the German nation. Rather, their ties belonged historically to the Czech people. To demonstrate this, the author offered a novel interpretation of Bohemian Jewish history, in much the same manner that František Palacký (1798–1876) had done for Czech history during the preceding decades. What resulted from this reinterpretation might be called the Czech-Jewish "myth." It went as follows: The natural inclinations of the Jews of Bohemia, linguistically and culturally, were Czech, but this "natural" orientation was disrupted by the forced "Germanization" of the Jewish communities of Bohemia and Moravia during the seventeenth and eighteenth centuries, especially in the aftermath of the reforms of Joseph II and his successors. Additionally, the premodern Czechs had always treated their Jewish neighbors with great tolerance. They learned intolerance and hatred only later, under the tutelage of the "German" Counter Reformation. Yet even at this point Czechs continued to behave toward their Jewish neighbors with more humanity than the Germans had ever managed to display.[32]

A historical scenario of this type performed a number of functions. First, by arguing for the artificiality of the German-Jewish relationship, it called into question the nature and direction of Jewish modernization and acculturation in the Czech lands since the late eighteenth century. Second, in proposing a natural alliance of Jewish and Czech interests—at least in the countryside—it sought to reestablish a basis for mutual understanding and cooperation which seemed to have gotten lost in the rush of urban migration.

Like the cultural movements of other national minorities in the Habsburg Empire, the earliest proponents of Czech-Jewish rapprochement acted as critics of the "notables" (*Honoratioren*) within their own social group. Members of the nascent Czech and Slovak middle classes, for example, most of them only a generation or two removed from the peasantry, had directed their attacks to a large extent against the nobility and members of the ecclesiastical elite who either had allowed themselves to become "Germanized" or "Magyarized" or who themselves consisted of a foreign implantation. The first generation or two of Jewish Czech nationalists may not have been able to point to the historical complicity of the first and second estates in the same manner. However, the urban Jewish patriciate as well as the Jewish communal establishment served as comparable foils. In the eyes of the author of *Die Juden und die Nationalen,* the Prague Jewish community deserved condemnation for the tiny regard that it took for the people around it. Moreover, the German-Jewish position of cultural separatism contradicted the very assimilationist premises on which it claimed to rest:

The Czechs are right when they say that the Jewish community of Czech Prague is—and must be—predominantly Czech, because . . . it, itself, advances the theory that the Jew belongs to that nation in whose midst he possesses the right of domicile, for he does not form a nationality of his own.[33]

The myth created a structural equivalent to Czech nationalist ideology which permitted incipient Czech-Jewish patriots to argue, no less convincingly than their Czech counterparts, that their's was a conservative enterprise. Cultural nationalism of the Czech and Slovak variety centered on the resuscitation of a natural language, the recovery of a peasant culture, the rediscovery of a proud history—all of which were threatened with extinction by the oppressive domination of a foreign culture. Revival equaled survival, and nationalism the preservation of a sacred heritage.

In his closing appeal the author referred once again to the ideals of humanitarian, liberal nationalism. He urged his coreligionists to offer their hands in friendship to the Czech nation. If they could not become good Czechs, at least they could try to cease being so overwhelmingly German, to become open to a plurality of affiliations.[34] Another anonymous publication, appearing this time in 1865 in the pages of the Old Czech—or National party—newspaper *Politik,* argued further for the acceptance of cultural pluralism among Prague Jews.[35] The letter in *Politik* protested the simplistic identification of Jewish interests with German ones, but also decried the growing climate of nationalism which required that individuals carry with them a single, all-encompassing loyalty. A more natural situation, the writer argued, would have been one in which the individual owed loyalties to a number of groups or social institutions:

Man represents the moral unity of the most diverse feelings and seemingly contradictory facts of consciousness. Despite his undivided individuality, he considers himself to be, at one and the same time, son, brother, husband, father, in-law—whatever member of this or that family—but also: citizen, artisan, artist, or scholar; friend and foe; and whatever all of the unending relationships might be called. . . . A deep and strong ethnic feeling (*Stammesgefühl*) does not hinder—indeed may even further—one's attachment to the nationality. To claim that the Jew cannot feel like a Czech because he feels like a Jew is in the end the same as to say that he who feels like Baron X or Count Y cannot consider himself to be a Czech.[36]

In addition to expressing sympathy for the growth and development of Czech culture, the writer of this letter also isolated what were to be the key problems for Jewish life in Prague and Bohemia over the next few generations. Did the rising Czech national movement require of the Jews a total and radical break with their long-standing attraction to German culture? Did intregral Czech nationalism allow room for a multifaceted identity on the part of Jews? Or did they have to make an absolute choice between Czech and German language, culture, and politics? Finally, was there no place for the cultivation of a Jewish cultural position in this nerve bed of national competition, or would such a tactic merely have represented a further, intolerable fragmentation of the country?

The anonymous voices of dissent from 1863 and 1865 went largely unheeded. Bohemian Jewry, and in particular the Prague community, could not be moved by the increasing vociferousness of a minority national movement or by isolated acts of violence against Jewish property to question the judiciousness of their overt loyalty to Austrian centralism. Indeed, the atmosphere of popular agitation might have strengthened Jewish resolve to support the institutions of the state and the prerogatives of the leading cultural group. For, while it is true that Bohemian Jews tended universally to place a high value on German language and culture in its own right, their attitude toward politics was more discriminating. They did not support German national politics pure and simple, but rather that form of German liberalism which was represented by the Verfassungspartei (Constitutional party) and which had been inspired by the democratic revolutions of 1848. By a kind of a fortiori argument, the Jews of Bohemia reasoned that in a time of political turbulence it was particularly important to maintain one's support for the forces of order, constitutionalism, and progress.[37]

For their part, Czech nationalist writers in the 1860s and 1870s seemed both to take for granted and to resent the notion that there existed in Prague a German-Jewish cultural alliance. The influential novelist and storywriter, Jan Neruda (1834–91) joined a chorus of urban, petit bourgeois, anti-Jewish sentiment with his pamphlet *Pro strach židovský* (On the Jewish fear), written in 1869.[38] Neruda revealed in several places his indebtedness to Richard Wagner's *Das Judentum in der Musik* (1850), in which the great German composer had declared the German and Jewish spirits to be inimicable. The Czech writer accepted this proposal, but added the insight that the Jews were equally—if not more—foreign to the Czech nation.[39]

Neruda also added a rather cutting historical correction of his own to the Czech-Jewish debate. Not only were the Jews a foreign national element in the Czech lands, but historically they had acted with malice and hatred toward the Czechs. Writing two years after the granting of full civic emancipation to the Jews of Austria, Neruda repeated a slogan that had once been used by Karl Marx more than two decades earlier: "The question is not the emancipation of the Jews, but rather emancipation from the Jews, so that we might be able to free ourselves from the exploitation of one's fellow man and cease being the slaves of tyrants."[40]

Czech historians of this period also began to consider the history of the Jews in Bohemia and Moravia from the point of view of the national controversy. One of the earliest tracts devoted entirely to this question was the 1867 publication of the soldier-historian Antonín Tokstein, *Židé v Čechách* (The Jews in Bohemia). In his opening pages the author placed his work squarely in the middle of the growing national conflict, explaining that his goal was to try to find in the history of the Jews in Bohemia the causes for their stubborn refusal to take part in Czech national life:

> Is there somewhere in history any kind of just reason which would explain their attitude toward us up to now—when in the period of general persecution of the Jews in foreign lands we were always more than benign toward them? History above all should be the judge for us, depicting impartially the life of the Jewish race in Bohemia and its relationship to the nation after several centuries.[41]

Tokstein's history had two main themes. The first was that, while the Jews were subject to persecution throughout Europe since the middle ages, this was the result of church and state policies. The local populations, particularly the Czechs, were neither responsible for this persecution, nor did they aggravate it. Second, the Jews prospered greatly over the centuries from their contact with the Czech populations of Prague and the countryside. In fact, Tokstein argued, the Jews profited from the Czech defeat at White Mountain at the start of the Thirty Years' War. In 1627, when Ferdinand II expelled the Czech nobility from Bohemia and Moravia, he simultaneously extended royal protection to the Jewish population.[42]

That Tokstein's book was intended, at least in part, for a Jewish audience is evident from the fact that he paused several times in the course of his narrative to exhort the Jews of Bohemia to change their attitude and behavior. They should demonstrate a greater love for the homeland, stop making exclusive use of German and Yiddish, and start to speak Czech outside of their business affairs, in the home and in the synagogue. The author criticized the Jews harshly for their isolation from the Czech nation, for their consideration of personal and "tribal" gain as opposed to the well-being of their Czech neighbors. Not surprisingly, the historical justification that Tokstein claimed to be looking for in his introduction turned out to be missing. The Jews themselves were responsible for their attitude toward the Czechs. They themselves had insisted on living as foreigners in the Czech lands.

But Tokstein held out hope. He tantalized the Jewish reader with the vision of a golden future, one of peace, brotherhood, and cooperation, the prerequisite for which was total surrender to "the nation":

> If they [Jews] were to approach the nation resolutely and with confidence, not as they have been acting up to now, "united in strength," but in the spirit of sacrifice and selflessness, if they would work toward the prosperity and wealth of the land, better days would lie ahead for them. Their descendants will praise them, and the nation will commemorate them. The land on which they were born and where the bones of their fathers rest will be more sacred to them. The history which both they and their ancestors lived through together will be more beloved to them. The Czech land will become a precious promised land. But the language, which they will have learned from the mother's lap—to call out both

to God and to one's fellow man—will forever unite them in friendship with the nation.[43]

The Emergence of Cultural Dissent:
The Association of Czech Academic Jews

During the winter semester 1875–76 a small group of Jewish students at Prague's as-yet-undivided university and its *Hochschulen* (technical colleges) began a series of regular but informal meetings. At the outset the members of this group had sought each other out for the purpose of companionship. They were looking for a social setting in which they could discuss issues of common concern, lend mutual psychological and material support, and also further the cultural aims of the Czech national movement. The group wasted little time in electing an executive committee, drawing up a set of bylaws, and submitting both to the Austrian authorities for approval. In March 1876, official recognition was granted to the new organization, and the Spolek českých akademiků-židů (SČAŽ, Association of Czech Academic Jews) came into existence.[44]

Just who the members of this association were, where they came from, why they felt the need to organize, and what their enterprise was all about, are questions worthy of close consideration. Together they point to the effects of several generations of profound social change among Bohemian Jewry and to the beginnings of a concomitant transformation in the self-perception of large numbers of Bohemian Jews.

The founding members of the Association of Czech Academic Jews consisted of university and technical-college students and recent graduates. They were by and large professionals and preprofessionals, members of or aspirants to the upper middle class. The first executive committee of the SČAŽ contained three law students, two medical students, and one engineering student; the group's *Protektor* (academic advisor) was the law professor and adherent of the Old Czech party Alois Zucker.[45] The other Jewish members of the organization in the 1870s and 1880s fit neatly within the middle class. Of the thirteen "founding members" (*členové zákládající*) of the society in 1878—those who contributed at least twenty crowns in two years—there were factory owners, businessmen, politicians, lawyers, journalists, a member of the Czech national theater in Prague, and even the director of the Czech symphony orchestra.[46] A second category of members, "contributing" supporters of the group who gave at least two crowns per year, included businessmen, journalists, and lawyers. The core of the organization, the "active" members, was composed of students and recent graduates who were professing Jews.[47]

In its first year of activity, the Association of Czech Academic Jews attracted 82 members, 28 of whom were students. Over the next six years the organization grew impressively. The number of "founding members" rose to a total of 51. They included, in addition to a number of Jewish religious communities outside of Prague, a large landowner, a banker, a master glass maker, the owner of a Prague brewery, and a deputy in the Bohemian Diet. A massive membership drive in the countryside enabled the association to sign on as "contributors" no fewer than 393 individuals and corporate bodies. Meanwhile, 56 students composed the "active" membership.[48] The artificially inflated figures for 1882–83 settled at a more reasonable level by the end of the decade. Thus we learn that in 1890 there were 71 "founding members," 117 "contributing," and 53 "active." Interestingly, the number of active members rose the following year to 71 and the year after that to 81, this during a period in which there were only 64 Jewish students at the Czech University of Prague and 6 at the Technical Institute. Hence, even though many more Jewish students attended the German University—450 between 1891 and 1896—some of these people must have considered themselves Czech nationals.[49]

Of the nonstudent heads of the association, Bohumil Bondy (1832–1907) and Jakub Scharf (1857–1922) came from long-standing Prague Jewish families. Bondy, the chief financial backer of the Czech-Jewish endeavor as well as its éminence grise, belonged to the Jewish patriciate of Prague. He was the owner of a machine factory in the suburb of Bubeneč—apparently the only firm in the city to retain all of its employees in the wake of the financial crash of 1873—member of the Town Council from 1864 to 1869 and from 1875 to 1878, and also the first Czech speaker to be elected to the presidency of the Prague Chamber of Commerce.[50] Scharf, both a lawyer and a publicist, did more than anyone else to ensure the early political successes of the Czech-Jewish movement. He was the founder of the Czech-Jewish National Union (Národní jednota českožidovská), the "political arm," so to speak, of the movement, aided in the establishment of the first Czech-Jewish newspaper in 1894, and served as its second editor.[51]

However, most of the young leaders of the Association of Czech Academic Jews came from towns and villages in the Czech countryside. Leopold Katz hailed from the town of Jistebnice near Tábor.[52] Alois Zucker was born in Čkyň, moved with his family to the larger town of Strakonice, and also studied in Písek in southern Bohemia before coming to Prague to attend the university.[53] The brothers Josef and Salomon Žalud, both lawyers active in the new Czech-Jewish movement, came from Stálec outside of Tábor.[54] August Stein, the son of a provincial rabbi, was born in Nový Knín.[55]

The membership lists of the Association of Czech Academic Jews, though extensive, do not provide for the places of origin of its members, so an accurate survey cannot be made. However, wherever more detailed biographical information exists, one finds over and again that most of those people who were active in the Czech-Jewish movement in Prague had themselves come to the city from the countryside. This continues to be a characteristic feature of the movement down to the second and third generation of leadership. The prewar triumvirate of Viktor Vohryzek (1864–1918), Eduard Lederer (1859–1941), and Bohdan Klineberger (1859–1928) consisted of migrants from Přestavlky, Chostovice, and Rataj, respectively. The post-World War I leader Jindřich Kohn (1874–1935) spent his childhood and youth in Příbram. Interestingly, all four of these figures set up professional practices outside of Prague after completing their education. Vohryzek practiced medicine in Pardubice, Lederer law in Jindřichův Hradec; Klineberger spent twenty-seven years in Milevsko after receiving a law degree from Vienna; and Kohn set up his law practice in Plzeň. The political nucleus of Czech-Jewish cultural activism may have been Prague, but the countryside provided the lifeblood of the movement and also served as the focus of many of its endeavors.[56]

The Association of Czech Academic Jews emerged as one of the more striking consequences of the uprooting of Jewish life in the countryside. It was an institution that tended to attract children of Jewish families who were on the move—geographically from village to town or from town to big city, and socially from such occupations as peddlers and small shopkeepers to the middle-class professions, business, and industry. Yet only a minority of young Jews who belonged to this broad social category actually joined the new movement. What was so unique to their situation as to induce them to do so while so many of their coreligionists failed to see either the desirability or the need? This question is indeed difficult to answer. A number of apologists for Czech-Jewish assimilation have argued that the original inclination to establish formal institutions along these lines stemmed from the quality of Czech-Jewish social interaction in the towns and villages of their childhood. In the process of migrating to the urban centers of Bohemia, the Jews from the villages lost this sense of wholeness and social well-being. Moreover, they now encountered a Jewish community that did not possess the same attitude of intimacy toward the Czech people, their language, and their culture, and which was not prepared to offer Jews an institutional life that would perpetuate such ties. In the course of the population movements of the 1850s and 1860s, the Jews of small-town and rural Bohemia had become culturally Czech. Once in the city they faced the prospect of becoming, as more than one Czech Jew has written, "de-nationalized." Thus, according to this view, the movement emerged in the first instance in order to shore up and defend a process of acculturation that had occurred naturally over a generation or two and which was in danger of becoming overwhelmed.[57]

The problem with such an explanation is that it attempts to put forward a rather amorphous, and ultimately unverifiable, emotional atmosphere as a causal factor. It is not enough to say that Jews felt close to Czechs in the small towns and villages and thus were compelled to recreate an urban environment in which the Czech-Jewish relationship might persevere. We know, first of all, that many rural Jews were quite satisfied to become integrated into the predominantly German Jewish community upon their arrival in Prague. Undoubtedly these people, too, tried to have as good relations with their neighbors in the city as they had had in the countryside. Moreover, the Association of Czech Academic Jews was a Jewish organization designed to serve the needs of Jews. It did not constitute a "small society" of Czechs and Jews and was, by its very structure, incapable of doing so.

What, then, did move these students and young professionals to act? What was it that made one Czech-Jewish family the willing object of German-Jewish acculturation and another a proponent of Czech-Jewish distinctiveness? Unfortunately, biographical information on the members of the Czech-Jewish movement has never been systematically assembled or analyzed. Nor, in all likelihood, could it be. The sources at our disposal are fragmentary. Nevertheless, a few points do stand out. First, the peregrinations of those families whose children later joined the Czech-Jewish movement seem to have taken them to the larger Bohemian towns and cities outside of Prague itself. These were places such as Tábor, Chrudim, Hradec Králové, Pardubice, Kutná Hora, and Příbram, centers of middle-class Czech nationalism in the second half of the nineteenth century. Young families who set up households directly in Prague, without making intermediate stops—Franz Kafka's father Hermann was a good example of one who made this type of move—were less likely to question the cultural tendencies or the social values of the established Jewish community in their new environment. On the other hand, those who paused in the "intermediate" phase of migration to raise and educate their children were more likely to provide young recruits to the Czech-Jewish tendency.

Among those families who made the "intermediate" stop, the critical factor in determining cultural allegiance appears to have been the secondary education of the youngsters. Community-run, German-language elementary schools—a heritage of Josephine times—continued to flourish in the Bohemian countryside until the 1890s. Their presence, though of much propagandistic significance in the Czech-German conflict, does not appear to have had an overriding impact on the national loyalties of Bohemian Jews. Rather, it was the next level of schooling that seems to have molded what were to become lifelong practices and convictions. Before 1848 no secondary schools existed in Bohemia in which Czech was the language of instruction.[58] Between 1850 and 1867 only ten Czech gymnasia (classical high schools) were functioning, although the Austrian government did insist that both Czech and German be taught at all secondary schools. Following the *Ausgleich* ("compromise" between Austria and Hungary) of 1867 and the considerable degree of local autonomy granted to the Czech lands in matters of education, the number of Czech-language high schools grew measurably. By 1877 there were twenty-six gymnasia and ten *Reálky* (*Realschulen,* science-oriented high schools) in Bohemia whose medium of instruction was Czech; there were four such gymnasia and two such Reálky in Moravia.[59]

A growing number of small-town Jewish families after 1860 chose not only to provide their children with a secondary education, which for many was a novelty, but also to send them to Czech-language gymnasia. The opening sentence in Maxim Reiner's (1864–1937) reminiscences reads, "It was in the year 1882 when I came to Prague as a gymnasium graduate to prepare for my future course of life."[60] This description characterized the situation of hundreds of Jewish eighteen year olds during the last quarter of the nineteenth century, people who found themselves in a new and strange environment as they began the final leg in their professional education. Every memoir and biography of Czech-Jewish activists before the First World War reveals one common element above all: each of these individuals went through a Czech-language gymnasium. Alois Zucker and August Stein attended the school in Písek, Josef Žalud and Bohdan Klineberger the Reálka in Tábor. Viktor Vohryzek attended the Czech high school in Chrudim and Jindřich Kohn the one in Příbram. Only Eduard Lederer appears to have remained outside of this critical pattern. Paradoxically, Lederer, who was one of the few Czech-Jewish patriots to enjoy the reputation of a Czech *homme de lettres,* attended a German-language gymnasium in Prague's Nové Město before studying law in both Prague and Vienna.[61]

In terms of geographic origins, migration patterns, and secondary education—though not religion—the members of the Association of Czech Academic Jews closely resembled student activists affiliated with the Young Czech or National Liberal party. They, too, had been flooding the centers of Bohemian industrialization since 1850. They, too, had benefited from the political and educational reforms of the 1860s which had allowed for considerable self-rule at the municipal level and for the flourishing of Czech-language schools. They, too, had learned their nationalism, so to speak, at the Czech gymnasia, which were staffed by patriotic teachers who instilled in their students a strong sense of linguistic and national consciousness. They, too, the sons of shopkeepers and peasants, were preparing for careers in the liberal professions, science, and engineering. And they combined their quest for social advancement with political demands for the safeguarding of Czech culture in the life of the state.[62]

Program of the Czech-Jewish Movement:
The Medium and the Message

German-speaking Jewish students in Prague who wished to affiliate with an extracurricular student organization normally chose that *Burschenschaft* (fraternity) whose colors were the red, gold, and black of the liberal nationalists of 1848, the Lese- und Redehalle der deutschen Studenten (German Students' Reading and Discussion Room). Before the 1890s at least, they did not seek out or create specifically Jewish fraternities. Jews found that they were welcome in the liberal German organizations of Prague, and their presence in these institutions was so common that the two categories, German and Jewish, were often seen as equivalents in the popular imagination. Why a parallel process did not occur with regard to Czech student fraternities is not clear. I have found no evidence to suggest that the Akademický čtenářský spolek (Academic Reading Society), to which almost half of all Czech university students belonged, refused to accept Jewish membership.[63] Yet the Jewish Czech nationalists who came to Prague consciously chose to create an organization whose "active members" (to use the group's own categorization) were to be students and recent graduates who professed the Jewish religion.[64] The group chose a name for the organization, Spolek českých akademiků-židů, which purposely accentuated the Jewish status of its membership. They did not call themselves "Jewish Czechs," or "Czechs of the Jewish faith," but rather Jews (from an academic environment) who were also Czechs.

The peculiar choice of name and the insistence on establishing a separate Jewish organization (the first self-consciously Jewish student organization in Bohemia) suggest two things. First, the Czech-speaking Jewish students maintained a strong, Jewish, ethnic identity even as they set about encouraging greater Czech acculturation and national assimilation among Jews. Moreover, they saw the relationship of Jews to the Czech nation as a problematic one. The vision that they all shared of national assimilation would proceed only in the wake of a concerted program of popular education aimed specifically at the Jewish population of the Czech lands. Hence the need for a separate Jewish organization aligned with the Czech national movement.

"The purpose of the Association," read the bylaws that were approved by the government, "is to spread love of the homeland and of the mother tongue among Czech Jews, to cultivate reciprocity among its members, and to lend material support to its less fortunate ones."[65] Cultural patriotism, social-psychological solidarity, and financial assistance, then, formed the cornerstones of the organized Czech-Jewish movement in its early years. Its leaders viewed the question of financial aid with particular urgency. A number of German-Jewish institutions within the organized Prague community existed for the sole purpose of supporting indigent Jewish students. But, according to nationally conscious Czech Jews, such organizations served additionally to transform Czech-Jewish immigrants to Prague into Germans. If charitable avenues could be established that did not entail the "denationalization" of poorer Jewish students from the Czech countryside, such individuals could be preserved for the Czech nation.[66]

During the first five years of its existence the Association of Czech Academic Jews contented itself with the rudiments of organizational work: attracting members both in Prague and outside the capital, providing for the psychological and material well-being of Czech Jewish students, and also soliciting the support—at times the collaboration—of distinguished figures in the Czech national movement. The group achieved a moderate degree of success in this last pursuit, winning the formal approval of such Czech dignitaries as Josef Bárak, Jan Strakátý, and Julius Grégr in its very first years. Bárak, a maverick politician and writer affiliated with the Young Czech party, together with Grégr, editor of the most influential Czech newspaper in Prague, the liberal-nationalist *Národní listy,* provided the movement with political balance. A number of the founders of the association had themselves been tied to the Old Czech party in Prague, but through individuals such as Bárak and Grégr, as well as through the Jewish students themselves, the ideology of the National Liberals was able to gain influence.[67] In years to follow, the Czech-Jewish movement succeeded in attracting to its cause such noted personalities as the playwright Josef Jiří Kolár, the poet Jaroslav Vrchlický, the writer Jakub Arbes, and the chairman of the Young Czech parliamentary club Emanuel Engel.[68]

Since its founding in 1876 the SČAŽ carried the implicit hope that its very existence would advance the cause of Czech national culture among the Jewish population of the Czech lands. It took the first practical step toward realizing this goal in 1881 when it began publication of a Czech-Jewish almanac, the *Kalendář česko-židovský* (KČŽ), thereby venturing into the domain of mass journalism and popular culture. The leaders of the Czech-Jewish movement seriously viewed themselves as educators, as "awakeners of national consciousness." They likened themselves to the great journalists of the previous century, such as Benjamin Franklin of Colonial America and, closer to home, Václav Matěj Kramerius. To the leaders of the SČAŽ, Franklin's *Poor Richard's Almanac* represented an instance in which popularly diffused literature had been able to mold the sensibilities of an entire nation. Kramerius's *New Almanac of Toleration for the Entire Czech Nation* (1787–98) not only had served the cause of enlightenment and religious toleration in Central Europe, but had also aided in rekindling the spark of Czech national feeling in an age in which very few Czech books—aside from religious tracts and collections of prayers—existed.[69]

Thus, to use the analogy often employed by Czech-Jewish writers themselves, the contributors to the *Kalendář česko-židovský* during the final decades of the nineteenth century resembled the enlightened "national awakeners" of the Czech people approximately one hundred years earlier. The Czech nationalist intellectuals of the eighteenth and nineteenth century had sought to reintroduce Czech language and literature for secular purposes, to wean the population away from its long-standing reliance on the German language and culture. The Czech-Jewish awakeners, for their part, had actually to introduce to the Jewish population of Bohemia and Moravia a national culture which would have been the natural target of acculturation had it not been for the deliberate interference of the Viennese government in Jewish affairs.[70]

With the publication of the *Kalendář česko-židovský,* the small Czech-Jewish movement took direct aim at Jewish cultural and behavioral patterns in the Czech countryside. The volumes of the Czech-Jewish almanac represented in most cases the first exposure that Bohemian Jewish families had to literature in the Czech language and certainly their only contact with topics of Jewish interest which were not presented in German. In an effort to ensure that their publication would in fact be read by large numbers of Bohemian Jews, the editorial board of the SČAŽ patterned their first literary project after the highly popular German-Jewish calendar that adorned virtually every provincial Jewish home, *Pascheles' israelitischer Volkskalender.*[71] Books such as these enjoyed great popularity precisely because they performed a very practical function for the average Bohemian Jewish family. They served as yearly calendars, providing on the one hand crucial information concerning the ritual cycle of the Jewish year and, on the other, a complete accounting of the Christian calendar, including all of the popular Czech "name days." Most important, the almanacs listed every fair and market in Bohemia, Moravia, and Silesia according to date and locality—an indispensable aid for the Jewish peddler, small shopkeeper, and wholesaler.

The *Kalendář česko-židovský* provided all of these services to the Bohemian Jewish public, but in a new form and with a radical message. In presenting all of the non-Hebraic parts of the calender in Czech, the young movement hoped to demonstrate to Bohemian Jewry that that medium of communication that everyone accepted as natural in commerce and daily life belonged just as naturally to the world of Jewish culture more narrowly defined. Implicit messages such as this were driven home with much force and even some artistry in the work's more extensive literary sections. It is here that one finds lasting contributions both to the development of Czech-Jewish literature and to the elaboration of Czech-Jewish politics in the post-emancipatory era.

The editors of the *Kalendář* could not openly espouse political causes. The charter of the SČAŽ limited the organization to purely cultural activity, and adherence to this limitation was a precondition to the group's continued operation under the Austrian regime.[72] Nevertheless, they were allowed to urge their coreligionists to cultivate Czech patriotic feeling, and they apparently did not overstep their bounds when they endorsed the efforts of the Czech school association, Ústřední matice školská, in the introduction to their first edition. The early volumes of the almanac were dominated by articles on aspects of Jewish life in Bohemia, biographies of important Czech-Jewish figures, and examples of mid-nineteenth-century Czech-Jewish poetry. Increasingly, however, the publication opened up to a wider variety of literary contributions and a steady stream of theoretical essays on the "Czech-Jewish problem." Karel Fischer (1859–1906), who succeeded August Stein as editor of the *Kalendář* in 1885, proceeded over the next twenty-two years to develop it into a fine literary publication. He invited the participation of non-Jewish Czech writers such as Jakub Arbes (1840–1914), J. S. Machar (1864–1942), Jaroslav Vrchlický (Emil Frída, 1853–1912), and Gabriela Preissová (1862–1946). It was also Fischer who painstakingly cultivated the literary career of Vojtěch Rakous (Adalbert Österreicher, 1862–1935), the self-educated clerk who was to become the first major Czech-Jewish writer of the turn of the century, a naturalistic portrayer of Jewish life in the Czech villages.[73]

The *Kalendář česko-židovský* occupied a position of some importance not only in the development of Czech-Jewish culture, but also in the field of modern Czech literature. It was in its pages, for example, that the writer Jakub Arbes first made the transition from the German to the Czech language. And it was also in the *Kalendář* that Vrchlický first published the early acts of his 1897 play *Bar Kochba,* based on the Jewish revolt against Rome in the second century C.E. [74]

August Stein (1854–1937), recently graduated from the University of Prague with a doctor of laws degree, assumed the position of editor of the Czech-Jewish almanac from its inception until 1885. Whatever ideological consistency the young movement managed to display in its early years it owed to Stein alone, as his programmatic essay in the first volume of the *Kalendář,* "Židé v Čechách" (The Jews in the Czech lands), provided the Jewish public with the clearest exposition to date of what his party hoped to accomplish.[75]

The fundamental goal, quite obviously, was national assimilation. In its loftier formulations group leaders interpreted this to mean nothing less than "the fusion of Czech culture and Judaism" (*češství a židovství*) within each Jewish individual. But they were quick to admit that in practical terms assimilation entailed a process of acculturation and national sensitization the end result of which would be for one to consider oneself a Jew from a religious perspective and a Czech from the point of view of national affiliation.[76] The question that Stein sought to address at the outset of "Židé v Čechách" was under what conditions and at what point in Czech-Jewish history ought this process to occur?

The answers that Stein proposed reveal his dual indebtedness to classical assimilationist theories and to the specific impact of the Czech national movement. He adopted as his premise the familiar refrain that since the destruction of the Second Commonwealth at the hands of the Romans, the Jews constituted a religious community without a nationality. However, Stein added, only as long as two conditions prevailed could the Jews be expected to remain "bez národnost" (without a nationality): (1) if they were segregated from the rest of society through special, restrictive legislation and religious intolerance; and (2) if the general population in whose midst they lived had not yet developed its own movement for national self-realization.[77] Both conditions, Stein argued, had existed in the Czech lands until the end of the eighteenth century. Thereafter, the Christian-Czech population began to emerge from the cultural stupor that had prevailed since the Thirty Years' War to reassert its distinctive culture, language, and national identity. Jews, however, had not been capable of interacting with the general population as full and equal members of society before the final emancipation was achieved in 1867. Up to that time Jew and Gentile in Bohemia did not share mutual rights and responsibilities; hence they could not be expected to view one another as brothers. Emancipation created a new moral community and a social contract which implicitly required of its Jewish members a complete national identification with the majority culture.[78]

Of course, Stein was not ignorant of the steady process of German-Jewish acculturation that had existed in the Czech lands since the time of Joseph II. Rather, he argued that acculturation and (national) assimilation could remain distinct social phenomena as long as Jewish emancipation was not a reality.[79] Thereafter they could be expected to merge. Moreover, it was wrong to assume that because one of the agents of emancipation, the state, acted upon society in a centralizing fashion, it was then incumbent upon the Jewish community to regard this agent as its sole benefactor and object of loyalty. Emancipation, Stein urged, might be proclaimed by governments, but it could only be realized in the context of the nations among whom Jews lived. It was the nations of the Habsburg monarchy, "fighting for enlightenment and freedom," who succeeded in achieving equality for the Jews in 1867. Consequently, in directing both their social aspirations and their political loyalties toward the state in contradistinction to the nation, the Jews of Bohemia could at best be said to have been profoundly confused.[80]

The record of Czech-Jewish assimilation in the intervening fourteen years since the emancipation was, in a word, dismal. Stein charged Bohemian Jewry with "national indifference," with standing alone among the European Jewish communities that had been emancipated since the French Revolution in refusing to integrate with the surrounding population.[81] He did not care to consider the possibility that citizenship in the Austro-Hungarian monarchy might entail a plurality of cultural affiliations, or that an inherent conflict might exist between identification with the multinational state on the one hand and single-minded affiliation with one of its component nationalities on the other. Emancipation may have been achieved through the auspices of the Habsburg monarchy, but the social arena in which the drama of Jewish-Gentile interaction was to be played out was Bohemia. And, although the province as a whole may have been multinational, the major areas of Jewish settlement—the Czech countryside and the city of Prague—consisted of an overwhelmingly Czech majority. Hence, in Stein's view, the national choices for the Jews of Bohemia ought to have been as obvious as those of French or German Jewry.

Stein's treatise in the opening issue of *KČŽ* actually belied the myth of Czech-Jewish symbiosis in two respects. Frequent references to the fact that

Czech-Jewish assimilation was not only possible but *necessary,* that "nationally indifferent," Jews risked provoking the ire of their Czech neighbors, contradicted the notion of the naturalness of the Czech-Jewish alliance. If Czech acculturation were simply a natural and reasonable historical process, it would not have required a self-conscious movement to bring it about and certainly would not have depended upon warnings of popular animosity if it were not realized.[82] Moreover, his charge of Jewish indifference to the national configuration in the Czech countryside ought to have put to rest the contention that the Czech-Jewish movement was engaged in an essentially defensive act of cultural preservation. Rather, Stein and his collaborators in the Czech-Jewish movement were in fact rebelling against the cultural patterns of their parents' generation, which they viewed with as much displeasure as the behavior of the German-speaking Jewish majority in Prague. The goal of the SČAŽ was not to preserve but to transform; its leaders were cultural revolutionaries, not conservatives.

The Czech-Jewish version of assimilation, emerging as it did toward the end of the nineteenth century, during a period of intense national competition in the Habsburg monarchy, could not avoid being itself an expression of Czech national aspirations. Nevertheless, the SČAŽ's conception of Czech nationalism differed considerably from the attitudes of the majority of politically active, middle-class Czechs. For example, Czech-Jewish theorists placed explicit limits on the scope of their national program. Unlike the advocates of "historic state right," the Czech-Jewish movement did not understand the word "Czech" to be a geographic formulation. It did not refer to the borders of the ancient Kingdom of Bohemia, but rather to those places where the Czech nation in reality lived in significant numbers. The Czech-Jewish movement did not seek to alter the cultural habits or national affiliations of Jews living in such demonstrably "German" areas of the country as Liberec (Reichenberg) or Chomutov (Chomotau). Nor could it in good conscience advocate the application of the principle of Czech national autonomy to areas that had a predominantly German population simply because they fell within the borders of the former Kingdom of Bohemia. The Czech-Jewish program of national education—in many cases reeducation—focused narrowly on those Jews "raised and living in a Czech region among the Czech people." This included the more than 20,000 Jews living in greater Prague, which was after all a "Czech" metropolis, but the ethnically German Sudetenland fell outside of its purview.[83]

The national theory of the Czech-Jewish movement also differed from the mainstream on the question of national identity itself. The Czech Jews, as members of a group which, they admitted, once possessed its own national identity, argued for fluidity and change in national affiliations. Historical and social, rather than "organic," factors accounted for the evolution of nations; these, in turn, were defined ultimately in cultural terms. Not biological descent, argued August Stein, but shared language, customs, morals, abilities, and attributes made up the main features of national existence; and of these only language was an absolutely necessary ingredient.[84]

Religion, customs, abilities, morals—all of these might change completely, and the nation would still remain a nation. On the other hand, Stein pointed out, a number of nations might share a common religion, common morals, customs, and abilities, yet they remain nationally distinct.[85] The fundamental ingredients that lend unity to human populations and create entities which we recognize as nations are language and common territory. All other features of national culture are free to interact in a limitless variety of combinations. Moreover, the combination achieved at any particular moment in history is valid as a description of the nation only for that given moment.[86] Thus, during the sixteenth century, the Czech nation possessed the shared characteristics of a feudal society in the throes of a religious reformation and enjoying the fruits of a highly original urban cultural renaissance. The same Czech nation a century and a half later had undergone a thorough Catholic Counter Reformation and was but a provincial outpost of a cultural world dominated by Vienna. The only ingredients common to both examples, immune, as it were, to the expanse of time, were language and territory, and the first of these, through a combination of neglect and Austrian intolerance, was at the point of collapse.

Before the period of the Enlightenment, when Czech society was defined in corporate and religiously exclusive terms, the nation was necessarily Christian. Although Stein does not mention this, one might add that within the Christian population of the country only those corporate groups that enjoyed political rights—roughly speaking, the nobility, the clergy, and the bourgeoisie—can be said to have taken part in the nation. With the growing secularization of society in the eighteenth and nineteenth centuries, the contours of the nation could not help but be altered. The absolutist policies of Joseph II sought to incorporate all useful members of society at large for the task of service to the state. In so doing he loosened the bonds that tied the peasantry to the land and invited the Jews to seek greater integration into the general society. Joseph's goals found their realization in the Revolution of 1848 (in which the last feudal obligations were abolished), the industrialization of the monarchy in the 1850s and 1860s, and the Ausgleich of 1867 (which witnessed the final emancipation of the Jews). This meant that the cultural features of the Czech nation after 1870 could no more resemble those of the eighteenth century than could the eighteenth-century nation duplicate the patterns of Hussite Bohemia. Instead, the post-Enlightenment, postindustrial Czech nation of necessity included members of all religions and of all social classes. Any person born in the Czech lands, living among the Czech people, who spoke Czech in his or her daily affairs, and who was committed to the propagation and defense of Czech culture, was a Czech national. National identity resulted naturally from the circumstances of one's existence as well as from free and conscious choice.

At its inception, the SČAŽ represented but a small voice within the organized Jewish community of Prague. Indeed, if one were to use as a measuring stick the simple criterion of group membership, one could argue that the Czech-Jewish movement before the First World War never commanded the loyalties of the majority of Czech Jews. On the other hand, cultural and social change is not expressed solely, nor indeed primarily, in terms of institutional affiliation. Starting with the 1870s, Jewish loyalties and identities underwent considerable fluctuation and generally resisted efforts at formal measurement. In a period of general demographic, social, and political instability, Bohemian Jewry showed itself to be both malleable and conservative, tied in important ways to the old alliance with Austrian-German liberalism, but simultaneously evolving new forms of affiliation. Clearly, a variety of factors—rapid population growth, migration from rural areas to the city, the culmination of Jewish emancipation, and the beginnings of political activity on a large scale—combined to place Bohemian Jewish society in a sustained state of flux. The SČAŽ did not represent the end result of this process, but rather was but an early manifestation of fundamental change.

The participants in the Czech-Jewish movement held much in common with the provincial middle-class professionals who spearheaded the Czech national movement during the second half of the nineteenth century. However, the two phenomena were quite distinct. The Czech-Jewish movement was not simply a subset of Czech nationalism. It was a specifically Jewish response to the problems of integration, social advancement, and group identity in a postemancipatory, multinational, and industrial society. Moreover, the fact that the Czech-Jewish movement became a focal point of cultural activity among the Jews of Prague ought to strike one as at least a little puzzling. For, unlike the tens of thousands of educated provincial Czechs, who found the existing avenues of social mobility and self-expression inadequate to their needs—and thus promoted national autonomy as an alternative arena in which these expectations might be realized—migrating Czech Jews faced no such barriers. The institutions associated with Jewish life in the Bohemian capital, both formal and informal, voluntary and obligatory, might easily have served as vehicles for integration, mobility, and advancement. But a segment of the Jewish community refused to follow the obvious course. Not only did it find the existing patterns of Jewish affiliation and group attitudes troublesome, and, indeed, intolerable, but it also sought to effect dramatic changes in these areas.

2

Communal Politics and the National Struggle, 1883–1900

The Battle Over Jewish Culture in the Czech Lands

Language and Religion

Nowhere—with the possible exception of the Jewish elementary schools—was the institutional identification of Bohemian Jewry with German culture more pronounced than in its synagogues. Public ritual throughout the Czech lands, whether in the cities or in the smallest of villages, shared one key feature: the language of discourse for everything but the ancient Hebrew texts was German. The Czech-Jewish movement saw as one of its primary functions the removal of German from public Jewish life, if not from the sphere of private discourse as well. But this was not going to be an easy task.

First of all, the more modern congregations in Bohemia were linked in some way to the moderate wing of the German Reform movement within Judaism. They depended upon German (or Hungarian) seminaries for the training of their rabbis, listened to German sermons, and read from prayer books that included a German translation alongside the Hebrew original. Moreover, we have already seen how German was associated in the popular imagination with enlightenment and religious toleration, with the social and cultural reforms that had been inaugurated during the reign of Joseph II, indeed with the very process of Jewish emancipation in the Habsburg monarchy.

To make matters worse for the Czech-Jewish activists, the century-long association of German with communal worship had endowed the language with an almost sacred status in the popular Jewish imagination. Small-town Jews in particular tended to assign one of the languages of Bohemia a weekday and the other a holiday status. Vojtěch Rakous, the Czech-Jewish humorist and storyteller, caricatured this situation in his short piece "Jak se u nás němčilo" (How we became Germanized).[1] The author recounted how his father, who spoke not a word of German during the week, would return home from prayer in the neighboring town on Saturdays, having picked up a few words of German and Yiddish here and there, and would speak only German for the rest of the day. Rakous's mother never understood a word but listened silently and attentively to everything her husband had to say:

> Father would explain each German or Yiddish word with such genuine piety, as though he were standing in the synagogue in front of the altar; and mother took in every word with awed reverence. These words may have been compensation for the Jewish worship which she neither heard nor saw in the synagogue.[2]

In a similar vein, the Prague Jewish lawyer Maxim Reiner once complained that he often came across Jews who openly professed the Czech nationality, but who, once they entered a synagogue, nevertheless spoke among themselves in German. It was as if, he suggested, German were more conducive to holy occasions than their everyday language, Czech.[3]

Jewish Slavophiles made few efforts to alter this state of affairs before the 1880s. Two early developments are worthy of mention, however. The first grew out of the Young Czech literary revival of the 1840s—itself inspired in part by Jewish intellectuals. Hynek Kraus, a postmaster in the town of Luštenice (near Mladá Boleslav), who had been impressed by Siegfried Kapper's overtures to the Czech cultural nation, issued the first Czech-Hebrew *Siddur*. Published in Vienna in 1847, Kraus's prayer book sought to fill the needs of those Czech Jews who, even by this time, felt more at home in the Czech language than the German.[4] Ultimately the book was to have very little impact on Czech-Jewish life. It was not widely diffused, and its numerous printer's errors and linguistic archaisms rendered it unusable within a few decades.[5]

Of more lasting significance were the efforts of Rabbi Filip Bondy (1830–1907), a student of Solomon Judah Rapoport and Aaron Kornfeld and a graduate of the University of Prague. Bondy served the Jewish communities of Kasejovice (1859–68) and Brandýs nad Labem (1868–76) traveling through many of the small towns and villages, preaching in Czech, and conducting religious services to Czech accompaniments. His early determination to use the Czech language as a vehicle for the popular diffusion of religious ceremony and education may have raised not a few eyebrows within the Jewish community. A number, however, were undoubtedly heartened and impressed by Bondy's actions. Vojtěch Rakous, whose sister was married in a ceremony conducted by Bondy, ironically remarked of the occasion, "It was certainly the first time in my life that I understood every word that was spoken from such a mouth."[6]

Bondy had directed his efforts at de-Germanizing the context of public ritual so that Jewish ceremony would become more understandable to village and small-town Jews. The SČAŽ meanwhile sought to employ similar means in order to heighten the national sensitivities of all Czech Jews—particularly those of the cities—as well as to showcase the cultural inroads made by their movement. In general, the smaller, largely isolated, Jewish communities of the countryside tended to be quite receptive to the program of the SČAŽ. They yielded readily to the pressure that was brought to bear by the movement's so-called rural secretaries. Jewish institutions in the capital proved to be much more resistant to change. Consequently, the SČAŽ decided to circumvent Prague's established congregations, to create a Czech-Jewish presence in the area of public worship without first challenging the legitimacy of the existing synagogues. In 1883 a number of the leading members of the association formed a new organization called Or-Tomid (Eternal Light) devoted to promoting "prayer in Czech and in Hebrew." Reform Judaism was not particularly popular in Bohemia, least of all among small-town Jewry. Hence the founders of Or-Tomid declared that they had no intention of changing or reforming the Jewish religion. An early programmatic statement of the organization explained:

> [The society] . . . does not want to change any [part] of that which up to this time has been performed in worship services in Hebrew. Only that which up to now has been conducted in German—such as sermons, the prayer for the royal family, occasional talks, public announcements, declarations, etc.—will from now on be given in Czech.[7]

Calling upon Bondy to become the rabbi of its new congregation, Or-Tomid began to hold services on a regular basis in 1886. No one who had occasion to observe this small group could claim that its aspirations were not high, nor that it was uncognizant of its potential role in the cultural transformation of the Jews of Bohemia. In a sermon to the congregation, Bondy himself likened the effects of the group to Jacob's ladder, and, in so doing, revealed just how strongly Or-Tomid perceived its national and educational mission:

> Just as that ladder stood on the earth and reached up to the heavens, so the Or-Tomid society joins together godly thought (religion) with human thought (nationalism). The religious ideal still moves the entire world in modern times; indeed it is said that, even now, the second thought, the idea of nationalism, has progressed farther precisely where religion in all justice has a great influence on people. Here it is necessary to uproot the prejudices which have arisen out of ignorance of our religious ceremonies. Thus, not wanting to change anything from our Hebrew prayers, we want only to work toward this: that in place of German, which was only introduced in the last century, our mother tongue be used.[8]

Within a few years this conspicuous arm of the Czech-Jewish movement had outgrown its original quarters. Josef Žalud announced in 1892 that a fund was being established for the creation of a Czech-Jewish "Temple," the construction of which he likened to that of the recently completed Czech National Theater. In both instances the physical structure was to assume an importance equal to that of the cultural enterprise going on within its walls;

it was to be a visible symbol of patriotic sentiment and national determination.[9] Or-Tomid did become a showpiece of Jewish sincerity toward the Czech national movement. Non-Jewish dignitaries frequently joined Jewish worshippers in its building on Jindřišská Street near the center of Prague as the contents of Judaism were transferred ceremoniously from a German to a Czech vessel.

Or-Tomid and the SČAŽ began an ambitious publishing campaign in the 1880s and 1890s designed to create as quickly as possible—often through simple translations of German originals—a sacred literature in Czech. Hynek Kraus, the author of the 1847 Czech-Hebrew prayer book, issued a book of prayers for women in 1881 based on a centuries-old adornment of traditional Jewish homes which up to now had been available only in German or Yiddish.[10] Cantor Mořic Kraus made herculean efforts to help transform Jewish worship in Bohemia into an entirely Czech and Hebrew affair through a long series of translations and occasional readings. His contributions began with an 1885 translation of the *Yizkor,* or memorial service, and culminated at the end of the decade with the publication of the first Czech-Hebrew Passover *Haggadah.*[11] In between he published a variety of miscellaneous pieces: *Psalms and Prayers on the Birthday of His Majesty* (the Emperor); *The Five Prayers for Sabbath and Holidays; Funeral Prayer;* and *Czech Prayers for Public Worship at the Synagogue of the Or-Tomid Association.*[12]

Certainly the most important and influential of the volumes that rolled off the presses of Or-Tomid was the 1884 Czech-Hebrew prayer book compiled by August Stein.[13] Stein made conscious reference to the larger political implications of his undertaking in the introduction to his work. The new prayer book, he hoped, not only would serve the needs of the young Czech Jew, who spoke Czech both inside and outside of the home, but also would carry the message to the Czech people with renewed emphasis that the only thing that separated them from their Jewish neighbors was religious faith.[14]

A major portion of the publications that Or-Tomid issued during the first decade and a half of its existence consisted of educational texts for use in Jewish religious instruction in the Czech schools. The leaders of the Czech-Jewish movement sought to nullify all possible excuses that Jewish parents might have offered for not sending their children to Czech, rather than German, schools, and they recognized that priority had to be given to the problem of religious instruction, an obligatory subject in the Austrian school system.

The earliest efforts in this regard were made by Rabbi A. Kohn of Hradec Králové (*Abstract of the Mosaic Religion* [1883]), August Stein (*History of the Jews,* 2 vols. [1885–86]), and Rabbi Lev Thorsch (*Instruction in the Mosaic Religion for Middle and Burgher Schools* [1884]), the last a translation of a German textbook. Filip Bondy's translation of selections from the Pentateuch (*Torat Mosheh. Moses's Teachings for School-Age Youth*) appeared in 1886. Hynek Baum published *Foundations of the Mosaic Religion* in 1890, and Bondy followed one year later with the most significant of the Czech-Jewish textbooks, *Beginnings of Instruction in the Mosaic Religion.* This book, which consisted of selections made by the Prague Jewish scholar Nathan Grün and translated by Bondy, was published by Prague's main Jewish publishing house, Jakub B. Brandeis, and was the first Czech-Jewish text to receive authorization from the Ministry of Cult and Education for use in the local schools of Bohemia and Moravia. Leopold Butter, a teacher in Nový Etínek, wrote the first Czech-Hebrew reader in 1892.[15]

The flurry of activity that was set in motion by Or-Tomid and the SČAŽ in the 1880s and 1890s did not radically alter the shape and content of Jewish culture in the Czech lands. To begin with, Or-Tomid's initial program consciously avoided dealing at all with the question of content, arguing that all that was required to improve Czech-Jewish relations and the chances for Czech-Jewish integration was a realignment on the basis of language. The Czech-Jewish movement concentrated in the beginning on finding opportunities for better communication with the Czech nation; it was not prepared to force changes upon an unwilling or indifferent population. In introducing new linguistic vehicles to formal Jewish culture, Or-Tomid was merely providing services for the already converted. Where resistance to such changes was met, the movement adopted a strategy of avoidance of direct conflict. If the major synagogues of Prague preferred to retain the traditional patterns of public worship, Czech national Jews would simply establish their own synagogue. They would create a niche for themselves, but would not as yet attempt to squeeze out rival forms of Jewish culture.

The tentativeness of this approach left the Czech-Jewish movement vulnerable to the charge that it provided only halfhearted support for Czech nationalism. If it was not prepared to challenge the heart of the German-Jewish cultural alliance, all it was doing was providing window dressing, tidying up the appearance of Jewish life in the Czech lands so as to make it less objectionable to the majority population. To the average Czech national politician of the 1880s and 1890s, eager to redress the balance of power between the two national communities in the Czech lands, such accommodation to the long-standing practices of Bohemian Jewry was inexcusable. If Jews were to demonstrate their genuine friendship and support, they could do no less than commit themselves fully to the national struggle; as members of a religiously distinct yet ethnically vague—albeit suspect—community, their duty was not simply to become converted themselves, but to bring over the bulk of their coreligionists as well.

The School Issue

Over the last decade and a half of the nineteenth century, the Czech-Jewish movement felt challenged to demonstrate its loyalty to the Czech national cause on one issue in particular: the schools. Czech nationalists of all political stripes, but in particular the liberals, represented by the Young Czech party, insisted on the preeminence of this question in the national controversy. The schools—and by this was meant the structure of both public and private education in the Czech lands—held the key to the ultimate determination of all national issues: the language of common use among the population; the success or failure of the Czech cultural renaissance; the national/political loyalties of future generations. As the Young Czech economist and political activist Karel Adámek remarked in his contemporary study of Czech national life,

> The blossoming of Czech education was and must remain for all time the principal political goal of all genuine patriots and true friends of the people, of the whole nation.
> . . .The question of schools is raised high above the interests of parties and of individuals; [it is] certainly the most widespread, important, national and cultural question.[16]

In fact, educational reform had been a prerequisite for the growth of Czech nationalism in the nineteenth century. Before the Revolution of 1848 only the elementary schools in the Czech countryside and in certain cities provided instruction in the Czech language, and in the urban institutions German was used exclusively after the second year. Gymnasium and university study was conducted exclusively in German.[17] Czech-language gymnasia began to emerge in the 1850s, but these too became highly Germanized during the Bach era (Alexander Bach, minister of the interior during the period of "neo-absolutism"). Religion and Czech language were in fact the only subjects actually to be taught in Czech. The 1860s brought considerable liberalization in political and civic life—and with this liberalization the emergence of organizations dedicated to the promotion of Czech national interests. However, the government's expressed policy of requiring the use of both national languages in all middle schools in reality worked against the establishment of new Czech-language gymnasia. As late as 1866, only ten Czech gymnasia had been granted license to operate in Bohemia; in Moravia no Czech middle schools existed before 1867.[18]

The real breakthrough for a fully nationalized system of education in the Czech lands came with the so-called May Laws of 1868 and the Imperial School Law of 1869. Promulgated during the heyday of Austrian liberalism, the May Laws revoked the Concordat of 1855, provided for state regulation of the Roman Catholic church, instituted civil marriage in the Austrian lands, and provided for the separation of church and state in all areas of public life, including education.[19] Up to this time, all elementary education in Bohemia and Moravia, and most secondary education as well, had been conducted under the purview of some religious body. State-supported elementary schools were administered by the Catholic church, while the Jewish communities, since the time of Joseph II, ran their own. As long as this association of school and church remained in force, Bohemian Jewry was loath to give up its separate school system. The legislation of 1868 provided not only for the secularization of elementary education but also opened the ranks of students and teachers in such establishments to members of all religious groups. The main reason for the perpetuation of separate Jewish elementary schools in Bohemia had vanished.[20]

The Imperial School Law of May 1869 established a system of state-run primary and secondary schools throughout the Austrian lands which were to be administered by local provincial governments. At the base of this network stood the *Volksschulen* or *Národní školy,* the primary schools, which in turn were divided into Volksschulen proper (*obecné školy* in Czech) and the so-called *Bürgerschulen* (*měšťanské školy*), urban schools designed to provide a sound education to children who did not intend to go on to a gymnasium or Realschule. The middle schools consisted for the most part of classical institutions (gymnasia) and technical institutes (Realschulen/Reálky); later a cross between the two, the so-called *Realgymnasium,* was added. A variety of specialized technical schools existed as well. Universities (of which the Austrian lands, or Cisleithania, had six in 1869) and technological institutes (*Hochschulen/Polytechniky*) composed the highest level of education in the kingdom.[21]

The liberalization of political life in Cisleithania and the establishment of a modern, secular school system coincided with the demographic revolution and the growing urbanization of Czech life. One measure of the collusion of factors behind the rise of Czech nationalism is the dramatic increase in the number of educational establishments, both primary and secondary. In 1860 there were 3,650 Volksschulen in Bohemia; in 1865, 3,875; and by 1885, 4,636. Barely 611,000 students were enrolled in 1860; by 1885 the number had reached 899,385. For the twenty-year interval between 1865 and 1885, the number of primary schools in Bohemia had risen by 19.7 percent, the number of teachers of academic subjects by 29.9 percent, and the number of registered students by 47.4 percent.[22]

The expansion of secondary education during this period was equally impressive. In 1861 there were 23 gymnasia and Realgymnasia in Bohemia (10 Czech, 6 German, and 7 bilingual or "utraquist") and 8 Realschulen (4 German, 4 Czech). By 1884 the number of gymnasia had risen to 53 (31 Czech, 22 German) and the number of Realschulen to 16 (7 Czech, 9 German). Altogether some 9,500 students enrolled in secondary schools in 1861. In 1884 the number stood at just under 21,000.[23]

Czech educators and national politicians could rightly point with pride to the major advances that had been made since the beginning of the constitutional era in educating Czech children in their own language and culture. In 1885 more than 560,000 children (72.5 percent of the school-aged population of Bohemia) attended Czech obecné or měšťanské schools. Meanwhile the number of students attending Czech gymnasia, Realgymnasia, and Reálky had grown from 4,273 in 1861 to over 14,000 in 1884.[24] Relatively few children attended private elementary schools, only 26,339 in 1884–85, or about 2.8 percent of the total school-aged population.[25]

Nevertheless, leading figures within the Czech national movement voiced dissatisfaction with the pace of national education in the Czech lands. In particular they worried about the persistence of German educational institutions in regions with an overwhelmingly Czech population and in the movement's inability to attract to Czech schools as high a percentage as attended German schools in the so-called Sudetenland. For example, 5,296 children attended German public schools in predominantly Czech regions, while only 2,131 went to Czech schools in German districts. Only 612 children attended Czech schools in urban areas other than Prague, but 7,410 went to German schools in large cities, including 3,662 in Prague.[26]

Even more troublesome was the situation in secondary and higher education. In 1883–84, 17.8 percent of the students in Prague's German gymnasium, 27.6 percent of the students in the German gymnasium in Smíchov, and 17.6 percent of those in the southern Bohemian city of České Budějovice, were Czech nationals. Moreover, the percentage of Czech students attending the German Realschulen of Prague, Litoměřice, and Karlín, respectively, was 35.3, 30.7, and 35.4.[27] Before 1882 there had been only one university in Prague attended by Czech students as well as by Germans. Thereafter the institution was divided into a Czech and a German branch. Over the course of the next decade, virtually no self-declared German nationals received their education from the Czech University. However, Czech students continued to choose the German branch in significant numbers: during the winter and summer semesters of 1889–90, for example, Czechs made up 19.4 and 21.4 percent, respectively, of the total student body of Prague's German University.[28] A similar situation prevailed in the city's technical institutes. During the academic year 1880–81, 99.5 percent of the students who attended the Czech Polytechnika were themselves Czechs. On the other hand, approximately 35 percent of the students at the German Technische Hochschule were also Czech nationals.[29] By the end of the decade the figure had dropped slightly to just under 24 percent.[30]

What caused these German "incursions" into Czech national territory? In part they were the result of uneven development. As late as 1886, one state-supported German middle school existed for every 25,000 Germans, but the Czechs could boast of only one middle school for every 119,000 of their own nationals. There simply may not have been enough Czech institutions to accommodate all of those who desired a secondary education.[31] Perceptions about the quality or ultimate utility of a German education may also have played a role. A significant minority of the population that lived in the Czech regions of the country—who may even have considered themselves to be ethnically Czech—nevertheless insisted upon a German-language education for their youth, because it was seen as providing a more useful vehicle for professional and/or social advancement. Lastly, one could point to the activities of German civic associations and educational alliances, such as the Schulverein (school association). Established in 1880, the Schulverein subsidized private German schools in areas where the actual number of German speakers did not warrant the establishment of state-supported institutions and, in so doing, made German-language education a viable option for families living in predominantly Czech regions.[32]

Since all elementary education before 1868 was connected to the Catholic church, it is not surprising that the Jews of the Czech lands should have felt little inclination before this time to abandon their separate school system. But with the secularization of the schools, the raison d'être of the Normal-schule would appear to have vanished. Did the Jews close their schools at this point in recognition of the completion of emancipation?

The answer, interestingly, is no. The Jewish communities of Bohemia continued to maintain 114 private elementary schools in 1884–85. True, the total population at these schools was only 4,470, approximately one third of the entire Jewish school enrollment in Bohemia, and barely 17 percent of the 26,339 children who attended private elementary schools of all types in the province.[33] Truly damnable in the eyes of Czech nationalists, however, were the following facts: 96 of the schools (84 percent) were located in Czech-speaking towns and villages, not including Prague; all but one of these institutions employed German as the language of instruction; and over 97 percent of the Jewish children who were enrolled in private schools attended German-language institutions.[34]

Clearly, during the early years of the national educational system, Jews in small towns and villages did not place much stock in Czech schools. Some did, to be sure—enough to create a critical mass of Jewish student supporters of Czech national culture. But the large majority, for reasons of traditionalism, religious conservatism, loyalty to the Austrian state, or expediency, chose to keep in place—at least for the time being—the old system of privately run Jewish schools. This traditionalism may have held true for the Czech countryside, but it apparently did not extend to the areas of new Jewish settlement, in particular the industrial centers of northern and western Bohemia. Most of these places had no official Jewish community before the 1850s or 1860s, and thus did not possess long-standing, private Jewish schools. In those cities and towns with a large German-speaking population, Jewish children tended to go to the state-run German-language schools. In some cases, formerly Jewish institutions were taken over as state-run schools.[35]

Surprisingly little is known about the precise state of affairs in Prague. Primary accounts do not detail the fate of the Jewish Hauptschule (and its subsidiary schools) following the secularization of public education at the end of the 1860s. My sense is that it was converted to the category of "private school recognized under public law," and gradually acquired a mixed Jewish and Gentile population. Apparently the Schulverein also helped to maintain some of its branches, but only a close examination of the manuscript records of the Prague Jewish community will yield a definite answer. We do know that on the eve of the educational reform, the Jewish community of the city maintained fifteen private elementary schools, ten for boys and five for girls.[36] Another source holds that the Prague Jews supported five such schools in 1885, but is silent on the existence of German-Jewish schools in Prague a decade later.[37]

What is certain is that the large majority of Jewish children in Prague avoided private education altogether in favor of the municipal school system. And most of these children, in turn, chose the German track. In 1890, 97 percent of the Jewish children attending public schools went to German-language institutions. In 1900 the figure stood at 90.5 percent; and in 1910 it was still 89 percent. Over the course of this period, the Czech cause made very small, but steady, progress both in terms of absolute numbers and as a fraction of the Jewish aggregate.[38]

The Josephine reforms of the late eighteenth century had provided for a system of secular Jewish schools at the primary level only. The Jewish communities were not expressly prohibited from establishing private middle and upper schools. Nevertheless, none did so. Jewish parents who wished to send their children to classical gymnasia in preparation for the university simply chose from among existing private or state institutions. Most of the former, particularly in places like Prague, were administered by religious orders, but this fact does not appear to have deterred Jewish attendance. Jewish students in Bohemia, as in most parts of Europe, attended secondary schools with far greater frequency than their non-Jewish counterparts. Thus, in 1880 the 1,716 Jews who attended gymnasia and Realgymnasia in Bohemia represented 11.5 percent of the student population, and the 586 who attended Realschulen, 10.6 percent.[39]

Because Jewish middle and upper schools per se did not exist in Bohemia, "Jewish separatism" could not have been an issue for Czech nationalists. Yet the secondary and higher education patterns of Jews still had political importance. Their conspicuously high presence in schools at this level meant that the "national" choices that Jews made carried extra weight. This was particularly true once the Austrian government began to award the benefits of cultural autonomy on the basis of precise nationality ratios. For their part, Jewish middle-school students appeared to "vote with their feet" in favor of the German minority. In 1882–83 (the first year for which accurate statistics are available), some 83 percent of all Jewish middle-school students attended German-language institutions. By the middle of the decade the figure settled down to about 80 percent, with the remaining 20 percent going to Czech schools. More significant, the 1,931 Jewish students who attended

German-language middle schools represented 23 percent of the student body in these establishments, while the 403 Jews attending Czech schools made up a mere 3.2 percent.[40]

Not surprisingly, Jews also tended to pursue higher education with greater frequency than the population at large. Thus, as was the case with the middle schools, Jews constituted a conspicuous presence in the universities and technical colleges of Bohemia, particularly the German institutions. Already by 1863, Jews composed 10 percent of the University of Prague. During the winter semester 1880–81, 11.7 percent of the student body at Prague's still unified university and 17.9 percent of the German Technische Hochschule were Jewish. Many other Bohemian Jews completed their schooling in Vienna.[41] In the winter semester 1885–86—after the University of Prague was divided into separate German and Czech establishments—the 404 Jews in attendance at the German branch made up 26 percent of the total student body whereas the 50 Jews who registered with the Czech University represented but 2.5 percent of that institution. They did comprise 11 percent of the Jewish university students in Prague, but their presence in an establishment that had over 2,000 students went virtually unnoticed alongside the Jewish position in the much smaller German school.[42]

The educational patterns of Bohemian Jewry provided much grist for the propaganda mill during the last quarter of the nineteenth century. The Jews offered an easy explanation for some of the shortcomings of the Czech national movement. They represented an irritating anachronism, a stubborn remnant of the imperial past that refused to take cognizance of the new *national* basis of social, political, and cultural life. If private elementary schools continued to flourish in the Czech countryside, denying the largely anticlerical Young Czech movement its vision of a completely secular, national school system, the fault lay with the Jews, who continued to maintain communal institutions that dated back to the times of enlightened absolutism. If German nationalists were able to threaten the integrity of the Czech regions of Bohemia through the agency of German minority schools, they owed their good fortune to Czech Jews who were both ambiguous in their national orientation and obsequious in their devotion to the Habsburg monarchy. And, finally, if Czech nationalism had failed to transfer to the cities of Bohemia the cultural dominance that it had achieved so decisively in the countryside, the blame once again could be placed at the doorstep of the Jews, who, unlike their non-Jewish counterparts, appeared as eager to trade national-cultural allegiances as they were to change domicile.

Karel Adámek, for one, held such views, He charged in *Z naší doby,* his important work on contemporary Czech politics, culture, and economic life, that the Jews in combination with the Austrian bureaucracy were "certainly . . . the strongest German factor in Slavic circles." Moreover, the Jewish confessional schools, "like the schools of the [German] Schulverein, [were] a dangerous lever in the Germanization of Czech cities and communities."[43]

This was not a new attack. Public opinion in the Czech lands had equated Jews with the German minority for many decades now. On the eve of the Revolution of 1848, the patriotic Czech journalist Karel Havlíček-Borovský had rejected an overture for Czech-Jewish cultural collaboration put forward by the Jewish poet Siegfried Kapper on the grounds that the Jews were a separate ethnic entity; if anything, they could ally themselves more naturally to the German nation than to the Czech.[44] At the end of the nineteenth century, however, such accusations against the Jews emerged from an entirely different perception of their role in the country's national relations. Simply put, the seemingly age-old German-Jewish alliance was no longer accepted as part of the natural state of affairs. The Jewish communities in the Czech countryside ought to have resembled more closely the cultural environment in which they were located. Jews ought to have behaved like Czechs. They ought to have demonstrated loyalty to the language and culture with which, in their day-to-day activities, they appeared to be completely at home. Above all, now that a national, secular system of primary education was in place, they ought to have been sending their children to local public schools.

Some within the Czech national movement accused the Jews who lived in the Czech lands not only of being blind and insensitive toward Czech national aspirations, but actually of colluding with the rival German national movement. Karel Adámek, once again prominent in his criticism of Czech Jewry, claimed that the German Schulverein had gone so far as to base its "operational plan" for the Czech countryside on the maintenance of Jewish confessional schools. To support this contention, he quoted the remarks made by a certain Dr. Kraus at the General Assembly of the Schulverein in 1882:

> In Bohemia there is a whole array of private German schools, with and without public legal status, which are maintained in purely Slavic localities by the Jewish religious communities there. We must look upon these schools in the purely Czech countryside as rare linguistic islands which must be preserved since in such regions these schools are often the only seedbeds of German culture.[45]

He then listed the names of Czech communities where private German schools were subsidized by the Schulverein: Holešovice, Libeň, and Josefov within greater Prague; Pardubice, Příbram, Slaný, Benátek, Jičín, Nový Bydžov, Zbraslav, Čáslav, and elsewhere. Singling out several specific examples of German-Jewish treachery, Adámek cited the case of Heřmanův Městec, where the formerly private Jewish school had been transformed into a public German establishment because Jews there "*freely* chose the German nationality" (emphasis in the original); and the private German school in the town of Nymburk, which had 230 students in 1884–85 although according to the 1880 census the town had 5,126 Czech residents and only 226 Germans. Of the 230 students enrolled in the school, only 39 were truly "German" (presumably Christian). "What would the Schulverein schools look like," Adámek asked rhetorically, "if they were not attended by Jewish and Czech children?"[46]

Josef Kořán, Czech journalist and deputy in the Bohemian Diet, appealed directly to the heart of the Czech-Jewish community when he used the pages of the *Kalendář česko-židovský* to pressure Jews to de-Germanize their communal institutions. The first that had to go, naturally, were the German-Jewish elementary schools. Not only did they prevent Jewish children from developing the proper Czech national sentiment, but they also stole non-Jewish children from the national camp. For, alongside the 4,073 Jewish children in the Czech towns and villages, who in 1885 continued to be educated in German schools attached to the Jewish religious community, were 192 Catholics and 17 Protestants.[47]

Kořán challenged Bohemian Jewry to admit to the untruthfulness of many of the rationalizations that it used to justify its cultural behavior. "The supporters of these schools," he wrote, "would certainly object to us that they are only intended for children to be educated in German from a young age, that they, however, are not educated in anti-Czech thought."

> But the mere existence of the schools is conclusive proof that Jews who establish and support them do not think as Czechs, have no love for our language, have no confidence in the victory of our cause, and even the knowledge of Czech [carries] less weight than the knowledge of German. These schools are a living protest against our national and political endeavors; indeed they are actually—even if their supporters did not have this in mind—demonstrations against our Czech culture.[48]

Additionally, some had argued that the Jewish communities were merely supporting confessional schools and not German schools per se. If that were so, Kořán asked, why were many of these schools interconfessional, particularly in Prague, where there were five German-Jewish schools? If these schools existed primarily for religious instruction, one would have expected to find them in German as well as Czech areas of the country. But such was not the case. There were only ten Jewish schools in all of the German-speaking towns of Bohemia, proof enough that they existed primarily to perpetuate German culture among the Jews.

Challenging the Jewish Community

The Czech-Jewish National Union and the Schools

The leaders of the Czech-Jewish movement were sufficiently uncomfortable with the linguistic favoritism of the formal Jewish community to want to do something about it. They did not need the prodding of Czech nationalist politicians, whether friends such as Kořán or opponents such as Adámek. Indeed, Jewish Czech nationalists, such as J. S. Kraus, had been agitating for the closure of the German-Jewish schools in the pages of the *Kalendář* since the early 1880s.[49] Kraus went so far as to offer a new reading of Bohemian Jewish history to account for the schools. Not only were they to blame for the abnormal assimilatory pattern of the Jews since the Enlightenment (the absorption of "state culture" over and against local, national culture), but they had been forced upon an unwilling population. Traditional Jewish society, no less than traditional Czech society, had been the victim of a despotic policy of Germanization.

Nevertheless, the movement was prodded, and none too subtly. And it is impossible to determine precisely which motives most influenced Jewish behavior in this hazy and tumultuous period in Czech-Jewish relations. The Czech-Jewish activists *were* committed nationalists; they naturally stood in opposition to the cultural policies of the Jewish establishment; and they also were recipients of a barrage of criticism from Czech national quarters.

Driven by this complex of factors, the Czech-Jewish movement turned increasingly during the last decade of the nineteenth century away from purely cultural tasks to the establishment of a political machinery to effect change within the Jewish community. Beginning in 1893, with the founding of the Czech-Jewish National Union (Národní jednota českožidovská), and followed in 1894 with the creation of both the first Czech-Jewish newspaper and an overtly political Czech-Jewish organization, the by-now veteran activists of the SČAŽ took aim at the Jewish communities of Prague and Bohemia. Their purpose was no longer simply to educate, to cultivate national feeling, but rather to mobilize Czech-Jewish opinion, to challenge directly the structure of Jewish life that had resulted from the Austrian-Jewish emancipation.

The establishment of the Národní jednota českožidovská indicated a subtle shift within the still relatively new Czech-Jewish movement. Whereas the student leaders of the SČAŽ had displayed no single political orientation, their faculty advisors and outside supporters generally had been devotees of the National, or Old Czech, party. Members of the urban upper-middle class, and inspired by František Palacký and F. L. Rieger, they tended to affirm the conservative nationalism that the Old Czechs had typified. Those who became involved in Czech politics themselves, such as Bohumil Bondy, Alois Zucker, and Josef Žalud, ran for office as Old Czech candidates. Bondy won a seat in the Bohemian Diet in 1883 as a representative of Prague's Staré Město. Žalud and Julius Reitler were sent to the Diet the same year from Josefov—the old Jewish quarter of Prague, long considered to be a stronghold of German power—and Zucker was elected to the Imperial Diet in Vienna in 1885.[50]

The recently graduated lawyers, doctors, businessmen, and journalists, however, tended to support the rivals of the Old Czechs, the National Liberal party, whose members usually went by the name of Young Czechs.[51] Jakub Scharf, Maxim Reiner, Ignát Arnstein, and others—all veterans of the Czech-Jewish student movement, and all supporters of the Young Czechs—took it upon themselves to broaden the base of Czech-Jewish activities, to create a statewide, coordinated network of Jewish patriotic societies. In establishing the Czech-Jewish National Union, they took as models the various voluntary societies that had been created by the Young Czechs during the previous decade to mobilize opinion and bolster nationalist policies in Prague and in the countryside. One of these was the Central School Foundation (Ústřední matice školská), founded in 1880 in response to the German Schulverein. Also important were the several *národní jednoty* (national unions) that had been established to improve the material and cultural situation of Czech families living in mixed or predominantly German areas.[52]

Like the SČAŽ before it, the Czech-Jewish National Union sought to "spread the news" of the Czech national movement to every corner of the country. To do so, it relied not only on public lectures and social gatherings, but also on the creation of an institutional network consisting, before the year was out, of a central organization flanked by thirty-four district chapters.[53] Like the Central School Foundation and its subsidiary organizations, the Czech-Jewish National Union regarded one of its principal functions to be the furthering of Czech national education. Yet its manner of operation was quite different from that of its Czech counterpart. The Central School Foundation had emerged to meet the challenge of the German Schulverein essentially by mimicking it, by performing parallel functions of its own, but in German areas. The Jewish *národní jednota,* on the other hand, represented a power that could actually negate the effects of the Schulverein in the Czech lands. Instead of simply providing increased opportunities for Czech children, the Czech-Jewish National Union would attempt to make Czech education universal in areas where a *Jewish* minority had in the past dissented from the norm.

Together with its fortnightly newspaper *Českožidovské listy* (Czech-Jewish press), established in 1894, the Národní jednota českožidovská called for the closing of all German-language Jewish schools in Prague and the Czech countryside. "We want to work so that every Czech Jew will become completely Czech," wrote the editors of *Českožidovské listy* in its opening issue, "will feel, think, speak, and act as every other loyal Czech."[54] The modern Czech Jews, the paper argued, felt themselves to be part of the nation in whose midst they lived, whose culture they shared. They had no reason *not* to send their children to local Czech schools; and to persist in the old practice of maintaining separate Jewish schools was to commit an affront not only against the Czech people, but against the "modern Jewish spirit" as well.[55] As to the argument that it was important for Jews living in the Austrian monarchy to know German in order to ensure success in business

Table 3. Private German-Jewish Schools in Bohemia

Year	Source	German District	Czech District	Prague	Total	No. of Students
1884–85	a	13	96	5	114	4,470
1885–86	b	(12)	96	5	113	4,436 (of whom 4,282 Jews)
late 1880s	c	10	92	2	104	Czech dist. only: 3,385*
1890	d	7	79	(0)	86	3,843
1894–95	b	10	80	(0)	90	2,587 (*sic*)
1896–97	e	3	72	(0)	75	Czech dist. only: 2,351**
1900	d	1	27	(0)	28	1,687
1910	f	not given	n.g.	n.g.	5	154

*Of these, 1,050 proclaimed Czech as language of daily use; 2,309 German.
**Of these, 1,128 (48%) proclaimed Czech as language of daily use; 1,223 (52 percent) German.
Derived from: (a) K. Adámek, *Z naší doby* (Prague, 1887), 2: 14. (b) J. Kořán, "Židovské školy v Čechách," *Kalendář česko-židovský* 16 (1896–97): 152–57. (c) Adámek, *Z naší doby* (1890), 4: 80. (d) Bureau für Statistik der Juden, *Die Juden in Österreich* (Berlin, 1908), pp. 83, 84, 87. (e) *Naše doba* 4 (April 1897): 670. (f) Bohemia, Statistisches Landesamt, *Statistická příručka království českého* (Prague, 1913), p. 131.

and professional careers, *Českožidovské listy* referred to a speech by the Prague physician and Young Czech politician Emanuel Engel: this could be accomplished through the establishment of special language schools which would be private enterprises, "not connected with either you or your faith." As for himself, Engel admitted, he was not so radical as to believe that one did not need to teach German to one's children. But he challenged the Jews of Bohemia to work toward a time when it would become less and less important for them to do so.[56]

Between 1894 and 1907 *Českožidovské listy* reported with great interest on the concerted efforts of the Jewish *národní jednota* to purge the German-Jewish elementary schools in the countryside. One by one it rattled off the names of small-town and village communities, like a gunfighter from the Old West carefully taking aim and picking off rows of standing targets: Benešov, Tábor, Hradec Králové, Kutná Hora, Mladá Boleslav, Plzeň, Slaný, and so on. Josef Kořán, the Young Czech deputy who had admonished Czech Jews in the pages of the *Kalendář česko-židovský* in 1886, made a second appearance in 1896 to report on the progress made over the past decade.[57]

In all of Bohemia, German areas included, the number of German-Jewish schools had declined from 113 to 90. In the Czech–speaking countryside, meanwhile, nine new German–language schools had been established, but 25 were closed, yielding a net decline of 16. (See Table 3.) The number of Jewish children enrolled in German schools had fallen by 39 percent—from 4,239 to 2,587—while the number of Catholic students in German schools declined during this period by only 9.4 percent, and the number of Protestants by 23.5 percent.[58] Not only did a greater percentage of Jews switch from German to Czech schools, but virtually all of the establishments that succumbed during the 1890s were schools whose student body was exclusively Jewish. Those that had a mixed Christian-Jewish student body enjoyed greater stability and resistance to closure.[59] The Jews of Bohemia appeared, then, to be responding more forthrightly than either German Catholics or German Protestants to the urgings of the Czech national movement. The truth of the matter was that Jews felt less secure than non-Jews in patterns of cultural behavior, which, because of their relative newness as well as the turbulence of the postemancipatory period, could be looked upon as still experimental.

Typically, notices of school closings in *Českožidovské listy* were brief and matter-of-fact, though colored with the editors' obvious satisfaction. Thus one reads in the 1 February 1898 edition of the paper of recent events in Zbraslav on the southern outskirts of Prague,

> German-Jewish school closed. From Zbraslav *Hlas Národa* [Voice of the nation, daily paper of the old Czech party] announces that the local German school, which has been maintained by the Jewish religious community, will be closed at the end of the school year. Jewish students attending this school will go next year to the Zbraslav public elementary schools.[60]

The newspaper was careful to add the last sentence to this brief notice. It was not enough to point out that the Jewish community had given up its practice of maintaining a separate primary school. One had to add that the families in this community would be taking the subsequent proper step of enrolling their youngsters in public Czech schools. They would not be seeking other, German, alternatives.

Occasionally, the editors of *Českožidovské listy* would come across Jewish responses to Czech nationalism which they could not wholly endorse, as they appeared to have been made halfheartedly or without sufficient understanding of the nature of the undertaking. One such case occurred in Humpolec early in 1898. The Jewish leaders of this small town decided not to close the local Jewish school but rather to change its medium of instruction from German to Czech. *Českožidovské listy* greeted the news with reservation, acknowledging the progress that this change signified, but complaining nevertheless that the period of time required to achieve a complete linguistic transition would be too long. The editors sought gently to cajole the Jewish community. If it insisted on maintaining a "confessional school," at least it could begin instruction in Czech before the end of the calendar year.[61]

Where gentle persuasion would not work, the Czech-Jewish National Union resorted to all-out attack. Such was its tactic with the city of Kolín in east-central Bohemia, which had one of the larger provincial Jewish populations at the time. In March 1898, *Českožidovské listy* devoted a series of columns to what it called "the situation in Kolín." It contended that the German-Jewish school there maintained its existence against the wishes of the majority of the city's Jews, against the statutes of the community, and

thus "as a provocation to the entire Czech nation without regard to faith."[62]
To support its charges, the paper published an open letter signed by sixty
voting members of the community:

> It was pointed out in the Jewish communal council that on the question of
> schools, [in the light of] present-day—in many respects, changing—conditions,
> neither the council nor the board of deputies *any longer represents the thinking*
> *of the majority of Jewish citizens,* and that therefore this citizenry must be given
> the opportunity to express its desires and aspirations in this regard. . . . We
> therefore demand that the larger directorate of the religious community be
> convened so that it might speedily decide upon the closing of the existing
> German school.[63]

The German-Jewish school of Kolín had educated 147 children in 1894–
95. Within six months of the start of the campaign in *Českožidovské listy,* it
had closed.

In 1906 the Czech-Jewish National Union announced with satisfaction
that, as far as it knew, fifty-two German-Jewish schools in Czech linguistic
districts had been closed since the organization first began its campaign in
1893. At least two public German schools, which were attended primarily
by Jewish students, likewise were closed. And, in at least two other localities, the German-Jewish private schools had been replaced by Czech-
Jewish institutions.[64]

In point of fact, the extent of German-Jewish school closings since the
early 1880s far exceeded the claims of the political leaders of the Czech-
Jewish movement. Whether or not these institutions disappeared solely as a
result of Czech-Jewish political pressure, however, is open to question. We
know that the movement specifically targeted a number of towns for school
closings and was, in most cases, successful. However, the data also show that
Jewish schools in rural Bohemia began to close of their own accord during
the 1880s and early 1890s, most likely because of declining enrollments.

Table 3 and Figures 1 and 2 reveal the steady progression in German-Jewish
primary school closings between 1884–85 and 1910. At the start of this period
some 4,500 children attended Jewish-sponsored, German-language schools
throughout Bohemia, over 88 percent of which were located in Czech-
speaking districts, including Prague. By the end, the total number of children
attending the German-Jewish schools had shrunk to 154. Of the 114 private
schools that had existed in 1885, only 5 remained.

The pace of school closings during the first decade of political agitation
(1885–95) was brisk. The number of German-Jewish schools dropped by
about 21 percent; the number of students attending them by 42 percent.
This, it will be recalled, was a period in which a small number of new schools
were actually opened while others were being closed. Moreover, in many of
those places where the schools did not actually close, they nevertheless lost a
high percentage of their enrollment. The Jewish school in Benešov, for

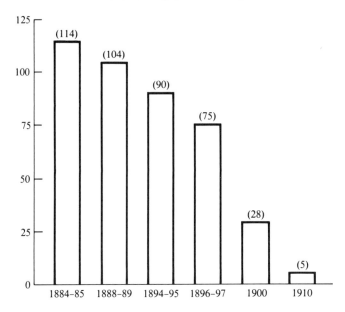

Figure 1. Number of German-Jewish primary schools in Bohemia

example, had had 60 students in 1885; a decade later the figure stood at less than half (26). Mladá Boleslav dropped from 105 to 67; Jičín, from 67 to 31; Brandýs from 52 to 30.[65] Even the important German-Jewish school in Kolín, the special target of Czech-Jewish criticism in 1898, had been losing population well before it became a political cause célèbre.[66]

The Jewish population of Bohemia had indeed been shifting away from the small towns and villages and toward the larger urban areas since the 1860s and 1870s, and the aggregate Jewish population did begin to fall after 1890. In neither case, however, was the pace of decline as rapid or as dramatic as that suggested by the statistics on primary-school attendance. One cannot escape the conclusion that Jewish parents in the Czech country-side began to remove their children from the German-Jewish school system of their own accord, long before the demise of that system would offer them no choice. And they took this action in more and more places and with growing frequency by the time the century was out.

The half-decade 1895 to 1900 witnessed a general intensification of politi-cal conflict as well as the outbreak of popular violence directed specifically against Jews in the Czech countryside, in the German towns of the Sudeten-land, and in Prague. It was indeed one of the most explosive periods in modern Czech history.[67] And during this time, a virtual tidal wave of school closings engulfed the Czech-Jewish countryside. Depending on which statis-tics one follows, the number of German-Jewish schools in this short period

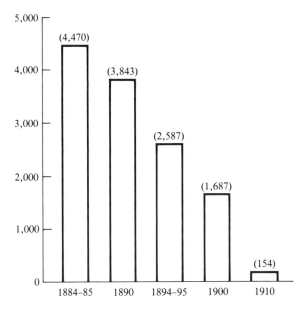

Figure 2. Number of students at German-Jewish primary schools in Bohemia

fell by as much as 69 percent, and the number of students by 35 percent. Only twenty-eight schools remained open in 1900. A decade later the German-Jewish school and, to all extents, the traditional German-Jewish alliance in the Czech countryside were dead.[68]

In the meantime Jewish children were swelling the ranks of public elementary schools in Bohemia. (See Table 4.) A total of 2,770 Jewish children attended public schools in Czech districts in 1880; in 1890 the number was 4,791; by 1900 it had reached 6,131. In German districts for the same years the number of Jewish students in public schools was declining (probably because their population in these areas was dropping): in 1880 the figure stood at 5,908; by 1900 it had slipped to 5,137.[69]

Despite its obvious victory in the redirection of elementary education, the Czech-Jewish movement failed to have as strong an impact on other areas of educational life. Changes in the patterns of Jewish attendance at the secondary-school and university level did occur, but they tended to take place gradually. At the highest levels, educational patterns showed remarkable stability through the first decade of the twentieth century. Gustav Otruba has compiled and published data comparing Bohemian middle-school attendance for 1882–83 and 1912–13. Over this period, the yearly total of Jews attending Czech-language gymnasia and Realgymnasia rose from 355 to 539; the Jewish share as a percentage of the entire student body climbed modestly from 3.3 to

Table 4. Jewish Attendance at Public Schools in Bohemia

Year	Czech Districts	German Districts	Total
1880	2,770	5,908	8,678
1890	4,791	5,439	10,230
1900	6,131	5,137	11,268

Derived from Büreau für Statistik der Juden, Berlin, *Die Juden in Österreich*, pp. 82–84.

4.5 percent.[70] Over the same period of time Jewish attendance at German-language gymnasia and Realgymnasia declined slightly, from 1,481 in 1882 to 1,225 in 1912. As a percentage of the whole, however, the decline was more profound. The 1882 figure represented 24 percent of the German student body; the 1912 figure only 15.8 percent.[71]

Thus, a twofold process appears to have been operating. On the Czech side, Jewish attendance increased gradually both in terms of absolute numbers and percentages. On the German side, the weight of Jewish presence was felt less and less, on the one hand because the real numbers of Jewish students were falling, and, on the other, because their relative numbers were declining even faster.[72] In the last analysis, the ratio of German-Jewish to Czech-Jewish gymnasium students provides the sharpest indication of the extent of cultural change within the Jewish community itself. And this measurement indicates clearly that progressively fewer and fewer Jews who received a classical secondary education were choosing to attend German schools. In 1882, close to 81 percent of Jewish gymnasium students took part in the German-language system. By 1912–13, however, this figure had been pared down to 69.4 percent, still the majority, but shrinking.[73]

The patterns of higher education among the Jews of Bohemia—attendance at universities and technical institutes—proved to be the most resistant of all to change. Between 1863 and 1881 Jews were able to increase their percentage at the University of Prague by only a small amount, from 10.3 to 11.7 percent, again because the increase in Jewish numbers was more or less offset by a parallel rise in the general student population.[74] Once the university split into separate German and Czech branches, Jewish attendance figures resembled those of the middle schools, but the differences were even more pronounced. Thus, in 1889–90, the 478 Jews who went to the German University made up more than 30 percent of the student body; while the 42 Jewish students at the Czech University represented a mere 1.7 percent of that institution.[75] Here, too, the actual number of Jews that attended the German University declined somewhat over the next two decades, while the absolute number of Czech Jewish students rose. Percentages, however, remained about the same, as the total population at the German institution dwindled while the reverse process occurred on the other side of the walls. Thus we find that during the winter semester 1899–1900, 413 Jews were enrolled at the German branch, 74 in the

Czech University, but the respective percentages were 31 and 2.4. In 1910, Jews continued to constitute about 20 percent of the German University and only 2 percent of its Czech counterpart.[76]

Since we know that the Jews of Bohemia possessed a declining population after 1900, and that even before this time the Jewish rate of growth did not keep pace with that of the population at large, the only true test of the effectiveness of Czech-Jewish acculturation with regard to higher education is one that measures attendance figures as a percentage of total Jewish enrollment. Yet even from this perspective, the results could not have been promising for patriotic Czech Jews. Between 1885 and 1901 as many as 92 percent—and never less than 82 percent—of Jewish university students in Prague enrolled at the German University. Perhaps some consolation could be taken from the fact that this figure was declining in steady, albeit minute, fashion over the course of the 1890s.[77]

Both the German and the Czech technical colleges (Technische Hochschulen/Polytechniky) succeeded in attracting ever-larger numbers of Jewish students between 1880 and 1900. But here, again, the Czech establishment could barely compete with the German school in popularity among Jews. Between 1881 and 1886, an average of 73 Jews attended Prague's Technische Hochschule each year; this was 25.4 percent of the student body. The number of Jewish students dropped somewhat for the remainder of the decade, but rose to 122 for the years 1896 to 1901 (26.2 percent of the student body), and jumped to 216 between 1901 and 1904 (30.5 percent). The Czech side showed a similar curve, with attendance dropping for some reason during the second half of the 1880s, but then rising dramatically in the 1890s. Between 1896 and 1901 an average of 27 Jewish students attended the Prague Polytechnika, composing 2.6 percent of the student body as a whole. Over the next four years the average grew to 34, but the Jewish share in total attendance dropped slightly to 2.3 percent.[78]

As we have found in the other areas of higher education, minor though perceptible change over time can be seen when the attendance records are considered from the point of view of total Jewish enrollment. The ratio of German to Czech enrollment hovered between 9.5 and 12 to 1 for the first part of the 1880s. In 1897–98 the ratio stood at less than 4.5 to 1, although in 1901–2 it had gone back up to 5 to 1.[79]

The Czech-Jewish movement enjoyed a mixed record on the question of the short-term transformation of Jewish educational patterns in Prague and Bohemia. Its only shining success came with the virtual elimination of the German-Jewish primary schools in rural and small-town Bohemia. This achievement resulted not only from secular demographic and social trends in the countryside, but also from the sustained pressure applied by both Jewish and non-Jewish Czech activists on the individual Jewish communities. The Czech-Jewish movement offered no such political program with regard to secondary education, relying instead on indirect persuasion and the natural inclinations of Czech-Jewish youth to do the job. Nevertheless, inroads were made in the patterns of Jewish gymnasium attendance; the percentage of German-Jewish students to Jewish students generally did drop; but by modest amounts and without causing any major disruptions.

Attendance patterns for higher education proved to be the hardest shell to crack. When it came to university and technical-college education, Bohemian Jewry chose by very wide margins perceived quality, utility, and prestige over other considerations. The German institutions of Prague enjoyed international renown. The education and training they provided—because of the German language—could be applied in many other parts of Europe. And the German University was, for all intents and purposes, the heir to the ancient institution of Charles IV (King of Bohemia, r. 1346–78). Deliberately to have chosen the lesser-known, relatively untested, provincially oriented Czech University would have required of most Prague Jews that they turn their backs on the very premises upon which a Jewish university education rested: the pursuit of scholarly achievement, the criterion of utility, and the promise of social integration and economic mobility.

Language and the Official Community

The establishment of the Czech-Jewish National Union in 1893 coincided with both government and Jewish communal efforts to shore up support for Jewish institutional life in the wake of the demographic disruptions of the past decades. Franz Josef issued a law in 1890 that reaffirmed the public status of the Jewish religious community in Bohemia (*Israelitische Kultusgemeinde/ Židovská náboženská obec*), and which reminded all Jews—particularly those who had changed domicile—that they were required to provide financial support to the official Jewish community of the district in which they resided. Only a public declaration of one's desire to be considered "confessionslos" (of no religion) could effect a divorce from the community and an escape from any financial obligation toward it.[80] At the same time the law instructed each new and existing Kultusgemeinde to draw up a set of bylaws defining the geographic scope and the functions of the community, and to submit it to the governor's office within three years.

The Czech-Jewish National Union saw this modest restructuring of Jewish institutional life as an opportunity to press home at least part of its national program, to bestow the blessings of public law on the Czech-Jewish revival. Its leaders hoped for some kind of statement in the new bylaws of the Prague Jewish community that would assert the equality of the Czech and German languages in communal affairs. However, the statutes ultimately proposed in 1893 were conspicuously silent on the question of language (though they were written in German).[81] Consequently, in a series of public addresses and printed pamphlets, the president of the Czech-Jewish National Union, Jakub Scharf, urged Franz Thun, the governor of Bohemia, to reject the bylaws of the Jewish community until they included the proper linguistic provisions.[82]

Unfortunately for the Czech-Jewish movement, the Bohemian governor's office interpreted this behavior as blatant political pressure and a violation of the organization's nonpolitical charter. In March 1894, the Czech-Jewish National Union was officially dissolved. The Czech-Jewish organization joined a long list of groups to have provoked Thun's displeasure during the early 1890s. The Akademický čtenářský spolek (Academic Reading Society) had been disbanded in 1889; the Moravian Peasant Union fell in 1890; and virtually every Czech student organization in Bohemia had to take cover during September and October 1893.[83] Not to be deterred, Scharf fought the ruling in court and won. After hearing what, according to all accounts, was a stirring speech by Scharf in defense of his organization, the Imperial Court overturned the action of Governor Thun in January 1895. The Národní jednota českožidovská was back in business.[84]

Now that the courts had declared such activity to be legal, "business" included renewed efforts to force the community to make linguistic concessions in its public affairs. The closing years of the nineteenth century witnessed sporadic assaults on the linguistic integrity of established Jewish institutions. *Českožidovské listy* attacked the Centralverein zur Pflege jüdischer Angelegenheiten (Central Association for the Promotion of Jewish Affairs) in 1898 for publishing a fortnightly newspaper with the ambiguous title *Israelitische Gemeindezeitung*.[85] *Českožidovské listy* warned its readers that the paper in question had no connection with the official Jewish community. Nor did it represent the "general interests" of Prague Judaism, as its title went on to claim, but was merely the mouthpiece of liberal, German-Jewish assimilationism.[86]

In 1899 the Czech-Jewish National Union attempted to have a resolution passed that would have guaranteed linguistic equality within the Prague Jewish community, but the board of trustees refused to go along. The leadership of the National Union then acted in the same manner that had gotten it in deep trouble only five years before. It wrote to the governor's office, asking it to intercede in the matter, as the Jewish community was about to renew its bylaws.[87] The movement did succeed in arranging for one upper and one lower class in the Prague Talmud Torah to be conducted in Czech beginning with the academic year 1899–1900. And it rejoiced over the fact that Julius Reich, a candidate for the post of rabbi of the Smíchov synagogue in 1900, delivered his sermon on Friday in German and on Saturday in Czech.[88] And so the battle progressed up to the start of the twentieth century. The Czech-Jewish movement enjoyed near-total victory in the countryside. In Prague, it met up with much greater resistance. But time, demography, and politics appeared to be on its side.

Language of Daily Use

Up to this point, we have brought together overt expressions of ethnic sentiment, examples of cultural politics, and a variety of indirect measurements of group identity in an effort to demonstrate the pace and overall direction of cultural change within the Bohemian Jewish community toward the end of the nineteenth century. Our arguments would have been much simpler had we been able to employ a series of direct and credible measurements of ethnic loyalties. Ordinarily, census returns might have provided just such an indicator. While a population was being counted, it could be given the opportunity to declare a national affiliation. Unfortunately, the Austrian government never created a census questionnaire that allowed for an unambiguous correlation between nationality and religion.

For one thing, Vienna never seemed to know quite what to do with the Jews. In mid-century, before full legal emancipation had been accomplished, both official and semiofficial censuses tended to treat the Jews as a nationality as well as a religion.[89]

With the creation of the Dual Monarchy in 1867, however, the Habsburgs appeared to have resolved the most obvious of their nationality problems and were not eager to promote the national claims of any ethnic minority. Jewish emancipation was completed the same year, and the official status of the Jews within the state now devolved to that of a religious denomination. Not surprisingly, when the next census was taken in 1869, Vienna refrained from recording national affiliations. Perhaps it hoped that silence on the issue would help to buy time for the Austrian half of the monarchy to achieve a national amalgamation of its own. This, as is well known, was not to be the case. The political confrontations of the 1870s resulted in provisions for partial cultural autonomy. Henceforth, schools, teachers, government subsidies, and the like were to accrue to the various nationalities on the basis of their representation within the population at large. From this point onward, censuses took on crucial political significance. Under the close scrutiny of rival national representatives, the Austrian government committed itself to measure periodically the size of each national group.

The first census following the Ausgleich to take national affiliation into account was that of 1880. The first to correlate ethnic preference to religious affiliation was the census of 1890. The authorities sought to lessen the political ramifications of the census by choosing a linguistic criterion—"everyday language" (*Umgangssprache/obcovácí řeč*)—for ethnic affiliation. They may have hoped thereby to avoid the potential for confusing ethnic and political loyalty, as well as to underline the fact that in a multinational empire language constituted the only acceptable basis for autonomy within the state.[90]

Austria's emancipated Jewry found that it had to acknowledge membership in a distinct religious community but could no longer claim national distinctiveness. This would have been difficult in any event in view of the government's insistence on language as sole determinant of nationality. But Vienna compounded the problem by refusing to recognize Yiddish as a separate national tongue. Instead, it considered Yiddish to be simply a subset of German and recorded it as such. The Jews, then, found themselves to be in a double bind. Not only were they prevented from claiming a unique ethnic identity, but the language that the Jewish masses in the East still spoke automatically placed them in the German national camp.[91]

Of course, Bohemian Jews had assimilated to the point that they were not likely to indicate Yiddish as their mother tongue. Their situation was nevertheless fraught with ambiguity. The vast majority being bilingual, Jews quite literally could simply choose between listing Czech or listing German. The census did not ask for the motives that lay behind one's choice, but these soon became a favorite object for speculation on both sides of the national divide. In 1890 about two thirds of Bohemian Jewry—and three quarters of the Jews of Prague—declared their language of daily use to be German.[92] Ten years later the situation dramatically reversed. Now more than 54 percent of both Bohemian and Prague Jewry proclaimed Czech as their daily language.[93] By 1910 the Jewish population had declined somewhat, and so had the size of the new linguistic majority among the Jews, but Czech clearly had become the official language of choice and would remain so up to the community's demise during World War II.[94]

Was this a sudden "conversion" on the part of Prague and Bohemian Jewry? Was the shift in linguistic affiliation an expression of political expediency? As we shall see in the next chapter, the years 1895–1900 witnessed the disintegration of German liberalism in Prague, the radicalization of Czech national politics, and also the outbreak of numerous antisemitic incidents. Perhaps the prudent Jewish residents of Prague or of the provinces simply wished to avoid the appearance of provocation and, hence, cast their lot, at least for the time being, with the more powerful national bloc. In their hearts they may have remained "German," but for the purposes of the official census they were content to play the "Czech."[95]

Such a reading of the situation does have some merit—census declarations were political acts of much symbolic importance—but it oversimplifies the Czech-Jewish phenomenon. It ignores, for example, not only the demographic movements of the previous decades but also the sustained political pressure exerted by Czech Jews themselves to alter the cultural patterns of the Jewish community. It also assumes incorrectly that national choices made before 1890 reflected the true intentions of the respondents whereas those made after 1890 did not. No such situation could be free of keenly perceived pressures, political or otherwise. The Jewish merchant or shopkeeper who wished to remain in good standing with the Czech street in one instance may have had equally compelling reasons to please the Viennese authorities in another.

The fact of the matter is that both the 1890 and the 1900 censuses represent valid indications of the cultural complexion of Czech Jewry. It was, to borrow a phrase, "ambidexterous." And it was this ability to move from one national camp to another that is just as important a fact as the move itself. One might wish to summon such factors as growing political pressure and the outbreak of popular antisemitism in order to explain why Bohemian Jews made the shift in 1900 rather than in 1890 or in 1910. But it is presumptuous to question the sincerity of 50,000 votes.

For the defenders of German culture in Prague, the national turnabout of the Jews in 1900 must have been a crushing blow. Jews were not the only ones to defect from the ranks, however. The 12,588 Jews of the inner city who declared German to be their everyday language in 1890 represented 46 percent of all German speakers in the city. Ten years later, the 8,230 Prague Jews who declared German still constituted 46 percent of all German speakers.[96] Obviously, a proportionately equal number of non-Jews had also changed their national colors. Alas, they appeared to enjoy a degree of anonymity not granted the Jews of Prague.

Recent research into the phenomenon of nationality transfer in Prague has argued that wealth was the single most important factor determining allegiance during this period. Gary Cohen has compared the ratio of German Jews to Jewish citizens with the percentage of the population living in housing with an annual rent of more than 400 crowns, and has found a fairly high correlation (0.58 for both 1890 and 1900). He conducted a similar test for Czech Jews, comparing this ratio to the percentage of the population living in housing of 200 crowns or less, and again came up with a high correlation (0.58 for 1890 and 0.52 for 1900).[97] Thus, at the extremes of the economic ladder the national loyalties of Prague Jews were fairly predictable.

Cohen's statistical correlations tend to leave a false impression, however, about the true sources of cultural change within the Jewish community. They do show that wealth and national culture went hand in hand during periods of relative stability. But they are much less clear on what was going on during periods of transition. For example, it would be false to conclude that those who switched national allegiances during the last decade of the nineteenth century were primarily poorer Jews. In fact the correlations between rent levels and language remained fairly constant at the two ends of the spectrum. Most of the Prague Jews who became "Czech speakers" in 1900 came from the broad middle class. Additionally, since the correlation between low rent and Czech language declined slightly in 1900, the relative wealth of the Czech-speaking group may actually have been rising.

In fact most of the Jewish newcomers to the Czech national camp were people who had a stake in the regional economy—small businessmen, shopkeepers, middle-class professionals, and the like. They were people of modest means, obviously bilingual, most often from a town outside of the capital, who may or may not have sent their children to provincial Czech gymnasia, may or may not have been interested in the nationality controversy themselves, but who shared at least one crucial characteristic: vulnerability, economic and psychological.

Cohen's own researches into three of the more prosperous parishes of inner Prague—St. Henry and St. Peter in Lower Nové Město and St. Gall in Staré Město—do bear out these points. Not only did the percentage of Czech speakers in these parishes rise from 71 to 79 percent between 1890 and 1900, not only did the Jewish share among Czech speakers increase from 4.3 to 17 percent, but the demographic base for these changes was clearly the commercial middle class. For example, the portion of German-speaking residents who depended on commerce for their livelihood dropped from 47 to 39 percent (the largest decline in any economic sector). At the same time, the number of Czech speakers involved in commerce rose from 30 to 38 percent.[98] On the surface it might have appeared as though the Czech population of Prague had gained a sizable portion of its middle class overnight. In reality, though, it was Bohemian Jewry, sounding an alarm, voicing its discontent with past cultural arrangements, flexing its ambidexterous limbs.

By 1900 the first fruits of a cultural transformation within Bohemian Jewry were readily apparent. They took the form of a demographic restructuring of the Prague and Bohemian Jewish communities, the progressive urbanization of Jewish life, a shift in the linguistic preferences of Bohemian Jews, and the break-up of the traditional system of German-Jewish primary education. These changes grew out of a combination of forces, two of which were paramount: demographic movement on a large scale and political pressure, both self-induced and external. There is no satisfactory way to isolate the factors in question in order to calculate their respective weights; any such attempt would be historically artificial as well as futile. What one can do is to freeze at a point in time the emerging profile of Bohemian Jewry. This, in part, is what the census of 1900 did; periodic measurement of Jewish school attendance between 1880 and 1910 could accomplish much the same thing. The making of Czech Jewry may have been incomplete in 1900, but the direction of change was becoming increasingly clear and the pace inexorable.

3

Breakdown and Reconstruction: Antisemitism and the Reorientation of Czech Jewry

The Radicalization of Czech and German Political Life

In 1891 the Young Czechs, representing the liberal wing of the Czech national movement, enjoyed their first decisive electoral victory. They now emerged as the strongest force in Czech politics both in Vienna and at home, vindicated in their decision seventeen years earlier to split with the National party over the issue of "passive resistance," that is, nonparticipation in the Bohemian Diet and the Austrian Reichsrat. To the Young Czechs, who formed a generally anticlerical and liberal bloc—though not exclusively middle class in composition—the Old Czech policy of noncooperation had seemed to be counterproductive. Some Czech nationalists might have taken comfort in the knowledge that they had not compromised the principle of historic "state right" (*státní pravo*) in order to share power in Vienna and in Prague. But the Young Czechs recognized all too well that loyalty to principle could leave one bereft of patronage and power.[1]

In 1879 the Young Czechs induced their more conservative rivals to abandon the tactic of boycott and to participate in the government of count Eduard Taafe (1879–1893). The new policy appeared to pay off handsomely during the following decade. Czechs for the first time began to translate their predominance in the population of Bohemia and Moravia into concrete political power. Already by 1882 the Czechs, together with their allies among the landed nobility, gained a majority in the Bohemian Diet. But the Czech national movement could also point to concrete changes in Austrian cultural policies that had occurred as a result of its new program of political participation and negotiation. The Austrian language law of 1880, known as the Stremayr Ordinance, had met the demands of the Czechs that any individual within the "lands of the Czech Crown" (Bohemia, Moravia, and Austrian Silesia) be able to use the Czech language in dealings with the courts and the bureaucracy. In 1886 the minister of justice bowed to further pressure from Czech nationalists and extended the use of Czech within the Prague High Court to include the internal workings of the body as well as contact with plaintiffs and defendants.[2] In 1881 the government agreed to the division of Prague's Karl Ferdinand University into separate Czech and German branches, the lion's share of the students destined to attend to Czech institution. Over the course of the 1880s, nationalist leaders managed to reduce the disproportionate advantage of numbers that German-language schools formerly had enjoyed over Czech institutions. They succeeded in building a complex, multilevel system of national education that not only inculcated a sense of cultural pride in a new generation of students, but also provided this Czech-speaking cohort with the advanced training required to assume positions of responsibility in an industrial society.[3]

The immediate context for the rise of the Young Czechs to power was a series of negotiations on nationality issues that the Taafe government had initiated in 1890. The Old Czechs, the old landed nobility, and the United German Left—but not the Young Czechs—met in that year to arrive at an Ausgleich (compromise) that, like the Austro-Hungarian Compromise of 1867, might have satisfied the demands of most Czech nationalists while preserving the integrity of the Habsburg monarchy. The agreement that eventually was signed failed to do this (the Czechs, for example, did not even achieve the recognition of Czech in internal government service or a general requirement of bilingualism for officials and judges), and the Young Czechs, who had not been party to the negotiations, astutely exploited the unpopularity of the so-called *Punktace* (Agreement). They not only ran against it in the upcoming elections to the Reichsrat, but also convinced enough deputies in the Bohemian Diet to change their party affiliation so that the Young Czechs became the largest party in this body.[4] In the Reichsrat elections of March 1891 the Young Czech party swept to victory—winning thirty-seven of thirty-nine Czech seats in Bohemia. It remained the largest Czech party in the Austrian Reichsrat until 1907 and in the Bohemian Diet until 1908.[5]

On the heels of the Young Czech victory of 1891, the leadership of the Czech-Jewish movement could point to the soundness of its political strategies of the past decade. It had aligned with what at the time was both the most liberal and the most fervently nationalistic of the Czech political parties. Now the veterans of the SČAŽ could view themselves as belonging, at least in spirit, to the ruling party in Czech politics. The 1890s appeared to promise the fulfillment of liberal Czech nationalism: cultural autonomy and free political development for the Czech people in an environment of secularism and tolerance that harked back to the 1848 revolutions.

Yet the optimism of the early part of the decade soon faded. Franz Thun, the Bohemian governor, instituted a state of emergency in Prague between 1893 and 1895 as a response to popular protests and a purported threat to the regime. Meanwhile, the Young Czech coalition of middle-class farmers and city dwellers, students, professionals, and intellectuals, proved to be unstable and began to split apart as early as 1893.[6] No longer members of the ruling coalition, the Young Czechs failed to create a genuine opportunity for national reform. Nor did their tentative combination of national and liberal ideologies lead to the establishment of a liberal, democratic society. The leaders of the party tended to compensate for lack of success in practical politics by allowing the terms of the national debate to become radicalized. Toward the end of the decade they made greater and greater use of antisemitism—a constant, but latent element in the Czech-German confrontations of the 1860s and 1870s—as a principal vehicle for the enumeration of Czech grievances against the government in Vienna.[7]

Life in the Czech countryside already had begun to worsen for Jews by the early 1890s. Nationalist politicians began an economic campaign against Jewish merchants and shopkeepers during the summer of 1892 that went by the name of "each to his own." "Svůj k svému" was a phrase first used by the nineteenth-century historian František Palacký, although in its original formulation it had been followed by the words "a vše dle pravdy" (and everything according to truth). Palacký's turn-of-the-century heirs apparently did not share his concern for the relationship between means and ends. To them, "svůj k svému" simply meant that the nation had to protect its own economic base, foster its own productive forces, and keep out foreign competition and exploitation. Most Czech nationalists in this period continued to view the Jews as members of the German camp, and, as such, their business was not welcome. Many Jewish establishments were ruined as a result, particularly those that had operated in small towns and villages and hence were totally dependent on Czech patronage for their survival.[8]

Industrial unrest, popular violence, and mass demonstrations in favor of universal suffrage combined during the first half of the 1890s to produce an atmosphere of crisis and turbulence. Much of this social unrest was directed toward Jews and took the form of a revival of the ancient "blood libel," the accusation that Jews murdered Christians in order to make use of their blood for ritual purposes. News of a ritual murder of a Christian servant girl broke out in Nový Benátech, near Mladá Boleslav, in 1892. In April 1893 anti-Jewish rioting erupted in Kolín following rumors that another young servant girl, whose body had been found in the Elbe, had been murdered by her employer and other Jews in order to obtain her blood for the making of Passover *matzot* (unleavened bread). These disturbances, in turn, set off a chain reaction of anti-Jewish rioting in other towns and villages, including Kladno and Kutná Hora.[9]

That such ancient superstitions as the blood libel should have emerged in postindustrial Bohemia is perhaps not so surprising. Accusations of ritual murder—still part of the popular imagination at the time—permitted small-town communities to ignore the prospect that they might be harboring a homicidal criminal in their midst. Just as important, the blood libel could shield from public view the problem of suicide among young, single females, many of whom may have been facing unwanted pregnancies, personal rejection, or both. And yet the rationalizations of public officials, made in the wake of these accusations, bestow an aura of unreality on these events. According to the Czech weekly *Krkonoš* (after the Krkonoše [Giant Mountains] in northern Bohemia), the Jews had brought the rioting on themselves through their economic behavior and their support of the German national cause. Most unlikely of all was the statement of the medical officer who examined the body of the dead servant girl in Kolín. In an odd juxtaposition of forensic science and political analysis, he concluded that the root of the problem lay in the maintenance of a German primary school by the Kolín Jewish community![10]

Unpleasant as they might have been for Jewish Czech nationalists, the events of the early 1890s paled in comparison to what was to occur during the final years of the decade. One could argue that the fortunes of Bohemian Jewry began to worsen dramatically in the aftermath of the first election of Karl Lueger (1844–1910) as mayor of Vienna in 1895. Lueger, leader of the Christian Social party in the Austrian capital, was an immensely popular politician and the first to run for office successfully on an overtly antisemitic plank. His rousing popular appeal alarmed the Emperor Franz Josef, who feared that Lueger might encourage popular unrest. For two years in succession the emperor refused to allow him to be seated as mayor. Faced with Lueger's third election in 1897, however, Franz Josef resigned himself to the realities of Viennese politics and recognized him in his new position.[11] During this period Christian Socialists in Bohemia and Moravia began to absorb Lueger's antisemitic rhetoric and use it to great advantage in combating the growing influence of Czech social democracy.[12]

At the same time that Lueger's Christian Socialists were overtaking the political establishment in Vienna, a crucial set of developments took place in imperial politics. In 1895 the Galician nobleman Casimir Badeni assumed the position of prime minister of Austria. He quickly embarked on a double strategy for prolonging the life of the Habsburg monarchy, promoting franchise reform on the one hand, and, on the other, seeking to entice the Czech nationalists back into the government by reaching a new agreement on the language issue.

Badeni proposed to meet growing demands for universal male suffrage by creating a fifth electoral curia—composed of all males over the age of twenty-four. This broad extension of the vote created an unprecedented situation during the election campaign for the Reichsrat in March 1897. The Young Czech party, which in the past had prided itself in having had broad popular appeal, now had to mobilize its membership to meet the challenge of a greatly expanded electorate. Together with the Christian Social party, the Young Czechs sought to gear their appeal to the workers, artisans, and small shopkeepers of the newly enfranchised population, thereby preventing it from falling into the hands of the recently established Czech Social Democratic party.[13]

It was in the course of the election campaign of 1897 that the Czech Jewish movement suffered its first major political shock. The Young Czech leadership in Prague decided to nominate its own version of Vienna's Lueger to run in the city's fifth curia—the popular crowd pleaser and vocal antisemite Václav Březnovský (1843–1918). The decision of the Young Czechs threw all of Prague Jewry—not simply the Czech-Jewish movement—into a spin. Březnovský had only two opponents, a representative of the Christian Social party, Father Josef Šimon, and Karel Dědič, the nominee of the Social Democrats. Prague Jews would never have voted for the clerical candidate (fiercely antisemitic in his own right), and most Jewish notables rejected the social and economic positions of the socialists. They had always thought of the Czech or German liberal parties, both of which had long traditions of anticlericalism, as their natural allies. Yet in the face of the Březnovský nomination, Prague Jews by and large chose a tactical alliance with Czech Social Democracy.[14] The *Israelitische Gemeindezeitung,* mouthpiece of the German-oriented Centralverein zur Pflege jüdischer Angelegenheiten, expressed the dilemma best:

> For the time being we will not discuss the economic program of Social Democracy. However, every true liberal can subscribe to [its] political program; and besides, "The enemies of my enemies are my friends!"[15]

The Prague elections, which were held in two rounds because no one garnered a majority on the first try, resulted in a resounding victory for Březnovský. He received virtually unanimous backing from the Catholic press and the Christian Social party in time for the run-off election despite the fact that he had a solid reputation as an anticlerical. Dědič, meanwhile, was castigated for having received both German and Jewish support and actually received fewer votes during the run-off election than he had on his first try.[16]

The new populist politics of 1897, coupled with what some Czech nationalists perceived to be unconscionable political behavior on the part of Jews, triggered a series of public denunciations of Bohemian Jewry. Addressing a public gathering in Prague, the Young Czech leader Edvard Grégr declared a state of enmity to exist between the two peoples:

> I shall not speak about the Jews; I will only go so far as to remark that it is good that this has happened . . . and that clarity finally reigns within our people. I was never an antisemite; it [antisemitism] repelled me from the humanitarian perspective. However, following the events of the last few days, from today onward all of Prague is antisemitic. The Czech people will learn how to deal with those who have repaid them for everything in this way.[17]

Various antisemitic books and pamphlets began to circulate in the literary marketplace at this time. Rudolf Vrba's *Národní sebeochrana* (National self-protection, 1898) was an extreme example of anti-Jewish diatribe. Heavily influenced by Éduard Drumont's *La France Juive* (Paris, 1886) and August Rohling's *Der Talmudjude* (1877), Vrba devoted some 400 pages to a crude and at times scatological attack on the Jews, their religion, their race, and their liberal and social democratic supporters within Czech society. A Catholic priest and economist of sorts, Vrba decried the Jewish control of industry, the banks, and the press (all common grist for the mill). "The *Neue Freie Presse*," he charged, "spouts out more poison at Christian people than the entire Babylonian Talmud."[18] Vrba even accused *Národní listy*, "that journalistic accomplice of the Jews," of verbally abusing the Czech priesthood while speaking approvingly of rabbis. And more:

> For the sake of Jewish advertising it brings very careful reports of where some Jew or Jewess had an engagement, a wedding, or where some Jew or Jewess died. Perhaps we can expect that the editors of *Národní listy* will carefully report whenever some genteel Prague Jewess has a migraine.[19]

By the end of his long tome Vrba had called for state control of the stock market and banks; banning of Jewish immigration and new Jewish settlement; removing Jewish students from public schools; forbidding Christian servant girls to work in Jewish households; instituting the death penalty for international trafficking in girls; banning of Jews from public office; requiring that Jewish doctors treat only Jewish patients and that Jewish lawyers have only Jewish clients; and a general review of the Talmud and the Shulhan Arukh (sixteenth–century code of Jewish law), among other provisions.[20]

Clearly, *Národní sebeochrana* constituted an extreme case of religiously and racially motivated antisemitism. It did not reflect the bulk of Czech national opinion, and Vrba himself does not appear to have enjoyed a great deal of popularity. He ran in the fifth curial elections in Hradec Králové in 1897 and received only 20 of 683 electoral votes.[21] Yet leaders of the Czech-Jewish movement could draw only a limited amount of solace from this fact. For the pamphlets and political statements that arose from the mainstream of the Czech national camp—including those of Young Czech writers—were scarcely more sympathetic to the Jews.

Jaroslava Procházková's *Český lid a český žid* (The Czech people and the Czech Jew), published in the working-class district of Žižkov shortly after the elections of March 1897, attacked the "Jewish question" from the purely secular, national viewpoint. Procházková acknowledged, albeit vaguely, that the group character of the Jews stemmed both from their religion and their blood ties; but her basic position was that, like it or not, the Jews formed a separate nation wherever they were and whatever they claimed to be.

> The Jew might become a Young Czech . . . he might become an Old Czech, a clerical, a socialist, a Christian of whatever belief . . . he might even become an

antisemite (which does occur today), but he can never become a Czech if he was not born a Czech.[22]

Nationalist political economy, heavily determined by anti-German and antisocialist sentiment, provided the basis for Procházková's condemnation of the role of the Jewish people in Czech life. The Jews, who were predisposed toward commerce and trade, dominated the capitalist structure of small-town and village life. They possessed no cultural ethic of morality in business affairs and dealt with outside groups according to dictates of opportunism and short-term advantage. Hence, as long as the German population of Bohemia appeared to be the dominant political force in the land, Jews voiced unanimous support for the German position. Now that the Czech national movement appeared to be gaining the upper hand, Jews were pretending to have discovered the virtues of Czech national culture. All along, however, they continued to exploit and demoralize the population at large.[23]

Prague Jewry's recent alliance with Social Democracy possessed special meaning for Procházková. On one level it represented an appropriate mating of interests: Jewry—at one and the same time national and international—allied with the socialists, who voiced allegiance to no nation, claiming to represent the interests of the international working class. And of immediate concern for the Czech national movement, both the Jews and the socialists strove to divide the nation at large. Socialists did this by encouraging social conflict based on economic class; the Jews through economic exploitation, the disposition of political and social privilege, and cultural demoralization.

What separated the antisemitism of National Liberals, like Procházková, from that of the Christian Social movement was the former's emphasis on political and economic arguments, their anticlerical views, and, paradoxically, their negative attitude toward antisemitism in contexts other than that of contemporary Czech society. Procházková argued that there was a great difference between French or German antisemitism, for example, and Czech anti-Jewish feeling. "In other countries Jews do not assume a hostile position with regard to the national endeavors of the rest of the population, which they do with us." In other cases, she explained, antisemitism arose either out of pure national intolerance or in defense of the class interests of one part of the population against the majority. In the Czech lands, however, antisemitism occupied a central position in the basic struggle for national independence.[24]

The devotion of mainstream Czech liberals to the democratic and secular ideals of the Revolution of 1848 created a basic ambivalence on the question of antisemitism. The essentially liberal ideology of nineteenth-century nationalism rendered antisemitism an odious by-product of the old monarchic and clerical order. There could be no room for such prejudice in a society restructured along secular, national lines. Thus, Young Czech writers were reluctant to accept the validity of anti-Jewish politics in countries that enjoyed national independence. But in the Czech lands the national question was still unresolved. Moreover, anti-Jewish feeling enjoyed great popularity among the newly enfranchised masses, and the temptation to exploit it for immediate political ends proved to be more powerful than mere ideological heritage.

This ambivalence helps to explain the contradictions that emerged from the "liberal" antisemitic publications of the late 1890s. Karel Adámek, the Young Czech politician and professional economist who had contributed a good deal to the external pressure to close German-Jewish elementary schools during the 1880s and 1890s, was convinced that Jews walked hand in hand with "our major enemies," that they were "the most zealous oppressors of the Czech minority in the mixed [linguistic] regions," and "the most zealous spreaders of Germandom (*němectví*) in the Czech regions."[25] Nevertheless, when he published his own account of antisemitism in 1899, he offered a sympathetic historical overview of Jewish life in Bohemia, emphasizing the restrictions under which Jews had been forced to live. His major conclusions, however, were condemnatory. The Jews as a group had consistently supported the interests of the German minority in the Czech lands and worked against the Czech nation. Together with the Germans, Jews had benefited enormously from the post-1848 industrialization of the country, invested their capital in factories, controlled markets and wholesale trade, and reaped enormous profits. Moreover, the concentration of economic power in the hands of Germans and Jews had prevented the Czech nation from undergoing more intensive cultural and economic development.[26]

The political economy of liberal Czech nationalism held simply that German and Jewish commercial concerns represented foreign domination. Procházková, Adámek, and a host of other mouthpieces of the Young Czech party insisted that the "svůj k svému" movement, the economic boycott of German and Jewish shops and businesses, was on these grounds justifiable. Procházková agitated for what she called "enlightened antisemitism," conceived of as a moral reform of Czech society, a defense of the national principle, and protection of the weak against the powerful.[27] Adámek refrained from including moralizing sentiment in his denunciations of Jewish economic and political behavior, but he was no less uncompromising. As to the argument that Jews who professed the Czech nationality should be exempt from the effects of economic antisemitism, Adámek countered that the achievements of the Czech-Jewish movement—which he did acknowledge—were up to this point quite meager. A great deal more would have to be accomplished before the Jews, "by their own endeavors," might remove the causes of antisemitism. The burden of change rested with the Jews, not with the Czech nation.[28]

Perhaps the most dramatic shift in the security of Jewish life and property, as well as in the position of Jews in the Czech national movement, occurred in the wake of the collapse of the Badeni government during the last days of November 1897. Following the elections to the Reichsrat, Badeni had issued a pair of language ordinances that were designed to meet the demands of the Czech nationalists for cultural parity while maintaining the Czech lands for the Habsburg state. Had they been successful the Badeni ordinances would have extended the principle of linguistic equality for Czech and German and applied it to the *internal* service of the courts and the bureaucracy. All administrative and judicial business falling under the purview of the Ministries of the Interior, Justice, Finance, Commerce and Trade, and Agriculture was to be conducted either in Czech or in German according to the requests of the petitioner who initiated an action. Moreover, in business not initiated by an outside party, either Czech or German could be used as the language of communication "according to the nature of the case."[29] Most controversially, the ordinance further stipulated that all civil servants in Bohemia and Moravia had to offer evidence, no later than 1 July 1901, of written and oral command of both German and Czech or face dismissal.

It was this last requirement that appeared to threaten directly the careers and livelihood of German civil servants throughout the Czech lands, since they were less likely to have been bilingual than their Czech counterparts. German deputies in the Reichsrat resorted to filibuster and other obstructionist tactics in an effort to thwart the new legislation and to overthrow the Badeni government. Mass demonstrations and popular violence erupted in the streets of Vienna, Graz, and the German towns of northern and western Bohemia. In the German Sudeten areas, this violence was directed against both Czech student groups and Jews. When Badeni himself was forced to resign, a new series of violent demonstrations erupted, this time in Prague and the Czech countryside.

For the three days following Badeni's resignation, the streets of Prague became the battleground for the rival armies of urban agitators. German university students may have precipitated the violence when they celebrated Badeni's downfall by singing German patriotic songs, including *Wacht am Rhein,* through open windows in the middle of town. Large, hostile crowds gathered, and tensions mounted as a group of Germans dressed in nationalist colors marched to the main German civic association, the Casino. By nightfall, angry mobs had gathered around Wenceslaus Square (Václavské náměstí); they marched to the New German Theater and bombarded it with stones; violence broke out in the suburb of Královské Vinohrady; the army was called in.[30]

More riots broke out on the second day. Masses of people who had assembled at Wenceslaus Square and the fashionable Na Příkopě (Graben) attacked German stores, coffee houses, and private homes. The crowds renewed their attack on the New German Theater until every plate of glass had been shattered. They destroyed the German Schulverein school in Královské Vinohrady and smashed the windows of synagogues in this neighborhood as well as in Žižkov. Vienna increased the military presence in Prague from two to four battalions of sharpshooters and two battalions of infantrymen.[31]

By 1 December large bands of young people were roaming through the streets of the city looking for any German institution, any symbol of German cultural nationalism, any German-speaking family, to attack. Similar outrages occurred in the Czech towns of Nový Bydžov, Beroun, Hradec Králové, Rakovník, Tábor, and Kostelec nad Labem.[32] Ultimately the government had to declare a state of martial law in order to restore peace in Prague, but not before the synagogue in Smíchov and many other private homes and institutions had succumbed to the popular fury.

The riots of November–December 1897 resulted, miraculously, in no loss of life. Nevertheless, they produced a measurable trauma within the ranks of the Czech-Jewish movement, to say nothing of the majority of the Bohemian Jewish community. The carefully constructed plans and cherished hopes of countless Czech-speaking Jews lay strewn along the sidewalks of Prague and tens of smaller communities together with the shards of glass and broken furniture of Jewish homes and shops. Predictably, the liberal Czech press did nothing to soften the blow of the "December storm." *Národní listy* made certain to report that the Prague disturbances had been precipitated by German and Jewish provocations, that the coffee houses from which German students had taunted the Czech population were mainly frequented by Jews, that "Semitic" faces could be seen outlining the doors of the cafes.[33] Among Jewish observers, the most charitable had to conclude that the Czech national establishment had abandoned the Jews in their hour of need. The less sanguine feared that much worse had occurred.[34]

Czech Jews barely had a chance to recover from the shocks of 1897 when a new calamity struck. On 1 April 1899, in the eastern Bohemian town of Polná, a nineteen-year-old dressmaker named Anežka Hrůzová was found murdered in a quarter of the town inhabited by poor Jews. Leopold Hilsner, a Jewish vagabond of apparently unsavory character, was arrested and charged with the crime. The prosecutor, in determining the probable motive for the killing, emphasized the fact the girl's body, which had obviously been stabbed or punctured, lay—as the indictment read—in "an insignificant pool of blood, no bigger than a hand." He did not speculate that the small amount of blood found with the corpse meant that she had been killed somewhere else and her body later moved.[35]

During the course of the ensuing trial, both the Catholic and the liberal newspapers of Bohemia charged that Hilsner had killed a young Christian woman in order to make use of her blood for ritual purposes. And, as the body was discovered in early April, generally the season in which Passover occurs, they presumed that the blood was used in the preparation of Passover matzot. To exacerbate matters, the opportunistic, former Young Czech politician Karel Baxa—who later became mayor of Prague—volunteered to

represent the dead girl's mother at the trial. He more than anyone contributed to the sensationalism of the proceedings, introducing the blood libel
whenever possible. In his charge to the jury Baxa urged it to consider carefully the "motive" behind the murder. "The murderers [it was assumed that
two other, unknown, assailants were also involved] were not concerned
simply with her life; everything depends on the method of the murder, which
is still unknown to us." The perpetrators, he concluded, had "murdered a
Christian person, an innocent girl, in order to obtain her blood."[36]

The court in Kutná Hora found Hilsner guilty of murder and sentenced
him to hang. This was not to be the end of things, however. Hilsner found
his Émile Zola in the person of Tomáš G. Masaryk (1850–1937), professor
of philosophy at the Czech University in Prague and head of a breakaway
progressivist faction within the Czech national movement known commonly
as the Realists. Largely in response to a brochure published by Masaryk, a
new trial was ordered, to begin in October 1900.[37] The same personnel
showed up to try the case the second time around, now at the regional court
in Písek. No new evidence was introduced, and another guilty verdict was
handed down. This time, however, the emperor commuted the death sentence to life imprisonment. Hilsner was finally pardoned under the new
Czechoslovak republic in 1918; he died, a poor peddler who went by the
name of Heller, in 1928.[38]

If the Czech camp proved to be increasingly inhospitable to Jews during
the 1890s, German groups in Bohemia did not offer much comfort either.
Georg von Schönerer's Pan-German movement, which enjoyed a peak in
popularity during the mid-1880s, had gained numerous adherents by this
time among German-speaking workers and artisans in northern Bohemia.
The large-scale migration of Czech-speaking peasants to the industrial areas
of the north alarmed traditional working-class elements there, who were
fearful of losing their jobs to settlers who might be willing to accept lower
wages. They formed a variety of defensive associations during the 1890s.
Some had the direct backing of Schönerer; others were merely inspired by
his Germanic, antisemitic ideology.[39] These forerunners of Austrian and
Bavarian National Socialism were joined by the Christian Social movement
of Karl Lueger and company in a chorus of denunciations aimed at Czech
workers, Jews, and socialists collectively.[40] The resentments of provincial
Germans living in the mixed districts of the Sudetenland erupted in physical
violence against both Czechs and Jews during the parliamentary stalemate
that greeted the announcement of the Badeni language ordinances in 1897.

Even the German political institutions of Prague proved to be susceptible
to the growing antiliberal and antisemitic tide. For the most part, as Gary
Cohen has shown, German institutions in the Bohemian capital until the late
1880s were shielded from the kind of radicalization that had occurred in
Vienna and provincial Bohemia. Thanks in large measure to the crucial

participation of Jews, German public life in Prague remained liberal and largely free of antisemitism during these years.[41] To illustrate this point, historians of late have been fond of quoting the impressions of Friedrich Jodl, a non-Jewish philosopher who left Munich in 1885 to become a professor at Prague's German University. Shortly after his arrival in Prague, he wrote the following to a friend:

> The entire social life here is completely dominated by politics, and if one has no inclination to join in, one can do nothing more than hold back as much as possible. Only two things are obligatory: no flirting with the Slavs and no hostility toward the Jews. Both are requirements for the existence of the local German society. Whether one happens to be a German-national, a German-Austrian, or an Old Austrian is totally immaterial.[42]

But the picture was not all rosy for Prague's German-speaking Jews. In the first place, though they represented approximately 45 percent of the "German" population of the city, Jews had only partially integrated into the larger German community. At some levels, residential housing patterns, for example, there was no integration at all. Cohen's own sampling of neighborhoods in both Staré Město and Nové Město reveals that German Catholics tended to reside in the same buildings as Czech Catholics, but they seldom lived with Jews. Jews—whether German-speaking or Czech—continued to reside among themselves until the end of the century.[43]

As for the major German associations, such as the German Casino and the Deutscher Verein, they may always have welcomed Jewish membership, but their boards of directors accepted only limited Jewish influence. In 1870 only one of the twenty directors of the Casino was Jewish; in 1883 the board contained three Jews out of nineteen members, yet Jews made up approximately 40 percent of the association. As late as 1898, by which time 45 percent of the Casino's members were Jews, it sat only four Jews on its board of twenty-five.[44]

The Pan-German movement did make some headway in Prague in the 1880s and 1890s. The Schulverein received a steady barrage of pressure not to accept Jewish members or support Jewish pupils, but the Prague chapter consistently opposed each motion. And *völkisch* (populist–nationalist) elements within the German Casino conspicuously espoused antisemitic platforms during the late 1880s. They forced a showdown with the board of directors and were eventually expelled from the society.[45] Middle-class Jews in the German parts of Bohemia responded to the rigidification of German club life in much the same manner as their counterparts in the German Empire and in Vienna: they created a new network of specifically Jewish fraternal organizations. It was in the 1880s and 1890s that Central European Jews first established chapters of the International Order of B'nai B'rith (IOBB) even though this organization had already been in existence for over four decades. Six chapters of the IOBB were established in Bohemia and

Moravia between 1892 and 1898 and all in cities that were either entirely or largely German speaking: Plzeň, Prague, Karlový Vary (Karlsbad), Liberec (Reichenberg), Brno (Brünn), and Opava (Troppau).[46]

However, Pan-German pressures made themselves felt most acutely in student life at the university. German student organizations increasingly came under the influence of radical nationalists, led by Schönerer and the Deutschnationaler Verein (German-National Club). Not only did they advocate the dissolution of the Habsburg monarchy and the association of Bohemia and the "hereditary lands" with the German Empire, but they also mouthed fashionable racial antisemitism and began to prohibit Jews from membership in their ranks. Teutonia was one such organization; it barred Jews as early as 1879. Others took informal action to exclude Jews during the height of Schönerer's popularity in the late 1880s.[47]

After 1891 the radical, nationalist students broke with their liberal counterparts. At this point all of the völkisch groups in Prague began to adopt constitutions with antisemitic clauses. Even the Lese- und Redehalle split apart, the nationalists breaking away and forming a separate association, Germania, which excluded Jews from membership.[48] The liberal Lese- und Redehalle lost almost half of its membership in the course of this shift. Meanwhile, the völkisch groups were fast becoming the majority. By 1911 the number of antisemitic, nationalist Burschenschaften was double that of the liberal bodies. Germania's membership alone had grown to around 700; the Lese-und Redehalle could boast only about half that number.[49]

The Lese- und Redehalle, like the Casino and the Deutscher Verein, stood its ground and refused to countenance explicit antisemitism. In so doing, however, it dramatized the paradoxical nature of the German-Jewish relationship in the city. As Ernst Pawel aptly points out in his biography of Franz Kafka, the Lese- und Redehalle was possibly the most dynamic and effective center of German culture in Prague at the time, with a library second only to that of the university, regular appearances by prominent German literary figures, and organized concerts, art exhibits, and discussion groups on various cultural topics. Yet, at the same time, it had become an identifiably Jewish institution.[50]

Perhaps this symbolized the dilemma of all of Prague Jewry at the turn of the century. They stood virtually alone as representatives of nineteenth-century liberalism. Those who had been actively involved in the Czech national movement since the 1870s found themselves squeezed to the periphery and their coreligionists abused in the name of tactical political advantage. German-Jewish liberals, on the other hand, grew more and more isolated, inheriting institutions and policies that non-Jewish Germans were abandoning. Thus, one finds that Jewish membership in the Casino pressed upward after 1897, while the total numbers of the group remained steady. Jews captured leadership positions in the Deutscher Verein after 1910; they accounted for at least one third of the officers and directors of the Lese- und Redehalle between 1897 and 1914. But by now these institutions had become unrepresentative of German associational life in the capital; in fact they were Jewish in all but name.[51]

Czech-Jewish Responses: Redefining the Relationship

Had the outpouring of popular antisemitism in 1897 and 1899 been confined to the fringes of respectability, leaders of the Czech-Jewish movement would have greeted it with stoicism. Pointing ominously to the potential for popular violence against German Jews, they might have agitated for speedier implementation of school closings and a more thorough bilingualism in the public life of the Jewish community. Most important, they would have remained convinced of the justness of their cause, of the effectiveness of their chosen careers. But the collusion of *Národní listy* and part of the leadership of the Young Czech party in the attacks against Jews stripped the Czech-Jewish movement of its confidence. What answer did it have to charges that Czech liberalism had abandoned Czech Jews? Indeed, what could the SČAŽ or the Czech-Jewish National Union offer in the way of consolation to their own adherents? The unspoken question in everyone's mind was "what now?"

On the whole, the public reactions of leaders within the Czech-Jewish movement to the demise of Czech liberalism showed remarkable courage. True, some of the institutions that had staked everything on the prospects of Jewish participation in the Czech national movement did attempt to deny the severity of the situation, contend that their vision was still viable, or, less plausibly still, argue that the basic problem continued to rest with the "German-Jewish elementary school."[52] This was to be expected. What is remarkable is how few individuals actually took such a position.

When the "svůj k svému" operation achieved its full force under the impetus the organization Národní obrana (National Defense), heads of the Czech-Jewish movement rose one by one to denounce it. They did so after some hesitation, as many admitted that they had been prepared to weather the storm in the name of national economic development and full autonomy. All they requested was that the policy of economic boycott be applied on an individual basis, that it be directed against those who either were German nationals or who supported the German national camp. But Czech politicians had betrayed the true meaning of Palacký's words. They had applied the tactic indiscriminately to Jews as a whole, ruining the livelihoods of thousands in the process. Thus, Czech Jews openly withheld support for the economic program of the national movement.[53]

Cries of alarm began to appear in the pages of *Českožidovské listy* as early as the spring of 1897. In April, Eduard Lederer, then a young attorney living in Jindřichův Hradec, expressed disgust at the fact that Viennese Catholic

intolerance—specifically Karl Lueger's antisemitism—was gaining a wide audience in the "land of Hus." He reported on a recent meeting that had been
held in Prague among Lueger's followers in Bohemia, listing as he did so the
names of various Prague dignitaries who were in attendance. The group had
included Březnovský ("that great lover of the nation in the fifth curia of
Prague and the great enemy of Prague's fifth district [i.e., Josefov]"), Father
Šimon (the Christian Social candidate who opposed Březnovský in the first
round), and Karel Baxa, who was later to achieve fame in the Hilsner trial.[54]
Lederer resolved to fight antisemitism wherever it was found, irrespective of
party, and never to allow it either to "reinstitute the ghetto" or thwart Czech-
Jewish cooperation.

Several months later Lederer took stock of the political relations of the
Czech-Jewish movement. The National Liberals, he acknowledged, spoke
for the majority of the Czech nation, and, up until recent weeks, Jews had
found in them a natural ally. However, memories of Březnovský's nomination and election and of the provocative behavior of *Národní listy* hung over
the heads of Czech Jews like a storm-cloud. The "liberal" parties in the
Czech lands were abandoning liberalism. Worse yet, they ignored or belittled the accomplishments of the Czech-Jewish movement. The Social Democrats in his view were not much better. They viewed the nationalist activity
of the Czech Jews as antiquated and a barrier to modern development. Only
the left wing of the liberal camp, made up of the Realists and the Progressives, offered some cause for optimism. The *Rozhledy* and *Samostatnost*
circles may not have jumped and cheered for Czech Jews, but they did at
least write about Lederer's movement with respect as a legitimate political
force.[55]

In the immediate aftermath of the December riots, Lederer publicly
lashed out at the Young Czechs, laying the blame for the violence in no
uncertain terms at their feet.[56] Subsequently, Maxim Reiner, leader of the
Czech-Jewish Political Union, denounced the Young Czech party for having
flirted with Vienna's racial antisemitism in collusion with the Christian Social movement. He expressed dismay that the mouthpiece of Czech liberalism, *Národní listy,* had gloated over the two convictions of Dreyfus in France
and had accused Dreyfus's supporters of having perpetrated a Jewish cabal.
And, in a revealing moment of self-criticism, Reiner admitted that the
Czech-Jewish establishment had seriously underestimated the effects of radical groups such as Národní obrana, whose agitation throughout Prague and
the Czech countryside greatly helped to prepare the ground for the December storm. On the other hand, he cautioned, the Czech political press was no
less myopic. Indeed, a considerable portion of it (again a reference to
Národní listy) preferred to pay lip service to the party's written program—
which abjured antisemitism—while encouraging the actions of the antisemitic movement.[57]

Reiner's analysis of the political relations of the Czech-Jewish movement followed a pattern that was characteristic of the difficult times in which he lived. He began with a litany of charges and accusations against the Czech nationalist establishment, but ended with a counterbalancing argument that he introduced with the word "nevertheless." Reiner proclaimed that his movement would hold fast to its long-standing position of working, as Czechs, for Czech national rights. But at the same time it would insist that Jews achieve full equality and freedom within Czech society.

> We wish to be equals among equals in both rights and duties. We shall gladly lend our strength to the service of the nation. We want to fulfill this obligation and shall, conscientiously and resolutely as in the past. On the other hand we do demand that we and our actions—our persons and our deeds—be judged according to truth and justice, not with glasses clouded by hatred.[58]

Following the shock of 1897, the major Czech-Jewish organizations had determined not to be taken by surprise should another outburst of anti-Jewish agitation occur. Thus, when the Hilsner murder trial began in 1899, they were prepared to respond with a coordinated publicity campaign of their own. The Czech-Jewish National Union published and distributed over 7,000 copies of a Czech translation of the Berlin theologian Hermann Strack's pamphlet "Against the Ritual Murder Superstition" (1892). The group attached to Strack's refutation excerpts from Anatole Leroy-Beaulieu's *Israel Among the Nations* (1893) as well as a communication from Tomáš Masaryk that had appeared in the *Neue Frei Presse* of Vienna.[59] Bohumil Bondy, Viktor Vohryzek, and others placed refutations of their own in Czech newspapers— primarily *Hlas národa* (Voice of the nation), the organ of the Old Czech party. And the movement received help from the Medical Faculty at the Czech University, which publicly debunked the purportedly "scientific" bases of the ritual murder allegations. Most impressive in the eyes of Czech-Jewish leaders, however, was the powerful stand taken by Masaryk himself, who, not for the first time in his career, risked tremendous unpopularity in the name of integrity and common decency. Masaryk rode in the forefront of those who demanded a retrial for Hilsner, and the Czech-Jewish National Union subsequently singled him out for having displayed "manly courage." "Professor Masaryk . . . stepped into the confusion of battle for truth and justice, unafraid of the abuse which he had to suffer. For that he has our fervent, genuine thanks."[60]

At the end of the century, the Czech-Jewish movement faced the major crossroad of its young career. To all intents and purposes, it had been abandoned and deceived. Czech-Jewish leaders realized their dilemma as early as the 1897 elections to the expanded Reichsrat. At first they chose to deal with the problem by demonstrating their determination to fight for Jewish rights and Jewish honor, by chastising the liberal wing of the Czech national movement, and by urging it to return to the ideals of 1848. But they did not challenge their own overall commitment to national-liberal politics. Jews throughout Central and Eastern Europe, in fact, had very little room to maneuver during this period of liberal decline. If Czech Jews were to abandon the Young Czech party, what camp would they join? The aristocratic and semifeudal Old Czech party? The Social Democrats who criticized the social basis of the nationalist movement? Certainly not the German liberals against whom Jewish Czech nationalists had staked their futures and that of their children.

The preferred tack during the initial regrouping of the Czech-Jewish movement was one of cajoling and admonition. We remain as committed as ever, Jewish leaders asserted repeatedly, but we must insist that you meet us halfway. Two or three of the more vociferous critics of Czech liberalism began at this time to investigate alternatives to the Young Czech-Jewish alliance. Eduard Lederer caused a small furor in 1898 when he published an expose in the pages of *Českožidovské listy* entitled "Židé a sociální demokracie" (The Jews and Social Democracy).[61] In it he urged that Czech Jews reevaluate their political relationship with the Czech nation in the wake of the recent outbreaks of antisemitism. Consider, he asked, the fact that the only neighborhood in Prague in 1897 in which Jews and their property were protected from the fury of the mobs—mobs composed, for the most part, of upstanding petit bourgeois citizens—was the working-class district of Holešovice, the camp of Social Democracy. Czech workers came to the aid of their Jewish neighbors because of their own experience with oppression. Might not Czech Jews, then, although clearly opposed to Social Democratic policy on the questions of national autonomy and state rights, adopt a friendlier attitude toward the socialists?[62]

It may have been Czech liberalism's treachery concerning the Jews that moved Lederer to question received orthodoxies about other groups in Czech society. Whatever the cause, he urged his readers to break ranks with the Young Czechs on the question of acceptance or rejection of Social Democracy. Why not follow the lead, he asked rhetorically, of Masaryk's Realists or of the student movement, the Young Progressives, and show sympathy for the rights of Czech workers. The just causes of Social Democracy, such as the prohibition of forced Sunday and nighttime work, the regulation of female and child labor, and the institution of health insurance, deserved general support and ought not to be blurred by differences on the national question. Jews ought to develop the confidence to make independent judgments and the tolerance to recognize and support social justice even when promoted by "internationalist" circles.[63]

Lederer's proposal immediately touched off a debate in the letters to the editors of *Českožidovské listy*. All of the correspondents took exception to the Lederer article, many of them heatedly so. Jakub Scharf, who at the time was serving as the head of the Czech-Jewish National Union, objected to what he inferred as a call for Jews to take a united political stand. Alluding to developments that already were beginning to worry the advocates of Czech-Jewish assimilation, he labeled such a position "political Zionism translated into Czech."[64] One reader pointed out that Jews were the natural political allies of liberalism. They could never support Social Democracy because of its commitment to economic collectivism and full social equality.[65] J. S. Kraus, a leading figure in Czech-Jewish religious culture, rejected Lederer's claim that the Social Democrats had in fact stood up to the roving marauders and had protected Jewish life and property. He admitted, however, that the workers themselves may not have participated in anti-Jewish demonstrations. Still, he cautioned, one must not idealize the Social Democrats, and one must recognize the fact that radical-liberal politicians such as Březnovský and Václav Klofáč had acted in contradiction to the party's true position. Moreover, their actions alone were not enough to cause Czech Jews to abandon the Young Czechs. "We do not believe that the Young Czech party has thrown down the banner of liberalism and civil equality. If such were to take place, however, I would support the new national liberal party that would certainly emerge."[66]

If Lederer managed to raise doubts in the minds of Czech-Jewish intellectuals about the desirability of continuing an alliance with the Young Czechs, he did not go so far as to advocate a formal separation. Up to this point he was content to suggest a more open-minded approach to the social and national questions of the day. The real foundation for an entirely new estimation of the Czech-Jewish relationship came in 1900 when Viktor Vohryzek used the pages of *Českožidovské listy* to publish a long and influential piece entitled "Epištoly k českým židům" (Letters to Czech Jews). In what was originally a series of articles published between March and June 1900, Vohryzek undertook to reexamine the entire problem of antisemitism and Jewish culture in the Czech lands.

Vohryzek departed radically from the position of most Czech-Jewish leaders of his day when he argued that, ultimately, the causes of Jewish suffering and persecution in all countries lay not in some misdirected historical evolution, in poorly conceived governmental policies, or in the stubborn refusal of Jews to assimilate. The basic factors lay in human nature itself. Antisemitism was in the end a psychological and a moral problem. Like other forms of hatred and intolerance, it arose from atavistic instincts in man, from some inborn defiance of his other, humanistic, nature:

> Just as the child, who has hardly learned to move about, breaks and destroys everything that comes into his hands; just as the hunter chases down and destroys game, not out of need, but for amusement based on inborn, destructive instincts; so too does the person who possesses power destroy those who are weak—as a pastime, for his own whim and amusement.[67]

Hatred, no less than love, was a basic human instinct.

By arguing that the chief causes of antisemitism lay within human nature and did not derive from any particular behavior on the part of Jews, Vohryzek conveyed two key messages to his readers. The first was that neither recent history nor patterns of cultural allegiance—whether alone or in tandem—could account for the manifestation of anti-Jewish behavior. The Jews of Bohemia and Moravia had done nothing to warrant or "deserve" the violence that was directed against them, a notion that many Czechs, Jews included, had been willing to entertain. The second, perhaps more important, message was that antisemitism ultimately was a Czech and not a Jewish problem. It reflected a moral defect in the character of the Czech people, one that was being exploited by nationalist politicians for selfish and short-sighted purposes. In the last analysis, the Czech soul, not the Jewish one, suffered from antisemitism's poison.[68]

Vohryzek added to the by-now-common Czech-Jewish condemnations of "svůj k svému." Reminding his readers that nationalism, like clericalism, could be exploited by social elites to cloud over social and economic inequalities, he pointed out that economic antisemitism had above all benefited the bourgeois competitors of the Jews. It was doubtful whether the practice improved the standing of the nation as a whole. In fact, he argued, Jewish economic activity in the Czech regions, such as his own home town of Pardubice, had benefited the Czech population generally, provided for large-scale employment, and enriched the land.[69] Rather than cut off from the Czech nation a population that possessed great productive capacities, would it not be better, Vohryzek asked, to assimilate the Jews, to buy from Jewish businesses, and take advantage of Jewish industry already in place?[70]

By way of conclusion, Vohryzek advised Czech Jewry to do two things. First, it should wait out the decline of the liberal party:

> If the Czech nation were once again to return to Hussite liberalism, I would not hesitate to proclaim that we would soon succeed in reaching that point in which all Czech Jews would be in the Czech camp as loyal sons; but it would have to be sincere liberalism, not the comical pre-elections kind in which Jews cannot and do not believe.[71]

No one expected a return to the ideals of the Czech past to be accomplished soon, however. In the meantime, Jews were to prepare an "antidote" to the poison that had infected the Czech nation. "Our antidote is the strengthening of all progressive influences . . . the battle against hypernationalism and clericalism. The antidote is the struggle against the dark."[72]

Vohryzek called upon Czech Jews to learn how to defend themselves—to straighten their backs, as he put it—and not to "fall down in the dust before every journalistic bandit." They had to act with dignity and pride in order that basic human consideration dictate the conduct of others toward them.[73] This was not to say that there was not a great deal wrong with the nature of Jewish cultural and economic life in the Czech lands. Vohryzek felt that it was just as incumbent upon Jews to examine their faults as to defend their rights. Jews continued to pursue dangerous and unsavory economic occupations such as moneylending and the production and distribution of liquor. Jewish life required a thorough, ongoing reform—a renewal, based on the spiritual purposefulness, the social ethics, and progressive outlook of the prophets of the Old Testament. But the issue of internal reform and redirection, Vohryzek warned, was for Jews to face on their own. Society at large was in no position to pass judgment.

The Emergence of *Rozvoj* as Heir Apparent

The first formal break between the Czech political establishment and the Czech-Jewish movement occurred not in the aftermath of the riots of 1897, nor in the polemics of 1899, but as a reaction to a generally uneventful interview with the aged Old Czech leader F. L. Rieger at the end of 1901. In response to a query by the Catholic journalist Dostal-Lutinov, Rieger apparently blasted the Jews for being "a disruptive element" in Czech life. He complained that they gave aid and comfort to the Germans in Bohemia and contributed nothing to the Czech cause.[74]

So what? In the context of 1900 Rieger's utterances were not radical. One would daresay that many Czech nationalists shared his views. What bothered individuals such as Lederer, Vohryzek, and Bohdan Klineberger—a group that represented the nucleus of a new generation of political leadership—was the Jewish response to this incident. By now activists within the Czech-Jewish movement had prepared themselves to meet every antisemitic challenge head-on, to counterattack in the press and in other public forums, to defend Jewish honor without hesitation. Thus, Lederer, Vohryzek, and Klineberger were astounded when *Českožidovské listy* and the Czech-Jewish National Union refused to condemn Rieger's remarks out of deference to his political stature. Instead, the paper contented itself with a lukewarm letter from Rieger explaining himself more fully.

Prevented from expressing their views in the Czech-Jewish press, Lederer, Vohryzek, and Klineberger wrote an open complaint to *Čas* (Time), the daily paper of the Realist (progressive) wing of the Czech national movement. And, in a follow-up piece entitled "Čeští židé a český nacionalism" (Czech Jews and Czech nationalism), Lederer announced the secession of his circle from both the Czech-Jewish National Union and the Young Czech party. Czech Jews had no choice, he concluded, but to ally with "progressive" elements within Czech society, and this no longer included the National Liberals.[75]

Lederer's 1902 work *The Jew in Contemporary Society* developed more fully the new progressivist manifesto. It combined two purposes: presenting on the one hand what he hoped to be a final apologia for Bohemian Jewry—

a substantive defense that would lay to rest once and for all the false charges that had been hurled at it—but also pointing the way to a new Czech-Jewish ideology.[76]

The emergence of a Czech-Jewish "opposition" and the collapse of the liberal-Jewish alliance within Czech nationalism signaled once again a struggle between the provinces and the capital. The most persistent calls for Jewish integrity and self-defense came from Czech-speaking Jewish professionals in their thirties and forties who were making their livings in Czech cities and towns to the south and east of Prague. Lederer, a writer of fiction and drama as well as an attorney, lived in Jindřichův Hradec in southern Bohemia. Bohdan Klineberger practiced law, wrote fiction under the pseudonym Antonín Rataj, and issued numerous philosophical and sociological works from Milevsko in south-central Bohemia. And Vohryzek had settled down to a career in medicine and journalism in the eastern Bohemian town of Pardubice. It was in Pardubice that the institutions and the journalistic vehicles were created around which this opposition could crystallize and eventually challenge the leadership position of the Czech-Jewish National Union.

In 1903 the Czech-Jewish youth organization in Pardubice decided to undergo a change both in name and orientation. It dropped the designation "Veselost" (mirth), adopted that of "Rozvoj" (development), and addressed itself to what it saw as the pressing cultural, religious, and economic matters of the day. The organization set for itself three main objectives: to deepen the sense of Czech national identity among the Jews; to reorient and modernize Czech Jewry socially and economically; and last, to transform Judaism itself, to teach Jews the difference, as the group put it, between religion and piety.[77]

"Rozvoj" inaugurated an educational program for adults that featured lectures on science, economics, business, and contemporary Jewish issues by some of its own members as well as distinguished speakers from Prague and the countryside.[78] In April 1904, the Pardubice group oversaw the first meeting of an organization called "Progressive Jewry" (*Pokrokové židovstvo*), which, it hoped, would serve as the nucleus for the Czech-Jewish movement of the future.[79]

Viktor Vohryzek, the main force behind "Rozvoj," epitomized the social and cultural evolution that had given impetus to the rise of the Czech-Jewish movement. Born three years before the Austro-Hungarian Ausgleich, Vohryzek was one of thirteen children, of whom seven ultimately survived. His father, Nathan, ran a hardware store in the small town of Přestavlky in eastern Bohemia; here Viktor attended the German-Jewish elementary school from age six to ten. In 1874 he began eight years of study in the Realgymnasium in Chrudim, the district capital and a provincial stronghold of the Young Czechs. The language of instruction, of course, was Czech. Presumably, by the time Vohryzek transferred once again—this time to

Prague to begin his medical studies—he had acquired a strong commitment to Czech language and culture and a desire to be a part of the Czech national movement. Vohryzek, we are not surprised to learn, had already assumed the post of secretary of the SČAŽ by 1883–84, one year after he arrived in Prague.[80]

Upon receipt of his medical degree in 1887, Vohryzek did what Lederer and Klineberger before him had done and what Jindřich Kohn in the next generation would also do: he left the capital to establish a professional career in a provincial city. Of course, Prague did not dominate Czech cultural life at this time to the degree that it would after 1930; and the provincial cities represented veritable strongholds of Czech language and culture, not to mention political power. Perhaps, too, this still-unusual group of Czech-speaking university graduates found it easier to make a career in the provinces than in Prague, where, as Jews, they remained suspect in the eyes of the Czech population. Whatever the reasons, it was in Pardubice that Vohryzek opened his medical practice and—like Arthur Schnitzler in Vienna—began his simultaneous career as a writer.

Vohryzek's activities in Pardubice extended far beyond the immediate circle of the local Czech-Jewish movement. For three years, between 1904 and 1907, he financed, edited, and did much of the writing for a new and independent Czech-Jewish newspaper. It too was called *Rozvoj,* and reflected the progressive and by now antiestablishment positions of Vohryzek, Lederer, and Klineberger. By 1907 *Rozvoj* had replaced *Českožidovské listy* as the paper of choice among Czech-national Jews. *Českožidovské listy* ceased publication. *Rozvoj* changed from a fortnightly to a weekly, expanded its format, and moved its editorial offices to Prague. From there it continued to publish the single most influential organ of Czech-Jewish opinion until the Nazi occupation of 1939.[81] Vohryzek completed *Rozvoj's* 1907 "putsch" when he formed the Association of Progressive Czech Jews (Svaz českých pokrokových židů). Designed to serve as an alternative to the Czech-Jewish Political Union—which coordinated Jewish support for the Young Czech party—Vohryzek's progressive association consisted primarily of Jewish supporters of Masaryk's Realist party and encouraged Czech Jews to support socially "progressive" political causes.[82]

Vohryzek made no secret of the fact that he had created *Rozvoj* out of a deep sense of frustration with the established leadership of Czech Jewry. He complained that his overtures to the Czech-Jewish establishment, his "Letters to Czech Jews," had been ignored for four years. *Českožidovské listy* may have been willing to publish examples of differing perspectives on the problems of Czech-Jewish existence—including the provocative essays of Lederer—but it then went on to bury them beneath a sheet of silence. The movement was overcome with "intellectual chaos," Vohryzek wrote; it was like a boat "which certainly had a sail, but no rudder and no sure direction."[83]

Vohryzek's overriding fear was that, with the loss of purpose and direction, the Czech-Jewish movement would eventually lose whatever influence it once had on Bohemian Jewry. "Our intellectual fund has not sufficed," he began in *Rozvoj*'s opening issue of 1904, "has not equaled the difficulties of our tasks. If our defense is to be successful, it will be necessary to advance further toward the revision of our program."[84]

Rozvoj invited Czech-Jewish intellectuals to redefine the goals of the assimilationist movement, to address issues that previous Czech-Jewish leaders—in their haste to achieve specific social and political objectives— had failed to resolve. For example, Masaryk had challenged Czech Jews to define precisely what type of assimilation they envisaged. How far was the merger of Czech and Jewish culture to go? The editors of *Rozvoj* felt it was time that a concrete response be forthcoming, one that took into account questions such as the future of Judaism itself as well as the ethical basis of the Czech-Jewish relationship.[85]

From the start *Rozvoj* marked a departure from the staid and cautious journalism of the recent past. It was introspective but persistently eschewed apologetics; positivist in tone, yet highly sensitive to religion and ethics. *Rozvoj* offered no excuses for the relative lateness of the emergence of a self-consciously Czech-Jewish movement. Nor did it provide comfort to Czech nationalists who continued to mistrust it. Vohryzek reminded his readers that the task of de-Germanizing the Jewish population of Bohemia had been an emormous one. Have no illusions on this score, he appeared to be saying: the Jews had been a thoroughly Germanized population; even the Yiddish that they spoke was a version of German. And yet, whatever difficulties the structural conditions of Jewish life had placed before the Czech-Jewish movement, the Czech people themselves had exacerbated. Their top literary figures had rejected Jewish overtures in the 1840s, and their urban masses had rioted against Jews in 1848, forcing many to flee. The collective Jewish psyche found it difficult to forget such outbursts of hostility.[86]

Throughout its criticisms and admonitions *Rozvoj* included a hopeful promise of reconciliation. The Czech-Jewish relationship could still be salvaged; with renewed effort from both sides, a future based on autonomy and freedom, cultural symbiosis and ethical perfection, could still be reached.

> The Czech nation may have spurned us for the moment, but it needs us urgently; and the day will come when it will acknowledge that. Its political struggle has had no success; its painstaking fight for its rights has not been crowned with good fortune. The nation draws upon all of its strength, but [gets nowhere]. There is no nation that needs the Jews more desperately than do the Czechs, and for this reason there must be a reconciliation sooner or later. This will happen that much sooner if the Jews allow themselves to be guided by the maxim *Charitas extirpet hostes*—love will rid us of our enemies.[87]

Religion and Moral Philosophy

Rozvoj's most clearly defined break from the previous liberal nationalism of the Czech-Jewish movement consisted in an impassioned plea for the religious revitalization of both Czech and Jewish society.[88] Up to this time Czech-Jewish intellectuals, educated in the 1870s and 1880s and greatly influenced by European positivism, had not considered religion in general to be a serious topic of concern. Rather, it was a matter of individual taste and had no bearing on one's status as human being and citizen. In fact, if people could better learn to conduct social relationships with complete neutrality on religious issues, Jewish integration into the Czech nation might proceed more smoothly. Yet this avoidance of "the religious question," Vohryzek now argued, this failure to investigate the religious underpinnings of modern culture, had been the greatest mistake of the Czech-Jewish movement to date.[89] Why? Because Czech Jews had overestimated the salutory effects of a liberally inspired national movement and had seriously underestimated the force of traditional antisemitic sentiment within the Czech population. As Vohryzek explained, nationalism devoid of religious content operates outside the bounds of morality and ethical purpose. Religion both transmits and makes manifest the ethical component of culture; as moral philosophy in the broadest sense, it defines the ultimate ideals of national activity.[90]

Rozvoj's religious agenda stands out as a curiosity on several counts. Not only did it run counter to the confidence of the founders of Or-Tomid that no changes in Jewish belief and practice were needed to move Bohemian Jewry into the mainstream of Czech national culture, but it also appears to have been an anachronism—arising virtually a century after the first stirrings of Jewish religious reform in Central Europe, over a quarter-century after the final emancipation of Austrian Jewry, and in the aftermath of a strong positivist movement in Czech science and letters.

In part the younger wing of the Czech-Jewish movement was simply responding to the writings and addresses of Masaryk on philosophy and history, echoing sentiments that were in vogue in certain academic and nationalist circles.[91] However, Vohryzek and his followers were pursuing their own ends as well. Though not religiously observant Jews themselves, they set out to issue their "anti-secularist" manifesto in order to cut the wind out of the sails of both the new antisemitism and the Zionist movement. A revitalization of the religious element in national life, they reasoned, would rehabilitate the purely religious definition of Jewish distinctiveness—a definition denied by both racial antisemites and Jewish nationalists. It might also provide a much-needed boost to the involvement of Jews as Jews in the Czech national revival. Since the real value of a people was determined by its spirit, its religion, a demonstration of the spiritual equality of Judaism to Christianity—indeed of Judaism's universality—might increase the desirability of Jewish cooperation in the eyes of the Czechs.[92]

Yet the chief concern of the assimilationists in 1904 was to correct the abuses of Czech national politics. In this regard they found Masaryk's oft-expressed call for an infusion of the spiritual values of the Czech Reformation of the fifteenth and sixteenth centuries most appealing.[93] When Eduard Lederer argued in *Žid v dnešní společnosti* that all of society needed to operate along radically different lines, that the idea of social justice as expressed in the Gospels must temper that of nationality, he was echoing the views of the Czech philosopher. The Czech Reformation as reformulated by its turn-of-the-century interpreters was said to rest on the foundations of religious and social democracy, the primacy of peaceful means and intentions, and the insistence on political and social justice.[94] Both the Masarykians and the *Rozvoj* circle were in basic agreement that true national renewal could emerge only from a kind of moral regeneration. In a speech delivered in 1910 in which he made constant reference to the moral example of Jan Hus, Masaryk insisted, "The leaders of our reformation have but one message for us all, repeated and reechoed over our land: regenerate, reform the individual, regenerate, reform the whole people."[95]

Lederer and Vohryzek echoed this call for spiritual renewal. *Rozvoj* dedicated many pages during its early years to a wide-ranging discussion of the moral transformation of Czech society. It did so not only out of devotion to Masaryk, but also because Vohryzek felt that Jews had a special contribution to make in this area. Czech Jews, he argued, were in a position to draw upon the resources of rabbinic and biblical Judaism, as well as nineteenth-century philosophy, to aid in the creation of a new moral consensus, a religious and philosophical synthesis which would "unite us in a single cultural whole."[96]

At the same time, a mounting pessimism appeared to break through the writings of Lederer and Vohryzek on the future of the Czech-Jewish relationship. They seemed to be suggesting that only an ethical revolution could overcome the considerable obstacles to full Jewish participation in Czech national life. The last ray of hope for the social and cultural aspirations of Czech-Jewish intellectuals lay in the taming of Czech politics under the reins of Masaryk's ethical and humanistic constraints, aided perhaps by the ethical teachings of the rabbis. As Lederer observed in the closing pages of *Žid v dnešní společnosti*, the Czech-Jewish experiment was not beyond salvation. The "new ethics"—which he viewed as being modeled on the teachings of Hillel, Jeremiah, and Jesus of Nazareth—could assure the survival of Czech culture:

> The demagoguery of our day, countenanced from above and below, eventually will peter out. It is a fever which does not consume society, an illness, out of which the people will emerge healthier than before. . . . A wave will once again roll which will lead society out of the depths of today's decay to a level of higher consciousness (*nazírání*). Likewise antisemitism—one of the manifestations of this demagogic fever—will pass simultaneously with it; and of its effects only a few fires on the field of culture will remain, nothing more.[97]

According to the *Rozvoj* circle, Czech Jews could not contribute to the expression of a new moral aesthetics for the nation at large until they had tended, as it were, to their own house. Judaism both as a religion and as a system of practical ethics was seen as being in drastic need of change. Indeed, this generation of Czech-Jewish intellectuals possessed much the same insecurity that had characterized the early Reform movement in Germany. As *Rozvoj*'s editors explained in 1904,

> We have felt instinctively for a long time now that there must be a moral improvement of the whole in order for there to be fewer transgressions on the part of individuals. The better the totality, the more noble the moral idea that governs the whole, the more "perfect" is each individual, and the more infrequent, then, the lapses of isolated individuals.[98]

Although both Lederer and Vohryzek called for far-reaching reforms within Czech Judaism, they did not always share the same attitude toward the faith of their fathers. Often their remarks alternated between vigorous anti-Orthodox polemic and prophetic statements about what a reinvigorated and progressive faith of the future might look like. Lederer seems to have been a moderate. He was reasonably familiar with the sources of traditional Judaism, citing them frequently in his works and with a certain sense of intimacy. Likewise, he showed himself to be more eager than some of his colleagues to defend the reputation of the classics of rabbinic literature—the Mishnah, Talmud, and Midrash—as storehouses of ethical teachings and wisdom, rather than as mere legal compilations.[99] Vohryzek, for his part, made a point of despising religious Orthodoxy. He urged his readers to fight against the kind of religion that conceived of a purely national, rather than a universal, God and which did not allow for the development of faith on the basis of reason.[100] In an article entitled "Away from Galicia," he condemned what he labeled "clericalism" within Judaism (although it is not clear whether he meant the influence of rabbis per se) and argued that the restrictions that were placed upon the individual by Jewish law no longer were valid.

> A progressive person is one who proclaims: in the fullness of your heart you do not believe this; you are unable to observe this. You are leading a struggle for existence, and these laws are a hindrance for you; they complicate your domestic life and make it more expensive. It [the law] is a dead weight which would throw your already burdened ship down into the high sea.

"Orthodoxy is our principal enemy," he concluded, "and we cannot spare anyone who proclaims it."[101]

To what "orthodoxy" was Vohryzek in the end referring? The Prague Jewish community by the turn of the century, though not particularly responsive to the ideology of the Reform movement, was nevertheless largely indifferent to religious practice. No rabbi since the death of Solomon Judah Rapoport could be said to have wielded much power and influence in the city. In any event, the leading representatives of the Prague rabbinate, such as Nathan Ehrenfeld, Alexander Kisch, and Heinrich Brody, were all fully-Westernized, university-educated clergymen and not at all representative of Galician Orthodoxy.

Orthodox Judaism for Vohryzek was simply a "straw man." His real concern lay not with uncovering the realities of Jewish religious life in Prague and Bohemia, but rather with the need to formulate a philosophy of Judaism that would match the categories of Masaryk's religious thought and which might serve as a partner in the cultural transformation of the Czech nation. "We acknowledge Masaryk's watchword," Vohryzek wrote, "that a new philosophical-religious synthesis is needed in which our world can be united."[102] For Masaryk and other Czech intellectuals anticlericalism—and specifically anti-Catholicism—represented important components of national self-awareness. If they frequently called upon the Czech people to reconstruct the intellectual tradition of Jan Hus, Jan Amos Komenský, and the Czech Reformation, they did so not only out of a concern for religious and social freedom, democracy, and justice, but also because Protestantism itself highlighted the historical distinctiveness of the Czech nation.[103]

Vohryzek applied similar rhetorical imagery to his analysis of Judaism. Galician Orthodoxy thus served much the same function as did Rome for Masaryk's philosophical allies. It was made to represent an obscurantist, backward, and repressive culture, which may or may not in fact have existed in Prague, but on whose doorstep one could lay responsibility for the thus-far unhappy integration of Jews into the Czech nation. Judaism then, like Czech culture, required a "Reformation" of its own in order that Czech Jews might join progressive Czech nationalists in a new, symbiotic relationship, a joint effort in the redirection of the national spirit.

In essence, then, the intellectual circle around Vohryzek, Lederer, and the newspaper *Rozvoj* set out to reform an abstraction, undeterred by the fact that Masaryk's religious critique had been aimed at Roman Catholicism and, in point of fact, unequipped with a suitable alternative with which to replace Jewish "orthodoxy." Hussite liberalism, whatever this term in the end may have meant to Czech Jews, lacked a specifically Jewish content and thus was never really a serious candidate. Nor was classical German Reform of the nineteenth century; having failed to move Bohemian Jewry through the 1860s, by 1900 German Reform appeared to be hopelessly out of date.

The Czech-Jewish movement did discover in the work of Moritz Lazarus—professor of philosophy at the University of Berlin—a suitable, if not compelling, reinterpretation of Judaism. His *Ethik des Judentums*, published in 1898, had set out to demonstrate the ethical basis of Judaism using only classical and rabbinic Jewish texts. In it he had argued that morality—God's Law—is accepted by man in a Kantian affirmation of duty, because man strives to resemble the moral quality of the Divine. Lazarus (1824–1903) insisted that it was possible to isolate a fundamental principle of Judaism: "Because the moral is divine, therefore you shall be moral, and because the divine is moral, you shall become like unto God."[104]

Armed with Lazarus's definition of an unchanging Jewish ethics, Vohryzek called for a paring of the rotten exterior of Judaism to get to its wholesome kernel. "The meaning of our religion, as Lazarus has demonstrated, is the hallowing of the name of God, 'kiddush ha-shem,' the raising of man to divine status (*zbožnění člověka*). All of our thoughts and deeds must be a celebration of His name, not a benefit or a profit, but rather a reaching out for the highest goal."[105] The question, thought Vohryzek, was whether or not all aspects of Judaism allowed for the moral perfection of the Jew. His answer, predictably, was No. Certain practices actually inhibited the individual from achieving this goal. Consequently, it was incumbent upon Jews to distance themselves from such practices. "Only he who believes and acts according to his convictions can be [called] a good person."[106]

This morally honed Judaism of the future, with its emphasis on the hallowing of the name of God through ethical behavior, was to perform a specific function in Czech society. *Rozvoj* endowed it with Hillel's well-known dictum: Do not do unto others what is hateful to yourself. The paper interpreted this to mean to believe in and support human progress, to struggle against asceticism and the suppression of one's humanity. "Everyone belongs to our camp; everyone is our brother. That is our confession of faith."[107]

Ethical Judaism was meant, on the one hand, to serve as a vehicle for the improved integration of the Jew into Czech society. But it was also the intention of the Czech-Jewish movement to effect the nature of Czech society itself. The Czech-Jewish elite was to help direct the nation along a more moderate course, to lead it away from the hypernationalism of the past toward a new humanism:

> The national patriotism of the Jews has a precisely determined path: it is and must be humanistic. Humanistic in this sense, that it must not deny the legitimacy of other nations in the face of its own individuality. For Jewry this is a ready-made cultural and political program . . . and it is allotted to the Jew as his own, let us say, political, station—in other words, his religious-cultural mission.[108]

Such descriptions of the role of Judaism in the Czech future possessed a decidely messianic flavor. In the end Judaism's task amounted to nothing less than the modulation, even the sublimation, of the national impulse. Judaism was to provide the basis for the resolution of national tensions, for the wiping out of ancient prejudices. It was in fact highly paradoxical that this redefined and reshaped Jewish culture, once it was directed back toward Czech society, would result in the blunting of precisely those national conflicts that had spawned it in the first place. Yet such was to be the ultimate task of Czech Jewry: to mediate the national struggle, eventually to overcome nationalism and to arrive at a humanistic solution to social conflict.

   Although the political message of *Rozvoj* represented a clear challenge to
prevailing attitudes and policies within the Czech-Jewish movement, the
religious views of Vohryzek's wing ultimately did not. The reformulation of
Judaism along the lines of Masarykian—and neo-Kantian—moral philosophy consisted for the most part of an intellectual exercise and remained the
domain of a small cultural elite. Or-Tomid in the 1880s had circumvented
the established religious institutions of Prague in order to realize structural
changes in Jewish worship. Now, a generation later, Czech-Jewish religious
thought also operated in a sphere of its own but without any kind of institutional supports. Just as Vohryzek once had been content to ignore the social
realities that lay behind his critique of Czech Judaism, he now demonstrated
equal indifference to the prospect of actually implementing his cultural program in a concrete fashion. Somehow the combination of independent, creative thinking and journalistic exhortation would simply work their magic on
the Czech and Jewish populations.
   From the point of view of the day-to-day practice of Judaism, the Czech-
Jewish reform "in the image of Hus" was a rather sterile program. It produced numerous echoes on the printed page—Otakar Kraus's rehabilitation
of the German Reform movement, and Klineberger's massive opus on religious sensibility, for example—but had little direct impact on organized
religious life.[109] Its ultimate significance lay in the larger arena of Czech
politics and political culture. Here the *Rozvoj* circle successfully accomplished both a practical and a philosophical realignment, which enabled the
Czech-Jewish movement to participate with confidence in progressive Czech
nationalism. Religious thought represented but one element in an extensive
process of cultural transformation. Yet it was this postpositivist obsession
with the religious dimension in culture that signaled most profoundly the
Czech-Jewish dilemma at the turn of the century. It articulated the frustra-
tions of Jewish assimilation in a postemancipatory, ethnically contentious
environment, but it also held out the hope for a peaceful resolution to
national strife, a vision of concerted social endeavor based on the positive
contributions of both Jewish and Czech culture.

Siegfried Kapper, Czech-Jewish poet (1821–1879). Reproduced from *KČŽ*, 29 (1909–10).

Eduard Lederer, lawyer and Czech-Jewish leader (1859–1941). Reproduced from *KČŽ*, 29 (1909–10).

Viktor Vohryzek, physician and
Czech-Jewish leader (1864–1918).
Reproduced from *KČŽ*, 34
(1914–15).

Jewish Town Hall and
Altneuschul (Staronová
synagoga) at the turn of the
century. Reproduced from
KČŽ, 35 (1915–16).

Rabínská ulice at the turn of the century. Reproduced from H. Volavková, *Zmizelá Praha* (Prague, 1947).

Advertisement for the Czech-Jewish newspaper *Rozvoj*. Reads in part: "The only Czech-Jewish weekly. . . . The paper offers articles in politics, culture, and economics. The only Czech paper that fights antisemitism." Reproduced from *KČŽ*, 28 (1908–09).

The Prague Castle from Valdštejnska ulice. Photo: H. Kieval.

Old Jewish Cemetery, Prague. Photo: H. Kieval.

Old Jewish Cemetery, Prague. Photo: H. Kieval

Franz Kafka, German-Jewish writer (1883–1924). Courtesy of Archiv Klaus Wagenbach, Berlin.

Jewish courtyard, Prague, turn of the century. Reproduced from H. Volavková, *Zmizelá Praha* (Prague, 1947).

Hugo Bergmann, Prague Zionist (1883–1975). Courtesy of the Jewish National and University Library, Jerusalem.

4

Zionism in Prague: Bar Kochba, 1899–1909

The Origins of Prague Zionism

If the forces of population explosion, urbanization, and ethnic nationalism began to mobilize portions of Bohemian Jewry after 1870, it was the exacerbation of the national struggle in the 1890s that dictated a momentary lull in the new alignments. Czech-speaking Jewish professionals agonized over the treachery of Czech liberalism and eventually cut their ties to the Young Czech party. They chose instead to identify with smaller, more progressive elements within the national movement, and eventually to redefine the cultural basis of the Czech-Jewish relationship. German-Jewish businessmen and urban professionals quietly sought out civic associations that had not abandoned their liberal premises—even as the social bases of these groups were shrinking. Alternatively, they created a new network of Jewish fraternal societies, most notably B'nai B'rith, to carry out social and charitable activities while emphasizing Jewish solidarity and cultural continuity.

When the militant German nationalists broke away from the Lese- und Redehalle der deutschen Studenten in Prague, they left the organization half-empty and ostentatiously Jewish. Most of the Jewish members of the Lese- und Redehalle apparently were content to let the matter stand at that, to continue their pursuit of higher education, professional training, and social advancement under the guise of German culture but in reality as a highly visible and distinct ethnic group. Not all could accept the new status quo, however. In the eyes of some, the division of the Burschenschaften according to the question of the admission of Jews had discredited the entire network of German fraternities. So, in 1893 a small group of Jewish students formed an association of their own, calling it Maccabäa. Some years later, one of the founding members of the group recalled the deep and abrupt emotional disillusionment that he had experienced during the events that had led up to its creation:

> It went through me like a bolt when I saw over there, on the side of the opposition, my best friends from the Gymnasium, people with whom I had been in close contact up until the last few days. . . . In this one moment I saw the wide, gaping chasm [that lay] between Aryans and Jews; I realized that everything that binds people together—common homeland, common language and culture—that personal sympathies and all of the West European forms of civility, are merely narrow, fragile bridges, but nothing which could [begin to] fill this gap.[1]

Like the progressive wing of the Czech-Jewish movement, Maccabäa rejected the type of liberalism that had characterized Jewish student associations up to this time. It also declared itself to be openly nonreligious and nonassimilationist. Maccabäa had no apparent ties to Ḥibbat Zion (Love of Zion), the Jewish national movement that had emerged the previous decade in the Russian Pale of Settlement and that advocated the immediate emigration—as pioneers—to Palestine. Nevertheless, it did view itself as *nationally* Jewish, founded on the premise that the Jews constituted a self-contained entity (much as the German and Czech radicals had been arguing). Honor, if nothing else, required of the Jewish student that he recognize this state of affairs and affirm his own national distinctiveness.[2]

Two of the students who led the tiny desertion from the ranks of German liberalism were in fact Russian Jews studying at the time in Prague. One of them, Israel Aronowitsch (Aharoni, 1882–1946), was sufficiently fluent in Hebrew to organize and run a club, Hebräische Propaganda, where the Hebrew language exclusively was spoken. Both students were familiar with Jewish political literature of the past few decades. Most important, they possessed none of the deep emotional ties to liberal German culture that held sway over Prague's German-speaking Jews. They considered themselves, quite naturally and unself-consciously, to be Jewish nationals, and had little trouble convincing the members of Maccabäa of the sensibleness of adopting a position of neutrality in the face of the German and Czech conflict.[3] Maccabäa's 1894 appeal to gymnasium graduates drove home this last point forcefully:

> Here in the German and Czech colleges of Prague, as in all institutions of higher learning in Austria and Germany, there exists a sharp division between Jewish and non-Jewish students. Despite the fact that the [Jews] were all busy giving themselves up entirely to Germandom or Slavdom, indulging in national chauvinism, and not wanting to know anything about their own people, the Jews— they were rebuffed with scorn and derision and closed out of organizations of which they themselves were often the founders. The Jews are not Germans, not Slavs, they are their own people. On this point everyone was in agreement except the Jews, who went on ahead performing the dirty work of foreign nations in order to reap contempt for their ridiculous importunity.

. . . Voices were heard which asked: "Should we force ourselves upon a society that does not wish to tolerate us in its midst? Have we really sunk so low that we cannot stand on our own feet? Are we not despised precisely because we do not respect ourselves as Jews?"[4]

Maccabäa did not succeed in maintaining the fervor and intensity of its Russian founders, and in 1896 it underwent a change both in name and in tone. It became known simply as the Association of Jewish University Students (Verein der jüdischen Hoschschüler) and appears to have allowed much of its Jewish nationalist character to be watered down. It differed from other middle-class Jewish organizations of the time, remarked one observer many years later, only in the desire of its members "to fill Judaism with reality and life."[5] The group did manage to hear a review of Theodor Herzl's *Der Judenstaat* by one of its members in 1896, but it steered clear of any formal association with the Jewish national movement. The Verein stagnated for three years, attracting progressively fewer and fewer members. Hugo Bergmann once remarked, perhaps facetiously, that by the end of 1899 the entire Jewish nationalist student movement consisted of three people.[6]

Two historical developments converged during the final years of the century to help revive Jewish nationalism in Prague. The first was the convening of the First Zionist Congress in Basel, Switzerland, in 1897 and the subsequent creation of an international political organization based in nearby Vienna. The second consisted in the temporary collapse of the Czech-Jewish consensus and the eruption of antisemitic violence in the aftermath of Badeni's fall. The Zionist movement in Vienna paid great attention to the deterioration of Jewish and non-Jewish relations in the Czech lands. It saw in the events of 1897–1900 an opportunity not only to spread its message of the failure of Jewish emancipation but also to establish formal Zionist institutions in demographically important Bohemia.

Theodor Herzl began the Zionist initiative with an article in the Vienna publication *Die Welt* entitled "Die Jagd in Böhmen" (The hunt in Bohemia). In it he warned Bohemian Jews not to identify with either party in the nationality controversy.[7] *Die Welt*'s propaganda efforts for the next few years echoed Herzl's theme, harping consistently on the Jews of Bohemia to stop playing "whipping boy" to the Czechs and the Germans. Reporting on the effects of the 1897 riots in 1900, one local observer castigated both the German antisemite and the Czech "Judenfresser," but directed his sharpest attack at Jewish assimilationists who allowed themselves to become entangled in one or the other of the competing nationalist movements:

The German stone throwings in Eger and Saaz ought to have been able to convince the German Jews that a crooked nose and the *Wacht am Rhein* [German patriotic anthem] stand in a contradictory relation; the Czech campaign . . . which occurred in Prague and in several nearby battlefields, such as Náchod and Plzeň, could for its part have made clear to the Czech Jews that the enthusiastic singing of *Kde domov můj* [Czech patriotic song] has a considerably ironic effect.[8]

As for the Jews of Prague, the author observed, only the breaking of shop windows managed to rouse them from the dream that their city was a kind of German El Dorado. Shortly after the riots of 1897 Jews began to take down store signs that were either bilingual or written exclusively in German and replace them with Czech advertisements. Czech nationalist Jews, for their part, may have survived the riots of 1897 as a test of strength and faith, but even they succumbed to doubts in the wake of the Hilsner trial:

> Thus the Prague Jews are in the uncomfortable situation of a person who sits between two chairs; they have gone through a school of political hard knocks, in which they might have experienced and learned a truth: namely that they must be Jews and only Jews, and that their former weakness—their Judaism—would and must be their strength in the future.[9]

The Zionist movement offered to both German- and Czech-speaking Jews the solution of a credible middle road in the nationality controversy. The path was not to consist simply of a renunciation of both German and Czech "chauvinism"—a retreat to a kind of Bohemian neutralism—but rather the affirmation of a positive, Jewish national identity, the contours and content of which had yet to be defined. Nor was the Zionist option designed (as some would charge) to provide an alternative home for Prague's German Jews, who knew enough not to stay behind in a crumbling building, but who could not bring themselves to seek shelter in the Czech camp. In fact, nearly all of the early advocates of Jewish nationalism in Prague were themselves Czech Jews. Many had spent time in the SČAŽ or in the provincial chapters of the Czech-Jewish National Union.[10]

Two such individuals, Filip Lebenhart and Karl Rezek, founded the first overtly Zionist organization in Bohemia, the Jüdischer Volksverein "Zion" (Jewish People's Association "Zion") in 1899. A branch of the Vienna-based World Zionist Organization, Zion was composed primarily of small merchants, office workers, and shopkeepers. Immediately popular among provincial Jewry, the organization set in motion in 1900 the first positive Jewish response to the "svůj k svému" campaign: a popular savings bank, which dispensed emergency funds to merchants who were in danger of financial collapse. Czech-Jewish leaders of the time offered grudging praise for a step that they themselves either dared not or simply had failed to take.[11]

And it was a handful of Czech-speaking university students in Prague who helped to transform the Verein der jüdischen Hochschüler into an explicitly Jewish, nationalist organization. Disgusted with the events of 1897 and 1899, and inspired in part by the example of Lebenhart and Rezek, young trans-plants to Prague such as Alfred Löwy, Arthur Klein, and Josef Kohn ab-stained from or left the SČAŽ. In 1899 they entered the ranks of the Verein der jüdischen Hochschüler, where, joined by Samo Grün, son of the Prague rabbi Nathan Grün, they inaugurated an internal debate on the viability of a separate national position for the Jews of Bohemia. Eventually they persuaded the organization to revise its charter and voice open support for the Zionist movement.[12] By the end of the year, the Verein had changed not only its charter, but also its name (once again). This time it adopted the bilingual Bar Kochba, Verein der jüdischen Hochschüler in Prag/Spolek židovských akademiků v Praze (Association of Jewish University Students in Prague).

Bar Kochba may have derived its name from the 1897 play *Bar Kochba,* written by the Czech poet and playwright Jaroslav Vrchlický, which investigated the Jewish revolt against Rome in 132 C.E. Filip Lebenhart, who had become a friend and associate of Vrchlický's by 1899, undoubtedly served as the intermediary between the Czech writer and the student Zionists. In 1901 he wrote to Theodor Herzl about a recent meeting that he had had with Vrchlický in which the topic of discussion was Zionism. Lebenhart explained to the Viennese leader that it was most important—"in view of the meaning of this person"—to receive him fully into the Jewish national movement, for which he had already demonstrated great interest. Keenly aware of Vrchlický's position in modern Czech literature, and of the esteem in which he was held by the Czech-Jewish movement, Lebenhart appreciated—appeared in fact to relish—the paradox that the lyric poet's endorsement of Zionism posed. Many of Vrchlický's most loyal admirers, meanwhile, could but suffer in silent confusion.[13]

Under Lebenhart's leadership, the early Zionist movement in Prague took to the cities and towns of the Czech countryside, the heartland of the Czech-Jewish movement, in order to propagandize and try to set up local chapters of Zion. Members of Bar Kochba and Zion were even so bold as to attend meetings of the Czech-Jewish National Union, to challenge assimilationist ideology on their opponents' own turf. At one such meeting, held in Kutná Hora in February 1900, Ignát Arnstein had been scheduled to deliver an address on the response of the Czech-Jewish movement to increasing antisemitism. Lebenhart and the young chairman of Bar Kochba, Alfred Löwy, were also given an opportunity to speak. Addressing the gathering in their native Czech, they presented the Jewish nationalist position, and received for their troubles a scornful review in the Czech-Jewish press. Apparently those present heard nothing more from the Zionists than "a couple of well-known slogans the likes of which are repeated over and again at every meeting."[14] The assimilationists must have been bothered by their newly found rivals, however; their newspapers and journals had been devoting much space to refutations of the Zionist position for a number of years.[15]

The assimilationists may in fact have had good reason to fear the inroads that Zionism was making in their own territory. The Zionists' insistence on self-defense and the maintenance of Jewish honor struck a responsive chord among provincial Czech Jewry, who had long maintained stubborn ethnic attachments that tended to mitigate the pace of acculturation. Czech-Jewish leaders may have recognized that some kind of Jewish national reawakening merited recognition as a legitimate response to the worsening of the national struggle; hence the defections from the SČAŽ to the Verein der jüdischen Hochschüler around 1899. In subsequent years the Czech-Jewish movement would see a number of other influential members slip through its fingers. Adolf Bergmann, the first president of the Pardubice chapter of the Czech-Jewish National Union, became a Zionist before the end of World War I.[16] Emil Waldstein, corresponding secretary of the SČAŽ in 1909, became active in Po'ale Zion and Jewish national politics in the First Czechoslovak Republic.[17]

More disturbing was the loss of the person who was to become the leading Jewish political figure in Czechoslovakia after 1918, Ludvík Singer (1876–1931). A native of Kolín, Singer took part in the activities of the SČAŽ while a law student at the Czech University in Prague. The Czech-Jewish press reports that he participated in a number of the early debates between Zion and the Czech-Jewish National Union.[18] At the same time he became embroiled in the national controversy in the northern Bohemian city of Liberec (Reichenberg), the hometown of the Sudeten German movement, where he was performing his legal clerkship. Apparently a group of German attorneys there demanded of their colleague, Hugo Reichmann, that he dismiss his law clerk, Ludvík Singer, on the grounds that he was a Czech nationalist, a member of the Association of Czech Academic Jews, and a speaker of Czech at home.[19] In 1906 Singer set up a law office in Kolín, and in 1907 he joined the Zionist organization.

None of Singer's contemporaries has offered a specific reason for his defection. One suspects, however, that he became disillusioned with the increasingly uncompromising positions of both the Czech and the German national movements, perhaps convinced that there was no future in either camp for the Jews. Two years after joining the Zionist movement, Singer settled in Prague, where from 1910 onward he served as chairman of the Zionist district committee. During these years he negotiated with Czech politicians concerning the future of the Jews in the Crown lands. Singer cofounded the Jewish National Council (Národní rada židovská) in October 1918, was a member of the Comité des Délégations juives at the Paris Peace Conference in 1919, and lobbied successfully with Edvard Beneš for the official recognition of the Jewish nationality in the Czechoslovak Constitution. Head of the Jewish party in the new Republic, Singer sat on the Prague City Council and was for a brief period sent to the Czechoslovak Parliament. During the last years of his life, Singer enjoyed the position of éminence grise of Czech Jewry; he was elected to the chairmanship of the Jewish community of Prague in 1930.[20]

Neo-Romanticism and Jewish Self-Discovery

With the transition from Maccabäa to Bar Kochba, the main impetus behind Zionism in Bohemia was about to shift. In the beginning the initiative had come from Zion, the popular association of traders, artisans, and shopkeepers; now the lifeblood of the national movement could be found in the Jewish student activists of Prague. As student life in general became politically more radical, Jews had greater and greater difficulty accepting older forms of association. For them, whether originally Czech-speaking or German, Jewish nationalism offered both a social alternative to an uncomfortable—often hostile—environment and an honest retort to cultural responses no longer tenable. The Prague student Zionists tended to apply the fervor of the "converted" to their new political and intellectual endeavors. Thanks in part to the dynamism of their leaders, and in part to the seriousness with which they approached the enterprise of "nation-building," the student Zionists of Prague were to dominate Jewish nationalism in Bohemia until the start of the First World War.

Did there exist a specifically "Prague strand" within Zionism at large?[21] This is difficult to say. The very structure of student organizations often militated against the development of consistent intellectual and political traditions. The average student spent five years at the university. Thus, during a relatively short period of time, twenty-five years for example, approximately five generations of student leaders would have had occasion to emerge. Moreover, the Zionist movement as a whole exhibited strong divisions during its early years. These, too, were reflected in the Jewish student associations of Prague. Perhaps if strong, charismatic leadership were to emerge within the student movement at an early stage, or, alternatively, if comparable personalities were to dominate the group from the outside, this built-in tendency toward inconsistency could be overcome.

In fact, Bar Kochba showed remarkably little ideological wandering. It may not always have had a clear sense of where it stood on issues, and it was at times shaken by controversy. Nevertheless, Bar Kochba did manage over the course of a decade to map out a distinct and original cultural position. It did so in three stages, represented by the three generational cohorts that spanned the years from 1901 to 1914.

The first stage lasted from around 1901 to 1905 and corresponded to the period of leadership of the philosopher and classmate of Franz Kafka, Hugo Bergmann (1883–1975). During this time Bar Kochba elaborated its first consistent position on cultural Zionism. This was followed by what might be called Bar Kochba's "political phase," during which time a countermovement to Bergmann's cultural Zionism achieved impressive results, not the least of which was the establishment of the weekly newspaper *Selbstwehr* (Self-defense) in 1907. The last stage began in 1909 on the occasion of the first of Martin Buber's three major addresses to the Prague Jewish community. It lasted until the start of World War I and was characterized by sustained collaboration between Bar Kochba and Buber. This period witnessed the definitive triumph of Bergmann's version of cultural Zionism, though perhaps in more romantic tones than before, and climaxed in the publication of Prague's Zionism's intellectual jewel, *Vom Judentum* (On Judaism), in 1914.

Bergmann, like Kafka, was a first-generation Prague Jew. His father's family stemmed from the Czech village of Chrastice—which had only two Jewish families—his mother's from the considerably larger town of Příbram. Following the predominant pattern in German-Jewish acculturation in the city, the Bergmann household spoke German in the home, sent the children to German-language schools, and generally ceased to observe Jewish religious practices.[22] Many years later Bergmann was to remark that he received his "Judaism" as a child, not from Prague's Jewish institutions, but from his uncle's home in Chrastice, where the family used to spend summers.[23]

Bergmann's educational career and family circumstances provide an excellent illustration of a superficially German cultural exterior masking a more variegated and complex reality. For example, at the same time that he was being integrated to a classical, German educational system, Bergmann enjoyed close social and cultural ties with Czech-speaking Catholics. In Bergmann's case, these people were the peasants and neighbors with whom the boy lived during the summers in Chrastice. Recalling scenes of his childhood in the Czech village, Bergmann stressed the great impression made on him by living in an environment of "mutual, multilingual and multireligious penetration." "We spoke two languages together," he wrote, "and lived not to an inconsiderable extent the religious life of a Catholic."[24] The Bergmann children, for example, not only witnessed the practice of "crossing oneself" before swimming or partaking of a meal (the family would often eat at a single table with Czech servants and hired hands), but frequently imitated it as well. Similarly, when a priest would appear on the street, not only the village youngsters, but also their Jewish playmates, would run to greet him and kiss his ring.[25]

Equally revealing of the weakness of the Bergmann family's German "exterior" was the early association of both parents and children with Jewish nationalism. The father, Siegmund Bergmann, joined the Jüdischer Volksverein "Zion" at its inception; the mother, Johanna, was a driving force within the women's Zionist movement in Prague; and the older brother, Arthur, worked actively for the nascent Bar Kochba upon his entry into the university.[26] Small wonder, then, that the younger son, Hugo, became a Zionist activist in 1898 while still a student at the Altstädter Gymnasium. His decision to join Bar Kochba in the fall of 1901 (when he, Kafka, Emil Utitz, Oskar Pollak, and the rest of his class entered the German University) had been a foregone conclusion for years.[27]

Bergmann rose quickly through the ranks of Bar Kochba; at the end of two years (1903–4) he was elected its chairman. In choosing Bergmann, Bar

Kochba turned for the first time to a person who possessed both a clear picture of what it meant to be a Jewish nationalist in Austria and the will to see his conception implemented concretely. The purpose of Zionism, according to Bergmann, was "to teach ourselves to be complete Jews, to finish the struggle against assimilation within our own selves in victory, to recognize the nation such as it is, even in our day-to-day lives."[28]

Bergmann's conception of Zionism focused almost exclusively on what was called "cultural regeneration." Bar Kochba placed a great deal of emphasis on regular public lectures and discussions, the study of Hebrew, Jewish history, and Zionist theory. Above all it stressed the need for its members to incorporate into their lives an active Jewish culture. Not only did Bergmann continue the Hebrew language course that had been initiated by Aronowitsch; he also encouraged all Bar Kochba members to learn Yiddish, as both languages constituted the vessels that carried the materials of a "living Judaism." He even pushed through a change in the bylaws of Bar Kochba requiring that henceforth any person aspiring to a leadership position within the organization first pass an examination in Jewish history![29] On the importance of recapturing an active knowledge of Hebrew, Bergmann wrote: "If you want to recognize the Jewish nation, if you want to give your opinion on the problems that determine its life, and if you want to relate earnestly to your Zionism—first learn to hear its tongue."[30] Bergmann's friends often repeated a favorite maxim of his at the time: "A student Zionist who does not know Hebrew is a contradiction in terms (*contradictio in adjecto*)."[31]

To the Jewish students of Bar Kochba, Zionism was a personal, spiritual revolution, a reappropriation of Judaism as a living culture. Superficially, this conviction resembled Theodor Herzl's famous formulation, made at the First Zionist Congress in 1897: "Zionism means the return to the Jewish people (*Judentum*) even before the return to the Jewish land."[32] Beginning with Bergmann, however, Bar Kochba's Zionism became decidedly non-Herzlian. It drew its main inspiration from the school of "cultural Zionism" originated by Aḥad Ha'am (Asher Ginzberg, 1856–1927) and transmitted to Bar Kochba through the mediation of Nathan Birnbaum (1864–1937), Berthold Feiwel (1875–1937), Martin Buber (1878–1965), and Bergmann himself.[33]

Nathan Birnbaum (pen name Mathias Acher) had been one of the founders of Kadimah, the first Jewish nationalist student association in Vienna, in 1882. A devotee of Leo Pinsker and the Russian-Jewish Ḥibbat Zion movement, Birnbaum began in 1885 to edit the first Jewish nationalist periodical in German, named *Selbstemancipation* after Pinsker's path-breaking pamphlet of 1882. Birnbaum's address to the First Zionist Congress in 1897, entitled "Zionism as a Cultural Movement," officially announced his endorsement of Aḥad Ha'am's vision of a modern Jewish cultural rebirth as the ultimate solution to the Jewish question.[34] Six years later he offered Western Jews the first systematic presentation of Aḥad Ha'am's thought in a work published by Jüdischer Verlag in Berlin.[35]

The Moravian-born Berthold Feiwel may have had the most direct role in Bar Kochba's formulation of Zionism as a "spiritual revolution."[36] In March 1901, at the Conference of Austrian Zionists attended by Alfred Löwy, and Siegmund, Arthur, and Johanna Bergmann, among others, he introduced the program known as *Gegenwartsarbeit* (work in the present)—which stressed the amelioration of current cultural, economic, and political conditions among diaspora Jewry—as a necessary first stage in the Zionist revolution.[37] Later that year, after Feiwel's program was rejected by the World Zionist Executive, he joined forces with Buber, Chaim Weizmann (1873–1952), and Leo Motzkin (1867–1933) in the establishment of the so-called Democratic Faction—a loosely knit opposition to the mainstream Herzlian Zionists that called for the preeminence of cultural activity, the democratization of communal institutions, and the immediate settlement of the Land of Israel.[38]

Virtually from the start, Bar Kochba felt inclined to align with the cultural Zionists and the Democratic Faction. Accepting Bar Kochba's designation as "presiding corporation" at the first conference of Austrian Student Zionist Organizations in 1903, Hugo Bergmann declared that his colleagues did not intend to follow Herzl's policies with respect to the noninvolvement of Zionists in domestic affairs. Instead, he stressed the importance of Gegenwartsarbeit. This, in the context of Austria, was to entail struggling for the recognition of the Jewish nationality in secondary schools and at the university; educating Jewish youth in Zionism; attempting to bridge the "gap" between Eastern and Western Jewry; and devoting oneself to the problems of the "Jewish masses."[39]

During the "Uganda Crisis" of 1903–4, which threatened to split the Zionist movement over the issue of whether or not to accept—even as a temporary solution—territory outside of Palestine as a homeland for the Jews, Bar Kochba threw its weight behind the Kharkov resolution of the Russian Zionists. They agreed that only the "Land of Israel" could hope to elicit a positive response from the Jewish masses. After Herzl's death, Bar Kochba continued a policy of opposition toward David Wolffsohn (1856–1914) and the leadership of the Zionist movement. This did not end until the Prague student Zionists found in Kurt Blumenfeld (1884–1963), general secretary of the German Zionist Organization after 1909, a figure who shared their views concerning the cultural component of the Jewish national rebirth.[40]

If Bar Kochba located its first ideological authority in Berthold Feiwel, it discovered its master teacher and advisor in Martin Buber. Only slightly older than most of the founders of Bar Kochba, Buber exercised a moral authority over the group far beyond his years. He was both path-breaker and mirror, a faithful reflection of the cultural temperament of most Bar Kochba members and an inspiration for what imaginative scholarship could provide to a generation out of touch with its past.

Buber shared with the prewar generation an intense dislike of nineteenth-century positivism. He and others of his age scoffed at that scientific optimism which argued for man's ability to measure exactly all aspects of his physical environment; they chafed at the positivists' predisposition to classify all reality according to "natural laws." Turning instead to the writings of Nietzsche—particularly *Zarathustra* with its imagery of activism and creativity—Buber called for the reintegration of man into nature, for the recovery of the individually determined and creative act.[41] The student Zionists of Prague tended to identify with this romantic impulse, expressing it alternatively in terms of religious quest and heroic striving. It, too, fed on the works of antirationalist writers such as Nietzsche and Henri Bergson, but corroborating voices could be found in the works of the romantics.[42] Dusty from the neglect of two generations of Europeans, the early romantics now spoke to emotional needs that were widespread and deeply felt. Hans Kohn (1891–1971), who joined Bar Kochba in 1910 and soon became a great popularizer of Buber's ideas, later acknowledged the debt that he and his colleagues owed to the romantics. Theirs had been "a battle of the concrete form against the abstract law, of the psyche against the word."[43] Kohn's generation took up the cudgel once again, pitting the individual and the individual's creative activity in the world against the natural and political order.

> Fichte interpreted the *I* as the ethical will, and the world as the material in which the will should create that which ought to be. We transferred Fichte's lectures on "The Vocation of Man" and on "The Characteristics of the Present Age" into the context of our own situation, and we accepted his appeal to bring forth the ideal community by placing all the power of the rationally and ethically mature individual at the service of his own nation.[44]

In 1903, during Bergmann's tenure as chairman of Bar Kochba, the group held its first *Festabend* (festive evening) to commemorate the tenth anniversary of student Zionism in Prague. The purpose of the Festabend—a deliberate substitute for the traditional fund-raising balls held by most fraternities once a year—was to bring important Jewish personalities to the attention of the community at large.[45] It will come as no surprise to learn that on this occasion Bar Kochba invited both Berthold Feiwel and Martin Buber to be the principal speakers. Feiwel spoke on the theme of "Jewish Writing"; Buber addressed the audience, as his Bar Kochba hosts had anticipated, on the topic of "Jewish Renaissance."[46]

The exact text of Buber's remarks that evening no longer exists. But echoes can certainly be found in his essay "Renaissance und Bewegung" (Renaissance and the movement), written in 1903 and published in 1905 in the volume of essays *Die Stimme der Wahrheit* (The voice of truth).[47] In this piece Buber handed his readers a compact and suggestive interpretation of the course of modern Jewish history on the European continent.

Up to the middle of the eighteenth century, Buber suggested, Judaism suffered both from the inability to determine its own destiny, that is, from external regulation, persecution, and fear, and from what he called the "despotism of the law," the stifling effects of rabbinic legislation (*halakha*) on the spiritual life of the community. At this point in his career, Buber frankly and pointedly disliked the norms of traditional Judaism. He painted them as a "misunderstood, ornate, distorted religious tradition, under the spell of a hard, unmoving 'ought,' alienated from reality, which brands as heretical and destroys everything that is instinctively light and joy, all that thirsts for beauty and is winged."[48] The laws and customs of normative Judaism rested like a dead weight on the Jewish community, crushing its spirit and vitality. This suffocating tradition was equally as pernicious as the forces of repression and persecution whose sources lay outside the community. Both external oppression and the "despotism of the law" worked toward the perpetuation of a "ghettoized" Jewish existence.

According to Buber's scenario, two eighteenth-century developments within European Judaism had undermined the force of law in Jewish life. They were Hasidism, the popular, pietistic movement of the Jews of Eastern Europe attributed to the figure of Israel ben Eliezer, master of the good name or "Baal Shem Tov," and Haskalah, the intellectual and political movement that grew out of the impact of the European Enlightenment on Jewish thought. Both "events" had the effect of undermining the authority of halakha, although each did so in a unique way. The Haskalah, through its vision of the free development of man's potential, insisted on the role of reason in determining behavior. Hasidism proved to be a subversive force because of its elaboration of the notion of a "higher law of life," properly understood as a higher purpose, or intention, behind the fulfillment of the *mitzvot* (commandments). This "higher purpose" aimed far beyond the individual's obligation to the legal system, per se, to a mystical appropriation of the Divine in the world of reality.[49] Twenty years before the publication of his *I and Thou,* Buber saw in Hasidism, not a guide to religious existentialism, but a "powerful and emotionally deep mysticism, which brings the Beyond (*Jenseits*) totally in to the Here (*Diesseits*) and allows the latter to be formed by the former. . . . It is the teaching of active feeling as the bond between man and God." Buber concluded, "Everything that results from a pure heart is service to the Lord. The goal of the law is that man himself become law. In this way the despotism is broken."[50]

Buber argued that the Jewish renaissance, like its more famous namesake, did not signify a return to old forms. It signaled instead the "rebirth of the whole man," the emergence of the "new" Jew, who no longer acted according to the law, but rather in response to his own reasoning and feeling; who, in imagery culled from Nietzsche, "strives toward the creative."[51]

Eastern Europe represented for Buber the clearest example of the interplay of both Haskalah and Hasidism on the traditional fabric of Jewish life. This was an area of the world where the "renaissance" had already made gradual, but steady, progress, its most concrete expression being the Jewish national movement. In Western Europe the renaissance had been stillborn. Assimilation—the all-too-sudden incorporation of European culture under the enticement of emancipation—had led to its early mortality. "In this way a portion of the nation was seduced into being untrue to its unspoken, natural ideals, and, instead of acquiring and adopting what was new slowly, took it from the hands of the civilized nations ready-made and at the cost of its own soul."[52]

The task, then, of those West European Jews who were interested in the spiritual regeneration of their people was to incorporate the example of Eastern Europe (as Buber portrayed it), to reintegrate into their lives the symbolic features of Hasidism and Haskalah, that is, the will to self-determination and to higher spiritual purpose. Jewish nationalism was the tool that could accomplish the desired synthesis.

> The Jewish movement is, in the last analysis, the striving after the free and perfect operation of the newly awakened powers of the nation. If one imagines the nation in the renaissance . . . in the image of an organism, then its consciousness is the national idea, its will the national movement.[53]

In "Renaissance und Bewegung" Buber provided what one might call a "working myth" of the recent Jewish past, a paradigm of the history of the Jews in Europe together with a promise for the future. Gershom Scholem has rightly pointed out that Buber in fact schematized and idealized Jewish history to the point that his portrayal bore very little resemblance to concrete historical reality.[54] Yet, certainly it was this very distortion that carried such tremendous appeal to the young, Central European, Jewish intellectual. These individuals, who tended to be emotionally and intellectually removed from traditional Judaism, nevertheless had come to reject complete assimilation as being somehow dishonorable or untrue to oneself. To them Buber proferred a valuable ideological service. Writing through the idiom of neo-romantic, *völkisch* vitalism, he dismissed the inaccessible forms of traditional Jewish practice as pernicious as well as irrelevant. He idealized the mystical elements of East European Hasidism into an abstraction that was attractive intellectually. Lastly, Buber called for the development of a new "Jewish type" (*neue Judentypus*), which the culturally estranged Jew actually could help to create. He, as it were, lifted postemancipation Jews out of the margins of Jewish existence and deposited them squarely within the mainstream of Jewish history through a creative, albeit heavy-handed, treatment of the Jewish past.

The Bar Kochba circle interpreted cultural Zionism to mean that the upheaval that was to transform assimilated Jews into national Jews would take the form of a personal, spiritual revolt. It was to take place within the consciousness of the individual, stripping one, as it were, of one's assimilationist personality and rendering one for the first time culturally active and creative. Thus, for all of the stimulation that the Czech and German national struggles might have provided, the Prague student Zionists were determined to pursue Jewish renewal in a context of social and cultural isolation. Zionism for this group provided a solution to the problem of the Jew and the individual self, rather than to that of the Jew and the environment.

Bergmann himself wrote of this feeling of isolation coupled with yearning for personal fulfillment in a letter to Franz Kafka in 1901:

> Do not believe that it was the feeling of compassion that changed me into a Zionist. My Zionism is replete with selfishness. I feel as though I want to fly, to create, but cannot; I have no more strength. For all this I feel that under other circumstances I could find the strength, that this uprootedness was not decreed to me from birth. And so Zionism is for me an expression of my yearnings for love. For I know that thousands are suffering exactly as I; I want to travel on their path, to work with them. . . . Perhaps one of these days we shall overcome [our] weakness. One of these days we shall stand firmly on our soil, and we shall no longer be lacking roots, detached and trembling as a reed. And perhaps, perhaps my strength will return again to me.[55]

Bar Kochba's preference for cultural over political regeneration might be compared to the position of Czech intellectuals in the first half of the nineteenth century. They, too, saw their role primarily in terms of didactics. The task was to teach people to reappropriate and revitalize the remnants of Czech national culture in Bohemia and Moravia, to breathe new life into debilitated cultural forms. On the other hand, Bar Kochba's attitude of spiritual isolation contrasts sharply with the Czech-Jewish vision of cultural symbiosis. For Lederer and Vohryzek the process of cultural development required of Czech Jews the ability to assimilate signals that they received from general Czech culture and to force a confrontation between their assumptions—their faith—and the elements of modern Czech thought. Eventually they would be able to influence the national debate through the medium of a refined Judaism whose face was faithfully Czech. The Czech-Jewish intellectuals saw their venture as one that intersected at every point with the Czech environment. Interaction between Jews and non-Jews was to be constant, although Jews would not be in a position to participate as equal partners in Czech cultural life until they had revised Judaism and brought it up to date.

The Prague Zionists, on the other hand—whether educated as Czechs or as Germans—saw no way for the time being in which they could take part in a cultural give-and-take. To begin with, they were determined to abstain from the partisan Czech-German controversy. Further, they could not hope to participate in society as Jews until they possessed a Jewish culture. The first task, then, was to appropriate and redefine Jewish cultural forms, Jewish values: to build a modern Jewish cultural tradition de novo. For this the members of Bar Kochba looked to Aḥad Ha'am, Buber, and Feiwel, to the mediated traditions of East European Jewry, and, above all, to their own imagination.

National Ideologies and Jewish Politics in Prague

Czech Nationalism and Bar Kochba

Abstention from the nationality controversy, however, did not mean that the Prague Zionists were unimpressed by the examples of Czech and German nationalism. Needless to say, the reverse was true. The Prague Zionist intellectuals shared most of the convictions that permeated the writings of turn-of-the-century nationalists. In Bergmann's 1903 pamphlet *Die Judenfrage und ihre Lösungsversuche* (The Jewish question and attempts to resolve it)—distributed to young Jews who were matriculating from secondary schools in Bohemia—he frankly rejected liberal cosmopolitanism as historically and politically unnatural. Jews who were indifferent to the "national problem" ignored the realities of history. In a paraphrase of Johann Gottfried Herder, the pamphlet concluded, "A truer, more fruitful cosmopolitanism is arrived at through the free development of all nations."[56]

The Prague Zionists acknowledged the fact that they were, if not a byproduct of the nationality controversy in the Czech lands, then certainly inspired by the great nationalist leaders of the century. Within the Czech national camp Tomáš Masaryk provided a most congenial and appealing model. He was known as a defender of Jewish rights and a staunch opponent of the blood libel (and hence already a hero to most Czech Jews); but his emphasis on the spiritual and moral components of nationalism struck a particularly responsive chord among the followers of Aḥad Ha'am, Birnbaum, and Buber. Masaryk's reference to the Czech Reformation as a model on which to base the values of the Czech national movement, and above all his insistence that nationalism must serve ethical ends, had a lasting influence on Bar Kochba's own development.[57]

To the chagrin of his faithful supporters within the Czech-Jewish movement, Masaryk could never fully accept either the philosophical or the moral basis of Jewish assimilation. As early as 1883, in a review of Ernest Renan's *Le Judaisme comme race et comme religion* (Judaism as a race and as a religion), he argued that the Jews did constitute a nation. Moreover, Jewish national self-awareness provided the best means of ensuring peaceful coexistence between Jews and non-Jews. It did not help much in the fight against antisemitism to argue, as Renan had, that the Jews were not a pure race or nation. The issue at hand was not that of racial purity but of character.

> Non-Semites as well as Semites must recognize what separates us and which of our character traits are unpleasant to us both. In recognizing our mistakes and

our faults we both should then work toward finding the cement which up to now has not been discovered.[58]

Masaryk and other writers involved in the Czech Realist publications *Čas* (Time) and *Naše doba* (Our times) began to follow developments within the world Zionist movement from as early as 1897. The moderate Czech nationalists gave their endorsement to Zionism the following year in an article entitled "Sionism," which appeared under the initials F.B. in *Naše doba*. The author of this piece (one wonders if it was not perhaps Berthold Feiwel) possessed a firm knowledge of Jewish history and liturgy. He introduced the argument in favor of Zionism with an overview of the history and persecution of the Jews during antiquity and the middle ages, then turned his attention to central passages in Jewish liturgy, including the ritual of the Passover *seder*. Every year, he emphasized, Jews pause in the middle of the seder meal to welcome the prophet Elijah, the harbinger of the Messiah, and pronounce in unison, "Next year in Jerusalem!" He pointed out, "They have always believed and felt that they are a special people; they have always held fast to the belief that from them would come the rebirth of the world."[59]

Turning to the specific recommendations of Herzlian Zionism, F.B. put forward both the cultural and the political goals of the movement. He stressed Herzl's admonition that Zionism was first and foremost a return of the Jew to Judaism and only then a return to the Jewish homeland. But the desire to establish an independent state in Palestine was sincere and, he added, legitimate. A neutral Palestine, like the neutral Switzerland in Europe, would serve as a bulwark of international peace and stability.[60] The article in *Naše doba* closed with a question: Is Zionism important to the Jews? Quite naturally the author answered Yes, explaining that Zionism's main task lay in lifting up the Jews morally:

> The life of the Jewish bourgeoisie, under the weight of circumstances, has been transformed into a desert. But now a breath of idealism has begun to blow—be it a mere fiction—which nevertheless is chasing away the evil spirits. We welcome it particularly because it has a democratic, progressive coloring.[61]

In his *Philosophical and Sociological Foundations of Marxism,* published in 1899, Masaryk revealed that he had read Herzl's *Judenstaat.* He also rejected Marx's resolution of the Jewish question in favor of Herzl's, explaining, "The Jews are a single nation even though they have already given up their spoken language. But language alone is not the ethnographic sign of nationality."[62] On this point, as on many others, the spokesman for Czech progressivism and the Zionists agreed.

The Czech members of Bar Kochba probably had been supporters of Masaryk even before they discovered Herzl and Aḥad Ha'am. And they eagerly sought to introduce the other members of the group to the ideas of this pivotal figure. Masaryk and his immediate circle appeared to be just as determined to sound out the young Jewish nationalists. Shortly after the founding of Bar Kochba, Alfred Löwy received a note from Masaryk in which the professor asked whether he would be interested in giving an "informational lecture" on Zionism to Slavia, the association of Czech university students. Löwy recorded the event in his diary: "The lecture took place last night. Followed by a lively discussion in which Prof. Masaryk himself affirmed our movement most strongly. The only opponents were the Czech-Jewish assimilationists."[63] Shortly thereafter Löwy was invited by a Professor Bartušek to hold forth on the same topic in front of the SČAŽ. This time Löwy's diary entry read: "I spoke before the society last night. We debated until 1:30 A.M. over the fate of the Jewish people."[64]

During Hugo Bergmann's chairmanship, relations between Bar Kochba and Masaryk grew closer still. The group had been forced to move its quarters from the fashionable Wenceslaus Square (Václavské náměstí) to Poříčí Street next door to the hotel where Masaryk was delivering a series of lectures to Czech workers. At the urging of Emil Oplatka, a Czech-speaking Jew from the village of Praskolesy, the officers of Bar Kochba sat in on Masaryk's talks.[65] They were doubtless impressed by what they heard. Significantly, one can infer from Masaryk's subsequent essays that some of the members of Bar Kochba conferred with him, pointed out the similarities that they believed to exist between the Czech and the Jewish national revivals, and brought to the professor's attention the writings of the Jewish cultural renaissance.

I draw this conclusion from an article that Masaryk published in *Naše doba* in 1905, a review of religious and ecclesiastical developments during the previous year.[66] In it Masaryk wrote, "I am indebted to several Jews, who understood my interest in their religious question and who brought to my attention a thinker from whom one can draw very positive instruction. I am referring to the Russian Jewish writer Aḥad Ha'am."[67] Who else but a cultural Zionist would have approached Masaryk in 1904 and urged him to read the works of Aḥad Ha'am? Who in Prague other than members of Bar Kochba?

Masaryk's article in *Naše doba* stands out not only for the fact that he had read Aḥad Ha'am, or for the light that it sheds on the Zionist and Czech Realist relationship, but because of the impact that the Russian Jewish writer appears to have made on the Czech leader. That Aḥad Ha'am was a master of Hebrew prose style and a major figure in the Hebrew literary renaissance did cause Masaryk to step back admiringly. But what impressed him the most was Aḥad Ha'am's critical stance toward Western liberalism, his cultural modernism which nevertheless was infused with spiritual concerns.

Aḥad Ha'am is in the first instance an opponent of liberalism and hence an opponent of Western Judaism [literally, "Jewish westernness"]. He is not impressed with the freedom of Western Jewry, its liberal blend of chauvinism and cosmopolitanism. "Should I envy these our brothers their rights? No, and again, no! I, it is true, have none, but neither have I had to give up my soul for them. . . ." Aḥad Ha'am is a Jew, simply a Jew; he does not understand at all the question of why he remains a Jew.[68]

Aḥad Ha'am's views appeared to Masaryk to highlight his own. Neither advocated that their people forsake the Enlightenment or remove themselves from European culture; but neither wished for their people to lose their "national nature" in the process of becoming "modern." Masaryk, who felt that one could be anticlerical without becoming antireligious, modern without abandoning traditional culture, showed particular interest in what to some must have appeared to be an arcane dispute within the Jewish national movement. It involved Aḥad Ha'am and writers such as M. J. Berdyczewski (1865–1921), who were strongly influenced by Nietzsche and his concept of the "transvaluation of all values." To this group, all elements of traditional Judaism had to be left behind in order for a true cultural renaissance to be achieved. To Masaryk's obvious satisfaction, Aḥad Ha'am denounced this anarchistic approach to culture, arguing instead for a renaissance of Hebrew language and literature which used the religious/literary tradition as a necessary base upon which to build.[69]

Most important for Masaryk, Aḥad Ha'am called upon the Jews to effect a "reawakening of the heart," an internal rebirth. In this Masaryk clearly recognized a kindred spirit. But he also found in Aḥad Ha'am a nobility of character that he felt was lacking in the Czech Jewish assimilationists, even those who had determined to stand up to antisemitism within the Czech national movement.

> Thus he approaches antisemitism in an entirely different way than do most Jews: antisemitism must not be the reason and motive for the efforts at national revival; these efforts must emerge from one's own deepest conciousness.[70]

"In a word," Masaryk concluded, "Aḥad Ha'am points to the improvement of Jewry through a spiritual and religious awakening."[71] This, Zionism's emphasis on self-improvement, provided the movement with unassailable moral strength. A second source of its ethical superiority over other Jewish cultural positions came, in Masaryk's view, from its uncompromising stance on the question of national assimilation. As Christoph Stölzl has correctly pointed out, Masaryk himself had started on a path of national assimilation in Vienna before he rejected it in favor of Czech national culture; from then on he interpreted the tension between assimilation and dissimilation in terms of an ethical struggle between integrity and dishonesty, good and evil.[72] In a 1905 work Masaryk used this dichotomy to condemn Czech assimilation to greater Austrian culture in the sharpest possible terms:

> That which is most holy within the nation is its moral character. . . . The Czech becomes a German only out of impure motives; he is without character, and what is amazing is the fact that the Germans take him in. . . . A person who possesses character will not be untrue to his nation under any circumstances.[73]

Such criticisms, even in the abstract, must have struck painfully at Masaryk's supporters within the Czech-Jewish movement. All the more so since he introduced his essay on Aḥad Ha'am with a brief overview of developments within the *Rozvoj* circle. The Czech-Jewish assimilationists—with their ties to the old "negativistic" liberalism and their "negative" obsession with antisemitism—served as a foil against which to contrast the Jewish national revival.

Indeed the Czech-Jewish movement's problems with otherwise sympathetic centers within Czech nationalism did not begin and end with Masaryk. Realist and Social Democratic intellectuals constantly aroused the frustration and bewilderment of the Czech-Jewish movement during the first decade of the twentieth century. Time and again in interviews and public utterances they voiced their approval of the goals of Jewish nationalism. Responding to a questionnaire of the SČAŽ in 1906, several writers—among them J. S. Machar and Jaroslav Hilbert (1871–1936)—answered in all innocence that they considered the Jews to be a nation. The ensuing turmoil within the Czech-Jewish camp was highlighted by a lengthy response in *Rozvoj* by the principal spokesman for assimilationism, Viktor Vohryzek.[74] Jan Herben, the editor of *Čas,* recalled the incident several years later in a manner that revealed his continued puzzlement over the affair:

> Several of my friends came to me with the question, "Are the Jews a nation or are they not? Are they only a religion, etc.?" I don't know; it isn't possible to answer such a question satisfactorily. I once said that they are nation, because they appear to be one (*je to na nich vidět*), but my friends looked at me with such sad eyes. Apparently what I had said was nonsense and painful.[75]

Clearly it was impossible for Czech intellectuals to view the question of Jewish existence in Bohemia in anything but a nationalist framework. Ironically, their willingness to see the Jews as an independent national group within the Austrian Empire—and not as mere Germans of a slightly different coloring—indicated genuine sympathy for Czech Jews. Essentially they were prepared to regard the Jews as victims of forced denationalization (much as they themselves had been) who nevertheless possessed the potential to realize their own national rebirth. This did not mean that the moderate Czech nationalists did not welcome the aid and participation of individual Jews, or that they were any less eager than others to see the elimination of the German-Jewish schools. These nationalists welcomed the Czech-Jewish overtures, but they were disturbed by the greater implications of cultural assimilation.

The philosopher František Krejčí (1858–1934), a disciple of Masaryk, expressed this concern before a gathering of the Realist party in 1909. Speaking on the Czech-Jewish problem, he refused to consider the proposition that religion and nationality were separate issues. Especially in Judaism, he argued, were faith and national identity tightly interwoven. What impressed him, in fact, was that the question of Jewish nationality could continue to be posed.[76]

To Krejčí, as to Masaryk before him, the issue of Jewish culture in Bohemia was straightforward. It was the duty of every individual "to hold fast to his nationality, to acknowledge it and to work with all one's strength toward furthering it." Every individual and every nation faced this moral obligation; the Jews were no different.[77] Nor did it matter what state of development the nation was in, whether advancing, stagnating, or declining, whether strong or weak, culturally mature or unformed. Quoting the famous statement of Palacký, Krejčí warned, "If I were a Gypsy, I would have to remain a Gypsy."[78]

The only ethically justifiable assimilation was that which occurred after one's own nation had lost the last remnant of its uniqueness—and even then only if this situation had occurred against one's will:

> For it is simply a question of either-or. Either the nationality is present or it is not. But a conscious effort at assimilation, a discarding of one's unique something—whose very existence, in so doing, is in fact proven—is for a thinking person . . . impossible, ethically incorrect, and thus immoral. For the desire to be someone other than who one is—a negation of one's own personality—is simply ethically false.[79]

Krejčí suggested that if the prime element in Czech nationality was the Czech language, the common denominator of the Jewish nation was its religion. Judaism was the unique possession of the Jewish people; no other "cultural nation"—of which the Czechs were one—had it or was in a position to create something like it. Consequently, the only real assimilation for the Jew was one that ended in baptism, the erasure of his or her most fundamental national quality. This, however, was neither expected nor desired by the moderate Czech nationalists. "My real sympathies," Krejčí concluded, "belong with those who proclaim their loyalty to their Jewish nation."[80]

The Bar Kochba circle matched the Czech Realists' affirmation of Jewish nationalism with its own attenuated endorsement of Czech cultural and political aspirations. The Prague Zionists were eager to show themselves to be receptive to the inroads made by Czech language and art in Bohemia. Indeed, the newspaper *Selbstwehr*—though written in German—bore no traces of cultural favoritism. While the major German-language dailies, *Bohemia* and *Prager Tagblatt,* rarely if ever commented on Czech cultural events or publications, *Selbstwehr* devoted much space to paid advertisements as well as announcements of public events in Czech. The paper regularly listed four establishments in its theater announcements: the Königliches Landestheater and the Neues Deutsches Theater, whose program listings appeared in German; and the Královské české zemské divadlo and the Městské divadlo Královských Vinohradů, whose announcements were given in Czech.[81] Nor was it unusual for *Selbstwehr* critics to review Czech books and plays. Hugo Herrmann, for example, greeted the performance of Lothar Suchý's *David* at the Národní divadlo in 1911 with much acclaim. He wrote about the production in glowing terms and added that it was a stark contrast to the sterile, mediocre offerings at the German theater.[82]

Hugo Bergmann, writing in 1904, went so far as to offer a qualified endorsement of the activities of the Czech-Jewish movement under the new leadership of Vohryzek and Lederer. Since the central point of Zionism for Bergmann was the confrontation between individual Jews and their Judaism, no serious effort on the part of Jews to define and live a Jewish life could be dismissed or belittled. Nor, he argued, could the *Rozvoj* circle of Czech-Jewish intellectuals be categorized alongside the previous generation of assimilationists. Their effort to transform Bohemian Jewry into a modern, Czech population represented a conscious, if preliminary, approach to the Jewish question. Bergmann applauded the Czech-Jewish revolt against the "pseudoliberal" and "pseudo-German" Judaism of the previous century. He recognized that this battle was being carried out by an energetic youth, for whom "the new Judaism" meant more than simply a philosophy of merger.[83]

At the same time Bergmann criticized Prague Zionism for not having shown the intellectual daring of the Czech Jews, for having been content to follow a comfortable middle road. Zionists had to remember that they were, first and foremost, revolutionaries and that they had a mission to convince others, as well as themselves, of their cause:

> We have not engaged our followers in hot battle, particularly in recent years. [They] have not first struggled within themselves and among themselves, so that they might defeat the assimilation within their souls and come to us saying: "Your ideas have won; you have me; I am yours."[84]

Nor did the Prague Zionists appear to be thinking through the problem of cultural affiliations in Bohemia. Here too they were advised to take a lesson from the Czech Jews. To be neutral on the nationality controversy required that one demonstrate no cultural preference whatsoever. It was unseemly, Bergmann charged, for Zionists to continue to issue proclamations in German and to listen exclusively to German lectures in this the capital city of Bohemia.

> Not out of regard for our opponents, but out of regard for ourselves and for Jewish life, we ought not to consider the Czech language a minor detail, a formal concession. *The Czech transformation of Bohemian Jewry is a necessary development, which we neither will nor want to hinder.*[85]

The poor German of rural Bohemian Jews, together with the polished speech of their cousins in Prague, constituted the remnants of a century-long process that saw the distancing of the Jews from their own culture and from their proper national existence. Both Czech Jews and Zionists could at least form an alliance of convenience in this regard. The German-Jewish synthesis had run its course:

> It is now lost; our Jews see that and frantically seek a new, living, Jewish content. Zionism must provide this living content if it does not want to write off a worthy portion of its people. And so the Jewish question here takes the form in the first instance not of an economic question, but of a cultural question, and our struggle with our opponets [is] a culture struggle (*Kulturkampf*).[86]

In his eagerness to castigate the German cultural orientation of Prague Jewry, Bergmann certainly overstated the case for a Czech-Jewish Zionist rapprochement. Bar Kochba and the Czech assimilationists remained divided on key issues concerning Czech national culture. Two questions in particular barred any effective cooperation between the two: the issue of obligation versus choice in national affiliation, and the relationship between the language of the general environment and Jewish nationalism.

The Prague Zionists were prepared to urge all Jews living in Bohemia to learn Czech, the language of the majority of the population, for their own well-being, but they refused to acknowledge any obligation to do so. Two languages were of use in the land, and it was the right of every Jew to employ whichever he or she preferred. Neither history nor demographic realities could demand that the Jews do more. In 1908 *Selbstwehr* advised its readers to become fully bilingual but not to get involved in the struggle for national supremacy. By 1911 the paper was placing more stress on the role that the Czech language ought to play in the further development of Jewish culture. Still, however, the Prague Zionists were prepared to lend their support for the Czech national cause only as sympathetic observers, not as participants in the struggle.[87]

Moreover, the linguistic criterion used by the Austrian government to ascertain national affiliation—*Umgangssprache* or *obcovácí řeč*—was but an arbitrary category. It had little bearing on the true, national features of Jewish life in the diaspora. This, of course, was a crucial point in the ideology of Western and Central European Zionism. Those who would argue for the perseverence of the Jewish nation through two millennia of diasporic life had also to establish a distinction between daily language and national consciousness. This was not always easily achieved, since it was precisely those Jews who continued to speak a Jewish language—the Yiddish-speaking Jews of Eastern Europe—who possessed a solid national consciousness. And Zionists themselves were often divided on whether or not Western Jews possessed a Jewish national consciousncss or could merely strive for one. Nevertheless, all were ready to assert, almost as an article of faith, that the two—language and nationality—were *not* inseparable.[88]

The Prague Zionists contended, contrary to the insistence of two generations of Czech-Jewish intellectuals, that the Czech people themselves did not expect the Jews to assume the trappings of membership in the Czech nation. Instead, the Czechs correctly viewed the Jews as being a nation apart and expected of them nothing more than honest neutrality in the nationality controversy.[89] Taking a cue from the Austrian Social Democrats, but going them one step further, the editors of *Selbstwehr* called for the creation of a federation of nationalities that would grant autonomy to all ethnic groups, Jews included. The Zionists came out against all forms of national domination. They decried the "Czechization" of the Germans, the "Germanization" of the Czechs, and the "Magyarization" of the Slovaks. But the Jews too, *Selbstwehr* urged, whether they chose to do honor to the German or to the Czech language, had to be able to devote themselves to their own cultural and economic pursuits, unhindered, as an equal, autonomous nation.

> This will make possible the establishment of harmony with the Germans and the Czechs on the basis of a modern, all-Austrian policy—never however the advancement of Pan-German or Pan-Slavic tendencies. Neither against the Germans nor against the Czechs, but for the entire Jewish nation—for understanding toward all modern [tendencies] on the basis of the idea of a nationally autonomous, social, Austrian Empire—[this] is our motto.[90]

Intramural Struggles

Under Hugo Bergmann's leadership, Bar Kochba rejected the various paramilitary trappings of contemporary Burschenschaft life in Germany and Austria. It eschewed swords and duels, the wearing of colors, the singing of marching songs, the rowdy processions along the streets of the city—which in Prague frequently provoked counterdemonstrations from rival national fraternities. Even the annual formal ball, a common fund-raising event and staple of the social scene in university towns, was dropped in favor of the more intellectually serious Festabend.

Bar Kochba's shift to purely cultural concerns was not intended to signal a retreat from real life, to the potentially sterile environment of the cafe. Rather, Bergmann would have argued, Bar Kochba members were to make Jewish spirituality and Jewish national culture active, living concerns in their own lives. To demonstrate this point, Bergmann set out for Galicia in the summer of 1903, there to act out the precept of loving one's people *as it is,* as it exists. To do this one had first to discover the living nation: those "authentic" Jews who had yet to be transformed by the West. In the Austrian context, this meant the Hasidic Jews of Galicia. Thus, Bergmann set off on a pilgrimage of authenticity, an eastward trek, which many who had read Buber and Aḥad Ha'am had already taken in their imagination.

Bergmann managed to spend some time at the court of the Rebbe of Czortkow; he also met with student Zionist groups in Galicia. Impressed with what he saw, Bergmann returned to Prague more determined than ever to instill in his collaborators a thorough knowledge of Hebrew and Yiddish.

Bar Kochba, too, seems to have been impressed with the results of the visit and established a fund that would permit other students to travel to Galicia or to Palestine in order to experience Jewish life firsthand.[91]

However, not everyone within the organization approved of Bergmann's leadership or of Bar Kochba's exclusively cultural orientation. A sizable faction feared that the group's insistence on *innere Ausbildung* (inner development) hampered its ability to reach and recruit non-Zionists. At a time when Jewish fraternities in Berlin, Vienna, and Czernowitz competed successfully with liberal associations for Jewish membership, Zionism made hardly a dent in the associational patterns of Prague's Jewish students.[92] The discontented faction urged that students be allowed to form a "color section" within Bar Kochba, whose task would be to challenge German-Jewish assimilationism both at the university and in the provinces. This new group—which described itself as a "fighting troop against Bohemian-German liberalism"—was to pattern itself directly on the German and Austrian Burschenschaft. It would "wear colors," organize itself as a *Verbindung* (a corporation, as opposed to the looser Verein or association), and impress upon the public the honor of Jewish national identification.[93] The group urged Bar Kochba to strike out simultaneously at the old-fashioned liberalism, the new fashion in right-wing antisemitism, and the traditional Jewish community. Only through a proud and deliberate display of its "colors" could Prague Zionism hope to convert the mass of the Jewish population.

Under great pressure from the leadership, the majority of Bar Kochba rejected the motion. Bergmann and others argued that the idea represented a blind appropriation of the worst aspects of non-Jewish academic culture. In a city such as Prague, they argued, there was no room for so aggressive a display of Jewish nationalism. It would merely exacerbate ethnic tensions, alienate the Czech population—including Czech Jews—and blur the distinction between German Jew and Zionist.[94] At this point the dissenting faction—led by Leon and Stanislas Stencel, Robert Neubauer, Hugo Löw, and Leo Kornfeld—walked out and formed the rival Zionist Verbindung "Barissia." Bar Kochba's leaders continued to wage war on the heretics, denying its members permission to affiliate with Barissia and trying, unsuccessfully, to block the group's entry into the Austrian and World Zionist Organizations.[95]

Thus Prague Zionism was divided in its early years between those who would appropriate "foreign forms" to combat openly against assimilation and those who sought to achieve the "inner renewal" of the individual. The one group strove to win over Jewish society, the other the Jewish personality.[96] In some respects, the split within Prague Zionism followed the lines of the basic cleavage between Herzlian Zionists and cultural Zionists. Barissia tended to side with the political wing of the movement, led by Theodor Herzl, while Bar Kochba, as we know, fell under the influence of Ahad Ha'am and Berthold Feiwel.[97] Both groups were serious in their Zionism, and the main differences between them appear to have been tactical. Barissia never hid the fact that it was a "fighting" society. It was not uncommon for it to challenge liberal student associations in debate one afternoon and then meet them with colors, songs, and fists on the fashionable Graben (Na Příkopě) the next.[98] Its members were single-mindedly determined to win recognition of the Jewish nationality in the Austrian Empire and to counter any and all attacks on the good name of the Jewish people.

Yet Barissia was neither anti-Czech nor antiintellectual. Consistent with its attitude on activism in the political arena, its members campaigned vigorously during the Landtag elections of 1908 for the candidates of the Czech Realist party. Barissia's involvement in the campaign may have been a factor in the victory of at least one Realist candidate running in Prague's Nové Město.[99] When violence broke out between Czech and German national student associations in the fall of that year, Barissia ended its policy of neutrality and sided with the Czechs.[100] The rivals of Bar Kochba appear also to have placed greater emphasis on cultural programs and lectures after 1906. The Moravian-born Alfred Engel, who later became a professor at Brno, and who joined the Verbindung in 1908, helped in this regard. He participated actively in a whole range of educational programs on Jewish questions and served for ten years as the head of the organization's "Zionism" seminar.[101]

Indeed, it was members of Barissia who founded the first Zionist weekly in Bohemia, *Selbstwehr,* in March 1907. Nearly all of the paper's editors and contributors during its first years either came out of Barissia or were sympathizers of the group. These included the German University docent and Reichsrat deputy Arthur Mahler, Julius Löwy—who was also an editor of *Prager Tagblatt*—and Heinrich Wittmann.[102] Following the urging of Alfred Engel, Barissia and Bar Kochba managed to call a truce during the fall semester 1908, which lasted long enough to establish a central association for nationally inclined Jewish students. This, the Lese- und Redehalle der jüdischen Hochschüler in Prag (Prague Jewish students' reading and discussion room), was designed to function as an obvious rival to the liberal, German Lese- und Redehalle and served as a central clearing house for all student Zionist activities in the city. In 1910 the Czech-speaking branch of Prague student Zionism, Theodor Herzl, joined its ranks.[103]

The ceasefire did not last long. Already by the winter of 1909 tensions between Barissia and Bar Kochba spilled over into open conflict. At issue was a confrontation that had taken place in Vienna between the heads of the two organizations, Leo Herrmann of Bar Kochba, and Heinrich Wittmann of Barissia. Neither was the type of individual to shy away from a good fight. The two had represented their respective groups at a special course on Palestine, and upon their return Herrmann issued a report that roundly criticized the behavior of his colleague. Insulted, Barissia acted true to its role as a *schlagende Verbindung* (duelling fraternity) and demanded satisfaction from Bar Kochba. Wittmann challenged Leo Herrmann to a pistol duel. This put Bar Kochba in an uncomfortable position. While it would never engage in militaristic or provocative acts toward non-Jewish student organizations, it found it difficult to resist a challenge from a rival Jewish group. Herrmann and Wittmann measured their paces in the Šarka Park outside of Prague; mercifully, no one was injured.[104]

The emergence of Jewish nationalism in Prague threatened the equilibrium of organized Jewish life no less than had the Czech-Jewish movement a decade or two earlier. Both developments posed major challenges to the Bohemian Jewish cultural synthesis of the nineteenth century. In some respects, however, the Zionist threat appeared to the leadership of the Jewish community to be the more insidious of the two. Rightly or wrongly, Prague Zionism was interpreted by many to have been a defection from within the ranks of German-speaking Jewry, an internal weakening of the German cultural edifice, and thus qualitatively distinct from the challenge posed by the Czech-Jewish movement.

In fact, all of the German institutions of the city—not only those identified with the Jewish community—reacted to the activities of the Prague Zionists with immediate displeasure. In 1901 Bar Kochba submitted a request to the academic authorities to grant recognition to the Jewish nationality at the universities and technical colleges. Predictably, both the Czech University and the Polytechnika approved the request; they had relatively small numbers of Jews and hence little to fear from a Jewish defection from the Czech national ranks. Moreover, they could easily see the positive effects of a trinational division of Bohemia. Deprived of substantial numbers of Jews, the Germans would be reduced from a strong to a much weaker national minority. Also not surprisingly, the German institutions rejected Bar Kochba's petition and would continue to do so to the eve of the First World War.[105]

In 1905 the Bohemian State School Council, an official government agency, forbad gymnasium and other middle-school pupils from joining Zionist organizations. It was commonly assumed by all concerned at the time that the council issued the order in response to a plea from a high official of the Prague Jewish community.[106] Equally irritating for the Zionists was a loyalty oath that the board of directors of the Prague Jewish community drew up, which had to be sworn to by all Jewish students who wished to receive financial aid from the community. In the oath students were required to swear loyalty to the "German people." The members of Bar Kochba refused, as a matter of principle, to make such an attestation; they, like the committed Czech Jews, forfeited their eligibility for financial assistance from this ready source.[107]

The Zionists also had ethical quarrels with the Israelitische Kultusgemeinde (Židovská náboženská obec). Its board of deputies consisted primarily of wealthy and powerful members of the Jewish community and was elected through a system which proportioned the weight of each vote on the basis of the taxes paid by the voter. Time and again Zion and the newspaper *Selbstwehr* called for electoral reform and the establishment of a one man, one vote system. No reform, however, was to be forthcoming before the outbreak of the war.[108]

Frequently the Zionists decried the state of Jewish education in the monarchy, which had dwindled to an insignificant two hours per week in all schools. They urged that the standards of teachers be raised and more time be devoted to the teaching of Hebrew and Jewish history (the staples of the Jewish nationalist diet). They even debated the pros and cons of setting up an independent Jewish school system in Bohemia, an action that would have represented a reversal of the process of Jewish acculturation since Joseph II. As in the other cases, little came of this notion before 1914. The Zionists did manage to create a Jewish School Association in 1907—a faint echo of the rival Czech and German school associations that had spearheaded their respective national revivals. However, it was not until 1914 that the Jewish School Association succeeded simply in introducing extracurricular courses in Jewish history and the Hebrew language for the students of Bohemian secondary schools. Full-time, national Jewish schools would not open in Bohemia or in Moravia until after the start of World War I.[109]

Selbstwehr: *Defiance in lieu of Autonomy*

In its inaugural issue, 1 March 1907, *Selbstwehr* voiced the combative and aggressive self-consciousness of its Barissia founders. Its pages exuded energy and confidence as the editors of the paper issued a battle cry for a new vitalism on the part of the Jews of Western Europe. *Selbstwehr,* they explained, represented both a program and a protest. "A protest—a declaration of war—against all that is rotten, incomplete, and decaying in Judaism, and a mighty, audible affirmation of the young, self-conscious, budding strengths and endeavors of the Jewish nation."[110] The era of meek acceptance, fear, and cowardice on the part of Jews was over. Gone was the time when Jews would do all that they could to hide their distinctiveness. "The Jewish nation has been woken, roused from its torpidity and relaxation, and stretches everywhere to new life."[111]

Self-esteem and the insistence on determining one's own existence stood out as hallmarks of the new Jewish awareness. No longer content to be the object of someone else's approbation or pity, Jews were claiming the right to express their own individuality fully and freely:

> "Self-help, self-service, self-defense: this is the first and the highest principle of every upright person and of every self-respecting nation. It has long been the call and watchword of the modern Jew, and it is our watchword."[112]

It was characteristic of *Selbstwehr* in its early years to emphasize emotional themes such as self-discovery and defiance toward Western bourgeois society. The editors of the paper had little patience for the subtler issues of ideology and culture. "We must help and defend ourselves; we must band together, declare and participate in membership in our nation proudly and freely." Only through the cherishing of one's own national inheritance could the Jews hope to find a way to live in peace and mutual regard with the other nations of Central Europe.[113]

The editors of *Selbstwehr* did express sympathy for what they called the "efforts at a young-Jewish renaissance," but they were careful not to spell out any specific intellectual program for endorsement. The Zionism which they held up was a stance, a proclamation of honor and independence, and not a coherent set of ideas. Nevertheless, over the course of the next few years the paper did present cogent arguments on a number of subjects. These included a critique of Western emancipation, the rejection of liberal, German culture, and the prospects for national Jewish politics within the context of the Austrian state.

Selbstwehr began its career at a propitious moment for the Jews of Eastern and Central Europe. The Revolution of 1905 had signaled the beginnings of Jewish participation in the political life of the Russian Empire. Moreover, the move toward a parliamentary system in Russia suggested an alternative path to Jewish emancipation, one which, unlike the Western model, promised to maintain the national integrity of the Jews while it paved the way for their integration into Russian society. *Selbstwehr* took note of the fact that in both the Austrian Reichsrat and the Russian Duma representatives of a Jewish national party had won seats in recent elections. Jewish national politicians, one writer remarked, faced an infinitely more difficult task in Austria than in Russia. For, however tragic the condition of the Jews in Russia, one thing was certain: they were recognized by everyone (themselves included) as composing a nation. When the time finally would come for the Jews to become full citizens of the state, they would do so as a nation. "Then it will not be Russians of the Mosaic faith who will be emancipated, but rather the Jewish nation there which will—as such—receive its rights."[114]

On the other hand, Western emancipation was a bankrupt process, because it required of the Jews that they forgo their national identity. The Jews of Austria, the paper wrote, would long suffer the effects of an emancipation that came at the price of "national emasculation," the erasure of all signs of distinctiveness. Assimilation was a lie that now had to be challenged by the newly aroused Jewish national consciousness.[115] In their critique of Jewish emancipation the young Prague Zionists neatly paralleled the arguments of the Czech-Jewish movement a decade or two earlier. It, too, had pressed for a redefinition of the terms of emancipation, charging that the process had been achieved over the course of the nineteenth century at an exorbitant and dishonorable price. Both groups in fact argued that modernizing and emancipatory pressures had twisted the *natural* inclinations of the Jews of Bohemia. Both could agree that the adoption of German cultural values had been foisted upon the Jews without regard for their genuine well-being. The Czech-Jewish intellectuals, however, viewed the Germanizing process itself as the culprit behind the national difficulties of the Jews, whereas the Zionists generalized that all avenues of acculturation—be they Czech, German, or any other—served merely as arrangements of convenience through which Jews might thrive in their immediate environment. These circumstances ought not to impede the free expression of the Jews' own national culture:

> They have given us civil equality. We can live anywhere, attend any school, and—at least theoretically—occupy any public function. We can freely confess our faith. But our most primitive and natural right, to show our true face, to preserve our national uniqueness, to develop and to achieve perfection—for this right we must first struggle hard and laboriously.[116]

Selbstwehr's frequent denunciations of Prague's German liberal establishment provide yet another indication of how close its editors came to appropriating at least some of the Czech-Jewish movement's critique of Prague Jewry. In May 1910 the paper used the occasion of a "Parteitag" of the German Progressive party to ridicule the very notion of liberal German culture. "German Progressive Party celebration! Can one find at present a more nonsensical collection of terms?" *Selbstwehr* asked sarcastically.

> There is no longer a German progressive organization, no more common contributions . . . no more inner life. . . . The party has been destroyed through halfheartedness, insincerity, and not least through its Jewish partisans. What remains today . . . are strictly national, often antisemitic Germans, who refuse all social intercourse with Jews.[117]

The paper declared its deepest admiration for German culture, but warned that it had not the least respect politically for the various spokesmen—proclaimed and self-proclaimed—of German interests in Austria and Bohemia. "We have ceased being the grateful and the duped. The German people do not need us, do not want us, and we need and want them just as little. We shall help ourselves."[118]

Selbstwehr's program of self-help included mobilizing the Jewish population of Bohemia to meet the challenge of the newly granted universal male suffrage, to vote their "interests" during the Reichsrat elections of 1907. The Zionists concentrated in particular on the campaign in Prague's first district (Altstadt/Staré Město), which pitted the antisemite Karel Baxa against a field of other candidates. The paper strove to maintain independence from all political parties and, thus, would not endorse any single candidate for the first ballot (held on 14 May). Instead it urged that the Jews of Prague act on the basis of two principles: (1) that Baxa be defeated, and (2) that they not waste their vote on someone who had no chance of winning. This second proviso meant that they could not possibly support the German liberal candi-

date Alexander Hoffmann. *Selbstwehr* seemed to waver at this point between support for the Young Czechs and the Social Democrats. Ultimately,
it could not approve the Young Czech candidate, because the party's parliamentary club had refused to disavow the support of the National Socialist
deputy—also an antisemitic agitator—Václav Březnovský.[119]

After the first round of voting, when only Baxa and a Dr. Houser, the
Social Democrat, remained, *Selbstwehr* trumpeted Houser's candidacy. The
paper argued that it was the moral duty of every Jew—be he German or
Czech speaking—to defeat Baxa and thus to end that political anomaly
which saw a predominantly Jewish district represented by an unrepentant
antisemite.[120] Baxa in the end won the election. Most Jews, however, had
voted for his opponent.[121]

The elections of 1907 did bring some successes to the Zionist movement in
Austria. The newly formed Jewish National party won four contests in Galicia and the Bukowina and subsequently formed the first "Jewish Club" in
the Reichsrat. One of the victors in the Galician elections was Arthur
Mahler (1872–1916), classical archeologist at the German University of
Prague. The Zionists in Austria looked upon Galicia and the Bukowina—
rural areas that had undergone little or no industrialization, and which possessed dense concentrations of Orthodox, Yiddish-speaking Jews—not only
as rich depositories of human resources, but also as testing ground for modern Jewish politics. Here, where the masses maintained traditional Jewish
solidarity, the political and intellectual elite might lead and direct the Jewish
people in its struggle for national integrity and cultural autonomy.

Galicia in particular seemed to offer the Prague Zionists a picture of what
one could hope to achieve for the Jews in a multinational environment. In
the western part of the province—around Krakow—Jews made up the only
large ethnic minority. In the larger eastern region, however, the predominantly rural, Ukrainian population had begun to challenge the preeminent
position of the Polish nationality. Non-Orthodox Jews throughout Galicia
identified on the whole with Polish language and culture; the Orthodox and
Hasidic leaders did so only in the political arena.[122] Galician Jewry, then,
like that of Bohemia and Moravia, occupied an increasingly untenable middle position between two strong, competing nations. Despite the otherwise
glaring differences between Galicia and the Czech lands, the Zionists could,
with some justification, gain inspiration from the Galician example, see it as
a triumph of Jewish national culture and modern Jewish politics in a multinational environment.[123]

If the Zionists resented the terms of Jewish emancipation in Western
Europe, they nevertheless appreciated the differences between nation states
in the mold of France and multinational entities like the Austro-Hungarian
Empire. The division of East and West—once based on cultural, now on
political, criteria—could not blur the fact that Central Europe occupied a

position of its own, that it shared both the Enlightenment heritage of its Western neighbors and the centrifugal tendencies of the small nations that dotted the Eastern landscape. In an unguarded moment of enthusiasm, *Selbstwehr* proclaimed:

> The best guarantee for the success of [our] national yearnings is the Austrian state, which is a pure nationality state, and which in no way is dying—despite what the false prophets are proclaiming on this side and that. Precisely the opposite is true. Austria is undergoing a rejuvenation and strengthening on the basis of national autonomy, a strengthening in which the Jews of Austria will doubtless also participate.[124]

Like the German-speaking Jews of the nineteenth and twentieth centuries, the Prague Zionists before World War I proved to be loyal to the Austrian ideal. But, whereas German-Jewish patriotism stemmed from its perception of Vienna as the agent of progress, enlightenment, and constitutional government, the Zionists' support emerged from a postliberal conception of the empire, from the promise of Austria as a federation of nationalities. As the Habsburg state grew to recognize the legitimate national aspirations of its constituent peoples and to grant them ever-greater cultural autonomy, nationally conscious Jews could not help but reap benefits as well. Zionism, the road to Jewish national self-determination, had a mission to perform in Europe as well as in Palestine. The multinational empire thus provided a potentially rich context for the Jewish will to be reborn.[125]

5

Martin Buber and the
Prague Zionists: Elective Affinities

Bar Kochba Under Leo Herrmann

The early struggle among Prague Jewish students between political and cultural Zionism concluded in apparent stalemate. Agreeing, at least in spirit, to live and let live, Barissia and Bar Kochba continued for several decades to offer potent alternatives within the Jewish national camp. In truth, however, Bar Kochba had gained the upper hand. It proved to be the source of whatever intellectual contributions Prague Zionism was to make for the Jewish national rebirth. But just as important, Bar Kochba began to produce individuals with great political and administrative talents. These people not only dominated Czech Zionism through the war years and into the First Republic, but also occupied key positions in the World Zionist Organization and the Jewish *Yishuv* (settlement) in Palestine.

Leo Herrmann (1888–1951) was one such product. He has received scant attention from historians of Czech Jewry and little more from those concerned with the history of Jewish nationalism. Yet he was the first major political figure to emerge from the ranks of Bar Kochba. At the age of twenty Herrmann assumed the leadership of Bar Kochba; he went on to become editor of *Selbstwehr,* serve as secretary of the World Zionist Executive in Berlin, and help to direct the Keren Hayesod (Palestine Foundation Fund) in Jerusalem. A talented organizer and committed intellectual, Herrmann began his career as a disciple of Hugo Bergmann and later established close ties to Martin Buber, Kurt Blumenfeld, and Berthold Feiwel.[1]

He hailed from Landskron, a German-speaking town in the Bohemian Sudentenland, a few kilometers from the border with Moravia. After his father died at an early age, Leo assumed the role of paterfamilias while still a schoolboy. Though he excelled in his studies, he appears to have led a lonely existence, alienated from his classmates, perhaps as a result of their antisemitism. This, in any event, is the judgment of his younger sister Emmy, who recounts in an unpublished memoir that Leo's only friend during his gymnasium years was his cousin Hugo Herrmann (1887–1940), who lived a few hours away in the Moravian-German enclave of Mährisch-Trübau, the original homestead of the Herrmann family.[2]

Leo Herrmann's school years were particularly trying not only because he shouldered family responsibilities in the wake of his father's death, and not only because he was one of the few Jews in his gymnasium. Herrmann also had to suffer Landskron's oppressive political climate. The local deputy in the Austrian Reichsrat was Karl Herrmann Wolf, a disciple of Georg von Schönerer, and founder of the radically antisemitic Freialldeutschen Partei (All-German Independent party). It was Wolf who, while at the university in 1879, had established the first German student association in Prague to bar Jews from membership. Later he served as editor of Vienna's antisemitic paper, the *Ostdeutsche Rundschau*. Wolf won election to the Reichsrat during the turbulent year of 1897; by 1901 his party had become the strongest and most outspoken German bloc in Parliament.[3]

During Herrmann's gymnasium years, Wolf made frequent visits to his constituency and delivered numerous public addresses denouncing the Jews of Bohemia and Moravia. Herrmann responded to such provocations with a studied air of defiance calculated to distract and disarm his enemies:

> In my schooldays I considered it my duty to stand in the front row at every meeting which he addressed in the small town in which everyone knew me by sight, so as to prove that a Jew did not fear to attend anti-Semitic election meetings.[4]

Not surprisingly, he became a Zionist during these difficult times. As in everything else, he guided his younger siblings' cultivation of a strong Jewish identity. Emmy recounts the following: "Leo impressed upon me since my earliest childhood that I was a Jewess, that I was to be proud of it, and that my true home was neither Landskron nor Prague, but Palestine and Jerusalem." When Theodor Herzl died in 1904, the elder brother declared a day of mourning in the Herrmann household.[5]

In Landskron Herrmann practiced a toughness that brings to mind the defiant attitude of Barissia's leaders. Yet he does not appear ever to have been attracted to this group. Perhaps he was too much the man of letters, committed to writing and the world of ideas, and ultimately unimpressed with the politics of power. Perhaps he never meant to be as provocative as his posturing at Karl Herrmann Wolf's political rallies would have led one to believe.

A few pieces of evidence suggest that Herrmann supported a policy of national conciliation even before he left his hometown to attend the university. His cousin Hugo had introduced him to Franz Spira, son-in-law of the German Agrarian party leader Peschka, and at the time Hugo's Czech-language professor in Mährisch-Trübau. Spira apparently was one of the rare German politicians in Bohemia-Moravia to preach to his conationals the need to learn and use Czech, to break down unnatural language barriers. Later he became professor of Slavonics at the German University in Prague and a confidant of Leo's. Recalling the irony of their relationship, Herrmann wrote: "I often talked to him, German that he was, in Czech about Zionism and our problems."[6]

In his "Recollections," Herrmann also pointed out that he had been impressed by Engelbert Pernerstorfer (1850–1918), an Austrian-German radical turned Social Democrat. It was Pernerstorfer who had risen at the Party Congress of 1897 to support the division of Austrian Social Democracy along national lines with the observation that one could be a good German, Italian, or Slav and still be a convinced Social Democrat. Despite the fact that the party officially advocated the reorganization of the Habsburg monarchy along federal lines, Pernerstorfer was one of the few Austrian socialists to give a sympathetic hearing to the claims of Jewish nationalism.[7] Herrmann began to correspond with the Austrian socialist leader shortly after joining Bar Kochba; he sent Pernerstorfer some of the articles that he had written for *Selbstwehr,* and eventually visited him in Vienna. Pernerstorfer, in turn, explained to his visitor that he had been following the course of the Zionist movement for the past ten years. Moreover, he had often discussed with " 'colleague Masaryk' the role of the Jews and of the Jewish national movement among the peoples."[8]

In all likelihood, Leo Herrmann came to Prague in 1906 a moderate socialist committed to a resolution of the national controversy on the basis of compromise and the mutual recognition of the rights of each group. Upon entering Bar Kochba, he adhered to Hugo Bergmann's vision of Zionism as a cultural movement. During his tenure as chairman, from 1908 to 1909, Herrmann worked to ensure that the quest for Jewish cultural renaissance would continue to occupy a central place in Bar Kochba's activities.[9]

His most concrete achievement in this regard may have been to bring the newspaper *Selbstwehr* under Bar Kochba's control. Herrmann began to write for the paper in 1907 and became its editor in December 1910. He held this position until called to Berlin by Kurt Blumenfeld in 1913, but Bar Kochba never relinquished control of the paper from this point on. Siegmund Kaznelson (1893–1959) assumed the editorship after Herrmann and held it throughout the war years. He was followed in 1919 by Felix Weltsch (1884–1964), philosopher and librarian at the University Library in Prague, and close friend of both Max Brod and Franz Kafka.

Shortly after taking over at *Selbstwehr,* Leo Herrmann issued a restatement of the paper's goals and positions. In so doing he underlined the distance that separated the *Selbstwehr* of 1911 from that of its Barissia founders. Whereas in its early years the paper had concerned itself with defending the honor of European Jewry, combating antisemitism, and criticizing

German-Jewish assimilationism, its editors now put forward a new set of priorities. They would continue to defend Jewry against its enemies—both external and internal—but this was no longer seen as *Selbstwehr's* most pressing task. "More important is positive work, active intercession for all of the modern endeavors that operate and thrive within Judaism."

> What we want is to secure the present and the future of the Jewish people; to struggle against all that is un-Jewish in Judaism, against all of the disintegrating tendencies within the Jewish community; to revive the Jewish idea, which has preserved our people intact.[10]

Selbstwehr pledged to mirror all of the goings-on within Bohemian Jewish life, to portray the social and economic circumstances as well as the cultural underpinnings of the community. It hoped to help place Jewish-Gentile relations in the Czech lands on a more secure footing, "to the offense of none, but to the defense and health of the Jews." And it invited all who had an interest in the furtherance of Jewish life in Bohemia to join them: "No one who feels Jewish and who wants to act Jewishly need deny us his help in this undertaking."[11] Under Herrmann *Selbstwehr* assumed the mantle of cultural Zionism, declaring itself to be engaged not only in the cause of the Jewish people and its defense, but "for Judaism, its preservation, and its revival."[12]

Drei Reden über das Judentum

Shortly after his election as chairman of Bar Kochba in the fall of 1908, Leo Herrmann's fellow board members assigned him the task of locating speakers to participate in the group's upcoming Festabend. It was in this connection that Herrmann first contacted Martin Buber and invited him to address Bar Kochba, thereby launching a collaboration that was to result in the publication of Buber's *Three Addresses on Judaism.* Given the emotional closeness that eventually developed between Buber and the Prague Zionists, it comes as something of a surprise to learn that he had not even been on Herrmann's first list of speakers. Nor does Bar Kochba appear to have known exactly what it hoped to achieve at the Festabend aside from reaching in some way the majority of Prague's culturally uncommitted Jews.

Bar Kochba originally had hoped to lure the writer Arthur Schnitzler, who only recently had published his novel of Jewish spiritual indirection in Vienna, *Der Weg ins Freie* (The road to the open). Schnitzler demurred, however, as did their second choice, Richard Beer-Hofmann. A third writer, Felix Salten (1869–1947), finally agreed to speak on the subject of urban Jewish alienation. Herrmann felt that he ought to balance this, the negative side of the cultural condition of Western Jewry, with a positive presentation of the same picture, one that would point the way to active participation in modern Jewish cultural forms. He thought at first of including recitations from contemporary Hebrew and Yiddish literature, and solicited Theodor Zlocisti (1874–1943) in Berlin for more help. Zlocisti suggested the names of two former collaborators of Bar Kochba, Buber and Feiwel. Thus the circle was completed, and Herrmann began what was to become an extended and intense correspondence with the Berlin sage.[13]

In his first letter to Buber, Herrmann explained that Bar Kochba was planning to host a Festabend on 16 January 1909, the chief purpose of which was to bring to the attention of "the broad, assimilatory public of Prague" representative figures in modern Jewish letters who would "remind them and us of our Jewishness."[14] Alerting Buber to the likely content of Felix Salten's lecture, Herrmann suggested that he might be able to round out the picture. Is there a "Jewish note" that can provide the Jewish artist with a unique set of "cultural values"? "How are the remains of Jewish existence in the West to be transformed into something [that one can call] one's own?"[15]

Herrmann apologized to Buber for disturbing his crowded schedule, but also assured him that he, more than anyone, understood the urgency of this quest. Then, by way of enticement, Herrmann appended a description of the peculiar conditions under which the young Zionists in Prague lived:

> We live in Prague under totally unique circumstances. A large, old Jewish community—for a long time now absorbed in German culture, and supposedly German itself. Meanwhile, however, all of the Aryan Germans have been subjected to "Czechization" (*Čechisierung*), [a process] which is also beginning to assail many Jews. Only the Jews continue to believe that it is necessary to defend German culture (*Deutschtum*). Since they live without any contact with national Germans, their character remains predominantly Jewish. But no Prague-dweller (*Prager*) notices this. And almost everyone guards against conscious Jewishness.[16]

The Jews of Prague, Herrmann explained, were caught in the middle of a conflict in which their own interests could not be served. They were tied to a German culture to which they had no real national bonds—of which, however, they appeared to be the only defenders. And, in the face of the dramatic spread of Czech culture in Bohemia, many of Prague's Jews had begun to profess it as their own. Yet neither culture truly "belonged" to the Jews; both were at best adoptive. What no one seemed prepared to do was to declare his or her "Jewishness" as his or her proper national identity. "This is why it is so important," Herrmann concluded, "to tell this social history of Judaism. They only listen to something when it is presented in an outstanding way. For this reason precisely you, honored Doctor, would perform this task best."[17]

Exactly why Buber accepted Bar Kochba's invitation is not known. Since his resignation as editor of the Zionist weekly *Die Welt* in 1901, Buber had removed himself from active political life. He spent the next seven years enmeshed in the study and "rediscovery" of Hasidism—the East European Jewish pietist movement that flourished during the second half of the eighteenth century—surfacing long enough only to deliver an occasional public lecture or guide a manuscript through to publication. Not until 1906, with the appearance of *Die Geschichten des Rabbi Nachman* (The stories of Rabbi Nachman), did Buber reveal the first fruits of his investigations into Hasidism.[18]

Thus, Buber's acceptance of the invitation to address the Prague Jewish community signaled the end of his self-enforced isolation. An admirer of the writings of Nietzsche, he probably did not miss the parallel between his own trek to Prague and Zarathrustra's descent from his mountain seclusion. Like Zarathustra, Buber may have felt that he had concluded his meditations successfully and was now prepared to deliver his message to humanity. Prague and Bar Kochba simply came at the right moment.

Yet one cannot help but ask whether a stronger affinity might have existed—even at this early date—between the master and his future flock. Was it perhaps the description provided by Herrmann of life in this multinational center that attracted Buber to Bar Kochba? Herrmann's words may have reminded Buber of his own childhood in Lwów (Lemberg), the multinational capital of Austrian Galicia. Buber had gone to live with his paternal grandparents in Lwów upon the separation of his parents, when he was four years old, and he remained there until he finished his gymnasium studies.[19] It was in Galicia that Buber absorbed so many languages: the German that was spoken in his grandparents' home; the Hebrew of the synagogue and of the rabbinic texts lovingly presented to him by his grandfather; the Polish of the streets and of the ruling circles; and the Yiddish of the Jewish quarter. Buber himself attended a Polish, not a German, gymnasium. Although he later became a master of German prose style and translation, he continued to identify himself up to the end of his life as a Polish Jew. He wrote many of his early essays in Polish and lectured, even as late as 1943, in the same language.[20]

Perhaps, then, it was multinational Prague and its similarity in Buber's imagination to his own Lwów, which drew the philosopher to Bar Kochba. Buber offered in his own person the mirror image of the Prague Zionist. From a corner of the Habsburg monarchy that was nationally ambivalent, yet Jewishly traditional, he had emerged to reaffirm, redefine, and recreate his Jewish national personality. Buber, barely ten years older than his Prague protégés, immediately asssumed the role of advisor. He wished, for example, to know the precise content of Salten's talk, so that he might tailor his own accordingly; he involved himself in the mundane details of the Festabend, suggesting names for additional participants, and seeing to the overall thematic harmony of the evening.[21]

The Bar Kochba group eventually persuaded Buber to come to Prague not once but three times to speak: in January 1909, and again in April and

December 1910.[22] Prior to the first visit, Herrmann tried to convey to Buber what it was that Bar Kochba was hoping to receive. His words rang true to the decidedly "cultural" orientation of the group, but they also betrayed an intense desire to escape from the political rough-and-tumble of the real world:

> You will not have misunderstood us if you foist upon us a striving for more than pure "hurrah Zionism." We feel the need to develop all that is Jewish in us; we do not wish our entire spiritual existence to be dependent upon the successes or failures of the actual, political plane.[23]

The Prague Zionists in 1908 wanted not only to discover and to nourish a Judaism that was at the same time intrinsic yet inaccessible; they wanted also to withdraw from the political controversies that surrounded them. They yearned for a living culture, which nevertheless existed independently of uncomfortable political choices, one that was real, but not of the real world.

In his first speech to the Prague Jewish community, Buber offered his young followers a philosophical base upon which to build their experimental Jewish structure. He proposed a theory of Jewish national identification that operated independently of those objective criteria that nationalists in the past had used to justify their claim to self-determination. Buber's concept of Zionism derived instead from the individual's perception of his or her own subjective reality. "Warum nennen wir uns Juden?" he asked. Why do we call ourselves Jews? One can begin to answer this question, he suggested, only by posing its corollary: "What is it that causes a man's nation to become an autonomous reality in his soul and in his life? What causes him to feel his nation not only around but within himself?"[24] How is it that a positive, national identity can emerge that is bound neither to the old, lifeless forms of Jewish religiosity nor to the exigencies of Jewish-Gentile strife?

Buber asked his audience to take a close look at the processes of perception, at the ways in which the individual comes to recognize the elements of his or her world. As a child, in one's mental interaction with one's surroundings, one develops an apprehension of oneself as a separate existence, distinguishable from the rest of the material world. After gaining a sense of one's own body first by separating oneself from the world around one (what Buber called *Wahrnehmungsorientation*), one later learns to distinguish not only one's body, but also one's self as "substance," as something that remains permanent despite the "changing world of impressions and influences" (this Buber called *Geistesorientation*).[25] Hence the subjective self, as well as the objective self, emerges from the individual's perception of the world about him or her. But it is the world of time, of occurrences, out of which this self takes shape. The objective, physical self is limited in space; the subjective self, constant through time.

In order for his perception theory to lead to a definition of Jewish nationalism, Buber also had to examine the way in which individuals "apprehend" their social relationships. Out of the world of "impressions and influences," Buber explained, the individual begins to discern two main regions: that of the home (*Heimat*)—"earth and heaven and their intimate particularity"— and the circle of people with whom one interacts through the mediation of language and mores. Ultimately one develops the feeling of belonging to a community composed of those people who share with one these constant elements of experience: homeland, language, and mores. The people who make up this *Gemeinschaft* one labels one's "Volk."[26]

Up to this point Buber had depicted a situation in which the individual both coexisted and interacted with a living community. But he had not yet crossed the threshold of relevance for the Prague Zionists, precisely because the Jewish community of their time had lost the glue of common language, mores, and landscape. To accomplish this, Buber returned to his original dichotomy of subjective versus objective perception. Consider, he explained, the person who goes one step further, who, driven by a desire for permanence, discovers not only that there is a constancy to the forms of experience, "but also a constancy of existence which steadily sustains all experience. As the child discovers the I of his physical being last, so the adult discovers the I of his spiritual being last, as an enduring substance."[27]

If individuals, through the discovery of the separateness of the self, encounter their limitation in space, each one now, through the discovery of that self which lies beyond the bounds of an individaul life, realizes one's own limitlessness in time. Each person confronts the immortality of the soul—of strength, work, and deed—most starkly the moment one discovers the "succession of generations":

> He perceives then what comingling of individuals, what confluence of blood, has produced him, what round of begettings and births has called him forth. He senses in this immortality of the generations a community of blood, which he feels to be the antecedents of his I, its perseverance in the infinite past. To that is added the discovery, promoted by this awareness, that blood is a deep-rooted nurturing force within individual man; that the deepest layers of our being are determined by blood; that our innermost thinking and our will are colored by it.[28]

At this moment the Jew no longer considers himself to be merely a part of that community with whom he shares the "constant elements of experience," but also part of the deeper community with whom he shares a common "substance."

> On the first level, his people represented the world to him; now they represent his soul. The people are now for him a community of men who were, are, and will be—a community of the dead, the living, and the yet unborn—who, together constitute a unity. It is this unity that, to him, is the ground of his I, this I which is fitted as a link into the great chain. . . . Whatever all the men in this

132 *The Making of Czech Jewry*

great chain have created and will create he conceives to be the work of his own unique being; whatever they have experienced and will experience he conceives to be his own destiny.[29]

This, then, is the true definition of "subjective" nationalism: the "placing of the self in the great chain." Buber labeled it "individual man's natural position in relation to his people."

Had Buber simply proposed a theory of nationalism that was derived from an individual's perception of his or her subjective reality, his talk would certainly have been warmly received, as it would have been attuned to the chords of current intellectual discourse. But he went further. He also argued that the subjective affirmation of Jewish nationalism was more important than its objective reality. On one level Buber glorified the subjective over the objective because of his own long-held prejudices against "form and external trappings." On another, however, he provided a genuine service to the young Jewish intellectuals of Prague. He showed them that they could legitimately claim a Jewish "essence" without at the same time having to point to a living Jewish nation with whom they shared common elements of experience. One can even venture a step further. Since the process of human self-discovery—which the subjective perception of nationalism paralleled— required in the first instance a separation of the self from the outside world, a withdrawal into the self, one could argue that it was not only legitimate to ignore the "given facts" of external reality when considering national identification; it was in truth an essential step.

On the most basic level, then, Buber was arguing that, despite what assimilationists of all stripes might say—and despite commonly held liberal definitions of nationalism—one did not need a common language, a common set of shared experiences, to justify the cultivation of a separate national identity. Jewish nationalism in the West was valid in spite of the fact that the very patterns of contemporary Jewish life appeared to deny it:

> [The Western Jew] does not see his substance unfold before him in his environment; it has been banished into deep loneliness, and is embodied for him in only one aspect: his origin (*Abstammung*).
>
> That his substance can, nevertheless, become a reality for the Jew is due to the fact that his origin means more than a mere connection with things past; it has planted something within us that does not leave us at any hour of our life, that determines every tone and every hue in our life, all that we do and all that befalls us: blood, the deepest, most potent stratum of our being.[30]

Still, a person can ignore the world around him or her only for so long. Inevitably one must try to overcome the contradiction that exists between the objective and subjective worlds. One must strive to create for one's life an objective national reality in order, in Buber's words, "to attain unity out of division."[31] "Whoever, faced with the choice between environment and substance, decides on substance," must now, *von innen heraus* (from within), begin to live his or her Jewishness, to affirm his or her identity in the world. In one's concern for the future of Judaism and the Jewish people, the individual must seek to create new forms of a viable Jewish life; one must reintegrate oneself and one's newly found culture into the outside world. Buber expressed this sentiment in a series of trancelike affirmations: "I want to go on living; I want my future—a new, total life, a life for my own self, for my people within me, for myself within my people."[32]

Judaism had yet to make its final mark on world history, and Buber's exposition of Jewish nationalism ended on a messianic, almost mystical, note. He called upon his nation to release its great storehouse of creative strength:

> What matters for the Jew is not his credo, nor his declared adherence to an idea or a movement, but that he absorb his own truth, that he live it, that he purify himself from the dross of foreign rule, that he find his way from division to unity, that he redeem himself (*dass er sich erlöse*).[33]

Thus Buber's vision provided not only for the separation of the subjective self from the world of reality, it also promised the reintegration of the substantive self, the spirit, into the world. It was this progression from separation to recognition to reintegration that spoke to the basic emotional and intellectual needs of the Prague Jewish intellectuals, cut off by time and place from the wellsprings of national Jewish culture, yet keenly sensitive to the urgency of promoting a national identity. Buber, in effect, provided them with a past and a future; he showed them why they were not tied to the prerogatives of the present. He offered both justification and hope.

Although fifteen months separated Buber's first and second addresses, he began his April 1910 presentation virtually at the point that he had left off. In "Judaism and Mankind," Buber focused on the problem of overcoming the contradictions in one's life. For him it was the overwhelming drive to achieve "unity" that characterized the basic, primal element (*Urelement*) of Judaism. And it was also this fundamental quest for unity that pointed the way toward a solution to mankind's social and political ills.[34]

Referring to his previous speech, Buber explained how individuals who live in the midst of a fully developed and sovereign nation acknowledge their membership in that nation naturally; they feel no need to justify or explain the fact of their "belonging." Such is not the case for individuals whose people cannot boast of their own land, their own living community. Such people become conscious of their belonging through an imaginative projection of the self into the community. The more they contemplate their uniqueness, their "otherness" from the world around them, the stronger their conviction grows.

This model, Buber argued, applied equally to the relationship between the nation and mankind in general. The group that occupies a "secure position" among the nations, that possesses a distinct language, land, and *Lebensform* (way of life), does not need to belabor the fact of its existence. It serves mankind according to its nature. Not so the Jews, who have lost their natural land, who speak no single national language, who do not at present constitute a *Lebensgemeinschaft* (living community). The Jews feel a particular need to demonstrate what is eternal and unique about them, to point to that aspect of the human spirit that they incorporate. Judaism, as a national culture bereft of nation and state, represents an ideal awaiting its implementation in the real world. It embodies one of the highest "elemental drives" of the human spirit.[35]

In Buber's mind Judaism could be reduced to a single abstraction: the striving to overcome duality and contradiction through unity. Judaism had carried out this struggle historically within itself. What is more, the Jewish people directed the idealism of this quest toward the outside world as well. "It is this striving for unity," Buber urged, "that has made the Jew creative."[36] It was, moreover, the Jews' natural task, their "mission," to seek unity in all spheres: to work toward the integrity of the individual, to unify their own nation, indeed to seek the union of all nations. In the end the Jew was called upon to achieve the ultimate union, that between God and the world.

If Buber's first address had been Kantian in tone, "Judaism and Mankind" clearly harked back to Herder. Earlier Buber had demonstrated how one first had to withdraw from the world in order to acknowledge one's own self and effect a creative reintegration. Now Buber tried to show that through this "withdrawal" into Jewish nationalism one would, in fact, be moving toward the eventual elimination of all conflicts and divisions. The struggle against disunity, then, had both an internal and an external function. It aimed at bringing to a close the "inner exile" of the Jew and also at reintegrating the nations of the world in brotherhood. The affirmation and practice of Jewish nationalism directed one on the path toward universal humanism:

> If, then, we relate ourselves to elemental Judaism's spirit, if we strive for unity within our soul and purify the people, we shall have helped to effect its liberation and to set Judaism free, once again, for its deed within mankind.
>
> This, as we have seen, has always been and will continue to be Judaism's significance for mankind: that it confront mankind with the demand for unity, a unity born out of one's own duality and the redemption from it.[37]

Because of its material weakness, Judaism could not affect the content of other national cultures, nor create new conditions for people around the world. But it could demonstrate the possibilities for unity through its own example. "Conscious as is no other community of the primal dualism," Judaism can point the way to a world in which it is overcome, "a world of God . . . the world of unity."[38]

Buber dedicated his third and last speech before Bar Kochba and the Prague Jewish community to the question of Jewish cultural regeneration.[39] What he meant by this was not a gradual or evolutionary "improvement" in the quality of Jewish spiritual life, but rather a revolutionary upheaval, "a true and total renewal." He took issue with both the contemporary advocates of reform in Judaism, such as Moritz Lazarus, and with those who called for a cultural regeneration, such as Aḥad Ha'am. Lazarus's call for reform was deficient, because it merely sought to "bring Judaism into line" with modern life, to unburden it of its ritual baggage, despite his lofty rhetoric of a return to prophetic ideals. This was a purely negative endeavor. Even Aḥad Ha'am did not really speak of a true rebirth of Judaism. The cultural center in Palestine, which was basic to his thought, could never instigate a regeneration of the Jewish spirit; it could only *stem from* such a development. Palestine as a Jewish cultural center would be an outgrowth of the renewal of Judaism itself.

On what, then, might the renaissance of Judaism be based? For the answer to this question, Buber once again turned to the "idealist" approach to Judaism, which defined the essence of Jewish culture according to those spiritual tendencies that could be discerned beneath the external forms of custom and institutionalized behavior. He argued that Judaism in its true sense represented the sum and interaction of three "tendencies" of the Jewish people. It was a "spiritual process" that manifested itself in history as the "striving for an ever more perfect realization (*Verwirklichung*) of three interconnected ideas: the idea of unity, the idea of the deed, and the idea of the future."[40] Buber depicted this process as an "ideological battle," a "struggle for realization." The "ideas actually struggle for their own selves, for their liberation from the narrowness of the people's tendencies, for their independence, and for their realization."[41]

Hasidism in its time had hoped to raise Jewish law from the "conditioned" to the "unconditioned," "to transform it from the rigidity of a formula to the fluidity of the immediate."[42] So, too, any renewal of Judaism had to return to the Jewish people the possibility of living life "absolutely," that is, in full consciousness of its ideals, its "immortal substance."[43] Buber left open for the present what the exact nature of the renewal would be. Renewal was to mark the beginning of modern Jewish creativity, the return of the spirit to the life of the nation; its forms and specific content were neither knowable nor immediately relevant.

Buber's *Three Addresses on Judaism* constituted a mystical declamation of neo-romantic, inward-looking, nationalist faith. Its stubborn refusal to acknowledge all but the most subjective criteria of ethnicity strikes one today as being vaguely absurd. At the same time, however, the *Drei Reden* outlined a theory of nationalism that was uniquely adapted to the needs of Central European student Zionists. Decidedly nonliberal, even racial, in tone, Buber's speeches justified the withdrawal of Jews from direct involvement in other peoples' national controversies and presented even the most marginal of Jews with an image of an ideal Jewish culture with which they could identify. Furthermore, Buber suggested that the very affirmation of Jewish nationalism—which included the cultivation of Judaism's highest ideals—would enable the Zionists to lead the nations of the world away from divisiveness and chauvinism and toward a humanistic future.

Lastly Buber urged his listeners to remake Jewish spirituality, to involve themselves in the creative transformation of Judaism. The only tools that they needed to bring to the task were honest intentions, a commitment to the realization of Judaism's ideals, and a willingness to work toward the future of Jewish culture. Not only were the Prague Zionists equipped to carry out such a mission, but, Buber argued, they were the only ones who could ensure their own redemption. At the close of his first lecture, Buber illustrated this point with a parable:

> When I was a child, I read an old Jewish tale I could not understand. It said no more than this: "Outside the gates of Rome there sits a leprous beggar, waiting. He is the Messiah." Then I came upon an old man whom I asked: "What is he waiting for?" And the old man gave me an answer I did not understand at the time, an answer I learned to understand only much later. He said: "He waits for you."[44]

Buber's Impact

Buber's hold on the intellectual youth of his generation is difficult to account for today. His early mystical and romantic writings appear to have lost much of their original integrity with the passage of time. Gershom Scholem, looking back on his youth in pre–World War I Germany, has made the following confession:

> I am among those who in their youth, when these speeches appeared, was deeply moved by them and who—even as happened to the author himself—many years later can now read these pages only with a deep feeling of estrangement.[45]

Troubled by the ephemerality of Buber's early work—as well as by his own fascination with it at the time—Scholem offered a psychological explanation for the popularity of the *Drei Reden* and emphasized the magic that it and works like it exercised over the younger generation.

> I would be unable to mention any other book about Judaism of these years, which even came close to having such an effect—not among the men of learning, who scarcely read these speeches, but among a youth that here heard the summons to a new departure that many of them took seriously enough to act on.[46]

Above all, Buber worked his "magic" on the members of Bar Kochba. Writing in *Selbstwehr* on the eve of Buber's third address, Hugo Herrmann tried to convey the extent his group's indebtedness to this great man:

Buber has done a great thing; he has given of himself; he has shown how Judaism—the poor, leprous Judaism of today—out of itself will become fruitful and creative. He causes us to hear the currents moving about deep within ourselves, [currents] which we had long believed to be dried up and evaporated. We listen to ourselves and are astonished: does so much of which we were not aware still live in us? . . . Into the darkness in which our souls lie he sends a thin, trembling beam of light, so that we may learn to recognize where our relics (*Heiligtümer*) stand. . . . Redemption is only possible if we descend deep within ourselves and find our way to what is deepest and most holy. We wait for Buber as one at the crack of dawn awaits the day.[47]

Herrmann's words testify to the fact that Buber's impact went far beyond the intellectual message of his talks. It was also Buber's charismatic presence, together with the messianic expectations of the Prague Jewish students, which combined to produce the sudden and powerful friendship between the two.

Leo Herrmann—Hugo's cousin—recorded his personal impressions of Buber in diary entries for this period. Apparently, in 1909 Buber surprised the members of Bar Kochba by arriving in Prague a day early, and made use of his time alone with the group to lecture privately on his views concerning Judaism and Zionism. "We knew then," Herrmann wrote, "that he would help us further along our way."[48] The following evening, when Buber fretted privately to Herrmann that he did not feel that he could match the lively tone of Felix Salten's introductory speech, the Bar Kochba leader advised him to ignore the public, "to speak only for us." That is precisely what Buber did, and at the conclusion of his words—aimed at the initiates to his romanticism— Herrmann greeted the master, speechless, hand outstretched.[49]

The following year Robert Weltsch (1891–1984) wrote to Buber inviting him to return to Prague. In his letter he described Buber's first address as an "experience" (*Erlebnis*) whose impact was indelible. "It placed our Zionist convictions on a truly solid—and for many of us, entirely new—foundation, upon which we can now build our work. . . . You can gather from our Semester Report how we are striving to develop in the direction that you have pointed."[50]

When Buber met with Bar Kochba for the second time, the group decided to formalize what previously had occurred by chance. A small welcoming committee, consisting of Robert Weltsch, Leo Herrmann, Viktor Kellner, and Alfred Kraus, met Buber and his wife at the station a day before the scheduled public lecture. The Bubers and their Prague hosts walked through the streets of the city, over the Charles Bridge, and on to the Hradčany—the castle district—from which point one could observe the blinking lights of the Czech capital as evening approached. The party then proceeded to the headquarters of Bar Kochba. Here Buber spoke informally with his young Zionist followers, touching upon themes that he had been discussing on the promenade: "the meaning of the concept of 'blood,' the specifically Jewish attributes, the solution to the personal Jewish question, our relation to Palestine, the hope for a great, religious convulsion. . . ."[51] The following evening Buber addressed the general community. His mythmakers would have it that the audience hung on to every word; not a person coughed; not a key rattled. By all accounts he was greeted warmly by the Jewish public, but nothing equaled the mesmerizing effect that his words and his personality had on the members of Bar Kochba. Another day of private discussions and long walks through Prague followed. Even as the Prague Zionists escorted Buber and his wife back to the station for their return trip, they prepared to discuss for several hours more the import of Buber's address, the words of which more than one could recite by heart.[52]

Several of Prague's German-Jewish writers, who up to this time had moved quite comfortably in the city's liberal, German circles, had their first contact with Jewish national culture during the years of Buber's greatest influence. Chief among these were the core members of the Max Brod-Felix Weltsch literary group, a small circle of friends, which included, in addition to Brod and Weltsch, Franz Kafka, Franz Werfel, and Oskar Baum. They had met one another during or immediately after their university years, and frequently came together to read from their own works and discuss the state of the art.[53]

Felix Weltsch began his lifelong involvement in Zionism under the tutorship of Buber and Hugo Bergmann (his colleague at the University Library) during the two years that preceded the war. Oskar Baum started a correspondence with Buber in 1910 in which he discussed the Jewish themes in his work and put forward his views on the Jewish national rebirth.[54] Max Brod (1884–1968) was drawn in to the Prague Zionist circle somewhat unwillingly in 1909 only to become fully converted to the cause by the eve of the war and thereafter a major figure in local Jewish national politics.

Brod's introduction to Zionism came when he received through the mail a review by Leo Herrmann of his latest novel *Ein tschechisches Dienstmädchen* (A Czech housemaid).[55] The book, which depicted the brief affair of an alienated German writer and a troubled, Czech servant girl, caused Brod no end of problems. He had intended the physical attraction between the characters—separated by barriers of class as well as nationality—to suggest a possibility for mutual coexistence and empathy. The narrator, recounting the moment of passion, mused:

> Everything that I experienced on this great afternoon passed through my mind: the Czech people in their villages, with their comforting songs. I understand it now; I understand the anxious, childlike soul in my beloved. . . . I understand the Czechs, this nation of many talents and things of beauty.[56]

Unfortunately for Brod, people took exception to the book from all sides of the national controversy. The Czech writer Růžena Jesenská (aunt of

Milena Jesenská, Kafka's future confidante) criticized Brod for perpetuating an uncomplimentary stereotype in his portrayal of the Czechs as sensual, unthinking beings. Many Germans, on the other hand, objected to the very idea of intimate union between the two nations and labeled Brod a "national enemy."[57] Yet it was the Zionist criticism that most affected the author. Herrmann pointed out that Brod's main character resembled most closely not the displaced Viennese intellectual that he was purported to be, but the quintessential Prague German, the German-speaking Prague Jew, not unlike Brod himself. Acknowledging the author's sincerity in looking for an ultimate solution to the national controversy, Herrmann nevertheless chided him for his political naiveté:

> Does Brod really know the German people? If so, he must surely know that the German and the Czech people are not going to be brought together through individual, erotic relations. . . . Perhaps Max Brod will come to find a context that will lift him out of the realm of the individual and will permit him to arrive at a solution [to such questions], which has a better foundation than a hotel bed.[58]

Herrmann's stinging irony had an unusual effect on Brod. He felt the remarks were intrinsically unfair and that Herrmann had drastically oversimplified his message. Yet at the same time Brod recognized that his artistic "indifference" did threaten to reduce his work to the ridiculous and the irrelevant. He met with Herrmann, then chairman of Bar Kochba, and listened for the first time to a serious, impassioned presentation of the Jewish national position. He attended Martin Buber's public address as "an invited guest" and began, around this time, to study the cultural dimensions of Jewish nationalism—which included a reading of Aḥad Ha'am—with Hugo Bergmann.[59]

During the years between 1909 and 1912 Brod suffered what he called "the pains of theoretical realization." New questions and doubts swamped his mind. It was a time of learning and cultural experimentation. The only thing of which he was sure, Brod later recalled, was that "of the three nations that lived in Prague—the Germans, the Czechs, and the Jews—it was the third to which I belonged."[60] Brod, in turn, played a major role in igniting Franz Kafka's interest in Judaism when he invited Kafka to accompany him on one of his cultural journeys—a visit to the Café Savoy to view the performances of a Yiddish acting company from Lwów.[61] The personalities of the Polish actors, their earthy, matter-of-fact Jewishness, seduced the young writer. Kafka sat in on performances of the Yiddish troupe—at least twenty by his own count—from October 1911 through the spring of the following year. More than 100 pages of his diary entries are taken up with descriptions of the actors, plot summaries of the plays, and stories recounted to him by Kafka's newfound friend, the head of the group, Yitsḥok Levi.[62]

Kafka devoted much energy at the start of 1912 to gaining the widest possible exposure for Levi and his actors. He sent fliers to local branches of the Zionist organization in Bohemia advertising his "clients," and eventually convinced Bar Kochba in Prague to sponsor an evening of songs and readings. The affair was held on 18 February 1912 at the Jewish Town Hall. Kafka, himself, looked after every detail, from the printing and distribution of tickets to the submission of an advance copy of the program for police—as well as community—censorship.[63] And Kafka introduced the evening's performers with a poised, articulate, and somewhat defiant address on the Yiddish language:

> I would like to assure you, ladies and gentlemen, that you understand far more Yiddish than you think. I am not at all worried about the effect of what we have prepared for you this evening, but I would like you to be free to properly appreciate it. And this you will not be able to do as long as some of you are so frightened by the sound of Yiddish that the fear is written all over your faces. . . . But you will already be quite close to Yiddish if you realize that, active within you, in addition to knowledge, are forces and junctures of forces that enable you to feel yourselves into an understanding of Yiddish. . . . And once Yiddish has taken hold of you—and Yiddish is everything: word, Hasidic melody, and the very essence of this Eastern Jewish actor himself—you will no longer recognize your former complacency.[64]

On the heels of his discovery of the Yiddish actors from Lwów, Kafka began to study Jewish history and literature seriously for the first time. He read Heinrich Graetz's *History of the Jews* (popular ed.?, 1887–89), Meyer Pines's *History of Yiddish Literature* (in French, 1900) and Jacob Fromer's *Organism of Jewry* (1909). He subscribed to *Selbstwehr* and began to study Hebrew.[65] Kafka never became active in the political side of Zionism, but he did develop an intense interest in the program of Jewish cultural renewal and an abiding fascination with the vitality and honesty of East European Judaism. As Ernst Pawel touchingly notes, the eight Jews on the stage of the Café Savoy represented for Kafka "eight messengers from the world in which his own father had himself been a son, kindred spirits to a spirit that was stirring within him, speaking his own lost language, rooted and secure in their unassailable identity as Jews, Jewish in the way the Czechs were Czech, the Germans German—and he himself was nothing."[66]

Eventually Kafka came to lose patience with the dramatic productions of the Yiddish troupe; their plot lines were thin and often implausible; the acting was sometimes quite poor; the content of the plays themselves offered little spiritual sustenance. But he held fast in his attachment to the actors, "these actors, who are so good, who earn nothing, and who do not get nearly enough gratitude and fame." Above all, Kafka recognized that his love for Levi and his band was "really only sympathy for the sad fate of many noble strivings, above all of our own."[67]

Though the folksy players from Galicia worked their magic on Kafka, Martin Buber apparently did not. Here—as in so many other ways—Kafka stood apart from friends and colleagues. He complained to his fiancée Felice Bauer in 1913 that he was to forgo writing for an evening in order to attend a public lecture by Buber:

> The thing is that Buber is lecturing on the Jewish Myth; it would take more than Buber to get me out of my room. I have heard him before, I find him dreary; no matter what he says, something is missing.[68]

Yet, much as he did with regard to the Yiddish actors, Kafka offered a more charitable judgment of Buber as a human being. "As a person he is lively and simple and remarkable," he reported to Felice, "and seems to have no connection with the tepid things he has written."[69]

There is much to suggest that the Prague Zionists took seriously Buber's exhortation to employ Jewish nationalism to rise above everyday chauvinism, in fact to mediate the national controversies of their age. Those who had grown up in predominantly German-speaking households looked upon their withdrawal into Jewish national identity as a rejection as much of German nationalism as of the incipient Czech movement. If on the issues of linguistic affiliation and education they took no stand, arguing that it made no difference what language Jews used, they nevertheless *did* reject explicitly any identification with the German political nation. And they took great pains to do this precisely because so many of them had been raised in German-speaking families and could easily be identified as German sympathizers.

Equally important in this regard is the fact that the Prague Zionists understood Buber to be in a comparable position to their own: a speaker of German (and Polish) who nevertheless insisted on a separate national posture for Jews and on openness toward the other national groups of East Central Europe. While preparing for Buber's first address, Leo Herrmann complained to Buber about the Prague writer Hugo Salus (1866–1929), a model of intense German-Jewish acculturation:

> It will perhaps once be understood, that it is necessary for us to declare before the world our—above all self-evident—Judaism, never, however, to make our "de facto" German culture—where it exists—a *sine qua non,* never to make it a dividing-wall of principle within one's own camp.[70]

In a similar vein, Robert Weltsch let Buber know three years later that a person Buber had suggested as a possible speaker would not be appropriate, as he represented the German assimilationist position of which Bar Kochba was trying to steer clear.[71] The Prague Zionist leaders sought to limit the implications of their German linguistic culture by labeling it "faktisch" (de facto) but nothing more; it was a matter of external reality, not an expression of conviction or value. Most of all, it must not be allowed to divide one Jew from another or the Jews from their Czech surroundings.

Worthy of note, too, is the fact that around the time of Buber's talks in

Prague, the number of Czech-speaking and Czech-educated members of the student Zionist circle appeared to be growing. Herrmann explained to Buber that if the number of Czech-speaking students in the organization grew to the extent that the exclusive use of German in their meetings and publications would be unfair (as well as unrepresentative), the group would split, and a totally Czech-speaking wing would be established. For purely tactical considerations, he added, not ideological ones.[72]

It did not take long for this development to occur. A Czech branch of Bar Kochba was formed in Prague in December 1909, under the name Theodor Herzl (Spolek židovských akademiků Theodor Herzl). The group put forward goals that were no different from those of Bar Kochba; only its needs were special. Even tactical requirements can be put to good use, however. What had originated out of a need to provide speakers and literature to an interested, but non-German, clientele, soon evolved into a renewed effort to reach the masses of Jews in the Czech-speaking areas of Bohemia and Moravia. As the activities report of 1909–10 made clear, the Theodor Herzl branch was determined "to make the values of Zionism available to Jews whose daily language is Czech, without [also] taking up German cultural elements."[73] Much as the Volksverein Zion had done in the 1890s, the Theodor Herzl branch ventured into the heartland of the Czech-Jewish movement, the middle-sized towns of the Bohemian country-side, to press its cause. "Zionist evenings" were set up in places such as Radnice, Pardubice, Kolín, and Kutná Hora, where lectures could be heard—in Czech—on contemporary Jewish literature, medieval philosophy, the Bible, and, of course, Zionism. Even Eduard Lederer agreed to speak before a Theodor Herzl gathering in 1912 on the topic of Palestine, which he had recently visited.[74]

A number of Zionist newspapers also appeared in Czech during the years that preceded World War I. The Bohemian branch of the Jewish Socialist Workers' party, *Po'ale Zion,* published *Židovský lidový list* (Jewish people's press) from 1910 through 1912. And the general Zionist organization issued *Židovské listy pro Čechy, Moravu a Slezsko* (Jewish press for Bohemia, Moravia, and Silesia) in 1913 and 1914. *Židovský lidový list* came out with a serialization of Buber's *Drei Reden* in Czech translation in 1912. The speeches also appeared as a single publication the same year.[75]

The eagerness of the Prague Zionists to establish a separate Czech branch, as well as their reluctuance to admit of any overtly pro-German sentiment, points to a determination to steer a middle course, away from both sides of the nationality controversy. They did, however, make overtures of general support to the leadership of the Czech national movement, refusing only to be pressured into joining forces with the Czech nationalists at the expcnse of their own national aspirations. As Hugo Herrmann wrote in 1911, "We Jews are Jews as a nation (*der Nation nach*) and do not want to assimilate with anyone."

We appropriate with thanks the influences of our environment and take pains ourselves to speak and think in Czech, even to speak and think Czech well. [But] that which we consider necessary for our development as Jews, we do not allow ourselves to take from anyone, even a non-Jewish Czech. We are certainly prepared to act in an upstanding way, for it corresponds to our own inclinations to take part in the action and struggle of the Czech nation, which has given so much to us, clearly not as leaders and flankmen—for we are not fanatical Czechs—but as reliable, true allies.[76]

Debating Jewish Renewal

When it came time to review the published version of Buber's *Drei Reden,* the task went to Hans Kohn, then a student in the Law Faculty who, together with his lifelong friend Robert Weltsch, was soon to emerge as a leading theoretician of the "Jewish renaissance" in Prague.[77] Kohn's article revealed the nature of the Prague Jewish students' understanding of Buber, and—like Hugo Herrmann's piece of the previous year—it too gave voice to the highly personal, emotional yearnings of the group. On one level Buber had issued an untimely call, "a bold and powerful sound . . . against our time, the time of materialism and mechanization, conditionality and smallness."[78] Yet he reached the Prague Zionists so profoundly precisely because he spoke in their idiom; he isolated and held up for viewing a keenly felt intellectual crisis. As Kohn explained some years later, "He said to us simply what we want and what we yearn for out of our deepest hearts."[79]

Kohn had no difficulty accepting Buber's definition of the national quality in Judaism as a "lasting substance," which was transmitted from generation to generation. He appreciated its phenomenological foundation, the "I-experience," "that breaking through of the empirically-bound I, a moment of the feeling of totality."[80] Neither did he object to Buber's abstracting from Judaism certain fundamental characteristics. Indeed he both confirmed and elaborated upon Buber's description of the "polarity" within Judaism, interpreting it as the division and conflict between "official, all-knowing, and critical" Judaism and the "unknown, 'underground,' absolute" Judaism of the prophets, the mystics, the early Christians, and the Hasidim. This much was vintage Buber, but Kohn managed to outdo the master when he anointed the true, underground Judaism with no fewer than eighteen modifiers, including "full of hot, burning fervor for God," and "the Judaism of the *ma'aseh ha-merkava* and the *ma'aseh bereshit.*"[81]

What truly attracted Kohn was the promise of redemption (*Erlösung*). In his descriptions of the process, Kohn envisaged both the individual and the material world around one; both the Jew and mankind; the limits of physical existence and the absolute possibilities of mystical experience. Never totally clear in his explanations, he nevertheless did confirm that redemption involved both the release of individuals from the specifications of their material environment and the removal of conflict from mankind generally. Salvation in the end consisted of the transformation of the diverse, divided world to one of unity and absoluteness. The spiritual regeneration of Judaism would be a first step on the road to a total renewal of the human spirit. The call was issued "that we not allow the great spiritual struggle to fade out, but rather take it up and carry it; not only a small portion of the nation, but the whole people must win it."[82]

Hugo Bergmann reviewed the *Drei Reden* the following year for Aḥad Ha'am's Hebrew periodical *Ha-shiloaḥ*. He seconded Buber's antipositivism, expressing impatience with the "scientific" view that held that humans were simply the product of their environment:

> Man . . . is nothing but a game in the hands of the state of things: he is created but does not create; is made but does not make. The laws of reality are a decree that has been imposed upon him and from which there is no escape.[83]

Bergmann longed for the man of action, the "hero" of old, who in times past had been prepared "to change the earth through his actions and to put his seal on reality."[84] Assimilation, heir to liberalism and positivism in the West, had amounted to what Bergmann called the "victory of the environment over our internal substance (*penimiyut*)." It was only with the advent of the national movement that new strength and creativity was born in the heart of Jewry. It was only now that Jews were learning that they had in their hands the power to choose: to be or to cease to be.[85]

Like Kohn, Bergmann, too, spoke of redemption. It would not come about through "external agencies," but rather as the result of a "revolution in the heart of the nation." Messianism, moreover, required that one turn one's eyes away from "practical and relational life," and direct them instead to the "absolute," that is, unconditioned, life of the nation.[86] Here again, what is most striking about the Prague Zionists' understanding of Buber goes far beyond their romanticism and antipositivism. It was the call to secede from the real world, the world of contingency and struggle, of relative truths and political decisions. Redemption was to be a spiritual process, carried out in the first instance by individuals acting "absolutely," unhampered by contingency. The nation, according to this view, consisted of the sum of its individual members, and its redemption depended upon the transformation of each individual. "Each person redeems his nation when he elevates himself."[87]

The Bar Kochba members did not confine such concerns to formal publications and intellectual reviews. Much of their personal correspondence during the years preceding the First World War brimmed over with interpretations of the *Erlösungsidee.* Hans Kohn agonized in a letter to Robert Weltsch over the role that the individual Jew was to play in the world's redemption:

The Jews . . . as the chosen nation, redeem the world to the extent that they become *God*-like, that is, become God (as so-called Ecstatics). "You shall be a *holy* nation, *for I* am holy, your *God*." "Therefore you shall be *complete* (*vollkommen*), *just as* your father in heaven is *complete*.[88]

Pondering the steps that man had to take in order to achieve union with the absolute, Kohn confided to his friend that "man must redeem himself from the [empirical] world of conditionality and multiplicity . . . into the metaphysical world of oneness and unconditionality."[89]

This tendency of Bar Kochba to intellectualize politics, as well as Buber's own vagueness concerning the content of Jewish renewal, combined to produce a prolonged internal debate on the direction of the spiritual upheaval. There was no argument about the need for a renaissance, but the Prague Zionists differed strongly over tactics and over the role of Jewish intellectuals in the process. Were they to engage in political activity at all? Were they to challenge the larger community to join in on the process of change? Were they to polemicize against those Jews who refused to accept the national definition of Jewishness? Or was the course of renewal to be internal, with each individual completing it in one's own right, of one's own volition, before it could have an effect on the nation as a whole?

Bar Kochba's activities report for 1912, written by Robert Weltsch, reveals just how much energy the organization spent setting the parameters for a program of Jewish renewal. Siegmund Kaznelson spoke at one *Vereinsabend* (club night) on the "Problem of Culture"; Oskar Epstein (1888—1940) and Robert Weltsch debated the question of "renewal" in the company of invited guests Adolf Böhm and Kurt Blumenfeld. Hans Kohn later delivered a lecture on the same topic. Leo Herrmann and Dr. Max Rosenfeld spoke to the group on the possibilities for national autonomy for the Jews of Austria-Hungary. And Weltsch, on the occasion of Fichte's 150th birthday, outlined the analogies between Buber's *Drei Reden* and those of the German national awakener.[90]

Hans Kohn, Robert Weltsch, and Siegmund Kaznelson propounded the view that *Erneuerung* (renewal) was both an internal and an individual occurrence. "Something like Buber's ideas," wrote Kaznelson in 1911, "cannot be carried over to general, objective life, cannot provide the basis for politics, and must not be propagated as a party program. Such ideas, which touch the deepest spot in the human soul . . . can at most be a direction post, according to which a subjective life can be formed."[91] Kohn seconded Aḥad Ha'am's position that Judaism's internal resurgence was to be accomplished in the first instance by a cultural elite. "Each such 'renewal,' " he wrote to Buber, "can for a long period of time only be the experience and yearning of a very narrow circle, before it can become a common possession and a realization."[92] Jewish intellectuals had to be content with their own spiritual transformation and with the conviction that the general process of renewal would come as a historical necessity. A year later Kohn wrote, "Judaism will be 'renewed' when one 'fulfills' *oneself;* the only revolutionizing that I recognize is that [which is done] through acts (examples), not through speeches, insults, [or] arrogant questioning of the goodwill of others."[93]

The references to "speeches" and "accusations" were meant for Oskar Epstein, an outspoken critic of Kohn and Weltsch, who believed that young Zionists had to translate Buber's message into political terms, engage actively in communal politics, and effect a "national renewal" at the group level. Although Epstein did not leave behind his own reminiscences or correspondence, one can glean this much from the accounts of his adversaries. He also stated his position clearly in an essay that he wrote for the anthology *Vom Judentum.* In this piece Epstein showed himself to be a great supporter of Theodor Herzl. Moreover, he was convinced that a working synthesis could be achieved between Herzlian political activism and the Buberian vision of Erneuerung. The utopia of a renewed Judaism could be reached through direct action on the part of committed Jews.[94]

Epstein would accomplish this synthesis first by defusing the debate on the nature of Erneuerung itself:

> The phases of the absolute life of a living nation are too large to be comprehended by an individual. What we see taking place before our eyes is not renewal itself, but something that unfailingly leads to it, namely, moral uprising (*sittliche Erhebung*), just as hunger leads to physical renewal.[95]

By "renewal" Epstein understood not a deliberative process, but the end result of a series of concrete steps. He saw it as the inevitable outcome of the "moral revolt" against the current physical and spiritual conditions of Jewish existence. And, whereas Erneuerung was not something that could be totally understood at this point, the actions that would lead to it could be both understood and directed. Consequently Epstein felt justified in requiring of committed Jewish intellectuals that they involve themselves directly in Jewish politics—challenge the smugness and complacency of the Jewish community—and not simply theorize about what Jewish renewal might mean for the individual consciousness.

Echoing Herzl, Epstein inveighed against what he called *Mauscheljudentum,* a term that connoted the cowardly, mealy-mouthed existence of "emancipated" European Jewry. The Mauscheljude was the epitome of the diaspora Jew, whether fully assimilated or rigidly Orthodox. He was the relic of a dead nation, living completely outside his element in modern European society. In Epstein's eyes this type of individual was identical to what Buber had called the *Golusjude;* and he had to be fought, opposed by the Jew who would choose his own destiny, who would be creative and vital—Buber's *Urjude.*[96] Epstein warned against seeing this struggle, this "moral uprising," solely in terms of theory and "pretty speeches." Above all, one had to avoid "theorizing mysticism"—a clear allusion to the intellectual proclivities of his chief antagonists within Prague Zionism. "The revolt (*Erhebung*) cannot be described *at all;* it must be lived." But the overall direction of the national upheaval was not a mystery: it would replace secrecy in Jewish affairs with openness; absence of character with courage; and compromise with consequence.[97]

Other voices of impatience chimed in from time to time with that of Oskar Epstein. Hugo Herrmann, while serving as editor of *Selbstwehr* in 1912, bridled at Robert Weltsch's persistent requests that Herrmann join him and his friends for discussions at the Café Central. "I simply have no time," he rejoined in one letter, "I simply *cannot.*"

> It is moreover unthinkable to write interesting articles . . . about empty books . . . if one is to remain in the Zionist reality. . . . Presently I am perhaps more Zionist than ever. I finally see what it means to "go out," to get to the "last Jew," and to "rouse" him. I now understand Epstein better.[98]

A year earlier Herrmann had returned to Weltsch an article that Hans Kohn had written for *Selbstwehr* with the remark "one cannot talk a nation into renewal" (*Ein Volk kann man zur Erneuerung nicht überreden*).[99] And yet many within the Bar Kochba circle felt that one could do precisely that. The debate itself—theory versus practice, the example of the individual versus political work among the people—was not unique either to Prague or to Zionism. They were issues that all political movements must consider sooner or later. European socialism in the nineteenth and twentieth centuries divided along similar lines. German Zionism itself was torn between those who would implement the vision of settlement in Palestine immediately and those who were content to allow the status quo to proceed for the time being.[100] In Prague the Martin Buber-Aḥad Ha'am faction prevailed over Epstein's isolated voice of opposition.

Buber himself helped to determine the outcome of the struggle when he chose to lend the weight of his personal prestige to the Hans Kohn-Robert Weltsch faction. During the second half of 1912, with Kohn at the helm of Bar Kochba, and the group busily planning for the upcoming commemoration of its twentieth anniversary, Buber once again involved himself in the activities of the Prague Zionists. He advised Bar Kochba at virtually every step in the preparation of its "scrapbook" (*Sammelbuch*), and eventually persuaded Kurt Wolff Verlag to publish it in 1914 under the title *Vom Judentum* (On Judaism).[101] Buber also accepted the group's invitation to give the major address at its Festabend in January 1913; he spoke on the theme of "Myth in Judaism."[102] At the end of January, Kohn reported confidently to Buber that his involvement in the intellectual life of Bar Kochba had achieved the desired result:

> After many discussions, our position in the society is . . . greatly strengthened; the need to hold fast to the metaphysical Bar Kochba over the empirical one—

that is to say, to allow the intellectual content of Bar Kochba, which determines its uniqueness vis à vis all other associations, to continue to mold Bar Kochba.[103]

The organization, Kohn concluded, would not loom "above the individual," as an ideal to be put into reality by party militants. Instead it was to be an expression of its members' spirit, the sum of each individual's cultural creativity, and not the determiner of where that creativity should lie. A beacon of light, a call to movement, but not a platform.

Vom Judentum

Vom Judentum (On Judaism), the anniversary anthology of Bar Kochba, represented the first official expression of the intellectual ferment that had overtaken the organization since Buber's first Prague address in 1909. It was a joint venture between Buber and Bar Kochba from the start. When Robert Weltsch informed Buber of the group's intention to issue a publication, he alluded to Buber's as-yet unfulfilled plan to publish a Jewish yearbook, and suggested that the Bar Kochba volume inaugurate such a series.[104] Later, Hans Kohn recommended to Buber that he be listed as the editor of *Vom Judentum* alongside the name of Bar Kochba. In fact, Kohn apologized for feeling obliged to include Bar Kochba at all:

> I would like to mention the name Bar Kochba less out of patriotic feeling toward the association than because, in my opinion, as of today it is forming a program within the Zionist movement. Precisely for this reason I would like to bring the association—which today certainly represents the only Zionist organization that strives for a pure and strong intellectual position—into a closer connection with the journal that is being founded.[105]

The members of Bar Kochba intended for *Vom Judentum* to accomplish three ends. First, it was to achieve for the group a measure of publicity. Second, in presenting Bar Kochba's intellectual position, it was to help establish a place for the organization in the world of contemporary Jewish thought. Lastly, *Vom Judentum* was to stimulate other Jews to engage in the process of cultural renewal. In fact, Kohn originally had wanted the title of the book to be *Erneuerung: Ein jüdisches Sammelbuch.*[106] In his introductory essay, he portrayed Bar Kochba as the mouthpiece for an entire generation, "which lives in the consciousness that, *in* its life and *through* its life, the fate of Judaism is going through a decisive turn."[107]

More than anything else, *Vom Judentum* was a collective work. Bar Kochba solicited contributions from a wide variety of writers, many of whom had no connection to Zionism, all of whom, however, lived either in Germany or the Austrian half of the Habsburg monarchy. Hans Kohn's criteria for choosing contributors had less to do with politics than with intellectual standing and cultural temperament. As he explained in his introduction:

We wanted to hear [from] people who, out of necessity and desperate rebellion, searched for a way, a way to the realities of the *new Jewish life*. A way which says no to today, because it is servile and unbearable, and which will *create* a tomorrow in community.[108]

Kohn suggested that the "new type" of European Jew—the one who stood at the transition to the future Gemeinschaft—could find inspiration and direction from *Vom Judentum*. He was not so bold as to claim that Bar Kochba had in fact offered a blueprint for the future Jewish community. Rather, *Vom Judentum* could but point the way, suggest in what direction lay that utopian, national community that was truly free and creative. "It ought to show us where and how we are, [and] from now on, *what we ought to do*."[109]

Yet even this limited goal was hindered by the collective nature of the publication as well as by its editors' distaste for all tests of ideological or political purity. Consequently, *Vom Judentum* could not put forward a consistent line of argument. It did manage to bring together some very distinguished individual pieces, such as Buber's "Der Mythos der Juden," Hugo Bergmann's "Die Heiligung des Namens," Margarete Susman's "Spinoza und das jüdishce Weltgefühl," Kurt Singer's "Von der Sendung des Judentums," and Gustav Landauer's famous essay "Sind das Ketzergedanken?" But of these contributors, only Bergmann and Buber had any direct contact with the intellectual concerns of the Prague Zionists. The others could at best try to conform to Kohn's loose requirements. The end result, of course, was a work of varied quality, marked here and there by spots of genius, but on the whole bearing little connection to Bar Kochba's program of Jewish renewal.[110]

Yet there was one theme that appeared to run through most of the essays in *Vom Judentum*. More a state of mind than a coherent idea, it can best be described as romantic antirationalism and antipositivism. Virtually all of the contributors wrote from the point of view of neo-romantic vitalism, which harked back to Nietzsche but also echoed the contemporary voices of Henri Bergson and the young Buber. Kohn himself set the tone for the rest of the volume when he wrote,

> Zionism is not a science, not a logical system of thought; it has nothing to do with racial theories or definitions of nationality (*Volkstum*). . . . Zionism lies in a completely different plane of being. It is not knowledge (*Wissen*) but rather life.[111]

Much as life did, Zionism took the form of constant struggle. It was for Kohn the struggle of youth against the older generation, of those who yearned for greater and greater heights against those who were too tired to strive, who could no longer grow. The theme of romantic striving, of the power of the creative will, repeated itself in many guises throughout the work. The novelist Jakob Wassermann introduced it when he juxtaposed two types of Jews: the cosmopolitan, intellectual, "European" Jew, and the

"Oriental" Jew, who possessed the power to transform reality and, hence, to be creative.[112] In his lengthy essay on the "mission" of Judaism, Kurt Singer contemplated the relationship between Jewish culture and Bergson's vitalism.[113] The German Zionist Moses Calvary praised the transformative power of "creative imagination" and urged that it become the central principle behind the "new Judaism" in the making.[114]

Yet it was Alfred Wolff's "Jüdische Romantik" that came closest to capturing the mood of the entire volume. It portrayed romanticism as "the redemptive and liberating force, which wants to [cross] over thought to action."

> One conceives of romantic power as a force, which is not always capable . . . of destroying worlds and putting new ones in their place . . . but which *is* capable, with tremendous pressure, of unbolting the locks that stand before oneself, and of clearly showing the way for the soul to reach the heights.[115]

One member of Bar Kochba, Hugo Bergmann, managed to produce a truly original essay that was both a reflection of the intellectual concerns of Prague Zionism and a contribution to contemporary Jewish thought. Indeed, Bergmann's fluency in both Kantian philosophy and the language of traditional Jewish sources enabled him to achieve the kind of creative synthesis that his other colleagues could only write about. In his contribution to the volume, he chose to examine a concept fundamental to Jewish spirituality, that of the hallowing of God's name by man, and applied it to the issue of national renewal.[116] Bergmann began by considering that paradoxical element of Jewish thought that allowed for both the perfectness of God and His "perfectibility" through the acts of righteous individuals. If God is, by definition, holy, how is it that He can be "sanctified" by man? How can absolute being be affected by a limited and contingent being?

Bergmann tried to show not only that this paradox lay at the heart of Jewish theology, but that it was one that allowed for the existence of a dynamic, living relationship between God and man. God's existence, independent of any human recognition of it, has always been beyond question in Jewish thought. But His realization, His fulfillment, even His unity, has been interpreted by Jewish tradition as being tied to human behavior. Judaism's mystical sources, for example, do not speak of the unity of God, but of the uniting of God, or more precisely, of the unifying of His name (*yiḥud ha-shem*).[117]

Illustrating his points with examples from Midrashic and kabbalistic literature, Bergmann sought to connect the concept of man's participation in the realization of God to issues in contemporary Jewish nationalism. For this he employed the category of *sittliche Handlung* (moral action), which he borrowed from Kantian ethics: God is realized in the world through acts that are the consequences of "moral judgments." In the Jewish tradition, Bergmann argued, God is conceived of as something that exists "for itself" (rather than "in itself"), that is to say, a reality that is dependent upon man's intuition in space and time.

> God is only "for Himself"; He is not something that exists "in itself," that can be grasped from the outside, that could be had, as one takes hold of a thing. Thus He is only for those united-in-God (*Gottgeeinten*). Hence the Jew asks, "How is God, then, for me?" And he answers, "In that He becomes your life, your act. In that you prove Him, does He become a reality in your life."[118]

To demonstrate his point that God requires man to be His witness if He is to be made real, Bergmann quoted a Midrashic comment by Rabbi Shim'on bar Yoḥai. " 'You are my witness says the Eternal, and I am God': If you bear witness for me, then I am the Eternal; if you are not my witness, then I am not."[119] Man, then, as freely acting spirit, is not only created, he is creator; he is the unifier of the name of God, that is, the fulfiller of God's potential on earth. Man is "merely a creation as long as he, like a thing, is pushed from without, must be determined in order to act. [He is a] creator, when he, releasing himself from the chains of alien coercion, rises up freely to the moral act."

> In every act in which we transform ourselves from a thing to an I, from a determined creation (*bedingten Geschöpf*) to a free essence; in every moral act, we act "like God," we realize the Godlike.[120]

Kiddush ha-shem, the sanctification of the name, is action directed toward this end, toward the realization of God's potential on earth. It is the truly free, undetermined, moral act. Here is where it merged with the concept of Zionism, for to be a Jewish nationalist was to insist on the pursuit of the absolute in one's life. It meant striving for "das unbedingte Leben," for totally free, undetermined existence. It was to realize God's name through moral action. Bergmann concluded, "Zionism is our *kiddush ha-shem.*"

Bergmann's essay bore distinct echoes of the romantic yearning that was so characteristic of *Vom Judentum.* It, too, voiced impatience with reality as determined by the accidents of history. It, too, identified Zionism in cultural terms as the power of the creative will to shape, and indeed, overcome the world of contingencies. Two elements, however, set Bergmann's work apart from most of the others in the volume: discipline and knowledge. The romantic activism that he expressed in "Die Heiligung des Namens" operated within the confines of Kantian ethics. Kant's categorial imperative defined what types of behavior the creative individual could legitimately engage in. Moreover, Bergmann's familiarity with the sources of traditional Jewish culture—as well as his dexterity in both Yiddish and Hebrew—provided content for the "creative imagination," a content that was missing throughout much of *Vom Judentum.* The concerns of historical Judaism informed and shaped Bergmann's concerns. Unlike a number of his colleagues, he stood far above any charges of moral recklessness or intellectual vacuity.

If the psychological foundation of the early years of Jewish nationalism in Prague was one of defiance, on the eve of World War I it was one of rejection—rejection of the bourgeois world of their fathers, rejection of the exigencies of social and cultural reality. Romantic activism had many attractions for a generation weaned on antipositivism and antirationalism. Equally significant, it justified a retreat from the immediate social and political environment. The romantic impulse allowed the Prague Zionists to turn a deaf ear to the taunts of both German and Czech assimilationists, close their eyes to an empirical world that argued for the unreality of Jewish national existence at every turn.

Prague's student Zionists could simply declare their revolt against the indignities of the present. If it were true that no visible Jewish nation existed in Western or Central Europe, one could nevertheless hold up the vision of the rejuvenated Jewish nation that existed deep within the breast of the individual Jew. Such considerations doubtless aided the growth of Zionism among the Jewish youth in other Central European capitals, most notably Vienna and Berlin. But nowhere was the impulse to flee the conflicts of the social and political plane stronger than in Prague. Zionism, on a basic level, was a way out of an untenable situation.

Inward retreat, however, was to be only the first step in the process of renewal and national redemption. Buber's was also a call to creativity, to the active, "heroic" life. With a few notable exceptions, Buber's protégés in Prague refused to establish any definitions for the nature of the rejuvenated Judaism of the future. The whole point of their endeavor was to allow the freely creative, national spirit to be just that: free and creative. The historic forms of Judaism had no lasting value and would, justifiably, be torn apart during the regenerative process. But whatever forms and content would subsequently emerge could not be predicted and ought not to be predetermined. The mainstream within Prague Zionism did not budge from its original conception of redemption as, first and foremost, an individual occurrence. And Judaism itself, whose handed-down structures imprisoned the creative spirit, could be defined only as that which serious, well-intentioned Jews say it is, what they create in their own lives. Bergmann himself expressed this view in his review of Buber's *Drei Reden:*

> It is impossible to give an answer to the question of the future in a meritorious sense, that is to say, "this is the road; let us take it." Because each one of us will choose his own way. And he who awakens us to choose can require of us only that each person choose his path in the feeling of great responsibility, in seriousness, and according to his inner law, not according to some kind of external, borrowed paradigm.[121]

The Prague Zionists, content to cultivate their individual spiritual growth as a prelude to a general national awakening, were nevertheless able to communicate their excitement to other young Jews. Bar Kochba, as we have seen, enjoyed much success in recruiting both Czech and German-speaking Jews from across Bohemia and Moravia. But this individual cultivation of the spirit, coupled perhaps with Buber's iconoclastic interpretation of Judaism, resulted in an unintended paradox. Though immersed in literature, and committed to writing as a vocation, the Prague Zionists before the war actually made very few contributions to twentieth-century Jewish thought. They had no model, as models were abolished. They were told that "Judaism" was what they, as free spirits, created, but they had little idea of what traditional Judaism had been before, and hence operated in a cultural desert.

Vom Judentum did little more than issue the call for the rebuilding of modern Jewish culture; even the starting point was shrouded in mystery. It was a reflection of the ultimate poverty of substance within prewar Zionism in Prague that the single member of the group who was conversant in traditional Jewish texts—Hugo Bergmann—was also the only one to engage fully in modern Jewish culture. For the rest, the cultural vacuum that they had tried to ignore smothered the creative impulse.

6

The Test of War, 1914–1918

The Decline of the Czech-Jewish Movement

Ideology and Politics on the Eve of the War

In 1912, while the student Zionists in Prague were in the throes of their embrace of Martin Buber, a new body of opinion began to appear within the ranks of the Czech-Jewish movement. A third generation of writers and educated professionals was now emerging, people who had been nurtured from early childhood in Czech national culture and who, for the most part, carried only vague memories of the unrest and anti-Jewish violence of the 1890s. Active in this third generation were individuals such as Otakar Guth (1882–1943), a close disciple of Vohryzek; Viktor Teytz (b. 1881), editor of both *Rozvoj* and the *Kalendář česko-židovský* from 1907 to 1914; Jindřich Kohn (1874–1935); and the much younger members of the circle, Alfred Fuchs (1892–1941), Arné Laurin (Arnošt Lustig, 1889–1945), and Josef Kodíček (b. 1892).

Czech-Jewish writing during the immediate, prewar years differed strikingly from the classical exposés of Lederer and Vohryzek. It was, on the whole, nonalarmist in tone, more self-confident in the authors' relationship to the Czech nation, and more tolerant toward other, competing forms of Jewish cultural expression. The new self-confidence in Czech-Jewish literature grew to a great extent out of the material successes of the Czech-Jewish movement itself. The political writings of this period mentioned less and less the need to overcome the "German" influences in Jewish cultural life. The new catchword was "national indifference," and it was not used euphemistically. In an era in which the German-Jewish primary school no longer existed, in which Bohemian Jews regularly declared Czech to be their language of preference, in which an ever-greater percentage of Jews were abandoning liberal German politics, Czech-Jewish leaders could honestly say that they were not nearly as troubled by overt Jewish allegiances to German culture as they had been in past decades.

Instead of dealing with the German Jew, Viktor Teytz wrote in *Rozvoj* in 1912, one now had to confront the "opportunistic" or "nationally indifferent" Jew. Such a person may no longer have advocated German cultural and political dominance in the Czech lands, but he lacked outward dedication to Czech nationalism. He may have known when to be silent and when publicly to voice allegiance, but he did not yet act out of conviction to the Czech cause.[1] The movement continued to be preoccupied with the nationally indifferent Jew in 1918, when the prospect of Czech political sovereignty looked very promising and the question of the relationship of Jews to the new state loomed large.[2] But the fact that Czech-Jewish leaders now worried about "indifference" and lack of commitment is itself an indication of the real accomplishments of the movement for Czech-Jewish acculturation.

Czech-Jewish writers on the eve of the war provided another, more basic, indication of their position within the assimilatory movement. For decades their older peers had consistently defined the so-called Czech-Jewish question *(českožidovská otázka)* as the weakness of Czech-Jewish acculturation compounded by the unnatural strength of German culture among Bohemian and Moravian Jewry. As late as 1911, Alfred Fuchs introduced his essay on the subject with the succinct statement, "The Jewish question is the problem of how to relieve the abnormal relationship of the Jews to the nation among whom they live. Where there is not an abnormal relationship (Italy [for example]), there is not a Jewish question."[3] In point of fact, however, Czech-Jewish intellectuals—including Fuchs—no longer put much stock in this definition of the problem.

What intrigued them was not the desirability of assimilation but rather the content of postemancipatory Czech-Jewish culture. Not only did everyone within the movement agree on the historical necessity of acculturation to the Czech nation, but for most of the younger writers the phenomenon of Czech-Jewish acculturation was a basic fact of life. The point did not need to be belabored. As Evžen Stern described his generation in 1915, "We . . . not only lived with the Czech nation, we were born to it; we were born Czechs, directly and uniquely."[4]

Stern's remark appeared in his essay "On Contemporary Czech Jewry," which he wrote for the *Kalendář* during the first year of the war. In it he recounted a gathering of the friends of Viktor Vohryzek and Eduard Lederer that had taken place before the outbreak of hostilities. Stern, the youngest person present, was asked what he felt would be the principal task of the Czech-Jewish movement in the future. The young man could begin to answer only by stressing the profound differences that separated his generation from that of his interlocutors.

> We did not live through the separate Jewish schools; our visits to the synagogue with the family and the [few] hours with our rabbis [in the public schools] belong

to the wasteland of our youth. The Hilsner and Dreyfus affairs went back to our earliest childhood; they did not inhibit us at the time, as they did some of our fathers. We are happily born children of the Czech national spirit.

Our relationship to Czech-Jewish culture (*českožidovství*) is clearly understandable; it has not been an emotional crisis for us.[5]

Adolescents of Stern's generation did not wonder whether or not they ought to be Czech but why their parents insisted on their remaining Jews. And it was out of a need to understand the Jewish component of their culture that they first became involved in organizations such as the SČAŽ. Stern and his friends, however, were basically of the opinion that the Czech-Jewish movement no longer had a social and political function to perform. It had "carried out its mission" and had now become superfluous.[6]

Most Czech-Jewish writers may not have been as sanguine as Stern in their assessment of the progress of Czech-Jewish acculturation. Nevertheless they did voice similar attitudes concerning the nature of the Jewish question in their own lives. Jindřich Kohn, writing in *Rozvoj* in 1912, explained that, as far as he was concerned, the primary task of the Czech-Jewish movement was to define the limits of assimilation and at the same time respond to the important challenges presented by European Zionism. Czech Jewry, he remarked, was beset by two contradictory cultural signals. One called for the completion of the process of assimilation, the other for breaking it off. Which signal was correct? This, he argued, was the real Jewish question.[7]

Viktor Teytz ventured to answer Kohn's query by suggesting the following distinction between Zionism and the Czech-Jewish movement. For Czech national Jews, Judaism constituted a historical fact, and Czech culture, a fact of life.

> In [our] lives and culture, we are Czech; in memory, Jews. We have completely merged with the Czech present, and the Jewish past gives us value. We feel that the Czech past, too, belongs to us, to the extent that the present has grown out of it; but we would never leave the impression that we lived it through our ancestors, and we cannot fully identify with it. We can truthfully say, "our Palacký," "our Havlíček, Neruda, and Vrchlický." But we would never call ourselves the descendants of the Hussites.[8]

As far as the present was concerned, the Czech-Jewish relationship represented a full partnership. Both the Jews and the non-Jewish Czechs, however, brought to the relationship separate historical pasts, neither of which could fully be shared by the group that did not live it, but each of which molded the overall cultural profile of its descendants. Jewish and non-Jewish Czechs formed two distinct entities because their pasts had run separate courses. Teytz appeared to be arguing that any honest Czech-Jewish integration in the present had to honor the historical distinctiveness of the two groups. He was silent, however, on whether or not the two historical memories might someday merge as the single heritage of an undifferentiated population. Was this or was this not a goal to which his movement ought to be aspiring?

Jindřich Kohn, Evžen Stern, and Alfred Fuchs offered little more in the way of concrete answers before 1918. But the fact that they formulated the question of Jewish distinctiveness in so personal a light, and so differently than the previous generation, indicates that they were speaking for an age cohort whose cultural concerns veered radically from those of their precursors. From time to time, the new generation of writers did examine contemporary Jewish cultural positions, searching for one that appeared to meet the needs of the postassimilatory Czech Jew. When it did so, interestingly, it demonstrated genuine interest in and tolerance of some of the very trends that had caused the earlier generation to arch away in disgust.

Zionism, Hasidism, and Buberian mysticism now became objects of sympathetic, if detached, inquiry. Long the political and ideological rival of the Czech-Jewish movement, European Zionism had also been an object of study and analysis in the pages of the Czech-Jewish press. Its reporters traced the development of Jewish nationalism in the 1890s, reviewed its major congresses, and generally missed no opportunity to refute, and sometimes ridicule, Zionist positions on European Jewish integration. During the prewar years, this fascination with Zionism did not subside, but the tone of the discussion certainly had changed. Czech-Jewish writers on the whole still looked upon the movement as a rival, to be sure, but a worthy rival, and—more important—a legitimate fixture of the Czech-Jewish landscape.

Presumably the legitimacy granted to Jewish nationalism by important segments of Czech national opinion, if nothing else, forced Czech-Jewish individuals to take the Prague Zionists seriously. But the reasons for their newly found estimation of Zionism went still deeper. Jindřich Kohn, for example, acknowledged that for any modern Jewish movement in the Czech lands to succeed, it had to be national in orientation. Moreover, it had to address the sensitive question of the assimilation of a weaker culture into a stronger one.[9] What progressive Czech nationalists such as Tomáš Masaryk and František Krejčí appreciated most about Jewish nationalism was the ethical stand that it took on the issue of assimilation and the apparent similarity between Jewish and Czech cultural defiance.

Kohn approached the relationship of Czech Jews to Zionism by stepping around the overt contradiction between cultural nationalism and assimilation and by arguing for the symmetry of both Czech and modern Jewish (nonnationalist) aspirations. The Czech nation, he explained, represented a part of humanity that had marched "from glory, through failure, to rebirth." The Jewish odyssey, he suggested, had followed a parallel, if not identical, course: from Golgotha to the ghetto, and from the disfigurement of a ghettoized existence to "the full raising of oneself in the sunny bath of better days."[10]

In point of fact this construction was meant to hide the more obvious symmetry between Czech nationalism and Jewish national rebirth. And it required some intellectual gymnastics on Kohn's part to propose that Jewish emancipation, and not Jewish self-determination, represented the counterpoint to the Czech national revival. If he succeeded in doing so, it was because he identified "freedom" and the natural development of human potential as the features common to both historical processes. Kohn just barely managed to hurdle the problem of the morality of assimilation. Using a bit of old-fashioned casuistry, he reduced the scope of the term to refer only to the unnatural and dishonorable appropriation of German culture by the smaller Czech nation. Both he and the Czech national movement could rightly condemn such a course.[11]

Beyond its opposition to German-Jewish assimilation, Kohn concluded, the Czech-Jewish movement was pointed securely in the same direction as every other modern Jewish movement, Zionism included. It wanted what everyone else wanted—the peace and serenity that comes from harmonizing Jewish nature with the forces of reality.[12] Kohn, who frequently lectured to Czech Zionist organizations, was even willing to concede to the Jewish national movement a role in the redemption of East European Jewry from the ravages of poverty and political oppression. Zionism constituted a "possible" program of renewal for many Jews. In the West, however—within which Kohn included Bohemia and Moravia—Jewish nationalism was not viable. Here the Czech-Jewish movement was a "necessity."[13]

At the close of the war, Kohn addressed the newly established Jewish National Council in Prague as well as the Zionist district committee in his home of Plzeň on the position of the Jews in the Czechoslovak state.[14] In these speeches he emphasized the common role that his own movement and Zionism had played in the cultural transformation of Bohemian and Moravian Jewry. Czech Jews, moreover, did not want to become mere creatures of assimilation, but rather the creators of its "living structure" and the cocreators of a common Czech-Jewish existence.[15] Both Zionism and the Czech-Jewish movement, Kohn asserted, were directed at a common human purpose:

> Whoever expresses his Czechness Jewishly, let him call himself a Jew. Whoever expresses his Jewishness as a Czech, is a Czech. Let us defend both currents, the purity of their ultimate intentions. Belonging to a Zionist or a Czech-Jewish organization means little; both indicate the will to be—for our whole lives—that which our basic experience has made us.[16]

To the local Zionists in Plzeň, Kohn was even more conciliatory. "Let it not be asked, which current will win. It is not a question of struggle; it is a question of growth. Let it not be asked, which movement the Czech state will support. It is a question of proper, natural development, and of internal, spiritual growth."[17]

Official Czech Jewry's declining hostility toward Zionism was the result, it seems, of three main factors: the sharply nationalistic contours in which all cultural activity in the Czech lands was expressed; the obvious sympathy displayed by both the Realists and the Czech Social Democrats for Jewish national aspirations; and the emergence of a new generation of intellectuals that, for the most part, had not gone through the political struggles of the 1890s and for whom the demise of the traditional German-Jewish alliance was a foregone conclusion. In many cases the attitudes of the younger Czech-Jewish writers infuriated their elders in the movement. Nowhere was the conflict of generations more acutely felt than over the question of the reception of Martin Buber and his brand of romantic mysticism.

Buber, quite simply, was a phenomenon, not only for German speakers and not only for Zionists and fellow travelers. The Czech-Jewish press covered every major publication of his and every local appearance, beginning with a review of *The Tales of Rabbi Nachman* in 1907. At that time the reviewer had found the stories interesting on the whole, but wondered aloud whether Buber's recreations of East European Jewish culture were not just a trifle artificial and removed from real life.[18] The editors of *Rozvoj* assigned Otakar Guth to cover the first of Buber's three addresses in 1909. Guth brought back mixed impressions from the evening. He described Buber as an "Old Testament prophet, visionary, and mystic, removed from the world, awkward and frightened, who spoke more to himself than to anyone else on the meaning of Judaism."[19] According to the vocabulary of the Czech-Jewish movement, it was never a compliment to be labeled "otherworldly." Yet Guth was quick to add that Buber's apparent honesty and integrity had impressed him.

When Guth reviewed the German edition of the *Drei Reden* in 1911, his earlier admiration for Buber had greatly decreased. He argued that the "religiosity" which Buber proclaimed bore little resemblance to Judaism as practiced by Jews themselves (though Buber would certainly have agreed with him on this point). Buber's faith was sui generis, owing its existence to his own unique personality and beyond the reach of the average person. "His meditations, aspirations, and dreams, removed from reality, are capable of living only a paper existence," Guth complained. While he acknowledged that the attractiveness of Buber's writings to so many people lay precisely in their "unreality," he failed to understand why anyone would think of turning the "poetic dreams" of an Otakar Březina or a Walt Whitman into a political program.[20]

Formal Czech-Jewish opinion of Buber combined fascination with suspicion. The informal proclivity of some of its younger members, however, was a good deal more positive. Apparently Josef Kodiček, Evrín Taussig, and Alfred Fuchs were genuine enthusiasts of Buber (also of the Viennese writer Otto Weininger [1880–1903]).[21] Fuchs, himself, originally had been inclined toward Zionism and was a friend of the Czech-Jewish writer Jiří Langer (1894–1943), with whom he studied Jewish mystical texts. The highest ranking member of the SČAŽ at the close of the First World War, Fuchs never lost his zeal for religious mysticism. But these interests eventually led him to abandon Judaism in the 1920s and convert to Roman Catholicism.[22]

The conflict of opinion within the Czech-Jewish movement came to a head with the appearance of the Czech edition of Buber's *Drei Reden*.[23] Viktor Vohryzek, determined to put a halt to the infatuation of his younger wing with the Berlin master, published a three-part attack in the pages of *Rozvoj*, which appeared under the provocative title "Buber's Absurdities."[24] Not only did he ridicule Buber for his imaginative, pseudoscientific, and psychological examinations of Judaism, but he castigated by implication both the Zionist intellectuals and those within the SČAŽ who listened to such theories. The article caused a serious split within *Rozvoj*'s editorial board; the younger group walked out and began to write for the paper *Přehled* (Survey). *Rozvoj* was left in such disarray that it failed to publish a single issue for the first five weeks of 1914. Thereafter it was forced to appear as a fortnightly, a format that it had abandoned in its early years.[25] The old guard had gotten the bloodletting that it wanted, but the process very nearly paralyzed serious Czech-Jewish writing.

The Impasse of the War Years

After the outbreak of the war, Czech-Jewish institutions lost much of their former maneuverability. They could not hope to be as active as they had been in the past, because nearly all of their young writers, editors, and activists had been called up to the army. What personnel they retained could not write or speek freely, since the Austrian government had clamped down on all forms of expression and now wielded the censor's scissors with abandon.[26] Nor could Czech-Jewish institutions be confident of the continued support of the Czech-speaking Jewish population. The war appeared to underscore for Jews the issue of loyalty to the modern state. In the Habsburg case, it provided Jews once again with a prime opportunity to ally with supranational, central authority in oppostion to the many centrifugal forces within. Overt support for Czech nationalism at this point lost its appeal to many, otherwise sympathetic, Jews. The lesson that the monarchy was at war, not only with the West but with the Slavic Russian Empire and with Serbia, was not lost.[27]

Its editorial staff depleted and subscriptions to the paper down, *Rozvoj* was taken over once more in August 1914, by the aging triumverate of Lederer, Vohryzek, and Klineberger. They waged a valiant effort to keep the enterprise afloat, but the paper managed to appear only intermittently and with large blank spaces in its columns where text had been removed by the government censors. In November 1915, a lack of resources and staff forced *Rozvoj* to shut down.[28] At this point point, Vohryzek retired to Pardubice where he published a new periodical called *České listy*. The name was an allusion to Siegfried Kapper's volume of Czech poems that had appeared seventy years earlier.[29] This venture, however, ended disastrously.

Klineberger wrote an article for *České listy* in which he remarked that there had been empires in history on which "the sun never set," and which nevertheless had become extinct. A punctilious censor noticed the statement and had both Klineberger and Vohryzek (as the paper's editor) arrested. The two were detained on remand in the fortress at Terezín for suspicion of high treason and eventually released.[30] Neither the town of Terezín nor its fortress-prison possessed the notoriety that was to be theirs during the next world war, but the episode of Vohryzek and Klineberger's imprisonment bears a gruesome irony all the same.

The other major Czech-Jewish organizations of Bohemia also slowed to a virtual standstill. Having lost nearly all of its officers, and most of its active members, to military service, the SČAŽ, for example, was not able to attract new members and resume any of its programming until the academic year 1916–17. Even then the problem remained as before, as the individuals with the most experience left one after the other to join the front.[31] All of the other groups, the Association of Progressive Czech Jews, the Czech-Jewish National Union, and the Czech-Jewish Political Union, simply closed their doors for the duration of the war. They were, by and large, to reemerge in late 1917 and 1918. But for the moment they were silent.[32]

To be a Czech nationalist in Austria during this time was certainly no easier than to be a Czech Jew. Most Czech young men went willingly, if not happily, to war for the emperor, but some resisted, and others deserted once in uniform. In April 1915 the twenty-eighth regiment from Prague went over en masse to the Russian side.[33] And, while many civilian leaders volunteered declarations of loyalty to the regime, others worked in varying degrees of secrecy for the destruction of the monarchy. Czech emigrés in Russia loudly voiced their desire to see the "free and independent Crown of St. Wenceslas shine in the radiance of the Crown of the Romanovs." Meanwhile, a group of nationalist politicians at home formed an underground organization known as "the Mafia" for the purpose of sabotage and passive resistance.[34]

By the spring of 1915 the Austrian authorities were engaging in severe, repressive measures against the Czech population. Václav Klofáč, the National Socialist leader, had been sitting in prison since September 1914. Karel Kramář, the National Liberal leader, was arrested on 21 May 1915, sentenced to death for high treason, but reprieved by Franz Josef to life imprisonment. Masaryk had barely escaped a similar fate by emigrating the previous December. But thousands of Czechs did face internment; the Court Martial alone passed death sentences on almost 5,000.[35]

The onset of the war did nothing to ease relations between the Jews of

Bohemia and a large portion of the Czech national movement. Many national leaders, suspicious of Jewish intentions in the past, now bristled at what they took to be the unrestrained enthusiasm of German-speaking Jewry for the war effort. Newspapers began to accuse Jews of denouncing Czech patriots to the Austrian authorities. As the war dragged on, and material shortages became more pronounced, the complaint shifted to Jewish profiteering.[36]

There must have been some truth to the charge of superpatriotism on the part of Bohemia's Jews. *Rozvoj* felt compelled to issue a front-page announcement condemning denunciations of one's fellow citizen by any civilian.[37] Max Brod, Franz Werfel, and the psychologist Max Wertheimer stumbled unconsciously into a den of ill will when they paid a visit to Masaryk in the fall of 1914 to solicit his support for the establishment of an international peace movement. Not only did Brod and his entourage underestimate Masaryk's determination to exploit the war in order to further the creation of an independent Czech state, but they apparently had been unaware of the messages that poured in to the Czech leader's office telling of the continuing denunciations and arrests of Czech nationals. Masaryk received the visitors with a distinct lack of sympathy, rejected their plea for collaboration, and suggested instead that their time would be better spent "restraining the patriotic zeal of their coreligionists."[38] The defender of Czech Jewry during the Hilsner affair was himself beginning to mistrust the Jews and despair of their political loyalties.

What Czech-Jewish writing did appear between 1914 and 1918 bore clear traces of the psychological strains that the war had produced. In the early months of the conflict, *Rozvoj* ventured to predict the final demise of Zionism. In a time of national crisis, it argued, Jews were called upon to declare their primary loyalties unequivocally. The wartime situation had produced what the Germans called a "reinliche Scheidung," a pure division. It required of everyone to stand firmly in a national camp, be it Czech, or German, or Hungarian, and to serve the monarchy together with the nation. There was no room in such a critical period for the disingenuous claim of Jewish nationality.[39] Six weeks later, however, the movement reacted with consternation to an article in *Národní listy* that had interpreted the war in precisely the opposite light. The international conflict, according to *Národní listy,* had put to rest once and for all any thoughts that the Jews could assimilate with the nations in whose midst they lived.[40]

Why? Had the Jews not met the call to arms with a unanimous, self-sacrificing patriotism? Did Jews not face one another on opposite sides of the lines, shoot at one another in fact in the name of the German, the French, or the British nation? Paradoxically, it was this very demonstration of patriotism on the part of the Jews that appeared to set them apart from their neighbors, that gave proof to the continued existence of a distinct

Jewish nation. In the words of *Národní listy,* the Jews were emerging from the conflagration "as a fighting nation." "Their ancient national character—a fighting spirit to the point of self-sacrifice—has been brought to advantage in every state that we have been able to follow."[41]

Thus, in the eyes of those who had always claimed that the Jews were unassimilable, or that they deserved their own political independence, the war was a vindication. Both *Rozvoj* and the Realist paper *Čas* protested the prognosis of *Národní listy,* but the assimilationists appeared to be trapped in a situation out of which they could not emerge uninjured.

The strains brought on by the war even caused as optimistic a figure as Evžen Stern to begin to doubt the extent of his assimilation to the Czech nation. For his 1915 contribution to the *Kalendář* had really been a fusion of two opposing moods. The first half expressed the cultural self-confidence of Czech-Jewish youth on the eve of the war. The second half consisted of a sobering reassessment, a taking of stock now that the war had shattered Jewish illusions of security and success. What had started out as a smug and clever retort to an irrelevant question ended on a desperate note. Apparently there still was a "Jewish question" in the Czech lands; assimilation was not a fait accompli; antisemitic feeling was not a relic of the past. The Czech-Jewish movement still had a primarily social task to perform: to integrate the Jews fully into the Czech nation.[42]

Stern pleaded with the Czech nation in the end to be receptive to this process, to act decently toward the Jews and to accept their offer of help in the national cause. The vision of self-determination for the small nations of Europe had yet to be realized, and the Czech movement itself was threatened by the expansionist aims of the major powers. All that the Jews asked for was a willingness on the part of the Czech people to accept Jewish aid and participation. In return, the Jews would march in the nation's *avant-garde* to help secure its rights. The small nation, Stern observed, needed to assemble all of its strengths in order to meet the aggression of the strong. It needed its Jews. Both Czech nationalism and the Czech-Jewish movement remained unfulfilled, but together the two could possess the future.[43]

Prague Zionism's Unsentimental Education

The Demise of Romanticism

Following the call to arms in August 1914, many of the young leaders of Bar Kochba—among them Hans Kohn, Robert Weltsch, Hugo Bergmann, and Oskar Epstein—set aside their teaching in Hebrew, Jewish history, and Zionism, enlisted in the army, and took their places along Austria's Eastern front.[44] They left the day-to-day affairs of Jewish nationalism in Prague to less than a handful of people. Siegmund Kaznelson, who was in his last year at the Law Faculty when the war broke out, avoided military service because he was technically "stateless." His parents were immigrants from Russia and he himself had never been naturalized.[45] Having already been the editor of *Selbstwehr* for a year, Kaznelson had to decide whether the paper should cease publication or continue to appear, even though this would have required him to publish it single-handedly and for no remuneration. Kaznelson chose the second course, rented a room from the Jüdische Frauenverein (Jewish Women's Association), which he used as an office, and, with the assistance of Lise Weltsch—his secretary and future wife—kept *Selbstwehr* alive. The only other help came from Max Brod, with whom Kaznelson met several times a week, often in the company of Franz Kafka.[46]

Those who did serve in the kaiser's army received strong encouragement from Martin Buber back in Berlin. As was true with most Central European intellectuals, Buber greeted the start of hostilities with naive elation. He wrote to Hans Kohn in September 1914, that the concept of the "Volk" had never been as real to him as it had in the past few weeks:

> If only we Jews felt—felt through and through—what this means for us: that we no longer need the old sign-post "Not by might, but by spirit." For might and spirit ought now to become one. *Incipit vita nova.*[47]

Buber's intoxication with the martial mood of 1914 had both a practical and a romantic side. On the one hand he viewed the conflict with Tsarist Russia as an opportunity to rescue the masses of East European Jews who were living in Russian Poland from the boot of oppression. Buber eagerly joined forces with German-Jewish socialists and the diaspora nationalist Nathan Birnbaum to create an Action Committee whose purpose was to receive and care for Jewish refugees in Poland, a kind of Jewish Red Cross working behind the German advance.[48] The goal was to ensure that the Polish and Russian Jewish masses would remain "nationalist" while being transported from an oppressed to an emancipated political status. "It is our hope," Buber confided to Kohn, "that the German-Austrian victories will soon give us the opportunity to carry over our work. If I cannot be on the front, I might at least be active in its vicinity."[49]

Buber never did move his Action Committee to the area of the front. Instead he remained for a year in Berlin and moved in 1916 to the small town of Heppenheim in Hesse. The lack of personal involvement in the fighting, however, did not dampen his enthusiasm for the war effort. His principal motivation from the start had been a spiritual one. For Buber saw the war as a symbolic turning point in the psychological development of European Jewry. It was the field of action on which Jews would discover and express their commitment, their sacrifice, to the community. The war was to serve as the threshold at which Jews would strip off their long-held sense of individuality and alienation and merge in unison with their fellow man. "What more can people convey to one another at this time than a greeting—a signal that one lives, thinks about the other, and is devoted to him," Buber wrote to Hugo Bergmann in the field in 1915.

> To the other, that means between actively living people; and always, in whatever way, the overarching cause and [the] community. A signal, then, of the one, unshakable [reality] in the midst of chaos: that out of the idea and out of friendship there is solidarity—not two, but one, single, great, strong, steady solidarity. It is the constructive power that manifests itself in this way, the guarantee of the coming day.[50]

The war, then, was to be the school that taught the true meaning of community. In line with a whole generation of Central European intellectuals, Buber had often contrasted the term *Gemeinschaft* (community) with *Gesellschaft* (society). The two concepts, he argued, stood for different types of social organization, one informal and vital, the other formal and lifeless, one communitarian and interdependent, the other atomized and self-destructive. Nationalism in the neo-romantic mold was to lead individuals away from their unattached and alienated existence in Gesellschaft to a new social unity in which their fate and yearnings would be bound up with those of every other individual. According to this optimistic scenario, nations that were in a state of war enjoyed a relative advantage over other states, because those forces that led to the creation of true community—altruism, self-sacrifice, common purpose, and so on—were intensified.[51]

In regions where several communities compete for power, however, the individual person might well find himself torn between rival claims to his allegiance. This was particularly true in the case of Jewish nationalists in 1914, who were not a direct party to the conflict, and who might easily have seen a contradiction between the interests of the state and those of the Jewish nation at large. Buber, surprisingly, did not address this issue in any of his correspondence during the early years of the war. He left unclear whether the "community" to which he referred incorporated the Jewish people and Jewish interests alone or rather an alliance of Jews with the people of the Central Powers. Nor did he give any indication that Jewish interests and those of Germany-Austria might not be the same over the course of the war. Lastly, he did not question what kind of community it was that pitted Jew against Jew on opposite sides of the trenches.[52]

In a speech that he gave in 1914, and which he still considered timely enough to use as the lead article in the first issue of his new periodical *Der Jude* (1916), Buber praised the Central European Jews for having discovered the true meaning of community through violence *(Gewalt)*. "He has not only seen it," Buber declaimed, "he has experienced it." In the past, the basic weakness of Western Jewry had stemmed not from the fact that they were assimilated, but that they were "atomized," shorn of all connections to the rest of mankind, including their own people. Their hearts, to use Buber's poetic imagery, "no longer chimed in with the heartbeat of a living community."[53]

Now, however—in the catastrophic event that he has experienced in the midst of the nations—the Jew has discovered in perplexity and enlightenment the great life of community. And he has grasped the fact that he is no longer an atom; he has been drawn in; he has glowingly linked up with the community that offered him in this way its life—the community which at this moment needed him the most.[54]

An oddly non-Zionist tone rings through these words. It was in fact non-Jewish society, that nation "which at this moment needed him the most," which taught the Jew in the first instance the meaning of community. War, then, held out the promise of genuine social integration, the completion of Jewish emancipation. Buber was quick to add, however, that in order for Jews permanently to enjoy the fruits of community, they had to transfer their feeling of solidarity from that group that needed them "at the moment" to the one that required them "in eternity," that is to say, to the Jewish people. "The feeling of community has glowed in" the Jew; "he has felt something burn within him; has experienced belonging. He has made the first step toward inner liberation."[55]

If Buber was to remain blissfully ignorant of the reality of war for a year or more, the same was not true of his Prague colleagues on the front lines. For them the horrible and disruptive truth of battle made itself known within the first year. They were impressed not only with the general ravages of war—shocking though they might have been—but also with the dramatic plight of the Jewish communities that lay directly along the length and breadth of the Eastern front. Galicia and the Carpathians, for example, alternated from Austrian to Russian and then back again to Austrian control, leaving their massive Jewish populations open to attack, sickness, and hunger. As the Central European Zionists watched the misery of the Jewish masses in the East, their cavalier attitude toward the conflict melted away. Hugo Bergmann wrote to Buber in 1915 of the surprisingly disorienting effect that the war was having on him:

> Like a guest in a strange house I am distanced from everything; I feel nothing other than my own being and security and do not venture to answer any question that deals with reality with a clear yes or no; I do not know where I belong—unless it be in that narrow circle of friendship and love in which I admittedly feel all the more strongly placed.[56]

The war had heightened Bergman's sense of individual isolation. His was a soul adrift, uncertain of that community at which he might lay anchor.

Robert Weltsch wrote to Bergmann in a similar tone in May 1915. His most important lesson from the war so far had been that his path lay far away from the general direction that the world was taking:

> I have experienced a great disillusionment, so much so that the feeling of growing rage has flattened out into deep contempt. I never thought that in times

which were to be the most earnest frivolity like this could celebrate such triumphs, especially if the triumph of unreason were involved.[57]

There was certainly no regeneration of mankind to be found here, he concluded. Between July and November Weltsch wrote to Buber from the Galician front and reiterated his experiences of disillusionment and disdain. He wrote that he no longer expected to see the "workings of the spirit" make themselves known through the course of the war, but instead was resigned to wait out a long, drawn-out, bloody conflict. His only hope was that the spiritual transformation that he had hoped to witness might take place once the war was over.[58]

Also strongly affected by the events of 1914 to 1918—though not necessarily by the fighting itself—was Hans Kohn. He had been in active duty only a short while before he was taken prisoner by the Russians in March 1915. And he was to remain in Russia (primarily in Siberia and Central Asia) until January 1920, when the eastward advance of the Bolshevik armies persuaded him to return to Prague. During his imprisonment in Russia, Kohn often found himself free to travel to local towns. Toward the end of his confinement, he had gained access to libraries and was allowed to organize classes and discussion groups on Jewish history and nationalism. In his spare time he learned Russian, English, and French, translated modern Hebrew literary works into German, and began to acquire a number of Asian languages, including Arabic.[59] He was particularly moved by the course of the Russian Revolution and by what he considered to be the brutalizing effects of Russian imperialism in Asia. Toward the end of November 1917, he sent a letter to Martin Buber in which he tried to explain that he was no longer the same person who had set off to war three years earlier:

> I have experienced a great deal in the [intervening] three years, more than in the twenty-three previous ones, seen, learned, read, and thought about much—all of this has in many respects made me riper, richer, more honest. I have experienced the orient, learned languages, gained much equipment for life. In fifteen months of solitary "imprisonment" I have had time to argue with myself, with God, and with the world. In so doing I must have become a different person, for, having been "released" two months ago, I have been able to exert a great influence on my comrades.[60]

Prague's Jewish soldiers transformed their wartime experiences into a measuring rod against which to judge prewar positions and occupations. In criticizing the immediate past, they emerged with one overwhelming conclusion: past concerns had not sufficiently dealt with reality or with the larger Jewish community. Prague Zionism of the *Vom Judentum* era had devoted all of its efforts to the intellectual cultivation of the individual. In truth it had sought to deepen Jewish consciousness and commitment, but had not bothered to attract or serve the mass of Bohemian Jewry. Nor had it shown the individual Zionists how to transform their Jewishness from an affair of intellectual contemplation to a living reality. When the Zionists reached the front lines, they realized how ill-prepared they had been to confront the actual conditions of a living, but suffering, and socially dislocated, Jewish nation. They needed desperately to discover how to breathe life into a "salon Judaism" cast cruelly out of its milieu.[61]

Hugo Bergmann—who before the war had been one of the few in Prague to be engaged in an active reconstruction of Jewish national culture—came to regard the war's only saving grace in the fact that it forced participants to distinguish between reality and illusion.[62] It forced Western Europeans to abandon their idealized picture of East European reality, for one thing, and it demanded of them that they create a Judaism that could function in everyday life. For his own part, the war had brought with it a partial alienation from the Jewish people. Fighting alongside Germans and Austrians, Bergmann realized that his own sense of nationalism owed more to Fichte than to Herzl. The common cause with German culture made him painfully aware of the fragility of his separate Jewish identity:

> Now that we have fought for German culture, we feel more than ever what it means for us and how we continue to stand in it with our whole being. . . . Only because we had Fichte did we find the corresponding movements of Jewish culture, only then did we understand Judaism. In the former we were raised; the latter we discovered.[63]

All of this indicated to Bergmann the need to redefine one's Zionism, to reintegrate it into one's daily interests and even one's profession. "I yearn for the noble way in which people of other nations grow and develop and precisely in so doing serve their people. I yearn for this not only because I . . . feel that we can serve our Judaism through our humanity, and that Jewish work that is not related to our development as men cannot be fruitful—I feel above all that such a life has no reality."[64]

For Hans Kohn the redefinition of Zionism meant reducing it from the grandiose proportions that it had enjoyed in his mind around 1913 to a size and scope that was more in keeping with the lessons of his confinement in Central Asia. His years of enforced leisure may have given him the luxury of continuing and expanding the intellectual pursuits of his youth, but his proximity to the cataclysmic events of the Russian Revolution and to the rise of various national movements among the Asian peoples convinced Kohn to direct his attention to what he referred to as "humanity's social problem." In a letter of 1917, which he asked Robert Weltsch to read aloud before the new members of Bar Kochba, Kohn explained: "Today I see human suffering more sharply; I feel more heavily the bonds that tie us to all that is human."[65]

Kohn ceased to consider Zionism to be a kind of intellectual confession that could be arrived at only from deep within the soul of the individual and whose chief function was to provide the individual Jew with a new, revitalized Weltanschauung. To his earlier fascination with philosophical questions he supplemented increasing attention to the economic and social factors at work in history. "I have realized more and more," he wrote to Buber, "that we must move forward from our 'conversation with God' to influence the foundations of society, that we also have to orient our Zionism in a more social-political direction."[66] The Russian episode in Kohn's life had radicalized him, and he began to elaborate a position that demanded of Zionism not only that it work to affect lives and events in the real world, but that it—as a true revolution—usher in the world to come:

> I hope very much that people at home have also become more honest, contemplative, more eager to take responsibility—that they are closer to the essence of the times—and that we will face a new humanity, the new dawn of our prophets, the coexistence of peoples in justice, truth, and peace. This era will also be just to us. And so I see the fate of our people bound up with that of humanity. . . . The conviction becomes stronger and stronger in me that the salvation of the nations once again will come forth from Zion if we are successful in allowing the new Sabbath to break forth, the Sabbath over which a "separation" will never again be made.[67]

Kohn used the Hebrew word for separation, *havdala,* which is also the name of the religious ceremony at the close of the Sabbath in which its distinction from the rest of the week is emphasized. In so doing, he was alluding to a letter that Buber had written to him in August 1917, in which Buber had enclosed part of his contribution to Bar Kochba's 1917 publication *Das Jüdische Prag.* It was, he wrote, "directed particularly to you." The passage involved the retelling of a well-known legend concerning the life of Rabbi Judah Löw ben Bezalel (ca. 1525–1609), known in Jewish tradition by the acronym Maharal. In the story the Maharal was forced to postpone the Sabbath, as he had forgotten to remove from the mouth of the Golem (an artificial being made of clay) the piece of paper on which was written the holy name of God. The Golem could get no rest—indeed would wreak havoc on the Jewish quarter—until the piece of paper were removed. Buber ended his own rendition of the legend with a reminder that the great Sabbath, the messianic era, had not yet been realized. "It is not yet the Sabbath. First we must pull the [holy] name from under the tongue of the Golem."[68]

Commitment to Gegenwartsarbeit

Over the course of the war and its aftermath, the Prague Zionists one by one turned their attention to the practical application of the national program. One sign of their sincerity in this endeavor can be found in the new occupations that many of them took, each of which represented a merging of career and political commitment. By the end of 1918 Hugo Bergmann was urging Buber to accompany him to Palestine, where together they might form a

committee for the establishment of a Jewish university—or at least a teachers' college—in Jerusalem. Buber, however, complaining that his Hebrew
was not yet fluent enough, was reluctant to leave Germany. Nevertheless,
Bergmann left his position as librarian at the University Library in Prague in
1919 in order to become secretary of the Cultural Department in the Zionist
Office in London. The following year he emigrated to Palestine and founded
the Jewish National and University Library, which opened officially in
1925.[69] Max Brod taught at a school for Galician refugees in Prague that had
been established by Alfred Engel, a professor at Brno. After 1916, Brod
became a regular contributor to Buber's journal *Der Jude,* helping also to
formulate its editorial positions. In 1918 he cofounded the Jewish National
Council (Národní rada židovská) of Czechoslovakia, which represented the
interests of the Jewish national minority in the new Republic.[70] Siegmund
Kaznelson, the mainstay behind *Selbstwehr* during the war, joined the editorial board of *Der Jude* after 1918; two years later he assumed the director-
ship of the Berlin-based Jüdischer Verlag.[71]

A number of Czech Zionists occupied key positions in the world Zionist
movement during and at the end of the war. Hugo Herrmann served as
editor-in-chief of the Berlin weekly *Jüdische Rundschau* from 1913 to 1914.
Following demobilization he was editor of *Jüdisches Volksblatt,* published in
Moravská-Ostrava (Mährisch-Ostrau) from 1919 until 1922—at which point
it merged with *Selbstwehr*—and the head of Keren Hayesod (Palestine Foundation Fund) in Czechoslovakia until his emigration to Palestine in 1934.[72]
His cousin Leo Herrmann was brought to Berlin in 1913 to assume the
position of secretary of the World Zionist Organization. As noted earlier, he
helped to establish the Keren Hayesod in 1919, together with the Moravian-
born Berthold Feiwel, and served as its secretary general in Jerusalem from
1926 until his death in 1951.[73]

Ludvík Singer, the most prominent of the Czech-speaking Zionists, cofounded the Národní rada židovská with Max Brod in 1918 and also edited
the Czech-language Zionist weekly *Židovské zprávy* (Jewish news). He attended the Paris Peace Conference at the close of the war, as did Hugo
Bergmann, to represent Jewish national interests, was chairman of the Jewish National party in Czechoslovakia, and in this capacity was also elected to
Parliament.[74] Robert Weltsch worked as a correspondent in Vienna during
the revolutionary crisis of 1918–19. Thereafter, until 1938, he occupied the
position of editor-in-chief of *Jüdische Rundschau,* thus becoming the most
visible Zionist journalist in all of Central Europe.[75] As for Hans Kohn, after
his return to the West, he held posts in the Zionist Organization in London,
Paris, and Jerusalem—the last from 1925 to 1929. Several years later, however, he moved to the United States where he would live out his life, alienated from the mainstream of the Zionist movement and increasingly suspicious of what he took to be the excesses of nationalism in all of its guises.[76]

The new political occupations of the Prague Zionists did not prevent them from continuing to engage in theoretical writing. But theory was no longer tied to the free flow of the imagination. Now it was to be disciplined, harnessed in order to serve the practical needs of Jewish nationalism. Although Buber, as we have seen, maintained romantic notions about the effects of war longer than did many of his younger contemporaries, he did conclude the opening essay in *Der Jude* with a more earthly analysis of the relationship between the war and the Jewish community. The illusion that one could live in a time such as this cut off from "community," he wrote, looking in from the outside or merely voicing formal allegiance to it, had been shattered. "Whoever wants to proceed with his existence on the earth must begin with his relationship to the community . . . he [must] feel himself to be responsible."[77]

Hugo Bergmann and Oskar Epstein started essentially from this position in their own assessments of the problem of Gemeinschaft. For them the war had not worked some kind of benign magic on the souls of assimilated Jews. It had confronted all people, Jews included, with the blunt realities of violence and suffering, and it had extorted from Zionist intellectuals a deathbed confession, a promise to give up the frivolities of the past in favor of real intellectual discipline and commitment. Bergmann made what was perhaps the most important statement on the need to redirect Jewish nationalism in his article "Der jüdische Nationalismus nach dem Krieg" (Jewish nationalism after the war), which appeared in *Der Jude* in 1916.[78] In it he accepted the notion that the war, however traumatic, had brought to its Jewish participants a taste of life in community. The individual did experience what it was like to devote all of one's energies to the collectivity, and, although it was unclear what the final outcome would be for Jewish nationalism, the war had at least taught the Jew to appreciate the movement of history and the role of the group in historical change.[79]

Furthermore, because the war had forced Jews to become active, to take up arms, it also encouraged them to respond to it through concrete action. The Jews had a choice: they could be overcome with grief at the sight of suffering and death—and thus continue a literary tradition that dated back to the Crusades—or they could respond with the determination to control their own destiny, to effect change in their own community in their lifetime. The choice, in Bergmann's eyes, was to react as refugees or as soldiers. But to become a Zionist soldier meant to set out to build a Jewish national reality in Europe as well as in Palestine. Above all it meant avoiding the trap of intellectual abstraction into which the prewar Zionists had fallen. Bergmann likened them to the European socialists who had preached internationalism and brotherhood only to be pulled apart by patriotic considerations at the start of the war:

What mistake did all of the intellectuals make—such well-meaning men and such bad politicians—who lulled us into a dream of peace out of which we awakened so cruelly? They did not take into account the true interests of man, but rather [those of] an illusory image, a holiday person *(Feiertagsmensch),* an abstraction. Clearly it was not the idea of peace or of the brotherhood of nations which was at fault, but rather the superficial psychology of many of their adherents, who felt that they could master reality through addresses at congresses, toasts, and the exchange of telegrams.[80]

The same was true of prewar Zionism. "It saw 'Jews' and preached a 'Judaism' that neither was the result of forces that moved actual Jewish life, nor gave direction to strengths at hand. Rather it was a theoretical abstraction, like the Socialist International."[81] Zionists, Bergmann complained, used to leave their real worries at home and allowed an unreal holiday spirit—their *neshama yetera* (additional soul)—to take control of their gatherings and debates. But when the holiday was over and the work week began once again, Jewish nationalism and real life parted ways. It was as if nothing had happened; no one was changed. The whole problem of Zionism, then, was to integrate itself into the everyday life of the Jews, to create a "Jewish reality." Thus far Zionists had been able to create such a reality only in Palestine, but had left Western and Central Europe virtually untouched. "I demand respect for facts," Bergmann warned, "an honest discussion with life."[82]

Bergmann's "honest discussion with life" referred to the *galut* (exile). The task of Zionism in the aftermath of the war was to nationalize Jewish life in Western and Central Europe. For if those who doubted either the feasibility or desirability of an autonomous Jewish existence in the exile were correct, then any division between Jews and non-Jews was purely artificial and, as such, could be discarded. If this were the case, Zionists would have no right to complain about assimilation or to disturb its natural progress. The only way, Bergmann concluded, morally to justify Zionist activity in galut was for this work to encompass everything that touched Jewish lives:

> Judaism is nothing other than the entirety, the integral of all that Jewish people do; and so nothing that is human should be foreign to our Jewish striving. All that is human must be at home in us, all that is Jewish should pulsate with the living blood of lived humanity. Second, comprehensive Judaism must be Zionist, that is, arranged in the will toward community.[83]

In general the war years strengthened the commitment of the Prague Zionists to what they called Gegenwartsarbeit, nationalist activity that aimed specifically at diaspora Jewry and that had no overtly political goal other than to permit Jews to develop a full national life. Hugo Bergmann had raised this theme back in 1913 in an address to the Bohemian Zionist *Distriktstag* (district meeting). Zionism had a responsibility, he argued then, not only to the construction of a Jewish home in Palestine, but also to the 85,000 Jews who were living in Bohemia. "Zionism must decide clearly and forcefully whether—alongside work in Palestine—it can also take upon itself the care for these needs or whether it must hand it over to others."[84] True national life, he argued, was organic and anarchic, and not to be confused with a political program of any kind. One of the major faults of the Zionist movement in the West had been the misconception that one could make real Jews out of people simply by bringing them to mouth a political confession. Bergmann acknowledged the argument of people such as Hans Kohn and Robert Weltsch that one had to allow people to come to a Zionist conviction freely, of their own choice. But that was no reason to stand idly by, with one's hands in one's pockets, waiting for the nationalization of the Jews to occur through some miracle.[85]

Rather, the example of other newly awakened nations, in particular the Czechs, pointed to the fact that the touchstone of national consciousness was to be found in the home, the school, and the club. Success in these areas far outweighed any defeats on the larger political front. The most important goal that Bohemian Zionism could accomplish, it followed, was an educational one: to raise its children as Jewishly as possible.

> What is the goal of our work in the *galut?* We want to leave the *galut* even if geographically we must remain in it. We want to have a living Jewish community which does not cling to the outside, but which concentrates on itself.[86]

Oskar Epstein joined Bergmann in 1916 to promote Gegenwartsarbeit even more forcefully than in the past. Publishing his own manifesto in the same volume of *Der Jude* in which Bergmann's work had appeared, Epstein defended Berdyczewski's position that Zionism had to be synonymous with a nondogmatic, and therefore vibrant, Jewish culture. Judaism did not have a specific intellectual content or direction; it was not a "way of looking at the world"; it *was* the world, that is to say, the world of Jewish cultural creativity. Hoping to free Judaism from the chilly clutches of both political Zionists and Jewish intellectuals, Epstein called for the creation of national Jewish institutions which would cover all activities and areas of life and obviate the need for Zionists to affiliate with any non-Zionist organizations.[87]

Epstein also turned to Ahad Ha'am's scheme for Palestine to serve as the cultural center for world Jewry. He pointed out, however, that Palestine would have no impact at all on a Jewish diaspora that no longer possessed the consciousness of belonging to a Jewish community. "The whole ideology of a national center in Palestine would be meaningless if in the diaspora itself Judaism did not little by little embrace and penetrate all of the interests of the individual."[88] Real nationalism, then, had to be based on the relationships of real life. The distinctive, external characteristics of the nation would arise more or less naturally; they required no deliberate push.

Hans Kohn, too, argued for the intensification of Gegenwartsarbeit following the war's end. Zionism had at stake the regeneration of the entire Jewish people. If it concentrated solely on the development of Palestine, it did so at its own peril.

> We do not need *Gegenwartsarbeit* solely because—as so often is said—without a
> strong diaspora Palestine cannot be strong . . . rather, cultural activity in the
> present [*Gegenwartsarbeit*] is Zionist work; it is an integral, unerasable element
> of the work of regeneration.[89]

If specific content matter did not determine the scope of Judaism, what
did? On this point Bergmann and Epstein agreed fully: it was not the message itself that could be called Jewish, but the vehicle through which it was
transmitted. Language, then, occupied a pivotal position; in the case of
Northern and Eastern Europe this meant either Hebrew or Yiddish. But in
addition they pointed to the building blocks of Jewish culture, the literary
sources of Jewish tradition—from the Bible down to contemporary speci-
mens of Hebrew and Yiddish literature. What made a person's culture Jewish was the fact that it was transmitted through the national language of the
Jews and was informed by the classical sources of Judaism. Bergmann offered this definition in an essay, which appeared in the fourth volume of *Der
Jude,* "The Hebrew Book and the German Zionists," and defended it in a
heated exchange of letters with Buber.[90] Because the bulk of the Jewish
population in Western Europe was cut off from its language, Bergmann
observed, the entire Zionist movement risked remaining what it had been at
the start: a literary society.

> How are we to be free of the awesome responsibility that we have taken upon
> ourselves with this Judaism of speeches (which were once actions) unless—if
> we cannot in fact become farmers in Palestine—we at least take a step toward
> reality: that we engage ourselves in Hebrew literature and free ourselves from
> that which is foreign, that we speak—as much as possible through the strength
> of education—to the lost sheep of Israel and not, in the first instance, to
> strangers.[91]

Eventually Buber himself came around to Bergmann's point of view. At the
end of October 1919 he conceded, "What you said to me a month ago
concerning our relationship to Hebrew I must [now] recognize as correct."[92]

Galicia in Prague, Prague in Galicia

To many within the Zionist movement "the lost sheep of Israel" were the
Yiddish-speaking, nationally self-conscious Jews of Eastern Europe. Since
the beginning of the twentieth century, Central European Jewish intellectuals had alternatively eulogized or idealized the *Ostjuden,* used them as a
frame of reference in their own cultural struggles, but few had any firsthand
knowledge of Jewish life "east" of Germany and Austria.[93] This situation
changed suddenly in 1914. With the Eastern front moving back and forth
across Galicia, Jewish refugees by the thousands fled westward. Late in 1914
the Ostjuden arrived in Prague. They provided the Jewish community there
what, for all intents and purposes, was its first real exposure to East Euro-

pean Jewish culture. The only other taste of this life had come by way of the
traveling theater troupe from Lwów, which played in the city in 1911 and
1912, and to which Franz Kafka had been so devoted.[94] At that time, however, the members of Bar Kochba did not show much interest in the Yiddish-
speaking actors. They were content, instead, to draw inspiration from
Buber's idealized portraits of Hasidic life. The more realistic and graphic
descriptions of East European Jewish culture lay buried in the pages of
Kafka's diaries.[95]

The Jewish notables of wartime Prague, including some Zionists, appeared to be more taken aback than pleased at the influx of their poorer and
less-educated brethren. They did set up an emergency committee to supply
the Galician and Bukovinian Jews with food, clothing, and shelter, but by
and large they were put off balance by the dirt and misery, which they never
before had associated with Jews. One old-time Zionist remarked to a colleague from Krakow, who was then residing in Prague, "this is the first time
that we have ever seen Jewish rabble in Prague. Before the war it was
possible to see German rabble or Czech rabble, but we didn't know anything
about a Jewish rabble."[96] This was probably one of the milder reproaches
leveled at the East European refugees at the time. Much less generous was
the remark made by the Czech-Jewish paper *Rozvoj* that the only thing that
bound Czech Jews to these refugees was a feeling of "patriotic sympathy" for
people who had been persecuted by a common enemy:

> No reasonable person would claim that they are our brothers. Their religion is
> certainly not ours; and if one takes a look at the physiognomy of these Jews, one
> could not even claim that we are members of the same race.[97]

A significant minority of Prague Jews, however, not only cared about the
welfare of the East European refugees but also used the opportunity of their
presence in the city to deepen their own understanding of Jewish national
culture. Max Brod stood out prominently among these individuals. Having
been able to serve out most of the war in the city's General Post Office, he
helped to keep Jewish politics alive in Prague while most of his colleagues
were away at the front. Brod was recruited by Alfred Engel to teach a course
on world literature to girls aged fifteen to nineteen at the Notschule für
jüdische Flüchtlinge aus dem Osten (Emergency School for Jewish Refugees
from the East). He discovered after a short time of teaching that he, too, was
a beneficiary of this experiment in national education.

Writing in *Der Jude* of his recent experiences as a teacher, Brod remarked
that now—following years of talk about the need to establish a system of
national Jewish education in Austria—Prague finally had a modern, national, Jewish school.[98] And it was attended by no less than 1,400 students.
Even the Orthodox circles, which had resisted sending their children to
government institutions in Galicia and Bukovina, gave their full support to
the Jewish school in Prague, where classes were held on Sundays instead of

Saturdays and where boys covered their heads in the traditional manner. The experience also convinced Brod both of the feasibility and of the necessity of creating more national Jewish schools throughout Central and Eastern Europe, particularly in areas recently freed from Russian control. National Jewish education was not only in the best interests of the Jews, but also worked toward the creation of better citizens, steeped in their own ethnic and religious heritage.[99]

The very art of teaching, Brod mused, was entirely different in an atmosphere such as the one at the school for Jewish refugees. Beyond being moved by the directness of the East European girls, their honesty, naiveté, and thirst for education, he was impressed by the naturalness of their national identity. "I feel that I can appeal to a tradition, a common feeling of all the students. I have a people, a community, before me, not atomized *(zersiebte)* individuals."

> And one can lecture on Homer much better to a nation than to such delicately formed individuals. Something of the national energy which the writer brings together in his work, something of the tragedy of the solitary figure, who is separated from his people but fervently reaches out to them, to the community . . . something of these ties of communal feeling is alive among these students.[100]

The war years permitted some within the Prague Jewish community to have direct, personal contact for the first time with that brand of East European Judaism known as Hasidism. Jiří Langer, born in 1894 a son of the Czech-Jewish bourgeoisie, served as personal guide to many a Westernized Prague Jew. Like Hugo Bergmann before him, Langer had sought out Hasidic life on his own, journeying to the congregation of the Belzer Rebbe in Eastern Galicia in 1913. Unlike Bergmann, however, he attached himself to the master's court and became a devout member of the community.[101] Langer shocked his middle-class family when he suddenly turned up at the railroad station after many months wearing a long black coat, fur-trimmed hat, beard, and earlocks. As his brother later explained, "[Jiří] had not come back from Belz, to home and civilization; he had brought Belz with him."[102]

Langer returned to the Galician Hasidim shortly before the outbreak of war in 1914, summoned apparently by the Belzer Rebbe, who appeared to him in a vision in the family kitchen. When the members of the Belz community found themselves in what amounted to the middle of a battlefield, they managed to escape for the time being to Hungary. It was here that Jiří Langer received his call-up orders, and he was compelled to return for the second time to the estranged city of his birth.[103]

Langer was no more willing to make life easy for the Austrian authorities than he had been for his own family. The army after a short time threw him into prison for refusing to take part in military exercises on the Sabbath.

Langer compounded the insult to his superior officers by refusing to speak during his court martial. Fortunately for him, his brother František (who was a physician as well as a writer) found himself in Prague on leave at an expeditious moment, and argued convincingly for Jiří's lack of emotional stability. Essentially, František Langer simply reported in detail on his brother's behavior over the previous two years. The army sent Jiří home as a mental case.[104]

Following his discharge, Langer could often be found in the company of Hasidic groups in Prague and the spa towns of Western Bohemia. On a number of occasions he invited his friends Max Brod and Franz Kafka to accompany him, to witness and perhaps take part in the lively singing and dancing that punctuated Hasidic worship. Kafka's diary entry of 14 September 1915 recounts a visit that he made with Langer and Brod on a Saturday afternoon to the house of a Hasidic rabbi in Žižkov, one of the working-class suburbs of Prague. The room in which the rabbi and his disciples sat bristled with humanity; directly outside armies of children scampered up and down the stairs; women huddled together in an adjoining cubicle, their heads shielded by white kerchiefs. The visitors hesitated momentarily as they were led to a table at the rabbi's right, only to be assured by an unidentifiable voice, "You are Jews too, after all." At the same time, Langer leaned over and whispered to Kafka, "All rabbis look ferocious."[105]

Kafka and Brod had no illusions about the gulf that separated their culture from that of East European Jewry. But they and many of their colleagues did set out to lessen the divide, to apprehend through direct experience what they saw as the natural and genuine Judaism of Eastern Europe. Kafka, having already tasted a strong dose of Eastern European Jewish folklore from Yitshok Levi of the Lwów theater troupe, established close ties with Langer after 1914. He made careful notes in his diary of the Hasidic tales that Langer told and eagerly accepted invitations from his friend to visit circles of Hasidic refugees in Central Europe. Once, while convalescing in Marienbad (Marienské Lázně) in 1916, Kafka learned from Max Brod that the Belzer Rebbe and his followers were also in town.[106] Kafka sought Jiří Langer out from among the Rebbe's entourage and requested that he be allowed to accompany the Hasidim on their walking rounds of the resort. The descriptions that he sent back to Brod are marked by the same combination of humor, detachment, and sympathy that characterized his impressions of the Lwów actors. Kafka was both attracted and repelled by the coarse, immediate reality of East European Jewish life. But few topics did he pursue in his diaries and letters with as much passion and devotion.[107]

Robert Weltsch's contact with East European Judaism was made on the battlefields of Galicia. He enjoyed neither the relative tranquillity of Kafka's walks with the Rebbe of Belz nor the long periods of intensive interaction between student and teacher at the school for Jewish refugees in

Prague. Weltsch could make only brief and periodic contact with Galician and Polish Jews, and for the most part what he saw was poverty, suffering, and the disruption of traditional Jewish life. He reported back to Jews in the West that the war threatened to tear apart the very structure of Jewish life in Poland. Young men were on the run, traditional patterns of authority within the family lay in ruins, and young girls were encouraged to fraternize with German and Austrian soldiers. "The Jewish girl is pulled into the whirlwind of this changing life; she is blinded by the glare of the unaccustomed surroundings."[108]

In Weltsch's view the problem of direct contact with the soldiers was all the more acute because the Orthodox girls of Eastern Europe had been cut off, by and large, from traditional Jewish education during their teenage years (unlike Jewish boys). Not only were they not as knowledgeable as the boys their age, but many also did not possess the same devotion to the rules and obligations of normative Judaism. In this regard, he thought, the school for Jewish refugees in Prague was performing a tremendous service in the perpetuation of Jewish culture in Europe during a period of great disruption.[109]

Not all that Weltsch had to report from the front was gloomy. He had much praise for the Zionist schools in Poland in which both boys and girls were taught to speak and read Hebrew fluently. Weltsch was amazed at how students who finished these schools were able to quote freely from modern-day poets such as Ḥayyim Naḥam Bialik and David Frischmann as well as from the prophets Isaiah and Jeremiah.[110] In a letter to Hugo Bergmann—the details of which were also published in *Der Jude*—Weltsch told of encounters with Hebrew-speaking girls in the town of Swodiecz. He learned, in conversation with one, of her attendance at a Hebrew language school over the objection of her parents and the open hostility of her Polish neighbors. Shortly before the war the school had been shut down, but a number of the students continued to make every effort to perpetuate Hebrew as their primary language. They even founded a Hebrew Association (Ivriah), which already possessed an impressive library:

> For all the terrible tragedy of the situation, I (nevertheless) could have shouted for joy that there were still such healthy and good examples of the national element. Of course there are also Hebraists who have gone another way, but in her I found the highest conception of Zionism—not that Zionism consisted of speaking Hebrew, but that above all [it] meant a feeling of moral responsibility.[111]

In his report to *Der Jude* Weltsch concluded that these girls truly understood what Zionism meant: not a program of slogans, but a *Lebensprogramm,* a directed course of action which guided one's daily life. In language that harked back to Bergmann's "Heiligung des Namens," he characterized their nationalism as "the will to hallow life, the will to stand alone for the health and purity of the community. . . . They know that nationalism above all means the truth and reality of individual life."[112]

Das jüdische Prag

In 1917, while Europe was bogged down in the third year of its war, *Selbstwehr's* skeleton staff prepared to commemorate its tenth anniversary.[113] Previous anniversaries of student Zionism in Prague (1903 and 1913) had occasioned the issuing of *Festschriften,* and the 1917 event proved to be no exception. Siegmund Kaznelson, *Selbstwehr's* editor, solicited contributions from diverse sources—soldiers on the front, Berlin and Viennese intellectuals, Czech poets and writers, and communal activists in Prague—to produce the slim but dignified anthology *Das jüdische Prag* (Jewish Prague). One could say that Prague Zionism's transition from the mystical, neo-romantic preoccupations of its earlier years to a less exalted, more pragmatic conception of Jewish cultural activity reached its symbolic consummation in this work. Unlike the two Bar Kochba Festschriften, *Neue Wege* (New paths) and *Vom Judentum, Das jüdische Prag* did not pretend to represent a revolutionary, cultural statement. It was not designed to "point the way" to a new form of Jewish expression, but rather to capture and preserve an existing quality. Kaznelson, the child of Russian emigrants to Bohemia and an adoptive son of Prague, sensed that the city's uniqueness derived in large measure from the centuries-long Jewish presence, and that this presence could be discovered in all areas of Prague cultural life. His main editorial preoccupation, then, was to uncover the chain of historical continuity in Jewish Prague and then to link it up to the cultural and intellectual activities of his own day.[114]

Despite the difficult wartime conditions, Kaznelson managed to solicit contributions from more than forty-five writers. He cast his net widely and imposed no ideological restrictions on the respondents. "In this work," he explained, "our only intention must be unpremeditation" (*unsere einzige Absicht die Absichtslosigkeit sein muss*).[115] Nevertheless, he did have a strategy that he hoped would ensure general thematic integrity. Those authors who were not part of "Jewish Prague" were asked to comment directly on this as a topic. Short scholarly essays on Prague Jewish history and culture also spoke directly to the chosen theme. But the contributions of Prague Jewish writers themselves were included without concern for subject matter on the assumption that they naturally, if indirectly, gave expression to the spirit of the milieu.[116]

Though produced in German, *Das jüdische Prag* went out of its way to include a large section of Czech poetry and prose on Jewish themes. Kaznelson himself was an intimate of Brod and Kafka, but he was determined to broaden the definition of "Jewish Prague" (for his Central European readership) to include the whole spectrum of works written in "that language . . . which the majority of the Prague population speaks." Only in this way, he argued, could the Jewish elements in Prague's cultural life make themselves fully known.[117] Thus the poems of Otakar Březina, J. S. Machar,

Jaroslav Vrchlický, K. H. Mácha (1810–36), and others—translated by some of the truly bilingual representatives of German-Jewish culture—stood along-side pieces by Kafka, Oskar Baum, Franz Werfel, and Rudolf Fuchs in a cross-cultural panorama of Prague's Jewish spirit.[118]

Bar Kochba's 1914 opus *Vom Judentum* had blatantly ignored questions of historical continuity. Its concern had been for Erlebnis and for the kind of heroic creativity that was to herald a new age for Jews. *Selbstwehr's Das jüdische Prag,* in contrast, celebrated history. Its pages were filled with illustrations depicting Prague's Jewish past: the Alt-Neu Synagogue, Rabbi Judah Löw ben Bezalel, the Jewish expulsion from Prague in 1745. Even examples from the mid-nineteenth century—the high point of German-Jewish assimilationism—were included, as if to avoid breaking the chain of events that linked the twentieth-century Prague Jews to their distant past.[119] Essays on Jewish history made up 20 percent of the volume, and another short section was devoted to the recent experiences of East European Jews in the Bohemian capital.

Vom Judentum's implicit rejection of history had stemmed from ideologi-cal presumptions concerning Zionism's antagonistic relationship to the Jew-ish past as well as from romantic impatience with the limitations imposed by "external" contingencies. Its ignorance had been a sign of naive optimism in the redemptive power of cultural creativity. *Das jüdische Prag's* obsession with history, or, more exactly, with the problem of historical continuity, reflected the sobering effect that the war had had on the young Prague Zionists. Mysticism and heroic striving had lost their credibility; the reality of a Jewish historical tradition, of a Jewish cultural continuum, represented a new point of reference, a genuine foundation upon which to build a Jewish future in the Czech lands. Their's was a hopeful, but not necessarily optimis-tic, attempt. They longed to know the past and to build a Jewish future upon it, but they were also aware that the history of Jewish Prague remained largely inaccessible to them. As Robert Weltsch wrote:

> We know an old cemetery and a synagogue, which are shown to strangers, the last remains of a once living Jewish quarter; we know of old family traditions, jokes, and riddles that have come down to us, which speak of a world of affection, goodness, joy of life, and, above all, of the strongest connectedness; a world in which our fathers still grew up, but which for us has disappeared. The entire chain of events, sorrows, and excitement, of striving and of laughter—this whole history of living, Jewish Prague—we do not know.[120]

Nevertheless, Weltsch argued, Jewish Prague is our cultural heritage. It is what consistently saves us and gives us direction in this manifold world. An entire generation has been cut off from its past, has sacrificed itself to Gentile society, taught itself to cultivate aesthetic refinements, to give voice to the pain of the world *(Weltschmerz)* while blowing rings of smoke in big-city coffee houses. It lives an empty existence because it has lost its spiritual homeland and "the life-giving strength of community." "The sons now know, however, that one thing is needed: the building of a new—to use an old Prague Jewish word—'old-new' society." The new Gemeinschaft will not recreate the life of the Prague ghetto, but will have silent, inner relations to it. "A web of strong, unbreakable spirit will bind the two together, just as it binds the fathers and the sons over and above all antitheses."[121]

In addition to the literary and historical pieces, *Das jüdische Prag* did include essays of a more theoretical nature. These, however, were directed toward the question of community and social ethics and coincided nicely with the authors' concerns for historical reconstruction. Max Brod's essay on community, the title of which recalled articles that appeared frequently in *Der Jude*, approached the issue from a serious, Kantian perspective.[122] Brod fixed his attention on the conflict between the right of individual freedom and the right of society to regulate itself and pursue harmony among its members. He suggested that one of the main functions of the community was to sharpen people's moral sensibilities; humanity was only as moral as it showed itself to be in its social contacts. Nowhere in Brod's analysis could be found the high-flung notions of the mystically founded Gemeinschaft that used to appear in the writings of the prewar Zionists. Instead Gemeinschaft lay somewhere between isolation and friendship, a complex of people that was essentially foreign to one's self, but nevertheless loving, forgiving, vital, and meaningful.[123]

Felix Weltsch's contribution, based on a philosophical examination of the Hebrew prayer "Shema Yisrael" (Hear O Israel), linked *Das jüdische Prag* both topically and temperamentally to Hugo Bergmann's earlier work on Kiddush ha-shem (sanctification of the name of God).[124] Bergmann's investigation into the core of Jewish spirituality had underscored man's responsibility in the realization of God in the world. Weltsch likened the recitation of the "Shema"—also basic to the Jewish religious outlook—to the phenomenon of the "good will."

The decision to act morally represented "an affirmation of the will in the widest sense." It was not merely "a passive 'being for something'; not a calm taking of interest, which simply accepts an event, but an effort to take action, a will to action, to activity."[125] Above all, the moral decision involved the preparedness to take part in the world, trustingly and absolutely. This kind of position taking also characterized the central prayer of Jewish worship. One who recited "Shema Yisrael" expressed the conviction that "there is a true unity to be realized." To "love God," the basic command of the "Shema" paragraph, meant to engage in the most fundamental of moral choices, to be "good," to direct one's will to the realization of God. It was, Weltsch concluded, "a trusting, limitless, action-prepared love."[126]

Prague Zionism, like the Czech-Jewish movement, underwent both a material crisis and a severe testing of will during the First World War. Both sets of institutions were forced to close, or (in the case of the Zionists) nearly close their doors. For both movements the war years occasioned a traumatic confrontation with untenable cultural aspirations. Unfortunately for the Czech Jews, the international conflict called into question their hard-won conviction that they had achieved most of their social and political goals, that they could begin to turn their attention to defining the contours of an integrated Czech-Jewish culture. The war produced a loss of confidence just at the moment that they might have cemented a permanent alliance with progressive Czech nationalism. And it discouraged creative approaches to modern Czech-Jewish culture at a time when a new generation of Czech Jews needed to know who and what they were.

For the Zionists the trauma proved to be less debilitating. What died on the battlefield was not their commitment to the Jewish national program but only that rarified version of it that had managed to sustain them during their student years, but which ultimately could not escape its own prison of intellectualization. The war forced Central European Zionists everywhere, but particularly in the Czech lands, to test idea against reality, to lower their sights on the question of cultural renaissance, and to work in the first instance for an amelioration of the social and political conditions in which most Jews lived. Cultural activity did not recede to the background, but it did change focus. No longer a revolt against the shackles of the past and the timidity of the present, *Kulturarbeit* (practical, cultural activities) became very much a part of Gegenwartsarbeit. It was reconstructive rather than revolutionary, directed toward the larger community rather than an affair of the sensitive spirit. And it was determined to incorporate and build upon the Jewish past rather than try to create a new world in a vacuum.

7

Epilogue: Politics of Integration in the New State, 1918–1920

The Czech-Jewish Movement

During the fall and winter months of 1917–18 the institutions of the Czech-Jewish movement slowly revived. The Association of Czech Academic Jews called a "general assembly" for November 1917 and managed to attract fifteen people. The SČAŽ reinstituted its program of public lectures and, by 1918—as more and more former members trickled into the city following their release from the army—the fortunes of the group began to pick up. In May the Czech-Jewish poet and professor of German literature at Prague's Czech University, Otokar Fischer (1883–1938), addressed the SČAŽ on the familiar theme of Czech culture and Judaism. Alfred Fuchs, the most visible of the younger activists at the war's end, welcomed new members in the fall of 1918 with an address "On the Goals of the Czech-Jewish Student Movement in Today's Times." The following February the SČAŽ commemorated the work of Viktor Vohryzek—long the mentor of progressive Czech-Jewish students—who had died shortly before the new year. Thus, as its four-year hiatus in activity came to a close, the Czech-Jewish student movement could be found picking up where it had left off.[1]

Yet in the intervening years the political conditions of Prague and Bohemia had undergone a revolution. Austria withdrew from the war a shattered power, its multiethnic empire disintegrating from the pull of centrifugal national forces. The independent Czechoslovak Republic was proclaimed on 28 October 1918. Two weeks later the National Assembly, meeting in Prague, confirmed both the new Republic and the presidency of T. G. Masaryk.[2] Hence, a good part of the political—if not the cultural—program of the Czech-Jewish movement had come to pass by the end of 1918. Czech-speaking Jews no longer needed to defend the legitimate aspirations of a national minority in a provincial capital. Their political purpose appeared

183

now to be reduced to ensuring Jewish support for the new state, their cultural program to achieving a more effective integration with the Czech national majority.

The SČAŽ and its sister organizations soon came to recognize these facts. Within a year after the establishment of the new Republic, the Czech-Jewish leadership determined to alter the structure of its organizations in an effort to reflect more faithfully the social and political context of independent Czechoslovakia. On the one hand, the Czech-Jewish community was eager to put forward a united political voice representing the national consensus of Czech-speaking Jews. To this end the Politická jednota českožidovská (Czech-Jewish Political Union) and the Svaz českých pokrokových židů (Association of Progressive Czech Jews), antagonists since the start of the century, sought to combine forces early in 1918 only to split apart before the summer over the old problem of how forcefully to protest antisemitism in official Czech circles.[3] The two bodies managed to conclude a second try at merger in October 1919, and henceforth were known as the Svaz Čechu-židů (Union of Czech Jews). Their respective newspapers, *Rozhled* and *Rozvoj,* likewise joined together under the second title.[4]

The SČAŽ meanwhile voted to change its bylaws to accept members from all religious groups. At its inception forty-four years earlier, the SČAŽ had taken care to underline its status as an organization created by and for Jews, with a specifically Jewish agenda. But by the time that the new bylaws were ratified, in December 1919, Czech-Jewish university students no longer viewed their cultural tasks as being substantially different from those of Czech society at large. The goal of the student organization—now renamed Akademický spolek "Kapper" ([Siegfried] Kapper Academic Society)—was to further simultaneously the well-being of the Czechoslovak state as well as Jewish integration into Czech society. Toward those ends it welcomed the participation of liberal-minded non-Jews.[5]

A third element in the modest redirection of Czech-Jewish institutions at the close of the war consisted in efforts to locate a precise area of activity in which Czech Jews could make a decisive contribution to the new state. Jewish business and political leaders met at the start of 1918 to create a new association—limited neither to Jewish members nor to Jewish causes—independent of all political affiliations, whose dual purpose was to bolster the economic foundations of the new Republic while promoting Czech national culture.[6] The Union for Economic and Cultural Relief (Jednota pro péči hospodářskou a kulturní), as the new body was called, sought to direct Jewish economic energy and acumen at the vacuum left behind by the withdrawal of Habsburg Vienna from the political and economic control of the Czech lands. Led by the Prague industrialist Leon Bondy, the Jednota sponsored lectures on the economic reconstruction of Czechoslovakia, contributed to Czech cultural projects, and generally encouraged investment in the new state.[7] One of its earliest efforts involved the sponsorship of a contest to alleviate the buildiing crisis in the Czech lands. The Jednota received designs from some fifty individuals, which were judged by a panel of architects and urban planners and exhibited to the public. The exhibition generated a good deal of public interest; even Minister of Public Works Antonín Hampl found time to pay a visit.[8]

Along similar lines, adherents of the Svaz českých pokrokových židů in Pardubice issued a call in the fall of 1918 (before the war had ended) for a daily Czech-Jewish newspaper that would reflect progressive opinion and also emphasize business and economic news.[9] Such a venture would fill reciprocal needs. "The Jews need a Czech paper," the appeal noted, "and the Czech nation needs a business paper." On a deeper level, the Association of Progressive Czech Jews hoped that such a newspaper would affect Czech popular opinion and guard against antisemitic sentiment more effectively than other defensive measures. And it would further the progress of Czech-Jewish cultural integration.

> The establishment and publication of a truly progressive and democratic paper will demonstrate to Czech Jews in practice that there is no difference between us and the rest of society . . . in our personal relationship to—and genuine love of—the fatherland. That we have the same aspirations, the same hopes, as the other non-Jewish sons of the Czech lands. That we attach the same burning love to it, and that it is only prejudice and mutual misunderstanding which, unfortunately so often in recent days, has erected barriers between us.[10]

Tribuna, a liberal Czech daily with an emphasis on business, was in fact founded in 1919. Edited through 1921 by Arné Laurin, its collaborators included the literary and theater critic Josef Kodiček, Alfred Fuchs, Jindřich Kohn, and Karel Poláček. *Tribuna* changed hands in 1922 and ceased publication in 1928.[11]

Paradoxically, the Czech-Jewish movement was unable fully to enjoy its honeymoon with the new political order. Two factors kept interfering in the relationship. One was the intermittent, yet troubling outbreak of antisemitic demonstrations in Prague and in other parts of the Czech lands. During the national revolution of October 1918, the Národní výbor (Czech National Committee) succeeded on the whole in maintaining social order, and Czech political leaders discouraged suggestions that Jews be excluded from active participation in the triumphant national movement.[12] However, in early December 1918, recently demobilized troops and other civilians together marauded down the streets of Prague physically attacking Jews and Jewish property.[13] Demonstrations in May 1919 against profiteering and high prices led to the looting of shops and businesses in Prague and the suburbs. Many, but not all, of the establishments affected were owned by Jews. The most disturbing acts of violence occurred in November 1920, when mobs broke into the ancient Jewish Town Hall, tore apart paintings and furnishings, rifled through desk drawers, and destroyed priceless documents relating to the history of the Jews in the city.[14]

According to a report of the *Neue Freie Presse* of Vienna, the rioting of November 1920 was so intense that the American Consul in Prague had the American flag flown over the Jewish Town Hall in order to protect Galician refugees who were being housed there temporarily.[15] One need only refer to Franz Kafka's letter to Milena Jesenská at the time to appreciate the disappointment and despair felt by Jews who were otherwise sympathetic to the Czech national cause:

> I've spent all afternoon in the streets, wallowing in the Jew-baiting. "Prašivé plemeno"—"filthy rabble" I heard someone call the Jews the other day. Isn't it the natural thing to leave the place where one is hated so much? (For this, Zionism or national feeling is not needed.) The heroism which consists of staying on in spite of it all is that of cockroaches which also can't be exterminated from the bathroom.
>
> Just now I looked out of the window: Mounted police, gendarmerie ready for a bayonet charge, a screaming crowd dispersing, and up here in the window the loathsome disgrace of living all the time under protection.[16]

On the whole the Czech lands proved to be much freer of antisemitism than any other part of East Central Europe between the wars. In fact, the disturbances of 1920 were the last public demonstrations of Jew hatred to appear before the Munich crisis of 1938. Ultimately more troubling for the Czech nationalist Jews were the growing political successes of the local Zionist movement. The Zionists sought to organize Czechoslovak Jewry along national lines and to represent Jewish national interests in the new state. Such policies on their face threatened the integrationist program of the Czech-Jewish movement. The fact that they received a sympathetic hearing from the heads of the Czech government was enough to throw the Czech-Jewish camp into alarm.

Prague Zionism's Political Offensive

The wartime experience, by and large, had consolidated both the ethical priorities and the practical politics of Prague Zionism. Newly demobilized Jewish soldiers returned to Prague determined to reduce national conflict in its Central European—as well as Middle Eastern—context. Just as important, the insistence in President Woodrow Wilson's Fourteen Points on the free development of national minorities inspired Jewish nationalists to work for Jewish autonomy in the areas of education, culture, and social welfare. It began to appear by 1918 that all of the writing and discussion on the question of Gegenwartsarbeit, cultural activity in the diaspora, might indeed bear fruit. Zionists might now be able to work on behalf of a legally recognized national minority, transforming the institutions of the former *Kultusgemein-de* (religious community) into a national, representative structure. The intensification of Jewish national feeling in interwar Central Europe could be accomplished not only with a view toward emigration to Palestine, but also for the direct purpose of furthering Jewish national culture in a diaspora setting.

The Zionists on the whole demonstrated a greater ability than the Czech-Jewish movement to rebound from the hardships of the war years. While Czech-Jewish leaders combed the streets for a few handfuls of individuals to attend lectures and public meetings, the Zionists reorganized for effective political negotiations with the future leaders of the Czech state. The political reorganization began in 1917. Siegmund Kaznelson, with the support of Max Brod, began a campaign in the pages of *Selbstwehr* for an all-Austrian Jewish congress to organize, represent, and defend Jewish interests after the war.[17] Earlier that year Kaznelson had learned of American plans to convene a World Jewish Congress to deal with the fate of Eastern Europe's Jews, and it was in fact news of the American congress movement that emboldened him to seek support for an all-Austrian Jewish body. Brod, for his part, wrongly saw the congress as a vehicle for a third-party mediation to the end of the war. Both men, however, agreed that popular sentiment in Bohemia was tilting dangerously against the Jews—largely because of an unwise display of rabid, German patriotism on the part of some—and that only a body that represented national Jewish interests could intervene credibly on their behalf.[18]

Ironically, Kaznelson's call for a Jewish congress met with violent opposition from Viennese Zionists. The head of the Central Zionist Committee for Western Austria informed him that "neither a 'provincial paper' like *Selbstwehr* nor a 'provincial city' like Prague" could intitiate the first steps in such an undertaking.[19] Kaznelson and Brod continued their campaign through the summer of 1917 when they addressed the issue in front of a national "Volkstag" meeting in Vienna. While in Vienna Brod visited with the Czech representative František Staněk and informed him of the position of the Bohemian Zionists on current national issues. Staněk in turn urged Brod to meet in Prague with Antonín Švehla, whom he felt was to become one of the more important Czech leaders.[20]

As part of its campaign to normalize Jewish nationalism within a Czech context, the Bohemian Zionists launched a new, Czech-language paper in April 1918, under the editorship of Ludvík Singer. *Židovské zprávy* (Jewish news) soon became the counterpart to *Selbstwehr* and faithfully presented the Jewish national position to the Czech-reading public down to the German occupation of 1939. Singer's conception of Jewish nationalism, akin to that of Brod and Felix Weltsch, hinged on three principles: the establishment of a Jewish national center in Palestine; the ability of Jews outside of Palestine (where they lived in sufficiently large numbers) to cultivate an autonomous, national culture; and the granting of full civil and political equality to Jews everywhere.[21] The political goals of Czech Zionism could not be fulfilled in the absence of full political emancipation. Neither would the Zionists accept an emancipation that did not accommodate Jewish cultural autonomy. In the postwar order, citizenship and loyalty to the state were to be bound to the coexistence of a distinctive—and active—Jewish national identity.

At the same time Singer sought to reassure the Czech national movement of the Zionists' readiness to cooperate with their immediate goals:

> We Jews, living in a Czech milieu, put forward our relation to the Czech nation: we respect it, as [one would] a culture that stands equal to [one's own]; we carefully acknowledge its national feeling and wish it success in its effort at a just solution to the national question on democratic principles.[22]

The basic message, then, that the Zionists brought before the Czech national leadership during the waning months of 1917 and throughout 1918 was one of reassurance. Whatever their linguistic patterns, whatever their educational preferences, the Jews as a body would be loyal to the Czech state. The Zionists did insist on official recognition of the Jewish nationality and on guarantees for Jewish autonomy, but autonomy was to be limited to realms of education and cultural life.[23]

For all of its political sagacity, the Jewish national movement in Prague might not have met with the success it did had T. G. Masaryk and his Realist party not emerged from the war as the chief representatives of the Czech national movement in the eyes of the Western powers. Masaryk, long friendly toward Zionism, had spent most of the war in exile in England and the United States. While in America, he received much political support from Jewish notables (including Bohemian Jews) and later acknowledged a sense of indebtedness to Western Jewry.[24] In September 1918, following verbal assurances from President Wilson that the "Czechoslovak nation" would enjoy independence in the new European order, the Zionist Organization of America sent a telegram of congratulations to the Czech leader. Masaryk, in turn, sent a reply in which he promised that the same rights that were to be granted the German national minority in Czechoslovakia would also apply to the Jews. "As regards Zionism," he added, "I can only express my sympathy with it and with the national movement of the Jewish people in general, since it is of great moral significance."

> I have observed the Zionist and national movement of the Jews in Europe and in our own country, and have come to understand that it is not a movement of political chauvinism, but one striving for the moral rebirth of its people.[25]

Masaryk also sent an unsolicited telegram to Max Brod, recalling their meeting at the start of the war, and guaranteeing that Jewish rights would be respected fully in the future state.[26] Some within the Zionist circle—including

Brod himself—came only slowly to the realization that there was no real hope for a multinational federation in postwar Central Europe.[27] Others, including Kaznelson, Ludvík Singer, and Karel Fischl, expressed great enthusiasm for the national independence of the so-called *Kleinvölker* (small nations), and predicted that the Jews could rightfully claim from the newly enfranchised states rights to cultural autonomy which Austria had always denied them. On the eve of the proclamation of the Czechoslovak Republic, the Jewish nationalists—including a number of non-Zionists—organized themselves into a Jewish National Council (Národní rada židovská/Jüdischer Nationalrat). Six days later, on 28 October, the council approached the Czech National Committee (Národní výbor) and presented it with the demands of the Jewish minority.[28]

The memorandum of the Jewish National Council called for state recognition of the Jewish nationality and the right of Jews to declare it in censuses and elections. No individual would be compelled to declare his or her nationality as Jewish, "but by the same token no one desiring to profess it [was to] be prohibited from doing so officially or unofficially."[29] The memorandum went on to call for the full civil and legal equality of the Jews. The minority rights of the Jews were not "to be construed as affecting those rights which are their due as Czech citizens." In other words, the Jews were not to be removed from or given another form of citizenship, as such an action would relegate them to a preemancipated status. Instead the Jews were to enjoy what had been denied them previously under the terms of the emancipation of 1867: full civil equality combined with full national rights.[30]

The Jewish nationalists demanded cultural autonomy in the areas of Jewish education, the cultivation of the Hebrew language, relations with Palestine, and social welfare. They asked for the right to establish Jewish elementary and high schools—"along modern (not sectarian) lines"—where circumstances permitted. The memorandum reiterated the long-standing Zionist call for the democratization of the Jewish religious communities, which were still regulated according to an imperial law of 1890. The system of class voting was to be abolished; the community was to be given the right to tax its members; and the democratically elected Jewish congregations were to choose a "joint representative body" with headquarters in Prague. Finally, to the extent that cultural projects were to be recipients of state funds in the future, Jewish cultural institutions would also be entitled to proportionate assistance.[31]

The presidium of the Jewish National Council met with Masaryk himself on 31 December 1918, and presented him with a proposal that called not only for the recognition of the Jewish national minority, but also its guaranteed representation in the country's National Assembly.[32] During the early months of 1919, the council increased its pressure on the young government, always careful to point out the many ways in which it was supporting the new regime in the international arena. Throwing their support behind the efforts of the Comité des délégations juives at the Paris Peace Conference to achieve international recognition of the Jewish nationality, representatives of the Jewish National Council sat down in April 1919 with Foreign Minister Edvard Beneš to try to gain Czechoslovakia's approval.[33]

The Czech Zionists worked the political fields both in Prague and in Paris during the first fifteen months of the new Republic with unusual sophistication and self-assurance. They had prepared themselves for this role during the last years of the war, and certainly gave the appearance of being seasoned political professionals. The secret to their work, it seems, lay not only in their sense of how and when to apply pressure, but, moreover, in their sympathetic appreciation for the underlying assumptions of Czech nationalism. Masaryk and his associates, the Zionists believed, would not readily deny the Jews the cultural self-determination that the Czechs themselves had valued so highly. In addition to hard work and empathy, however, the Czech Zionists also relied on the self-interest of the Czechoslovak government to achieve recognition of the Jewish nationality. If the Jews of Bohemia and Moravia were given the opportunity to register their nationality as Jewish, the result might be a significant reduction in the size of the German national camp. Similarly, the Jews of Slovakia might thereby be induced to abandon the Hungarian cause. Hence to some within the government, accommodating the Zionists made good political sense, if only to weaken the national rivals of the Czechs and Slovaks.[34]

By the spring of 1919 the Prague Zionists became convinced that their efforts were going to yield some form of official recognition for the Jewish national position. In March, Max Brod reported that he could find no difference of opinion between the position of the Jewish National Council and the views of President Masaryk on the issues of the democratization of the religious community as well as the national representation of the Jews.[35] Masaryk moved closer to granting the wishes of the Jewish nationalists in a June address to the Lese- und Redehalle der jüdischen Hochschüler in Prag (Prague Jewish Students' Reading and Discussion Room). The president announced that he could see no reason why in a country like Czechoslovakia—where so many different nations lived side by side—the Jewish nation should be hindered from developing freely. "I can assure you that if I have the opportunity with regard to the Constitution, I will apply my views to the practical, political realm."[36]

The road to national recognition, however, was not to be free of obstacles. Beneš resisted all efforts to include specific reference to Jewish minority rights in the treaty signed in September at St. Germain en Laye, which recognized Czechoslovakia's independence. In a formal letter to Ludvík Singer, head of the Jewish national delegation for Czechoslovakia at the Paris conference, Beneš explained:

> I opposed the incorporation into our treaty of any specific clause pertaining to the protection of the Jews. I did so for a number of reasons. To begin with, a

clause of this sort would imply a certain mistrust on the part of the Allied Powers toward the State concerned, a suspicion that the said State might fail to respect certain human rights which are regarded as a matter of course. Our State and our people enjoy universal sympathy and the trust of all the Allies in this regard. We have fulfilled all our obligations thus far and will continue to do so. Furthermore, our attitude toward the nationality problems has been more liberal than that of any other country.

. . . In my opinion, the clause which clearly states that full satisfaction will be given to the national and religious minorities in matters of education, language and religious liberties should take care of your problem in its entirety.

. . . I do not think that I can request the Conference to decide on the acceptance of the proposal which you submitted to me, for that would be tantamount to requesting the Conference to render a decision on a question of principle: namely, Zionism versus assimilationism. The Czechoslovak delegation is not competent to broach this question and therefore cannot broach it.[37]

Several days later, meeting with Nahum Sokolow, chairman of the Comité des délégations juives, Beneš tried to reassure the Zionists of his sympathy for Jewish nationalism. He insisted, however, that to sign the so-called Jewish articles of the Polish treaty would represent a "yellow badge," for Czechoslovakia, a stigma of which only Poland and Romania—because of their history of antisemitism—were deserving.[38] Unable to convince Beneš to change his mind concerning the treaty, Sokolow at last suggested that he correspond with Masaryk about the issue. Beneš promised to write to Masaryk and added, "I think we'll issue something—a proclamation, perhaps, or a letter."[39] But in the end neither Masaryk nor Beneš agreed to the inclusion of the "Jewish clauses" in the Treaty of St. Germain.

It was not until the promulgation of the Czechoslovak Constitution in February 1920 that the government formally announced its recognition of the Jewish nationality. It did so not in the Constitution itself—which did not expressly indicate who the legally recognized national minorities were—but rather in documents that accompanied and clarified the Constitution. Ultimately the Jewish National Council received the concessions that it had sought. Jews who regarded themselves as members of a separate nationality had the right to express this choice in censuses and at elections. Yet they could not be required to do so. Moreover, Jews were the only national minority not to be tied to a linguistic criterion. Nor did "national" Jews necessarily have to identify with the Jewish religion.[40]

Czechoslovakia's concessions to Jewish nationalism were in fact unprecedented. For the first time in European history, a highly industrialized, parliamentary democracy with a long history of Jewish emancipation recognized the claim to Jewish national distinctiveness. The state, moreover, made room for Jewish cultural and national self-expression without diminishing the value of emancipation and free of any underlying motive to reduce Jewish social and political integration. Masaryk's government had, as it were, fulfilled the demands once voiced by Simon Dubnov's "diaspora nationalists"—to realize emancipation for Jews not as individuals, which had been the model of the French Revolution, but as a nation.[41]

In legitimizing Jewish national politics in the new state, Masaryk and the Realists continued to equivocate on the question of Jewish participation in the Czech national movement. The Czech leaders clearly expected—and welcomed—Jewish loyalty to the state, and they never publicly questioned the actions of Czech-Jewish assimilationists, but time and again they proved unwilling to deny the Zionists their claim to autonomous Jewish development. The independence of Czechoslovakia should have represented to Czech nationalist Jews a vindication of their half-century-old movement. Instead the state appeared to disappoint them at every turn. On the basis of their own ideology, the assimilationists might have been willing to recognize the Yiddish- and Hebrew-speaking Jews of the eastern portions of Czechoslovakia as members of an as-yet-intact Jewish nation. Yet the government specifically excluded language and acculturation (not to mention race and religion) as criteria of Jewish nationality, recognizing instead the same "subjective" definitions held by the Prague Zionists before the turn of the century, which the Czech Jews roundly ridiculed at the time. Thus the Czech-Jewish movement found its own theoretical foundations contradicted by state policy. In the eyes of Czech nationalist Jews the right to proclaim any nationality whatever, irrespective of spoken language, was an invitation to political opportunism of the worst kind. To Masaryk, on the other hand, whose own fluency in Czech had lagged behind his national convictions at the end of the nineteenth century, freedom of choice was an essential ingredient in the process of self-determination.[42]

The Zionist successes of the first years of the Republic provoked responses of anger and jealousy on the part of Czech-Jewish leaders, people who in 1918 had good reason to believe that "their time" had arrived, that their movement would enjoy at least a symbolically privileged position in the new order. A front-page article that appeared in *Rozvoj* in June 1919 complained bitterly of Zionist policies in the new state. The article, which was unsigned, contended that Zionist support for the state and its overt neutrality on the Czech-German issue was a masquerade designed to conceal its basically German makeup. Sardonically it recalled how the Czech Zionists had demonstrated in favor of Masaryk and an independent Czechoslovakia after the national revolution (in Czech, *převrat*) had already taken place, how everyone was careful to speak only Czech at the meetings of the Prague Zionists, though their Czech was really quite hopeless.[43]

Czech Jews at the time were prepared to see Zionism work, according to *Rozvoj*, if only to diminish the German influence within Bohemian and Moravian Jewry. But this did not come about. German Jews affiliated with the Zionist movement as an alternative, less-controversial form of German identification.

Table 5. Jewish Attendance at Public Elementary Schools in Bohemia During the First Republic

Year	Total Jewish Students	No. Attending		Percent Attending	
		Czech Schools	German Schools	Czech Schools	German Schools
1921–22	6,016	3,143	2,873	52.2	47.8
1924–25	4,310	2,555	1,755	59.3	40.7
1927–28	4,149	2,467	1,682	59.5	40.5
1930–31	4,706	2,822	1,884	60.0	40.0

Derived from: František Friedmann, "Židé v Čechách," in Hugo Gold, ed., *Židé a židovské obce v Čechách v minulosti a v přítomnosti* (Brno and Prague, 1934), pp. 733–34.

Zionist enthusiasm for Czechoslovakia manifested itself falsely, insincerely; from that point on the Zionists remained German-oriented even though their four, Czech-speaking, Prague leaders publicly abuse the German community more than is seemly. . . . They know of no interests other than their special Jewish interests.[44]

This last sentence pointed to a second, deeper concern of the assimilationists. What truly worried them was not so much the fact that German Jews were masquerading as Jewish nationalists but that Zionism had placed back on the political agenda issues which, according to liberal theory, belonged to the preemancipation era. The Zionist demand for recognition of the Jewish nationality, for autonomy in cultural affairs, for state support of a Jewish national, primary and secondary school system, evoked fears among Czech nationalist Jews of a "return to the ghetto." Small wonder that, alongside accusations of German-Jewish collusion, organs such as *Rozvoj* published emotional attacks on the educational program of the Jewish National Council.[45]

In a two-part 1919 editorial, *Rozvoj* appealed to its readers to recall the "heroic" period of the Czech-Jewish movement, the 1880s and 1890s, when so much energy was expended shutting down what at the time amounted to a Jewish school system. The editors even reproduced parts of Josef Kořán's 1886 piece in the *Kalendář česko-židovský*, the clarion call from the liberal wing of the Czech national movement for Czech-speaking Jews to put their ideals into practice and do away with the age-old German-Jewish elementary school.[46] The private German-Jewish school, of course, had long since ceased to exist. Moreover, roughly 52 percent of the Jewish children enrolled in public elementary schools in Bohemia were attending Czech institutions. This figure would grow to 60 percent over the next decade (see Table 5). Secondary education provided a somewhat less successful picture. Only 37 percent of Jewish secondary school students attended Czech gymnasia

Table 6. Jewish Attendance at Bohemian Gymnasia and Reálky During the First Republic

		No. Attending		Percent Attending	
Year	Total Jewish Students	Czech Schools	German Schools	Czech Schools	German Schools
1921–22	3,156	1,178	1,978	37.3	62.7
1924–25	2,925	1,189	1,736	40.6	59.4
1927–28	2,449	1,046	1,403	42.7	57.3
1930–31	2,063	890	1,173	43.1	56.9

Derived from: František Friedmann, "Židé v Čechách," in Hugo Gold, ed., *Židé a židovské obce v Čechách v minulosti a v přítomnosti* (Brno and Prague, 1934), pp. 733–34.

and Reálky at the start of the Czechoslovak Republic, but this figure would climb to 43 percent by 1930 (see Table 6).

The Zionists did achieve some noteworthy successes in their efforts to build a national, Jewish educational system. The first elementary school of this type in Prague opened on 6 September 1920 on the premises of the community's Talmud Torah, the very spot which, from the 1780s to the 1860s, had housed the community-run German-language school. Unlike the older Jewish elementary school, however, and unlike the school for refugee children that had been established during the war, the language of instruction in the Jewish national school was Czech. The realities of Jewish life in Bohemia were such that the Prague Zionists could not hope to transform the community into a Hebrew-speaking population. They did, however, acknowledge the Czech character of the postwar order and assiduously stayed clear of institutional efforts to perpetuate German-Jewish cultural and political ties.[47]

The Prague Jewish school began with one grade. By 1924 it had reached its full complement of five classes. One of the instructors in the school was Valli Pollak, a sister of Franz Kafka. Kafka himself attended the school's organizational meetings and showed unusual enthusiasm for the enterprise. He followed its progress closely during the last years of his life, sending periodic encouragement to his sister and reminding her of her important role in the formation of a new generation of culturally active Jews.[48]

Jewish national schools were also established in Brno, the Moravian capital, and in Toruň and Mukačevo in Subcarpathian Ruthenia (Podkarpatská Rus). Reflecting the slower linguistic transition of Moravian Jewry, the school in Brno opened as a German-language institution but soon switched over to Czech. The schools in Subcarpathian Ruthenia, on the other hand, where Jews continued to live in traditional communities of compact settlement, used Hebrew as the language of instruction. By 1925 no less than nine Hebrew-language elementary schools were functioning in Podkarpatská Rus.[49] A Jew-

Table 7. National Declarations of Czech Jews, 1921 (by percentage)

	Bohemia	Moravia	Czechoslovakia (all)
Jewish	13.8	48.7	53.6
Czecho-Slovak	46.7	15.7	21.8
German	32.7	35.0	14.3
Other	6.8	0.6	10.3

Derived from: Jan Heřman, "The Development of Bohemian and Moravian Jewry, 1918–1938," in U. O. Schmelz, P. Glikson, and S. Della Pergola, eds., *Papers in Jewish Demography, 1969* (Jerusalem, 1973); and *Encyclopaedia Judaica* 5:1190.

ish *Reformrealgymnasium* (gymnasium that emphasized the modern rather than the classical languages) operated in Brno, while Hebrew-language gymnasia could be found in both Mukačevo and Užhorod.[50]

The Jews of Czechoslovakia had their first opportunity to declare a national affiliation in the census of 1921 (see Table 7). In Bohemia the number of self-proclaimed "Czecho-Slovaks" declined slightly since the last census in 1910, from 43,181 to 37,234, a drop of about 13.8 percent. Over the same decade the overall Jewish population of Bohemia had fallen by about 10 percent. The fall in the number of "German" Jews was a good deal steeper, from 40,647 to 26,058, a decline of 35.9 percent. Meanwhile, just under 11,000 Bohemian Jews now declared themselves to be "Jewish" by nationality.[51] If one assumes that the loss in total Jewish population was distributed equally among Czech speakers and German speakers, the nationality figures for 1921 suggest that the vast majority of the newly proclaimed Jewish nationals came from among Jews who in the past had called themselves German. The body of self-consciously Czech national Jews remained relatively stable from 1910 to 1921, but the older German strata displayed great weakness.

In Moravia the same overall pattern held true, although Czech nationalism historically had made fewer inroads here than in Bohemia. There was remarkably little change in the number of Czech national Jews: 7,055 in 1900; 7,205 in 1910; and 6,087 in 1921. The number of German Jews remained steady in 1900 and 1910 (43,942 and 43,299, respectively), but dropped precipitously in 1921 to 13,623, a decline of 68.5 percent in eleven years. The Jewish nationalists picked up most of this slack, winning almost 19,000 declarations of Jewish nationality.[52] The further east one went, the higher the percentage of Jews who opted for the Jewish nationality. In Slovakia, over 54 percent chose it (compared to about 22 percent who wrote down Czecho-Slovak); and in Subcarpathian Ruthenia the number was an astounding 86.8 percent. By 1930 the number of Jewish nationals in Bohemia would grow from 13.8 to 20.5 percent, while both "Czech" and "German" Jews would decline. In Moravia, following a similar pattern, the number of Jewish nationals would grow from 48.7 to 51.6 percent.[53]

In terms of demographic ratios, the real loser to the upsurge in Jewish national activity and consciousness at the close of the war was the German community. The Czech Jews may have begun to run low in intellectual creativity during this time, and they certainly were outmaneuvered politically by the Zionists. But the social and demographic foundations of the Czech cultural position were so firmly in place by 1920 that no poverty of ideas, no amount of political unpreparedness, could shake them. Czech Jewry could maintain only two viable cultural strands into the 1920s and 1930s: one was self-consciously Czech, the other Jewish—both were in many respects complementary—but the German-Jewish alliance of the nineteenth century had breathed its last.

The multifaceted decline of German-Jewish culture, however, constituted only one broad aspect of the transformation of Jewish society in Bohemia during the last third of the nineteenth and the first decades of the twentieth century. The other part to the story was the progressive integration of Jews into virtually all levels of Czech society, political, cultural, linguistic, and national. Even an extreme measure of Jewish integration, that of mixed marriages, indicated a dramatic shift after 1918. In the city of Prague, the percentage of mixed couples (Jewish-Gentile) in all marriages involving at least one Jewish spouse stood at 9.8 between 1911 and 1914. In 1921–22 the figure rose to 16.4 percent; it jumped to 40.1 percent in 1925, and by 1930, had reached 43.6 percent.[54] Such numbers would have alarmed the leadership of the Czech-Jewish movement as well as the Zionists. At the very least, they pointed out that on the most basic of levels, Jewish integration into greater Czech society was a reality.

The intensity of the integration process after 1918 contained a double irony. It meant on the one hand that, despite the poverty of ideas, despite its apparent political failures at the hands of the Jewish nationalists, the Czech-Jewish movement had possessed a vision of Czech-Jewish relations that was essentially correct. It had indeed pinpointed in the 1870s and 1880s the direction that Jewish acculturation would inevitably take. On the other hand, Prague Zionism—though it argued for Jewish autonomy and self-development in cultural matters—did not erect any barriers to Czech-Jewish integration in the areas of politics, economics, and social relations. One even could argue that the Zionist movement's early political triumphs under the Czechoslovak Republic, by winning legitimacy for Jewish national involvement in constructing and defining the new state, actually helped to ensure Czech-Jewish integration at various levels.

Thus both paths of postemancipatory transformation, that which promoted Czech-Jewish assimilation and that which sought to create a Jewish national reality in the Czech lands, combined in the end to make—or rather, remake—the modern Czech-Jewish community. The two movements may have offered radically different visions of Jewish self-definition and culture, but they each had essentially the same positive effect on the social processes of Jewish integration. Each served as a principal agent of Jewish development in the Czech lands, and each proved to have been a timely and—in the short run— successful response to the dilemma of Jewish existence in a post-liberal, nationally contentious environment.

Conclusion

The transformation of Bohemian Jewry, from a village and small-town to a predominantly urban society, and from a German-centered, cosmopolitan culture to one overdetermined by national considerations, took place over the course of a half-century, roughly from 1870 to the first years of the Czechoslovak Republic. During this time Bohemian Jewry went through a complex process of change and adaptation, a "secondary acculturation" that had not been predicted by the Enlightenment model of Jewish emancipation.

By the 1860s the Jews of Bohemia had already gone through one modernization. The cultural and economic restructuring that had been set in motion by the absolutist reforms of the 1780s was carried through to completion during the 1850s and 1860s, the early decades of Austria's industrial revolution. Though still predominantly rural (over 80 percent lived in towns and villages outside of Prague), Jewish society had long since abandoned most of its premodern forms. The community had no juridical autonomy; traditional Jewish education had fallen into disuse—as had the Yiddish language; and Bohemian and Moravian Jews no longer suffered from residential, demographic, or occupational restrictions. Thanks largely to the agency of the state-supervised German-Jewish school, Prague Jewry exhibited thoroughly German linguistic and cultural patterns. Provincial Bohemian Jewry was bilingual, employing Czech in daily intercourse with the local population, but educating their children in German and preferring German for use in Jewish institutions.[1]

By 1910, however, a complex of social, cultural, and political factors had altered the face of Bohemian Jewry once again. Demographic upheaval and migration; the urbanization of Jewish communities and of Jewish culture; the realization of secular, universal education; Czech nationalism's challenge of German dominance; and the general radicalization of national politics, combined with an array of specific Jewish responses to produce a new social and cultural entity, modern Czech Jewry. If Bohemian Jewry had been predominantly rural and small town, Czech Jewry was decidedly urban. Over a third of the Jewish population lived in Prague; close to 70 percent lived in towns of more than 10,000 people. Seven decades earlier there had been 347 separate Jewish communities in Bohemia, only 22 of which had a population of more than 50.[2] If Bohemian Jewish culture had been colored largely by the German-Jewish alliance of the late eighteenth century, the Czech Jewish orientation was highly nuanced, increasingly alienated from Austrian-German liberalism, and self-consciously bilingual. This indeed is the real significance of the about-face recorded by Czech Jewry in the census returns of 1900 and 1910: not that the Jews had become committed Czech patriots overnight, but as a declaration of their inherent bilingualism, and of their quest for integration in a divided society.

Whether Czech in political orientation or Zionist, the culture of Bohemian Jewry after 1870 could only be elaborated in national terms. The arena of party politics certainly required this, but so too did the school system, the courts and the bureaucracy, and even voluntary associations and religious institutions. In the context of modern Czech society, cultural development, social integration, and personal growth were all tied to the relationship of the individual to the nation. Virtually no spheres of cultural and social life existed that did not define themselves in nationalist terms. Austrian Social Democracy and workers' institutions in the Czech lands were among the first in Europe to advocate the division of the state along federalist lines. Even those institutions, which in an earlier century had identified liberal politics and liberal German culture with a kind of cosmopolitan well-being, had devolved into mouthpieces for the German national position within the monarchy.

Processes of secondary acculturation, similar to that which transformed Jewish society in Bohemia, occurred in all regions of East Central Europe at approximately the same time. Each transformation was set in motion by a coherent set of factors, variables which, in general terms, might be applied to all the situations. Regional variations, however, were inevitable. Unlike the situation in the Czech lands, for example, national competition did not play as decisive a role in the evolution of the Jewish population of Central Hungary, where Magyar hegemony had occurred relatively quickly. German cultural and political elites had never been very strong in modern Hungary, having had to contend traditionally with a powerful Hungarian landed class and, after mid-century, with an urban, Magyar-speaking bureaucratic and industrial elite. Accordingly, Jewish acculturation moved naturally and quite painlessly from a German to a Magyar model. By the turn of the century, virtually all of Hungary's Jews were fully Magyar-speaking.[3]

In Hungary, unlike other parts of East Central Europe, real economic and occupational integration accompanied—and in many cases preceded—legal emancipation. Jews participated actively in the industrialization of the kingdom, enjoyed the fruits of the educational system, swarmed the ranks of the professions, and enjoyed a long period in which liberal politics dominated. They had, as it were, discovered a version of France along the Danube. It is not surprising that Zionism made such little headway in this country.

In Bohemia and in Galicia, on the other hand, national struggle played a key role both in Jewish integration and in the elaboration of modern Jewish identities. The overwhelmingly Czech character of the Bohemian countryside led to the political transformation of the province at large once large-scale migration of Czech speakers to the cities had begun. Similar demographic factors lay at the root of Jewish cultural and political changes. The movement of rural Czech Jews to Prague and also to the larger, industrializing towns—during a period when Czech speakers not only dominated local politics but also helped to direct the installation of public education—eroded the century-old German-Jewish alliance and encouraged the adoption of new cultural and political loyalties. With each triumph of the growing Czech national movement, Czech-speaking Jews challenged both the political assumptions and the cultural strategies of the larger Jewish community, effecting what in the end amounted to a veritable sea change in Bohemian Jewish life.

Unlike both Hungary and Galicia, the outcome of the national conflict in Bohemia in the late nineteenth century was by no means certain. For one thing, the German presence was more entrenched than in Hungary, as was the influence of the central government in Vienna. German-Jewish cultural patterns, as a result, enjoyed greater longevity and vitality than in either Hungary or Galicia. It was just as significant that the intensity of the national conflict resulted in an undercurrent of hostility toward Jewish participation in both national camps. Consequently, Zionism emerged as a serious cultural "option" for large segments of the educated and professional class even though the relative "westernness" of Bohemian Jewry in other respects appeared to militate against it. Zionism offered both German- and Czech-speaking Jews the solution of a credible middle road. It was a movement which on one level sought to shelter the Jews from the ravages of the national wars, but which ultimately spoke in the same idiom as Czech and German nationalism, offering Jews the chance to affirm a positive, Jewish identity, the contours and the contents of which had yet to be defined.

The fact that both Prague Zionism and the Czech-Jewish movement stood poised in the autumn of 1918 to claim their rightful place as representatives of the Czech Jewish community revealed the dimensions of the change that had taken place over the past half century. Both groups regarded the national unification of the Czechs and Slovaks, in the spirit of Wilsonian democracy and under the tutelage of Masaryk, to have accorded with their own political programs. In fact, Prague Zionism and the Czech-Jewish movement demonstrated remarkable similarities in their respective developments. Both represented an about-face in cultural and national loyalties, a conscious rejection of liberal prescriptions for Jewish emancipation. Both, moreover, were the natural children of the postindustrial, social, and cultural modernization of Bohemian Jewry.

The Czech-Jewish movement had grown out of the dislocation of rural and small-town Jewish communities and the migration of tens of thousands of these Jews to the industrial centers of Bohemia. Though centered in Prague, it never lost its provincial roots. Instead, it depended on progressive migrations of Jews through the Czech cities and towns of Bohemia to provide a critical mass of activist members. Czech-speaking shopkeepers, merchants, and educated professionals reacted critically to the cultural and institutional structure of the Jewish communities that they encountered in Prague and in other cities. They were, moreover, sensitive to political pressure from the Czech national camp to remove all visible signs of the century-old German-Jewish cultural alliance.

What emerged from this process was a movement to clarify the national position of provincial, Czech-speaking Jews, and to rectify the cultural imbalance of Jewish life in Prague and the larger cities. At issue was the relationship of Czech Jews to their social environment. On a deeper level, however, the movement engaged in an effort to transform both the content and the thrust of Jewish culture itself. The intellectual leadership grouped around the publication *Rozvoj* envisaged the creation of a cultural partnership with the progressive elements of the Czech nation. It sought to combine the teachings of a refined, Masaryk-inspired Judaism with the values of Czech, reformed, Christian culture to produce a modern, Czech national ideal, a kind of cultural declaration conscious of both its Jewish and its Christian components.

Jewish nationalism owed its popularity in Bohemia and Moravia not to the encouragement of any single national movement, but to the national conflict itself. The contradictory demands of Czech and German nationalism, compounded by a growing intolerance toward Jews in the social and political institutions that had once welcomed them, helped to produce the Jewish responses of abdication and self-affirmation. In small-town Bohemia Jews such as Filip Lebenhart and Karl Rezek joined the Zionist movement in the 1890s partly as a result of the disappointing reception accorded them in the Czech national movement; in the Sudetenland the excesses of German nationalism took their toll on middle-class, German Jews.

Zionism in Prague—particularly student Zionism—represented a deliberate turning away from the liberal German culture of the Jewish community, however. The largely German-speaking Zionists of Bar Kochba were quick to criticize Jews who clothed themselves in Czech national culture, much as their own parents had worn German. Nevertheless the Zionists engaged in a campaign that paralleled that of the Czech-Jewish movement. Theirs was fundamentally a revolt against the course of Jewish history in Central Europe since the confluence of Enlightenment and absolutism. Both movements rejected the historical identification of Jewish and German culture as having torn the Jewish community from its natural course of development and as having been imposed upon the Jews by an imperial government more concerned with order and homogeneity than with the real interests of its Jewish population. The traditional affiliation of Jewish and German interests in the Czech lands was not simply the result of the gradual emergence of the Jews from the ghetto over the course of the eighteenth and nineteenth centuries; viewed polemically, it was their ticket of admission to Gentile society, a precondition of emancipation in the Habsburg lands.

Both Prague Zionism and the Czech-Jewish movement agreed that emancipation had been the natural right of the Jews, a right to which no conditions ought to have been attached. Both, moreover, were convinced that full equality had to include the freedom to develop one's natural, national culture. The extent to which both movements regarded history as having imposed itself upon and perverted the "natural order" is indicative not only of the environment out of which both groups grew, but also of a similarity of purpose which ought not to be overlooked.

Prague Zionism mirrored its rival also in its determination to rework Jewish culture, although the Zionists tended to employ romantic imagery and spoke in terms of "revitalization" and "renaissance," whereas the Czech Jews for the most part remained true to Enlightenment rationalism and focused their energies on religious reform and refinement. Both cultural strands, however, looked ultimately to moral philosophy to answer the pressing questions of the relationship of the individual to his or her environment. And both Prague Zionism and the Czech-Jewish movement intended to introduce this reworked Judaism of the future—whether infused with Buberian mysticism or Masaryk's religious sociology—to European civilization in order to change Europe, to tame its national temper, to mediate and eventually overcome those cultural tensions out of which the two strands had developed.

It might strike one as odd, in a work that stresses the importance of social and cultural environment in the evolution of new Jewish forms, that an "outsider" like Martin Buber can be portrayed as having played so decisive a role. Buber, however, was in many ways a kindred spirit of the young Jewish intellectuals of Prague, if not in fact a mirror image. It was not the "sage from Berlin" who met with Bar Kochba between 1909 and 1911 but the student from Lwów, the graduate of a Polish gymnasium and of a German university, grandson of a rabbinic scholar, student of East European Hasidism, and assimilated Jew. Buber provided Bar Kochba with an intellectual structure that they had lacked up to that point. He traced for them a map of national self-discovery, which had as its starting point not the social environment but individual consciousness, and which proclaimed the self-indulgent act of personal withdrawal to be not only legitimate but an essential first step in the elaboration of Jewish nationalism.

Buber's theory of Jewish nationalism was undeniably subjectivist; but it was also a stage theory. Though the individual begins by choosing "substance" over "environment," the next step is to fashion a way of living one's Jewishness in concrete terms, of affirming one's identity in the world of appearances and relationships. In later stages, this revitalized Jewish culture leads to the reintegration of Jews to the world around them. The example of the Jewish national renewal points the way to the elimination of fraternal conflict in general.

Indeed, for all that separated the Czech-Jewish movement from Prague Zionism, they were united in their common preoccupation with redemption. Czech-Jewish thought identified the redemptive process with the division of European society into self-determining, national communities—infused with a healthy dose of ethical humanism. Redemption for the Prague Zionists was to be a "spiritual process," carried out in the first instance by individuals acting "absolutely," unhampered by contingency. Both groups may have rejected the liberal model of emancipation as a palliative for the modern Jewish condition, but they nevertheless looked ultimately toward a reintegration of the Jews into the European environment. Their "corrective" to emancipation derived from national formulas; but its ultimate aim harked back to traditional Jewish yearnings.

Abbreviations

BLBI	*Bulletin des Leo Baeck Instituts*
CZA	Central Zionist Archives, Jerusalem
JGGJČR	*Jahrbuch der Gesellschaft für Geschichte der Juden in der Čechoslovakischen Republic*
KČŽ	*Kalendář česko-židovský*
LBIYB	*Leo Baeck Institute Yearbook*
SČAŽ	Spolek českých akademiků-židů (Association of Czech Academic Jews)

Notes

Introduction

1. Some of the most recent historical scholarship on Prague, I fear, has in fact bolstered the Germano-centric interpretation of Bohemian Jewish life. See, for example, Gary B. Cohen, "Jews in German Society: Prague, 1860–1914," *Central European History* 10 (1977): 28–54; and *The Politics of Ethnic Survival: Germans in Prague, 1861–1914* (Princeton, 1981). For a critical review of the second work, see Hillel J. Kieval, "Gary B. Cohen, *The Politics of Ethnic Survival,*" in Jonathan Frankel, ed., *Studies in Contemporary Jewry,* vol. 1 (Bloomington, Ind., 1984), pp. 424–27.

2. See Conclusion.

3. On Jewish emancipation in Austria and Bohemia, see Wolfgang Häusler, "Toleranz, Emanzipation und Antisemitismus: Das österreichische Judentum des bürgerlichen Zeitalters (1782–1918)," in *Das österreichische Judentum: Voraussetzungen und Geschichte* (Vienna and Munich, 1974); Ruth Kestenberg-Gladstein, *Neuere Geschichte der Juden in den böhmischen Ländern, Erster Teil: Das Zeitalter der Aufklärung, 1780–1830* (Tübingen, 1969); and Hillel J. Kieval, "Caution's Progress: The Modernization of Jewish Life in Prague, 1780–1830," in Jacob Katz, ed., *Toward Modernity: The European Jewish Model* (New Brunswick, N.J., 1987), pp. 71–105.

4. See Kieval, "Caution's progress," pp. 79–81; also Ludvík Singer, "Zur Geschichte der Toleranzpatente in den Sudetenländern," *Jahrbuch der Gesellschaft für Geschichte der Juden in der Čechoslovakischen Republik (hereafter JGGJČR)* 5 (1933): 231–311.

5. Singer, "Toleranzpatent"; Paul P. Bernard, "Joseph II and the Jews: The Origins of the Toleration Patent of 1782," *Austrian History Yearbook* 4/5 (1968–69): 101–19; and Jacob Katz, *Out of the Ghetto: The Social Background of Jewish Emancipation, 1770–1870* (Cambridge, Mass., 1973), pp. 161–67.

In a Resolution distributed by the emperor on 1 October 1781, he assured the Staatsrat the following:

> Meine Absicht gehet keineswegs dahin, die Jüdische Nation in den Erblanden mehr auszubreiten oder da, wo sie nicht toleriert ist, neu einzuführen, sondern nur, da wo sie ist und in der Maass, wie sie als toleriert bestehet, dem Staate nützlich zu machen (Quoted in A. F. Příbram, ed., *Urkunden und Akten zur Geschichte der Juden in Wien* [Vienna and Leipzig, 1918], 1: 137).

The documents reproduced in Příbram indicate that the emperor and his advisors were in fact not well informed of the occupational distribution of the Jews of Bohemia. While the government in Vienna conceived of the Jews mainly as moneylenders, the Bohemian census of 1724 and the Prague census of 1729 indicated that over 27 percent of Prague Jews and 19 percent of Bohemian Jews worked as artisans; some 50 percent of Prague Jews and 52 percent of Bohemian Jews were listed as being involved in trade (Kestenberg-Gladstein, *Neuere Geschichte,* p. 12).

6. Příbram, *Urkunden und Akten,* pp. 494–97; Singer, "Toleranzpatent," p. 258–61. The universities had been removed from Jesuit control in 1773; they were formally secularized in 1782.

7. Kestenberg-Gladstein, *Neuere Geschichte,* pp. 66–85; Ludvík Singer, "Zur Geschichte der Juden in Böhmen in den letzten Jahren Josefs II. und unter Leopold II.," *JGGJČR* 6 (1934): 197–99.

8. Ludvík Singer, "Die Entstehung des Juden-Systemalpatentes von 1797," *JGGJČR* 7 (1935): 199–263; František Roubík, "Drei Beiträge zur Entwicklung der Judenemanzipation in Böhmen," *JGGJČR* 5 (1933): 313–428.

9. On the period 1848 to 1867, see Wolfdieter Bihl, "Die Juden," in Adam Wandruszka and Peter Urbanitsch, eds., *Die Habsburgermonarchie, 1848–1918,* vol. *3: Die Völker des Reichs* (Vienna, 1980), pp. 890–96.

10. Naphtali Herz Wessely (1725–1805) is an oft-cited example of this phenomenon. His pamphlet *Divrei shalom ve-emet* (Words of peace and truth) appeared shortly after the issuance of the Toleranzpatent and included a plea for the Jewish communities of the monarchy to put the provisions of Joseph's education reforms into place (see Katz, *Out of the Ghetto,* pp. 66–69).

11. Kieval, "Caution's Progress," pp. 81–99; Kestenberg-Gladstein, *Neuere Geschichte,* p. 48 (her figures are based on Wanniczek, *Geschichte der Prager Haupt- Trivial- und Mädchenschule der Israeliten* [Prague, 1832]).

12. Singer, "Toleranzpatent," p. 270.

13. Christoph Stölzl, "Zur Geschichte der böhmischen Juden in der Epoche des modernen Nationalismus," pt. 1, *Bohemia* 14 (1973): 198–200.

14. Quoted in Stölzl, "Geschichte der böhmischen Juden," pt. 1, p. 199. This and all other translations, unless otherwise indicated, are by the author.

15. Stölzl, "Geschichte der böhmischen Juden," pt. 1, pp. 200–201. See also "David Kuh," in *Pascheles' Illustrierter Israelitischer Volkskalender,* 5640 (Prague, 1879–80), pp. 87–88.

16. Quoted and translated in Guido Kisch, *In Search of Freedom: A History of American Jews from Czechoslovakia* (London, 1949), p. 209. The best study of Kapper to date is still that of Oskar Donath, "Siegfried Kapper," *JGGJČR* 6 (1934): 323–442.

17. Quoted and translated in Kisch, *In Search of Freedom,* pp. 37–38. See also Stölzl, *Geschichte der böhmischen Juden,* pt. 1, pp. 208–10.

18. Christoph Stölzl, *Kafkas böses Böhmen: Zur Socialgeschichte eines Prager Juden* (Munich, 1975), pp. 28–29; based on contemporary reports in *Der Orient* 5 (1844) and 9 (1848).

Chapter 1

1. In fact the Jews had been expelled from Prague in 1541 and again in 1557, but each purge lasted only for a few years. With each return the Jewish community was able to reconstitute itself and subsequently flourish. On the expulsion of 1541 see Samuel Steinherz, "Gerush ha-yehudim mi-beim bi-shnat 1541," *Zion* 15 (1950): 70–92; and Jan Heřman, "The Conflict between Jewish and Non-Jewish Population in Bohemia before the 1541 Banishment," *Judaica Bohemiae* 6 (1970): 39–54.

2. A recent study has estimated that there were 11,618 Jews living in Prague in 1702, representing some 30 percent of the general population of the city. See Jan Heřman, "The Evolution of the Jewish Population in Prague, 1869–1939," in U. O.Schmelz, P. Glikson, and S. Della Pergola, eds., *Papers in Jewish Demography, 1977* (Jerusalem, 1980), p. 54. The

Jewish population of Amsterdam in the early eighteenth century stood at around 12,000; that of Salonika (the largest Jewish center in the world) hovered between 25,000 and 30,000. See Jonathan I. Israel, *European Jewry in the Age of Mercantilism 1550–1750* (Oxford, 1985), pp. 238–40.

3. Tobiáš Jakobovits, "Das Prager und Böhmische Landesrabbinat Ende des Siebzehnten und Anfang des achtzehnten Jahrhunderts," *JGGJČR* 5 (1933): 79–136.

4. *Encyclopaedia Judaica*, vol. 10, col. 1403 (Jerusalem, 1972); Jakobovits, "Das Prager und Böhmische Landesrabbinat."

5. The intent of the laws was to freeze the Jewish population of Bohemia at its present level. Since the census of 1724 had accounted for 8,541 families, this was the legal limit proclaimed by the Familiantengesetze. See Anita Franková, "Erfassung der jüdischen Bevölkerung in Böhmen im 18. und in der ersten Hälfte des 19. Jh. . . ." *Judaica Bohemiae* 6 (1970): 55–69; and Kestenberg-Gladstein, *Neuere Geschichte*, pp. 1–2.

6. The collusion of the landed estate in Jewish efforts to circumvent the effects of Vienna's restrictive legislation has yet to be studied closely. For literature that does exist on the subject, see Josef von Wertheimer, *Die Juden in Österreich* (Leipzig, 1842), 1:187–94; Singer, "Toleranzpatente," pp. 236–37; Karel Adámek, *Slovo o židech* (Chrudim, 1899), pp. 5–8; and Adolf Stein, *Die Geschichte der Juden in Böhmen* (Brno, 1904), pp. 86–90.

7. A government estimate in 1754 put the total Jewish population of Bohemia at 30,000, about one-third of whom lived in Prague. Kestenberg-Gladstein argues that the Prague figure of approximately 10,000 individuals should be added to the 30,000 rather than form a part of it (Kestenberg-Gladstein, *Neuere Geschichte*, pp. 1–3, 8–12). Given the general unreliability of all official censuses in this period, one thing nevertheless seems clear: the Jewish population of Bohemia at worst was remaining steady.

8. Ruth Kestenberg-Gladstein, "Mifkad yehudei Beim she-miḥuẓ le-Prag bi-shnat 1724," *Ẓion* 9 (1944): 1–26.

9. "Statistische Tabellen über alle israelitische Gemeinden, Synagogen, Schulen und Rabbinate in Böhmen," in Albert Kohn, ed., *Die Notablenversammlung der Israeliten Böhmens in Prag* (Vienna, 1852), pp. 383–414; Jan Heřman, "The Evolution of the Jewish Population in Bohemia and Moravia, 1754–1953," in U. O. Schmelz, P. Glikson, and S. Della Pergola, eds., *Papers in Jewish Demography, 1973* (Jerusalem, 1977), p. 259.

10. Heřman, "The Evolution of the Jewish Population in Prague, 1869–1939," p. 54.

11. On the gradual emancipation of Austrian Jewry between 1848 and 1867, see Bihl, "Die Juden," pp. 890–96; and Häusler, "Toleranz, Emanzipation und Antisemitismus," pp. 89–108.

12. Heřman, "Evolution of the Jewish Population in Bohemia," p. 261.

13. *Encyclopaedia Judaica*, vol. 4, col. 1179. Ruth Kestenberg-Gladstein has offered a further index with which to measure the decline of small-town Jewish life in Bohemia. Making use of the government census of 1724, a survey of 1849 sponsored by the Landesjudenschaft, and the 1893 report of the Bohemian Kultusgemeinden, she demonstrates how most of the medium-sized communities grew between the first and the second censuses only to decline dramatically by the last decade of the nineteenth century. Kolín, for example, which lies about 70 kilometers east of Prague, possessed 99 Jewish families in 1724, 313 in 1849, and only 215 in 1893. The town of Polná, on the Bohemian-Moravian border, had no Jewish settlement in 1724, 128 families in 1849, and 58 in 1893. Unfortunately Kestenberg-Gladstein makes the erroneous assumption, based on a misreading of her second source, that the original expansion in the Jewish population occurred within a span of only three years, between 1849 and 1852! See Kestenberg-Gladstein, "The Jews Between Czechs and Germans in the Historic Lands, 1848–1918," in *The Jews of Czechoslovakia*, vol. 1 (Philadelphia, 1968), pp. 27–32.

14. Heřman, "Evolution of the Jewish Population in Bohemia," p. 259.

15. Heřman, "Evolution of the Jewish Population in Prague," p. 54. For slightly varying figures, see Bohemia, Statistisches Landesamt, *Statistická příručka království českého*, 2d ed. (Prague, 1913), pp. 32–33. "Greater Prague" is taken to mean the five districts of the inner city

(Staré Město, Nové Město, Malá Strana, Hradčany, and Josefov), Vyšehrad, Holešovice, and Libeň (incorporated into the city between 1883 and 1901), and the four contiguous suburbs of Karlín, Žižkov, Vinohrady, and Smíchov. These, together with outlying areas, became part of Prague in 1922.

16 Heřman, "Evolution of the Jewish Population in Prague," p. 54.

17. Ibid., p. 58. The total increase was 13,384 of which 9,269 came from immigration and 4,115 from natural increase.

18. Ibid., p. 57.

19. Gary B. Cohen, "Ethnicity and Urban Population Growth: The Decline of the Prague Germans, 1880–1910," in Keith Hitchins, ed., *Studies in East European Social History*, vol. 2 (Leiden, 1981), p. 10.

20. Cohen, "Ethnicity and Urban Population Growth," p. 10; also Cohen, *Politics of Ethnic Survival*, p. 95. The total number of immigrant citizen residents in 1900 was 234,626. Of these 199,612 came from the predominantly Czech portions of Bohemia; moreover, this figure represented 93 percent of the immigrants from all parts of the province.

21. Elizabeth Wiskemann, *Czechs and Germans: A Study of the Struggle in the Historic Provinces of Bohemia and Moravia*, 2d ed. (London, 1967), pp. 216–17.

22. Heinrich Rauchberg, "Der nationale Besitzstand in Böhmen und die Wanderbewegung," *Deutsche Arbeit* 2 (1902–3): 600.

23. Cohen, *Politics of Ethnic Survival*, pp. 95–96; Bruce M. Garver, *The Young Czech Party, 1874–1901, and the Emergence of a Multi-Party System* (New Haven, Conn., 1978), p. 27.

24. See Kestenberg-Gladstein's magisterial study of the period in her *Neuere Geschichte;* also Kieval, "Caution's Progress."

25. See the discussion and figures in Cohen, *Politics of Ethnic Survival*, p. 96.

26. Some 9,880 (about 54 percent) of the Jewish residents of Prague I–VII declared their language to be Czech, only 8,230 proclaimed German. Statistics that relate language of daily use to religion can be found in Bohemia, *Statistická příručka Království českého*, pp. 30–31; and Jan Srb, ed., *Sčítaní lidu v Král. hlavní městě Praze a obcech sousedních provedené 31. prosince 1900*, 3 vols. (Prague, 1902–8), cited in Cohen, "Ethnicity and Urban Population Growth"; see also Cohen's *Politics of Ethnic Survival* and "Jews in German Society: Prague, 1860–1914." For Bohemian Jews generally, see Bureau für Statistik der Juden, Berlin, *Die Juden in Österreich* (Berlin, 1908), p. 109.

27. Cohen, "Ethnicity and Urban Population Growth," p. 11.

28. On the Hánka forgeries, see Christoph Stölzl, "Zur Geschichte der böhmischen Juden in der Epoche des modernen Nationalismus," pt. 2, *Bohemia* 15 (1974): 138–40.

29. Stölzl, "Geschichte der böhmischen Juden," pt. 2, pp. 146–48.

30. On Teller, see Stölzl, "Geschichte der böhmischen Juden," pt. 1,p. 200; pt. 2, p. 141. In 1848 Teller published an essay in *Österreichisches Centralorgan für Glaubensfreiheit, Cultur, Geschichte, und Literatur der Juden* entitled "Toleranz der Tschechen," in which he laid to rest once and for all the dream of Czech-Jewish symbiosis.

31. *Die Juden und die Nationalen: Ein Gegenstück zur Broschüre: "Die Juden in Böhmen." Von einem Juden* (Prague, 1863).

32. Ibid., pp. 13–14.

33. Ibid., p. 15.

34. Ibid., p. 16.

35. "Über die wahre Stellung des Judentums zur nationalen Bewegung. Von einem Juden," *Politik* (14, 24, and 26 October 1865). Quoted in Stölzl, "Geschichte der böhmischen Juden," pt. 2, pp. 150–51.

36. "Über die wahre Stellung des Judentums," *Politik* (26 October 1865); Stölzl, "Geschichte der böhmischen Juden," pt. 2, p. 151, n. 129.

37. On the Constitutional party in Bohemia in the 1860s and 1870s, see Cohen, *Politics of Ethnic Survival*, pp. 60–72.

38. Jan Neruda, *Pro strach židovský* (Prague, 1870); all references are to the 1942 Prague edition.

39. "Jews live everywhere as a foreign nation; to us they are the most foreign" (*Pro strach židovský*, p. 16).

40. Ibid., p. 9.

41. Antonín F. Tokstein, *Židé v Čechách* (Prague, 1867), p. 6; references are to the second edition, published in Prague by E. Beaufort, 1939.

42. Ibid., p. 32.

43. Ibid., p. 34.

44. Jakub Scharf, "Deset let," *KČŽ* 6 (1886–87): 138–46; Vlastimila Hamáčková, "Débuts du mouvement assimilateur tchéco-juif," *Judaica Bohemiae* 14 (1978): 15–17.

45. According to contemporary accounts and reminiscences, the following individuals took active leadership roles in the early years of the association's existence: Original executive committee: Luděk Fischl, Alexander Frank, Josef Podvinec (law); Eduard Kohn, Hynek Brumlík (medicine); and Josef Weinberg (engineering). Other active members: Adolf Stránský, Leopold Katz, Jakub Scharf, August Stein, Josef Žalud, Vondörfer (law); Karel Fischer (journalist-editor); Bohumil Bondy (factory owner, Prague Town Council, Prague Chamber of Commerce). See Hamáčková, "Débuts," pp. 15–17; Scharf, "Deset let," p. 139; Josef Vyskočil, "Die tschechisch-jüdische Bewegung," *Judaica Bohemiae* 3 (1967): 41–42; *Dějiny českožidovského hnutí* (Prague, 1932), p. 7; and August Stein, "Zidé v Čechách," *KČŽ* 1 (1881–82): 103–6.

46. Spolek českých akademiků-židů v Praze, *Výroční zpráva spolku českých akademiků-židů v Praze, 1878–79.*

47. Ibid., 1878–79.

48. Ibid., 1882–83..

49. Ibid., 1878–79; 1882–83; 1890–91; 1892–93. For the number of Jewish students at Prague's Czech and German universities between 1891 and 1941, see the tables in Stuart Borman, "The Prague Student Zionist Movement, 1896–1914" (Ph.D. Diss., Univ. of Chicago, 1972), pp. 161–68.

50. "Bohumil Bondy," *KČŽ* 4 (1884–85): 57–59; also "Bohumil Bondy," *KČŽ* 12 (1892–93): 51ff.

51. "Dva přední buditelé českožidovství," *KČŽ* 16 (1896–97): 74–76.

52. Vyskočil, "Die tschechisch-jüdische Bewegung," p. 42.

53. Born in 1842, Zucker entered the university in 1859 and received the doctor of laws degree in 1864. An expert in criminal law, Zucker was named docent at the law faculty in 1870, lecturer in 1874, and professor in 1881. He generally chose to lecture in Czech, and, when the university split in 1882, he joined the Czech branch. Zucker became dean of the Czech law faculty in 1884. (Josef Žalud, "Prof. Dr. Alois Zucker," *KČŽ* 6 [1886–87]: 58–63.)

54. Karel Fischer "J.U.Dr. Josef Žalud," *KČŽ* 8 (1888–89): 55–58.

55. "Dva přední buditelé českožidovství," pp. 72–74.

56. For Viktor Vohryzek see Introduction *(Úvod)* to *K židovské otázce* (Prague, 1923), pp. 7–10; and O. Guth, "Dr. Vohryzek k 50. narozeninám," *KČŽ* 34 (1914–15): 136–40. For Lederer see Oskar Donath, *Židé a židovství v české literatuře 19. a 20. století,* (Brno, 1930), 2: 204–5, and O. Guth, "K 50. narozeninám Dra. Eduarda Lederera," *KČŽ* 29 (1909–10): 70–72. For Klineberger see Donath, *Židé a židovství,* 2: 202–3. And for Jindřich Kohn, see Zdeněk Tohn, "Dr. Jindřich Kohn," *KČŽ* 55 (1935–36): 14–32.

57. Perhaps the strongest evocation of this sentiment can be found in Jakub Scharf, "Deset let," pp. 141–42; but it appears in various forms throughout the literature of the Czech-Jewish movement, particularly in the reminiscences and short stories of Vojtěch Rakous. It was not only the assimilationists who idealized the Czech-Jewish relationship in the countryside. The Zionist philosopher Hugo Bergmann, recalling scenes of his childhood in the village of Chrastice, also argued for the existence there of a symbiotic Czech-Jewish culture. He reports

that he not only grew up fully bilingually, but also experienced rural Catholic culture as a natural element in his life. Jewish children raced to kiss the ring of the local priest when he was spotted on the street no less quickly than their Christian counterparts, and when a village Jew was greeted by his Czech friends with the customary "Blessed be Jesus Christ," he would routinely answer "for ever and ever." See Hugo Bergmann, "Prag," in *Yahadut Czechoslovakia* (Jerusalem, 1969), p. 88; also his "Petaḥ Davar" (Foreword) to the same volume, p. 9.

58. Stanley Z. Pech, *The Czech Revolution of 1848* (Chapel Hill, N.C., 1969), pp. 31–32.

59. Friedrich Prinz, "Das kulturelle Leben," in Karl Bosl, ed., *Handbuch der Geschichte der Böhmischen Länder,* (Stuttgart, 1969–70), 4: 160–61. By 1914 of the 171 state secondary schools in the Czech lands, 77 (45 percent) were German and 94 (55 percent) Czech; of 61 private schools, 27 (44.3 percent) were German, 33 (54.1 percent) were Czech, and one (1.6 percent) was Polish (Prinz, "Das kulturelle Leben," p. 161).

60. *Českožidovské listy,* 15 December 1898, p. 2.

61. Žalud, "Prof. Dr. Alois Zucker," pp. 58–63; "Dva přední buditelé českožidovství," pp. 72–74; Fischer, "J.U.Dr. Josef Žalud," pp. 55–58; Donath, *Židé a židovství v české literatuře,* 2: 202–5; Guth, "Dr. Viktor Vohryzek k 50. narozeninám," pp. 136–40; and Tohn, "Dr. Jindřich Kohn," pp. 14–32.

62. For an examination of Young Czech politics in the 1880s and 1890s, see Chapters 2 and 3. On the social, economic, and demographic background of the Young Czech party, see Garver, *The Young Czech Party,* pp. 6–120.

63. See Richard Wolf, *České studentsvo v době prvního třicetiletí české univerzity (1882–1912)* (Prague, 1912).

64. Vyskočil, "Die tschechisch-jüdische Bewegung," pp. 41–42; Stein, "Židé v Čechách," pp. 104–6.

65. Spolek českých akademiků-židů v Praze, *Stanovy spolku* (Prague, 1891).

66. Stein, "Židé v Čechách," pp. 105–6.

67. Spolek českých akademiků-židů, *Výroční zprávy, 1878–83.* In most cases, the non-Jewish dignitaries were listed as "honorary members" of the association. However, Julius Grégr was actually one of the "founding members" of the group.

68. Spolek českých akademiků-židů, *Výroční zprávy, 1890–91* and *1902–03.*

69. See the recapitulation of Josef Žalud, "Náš Kalendář," *KČŽ* 10 (1890–91): 121–22.

70. Jakub Scharf, "Deset let," p. 143; also Žalud, "Náš Kalendář," pp. 121–22; and Hamáčková, "Débuts," p. 18.

71. Hamáčková, "Débuts," p. 18. It was officially known as *Illustrierter israelitischer Volkskalender,* published by Wolf Pascheles and his successors from 1852 to 1939. A German-language rival appeared in 1881, the same year as the *Kalendář.* It was published by Jakub B. Brandeis of Prague and called *Brandeis' illustrierter israelitischer Volkskalender.*

72. Hamáčkova, "Débuts," pp. 16–17; Donath, *Židé a židovství v české literatuře,* 2: 182.

73. Fischer served as editor of the *KČŽ* from 1885 to his death in 1906. On his wide-ranging influence in the literary wing of the Czech-Jewish movement, see Vyskočil, "Die tschechisch-jüdische Bewegung," pp. 42–43, and V. Rakous, "Karel Fischer," *KČŽ 26 (1906–7): 71–74.*

74. Arbes wrote originally for the Old Czech paper *Politik,* which was issued in German. His first Czech literary works appeared in the 1880s. Of these, "Jedná z těch, které mně zajímaly" (One of those who interested me) was published in the *Kalendář* in 1883. He also translated a story by the Bohemian Jewish writer Leopold Kompert for the 1888 volume of the almanac, 'Lovkyně duší" (Huntress of the spirit). Apparently Fischer himself urged Vrchlický to undertake the writing of *Bar Kochba.* See Donath, *Židé a židovství,* 1: 63–118; and Egon Hostovský, "The Czech-Jewish Movement," in *The Jews of Czechoslovakia (Philadelphia, 1971),* 2: 151.

75. Stein, "Židé v Čechách," pp. 83–107. On Stein's contributions to Czech-Jewish ideology, see "Dva přední buditelé českožidovství," pp. 72–74.

76. See, for example, the reminiscences of August Stein, "Ze začátku Spolku českých adademiků-židů," in O. Guth, ed., *1876–1926: Vzpomínky a úvahy* (Prague, 1926), p. 6.

77. Stein, "Židé v Čechách," p. 83.

78. Ibid.: "Z té rovnoprávnosti občanské vyplývá pak židů povinnost a právo, aby se přihlásil k té národnosti, ku které znají se ostátní jeho spoluobčané, v jichž středu stejných s nimi práv a povinnosti požívá." (As a result of this civil equality, the Jew assumes both the obligation and the right to proclaim that nationality which his other fellow citizens—in whose midst and together with whom he partakes of mutual obligations and rights—acknowledge as their own.)

79. At least one contemporary social historian, Ezra Mendelsohn, has argued that the distinction between acculturation and assimilation does indeed apply to East Central Europe and to the Czech lands in particular. However, he attributes the disjunction to the existence of competing secular ideologies, in this case German and Czech nationalism. See Mendelsohn, *The Jews of East Central Europe Between the World Wars* (Bloomington, Ind., 1983), pp. 1–8 and 131–42.

80. Stein, "Židé v Čechách," pp. 98–99.

81. Ibid., pp. 84, 86–87.

82. Stein put forward the wish to avoid incurring the hatred of the Czech masses as one of the practical reasons for allying with the Czech nation (ibid., pp. 88–89).

83. Stein, "Ze začátku Spolku českých akademiků-židů," p. 6.

84. Stein, "Židé v Čechách," p. 90.

85. Ibid., p. 91.

86. See ibid., pp. 91ff.

Chapter 2

1. Included in Vojtěch Rakous, "Drobné vzpomínky," *KČŽ* 38 (1918–19): 21–23. Parts of this chapter, condensed and rearranged, first appeared in my article "Education and National Conflict in Bohemia: Germans, Czechs, and Jews," in Ezra Mendelsohn, ed., *Studies in Contemporary Jewry,* vol. 3 (New York, 1987), pp. 49–71.

2. Ibid.

3. *Českožidovské listy,* 15 December 1898, p. 2.

4. "The need has long been felt, but up to now not fulfilled, that the prayers of the Jews—professors of the Mosaic faith, living in the Czech lands and having command of the Czech language—should for once appear in the national tongue." (From the introduction to Kraus's 1847 *Siddur;* quoted in August Stein's foreword to *Maarche-lew. Modlitby Israelitův* [Prague, 1884]). See also Viktor Teytz, "Trochu retrospektivy a vzpomínek," *KČŽ* 28 (1908–9): 155–59, on Hynek Kraus and Siegfried Kapper.

5. August Stein, "Předmluva" (Foreword) to *Maarche-lew. Modlitby Israelitův.*

6. Vojtěch Rakous, "Hrst vzpomínek," *KČŽ* 25 (1905–6); also in *Vojkovičtí a přespolní* (Prague, 1910), pp. 127–28.

7. J. S. Kraus, "Or-Tomid: Spolek českých židů pro pěstování bohoslužby jazykem českým a hebrejským," *KČŽ* 4 (1884–85): 112.

8. Quoted in Kraus, "Or-Tomid," *KČŽ* 5 (1885–86): 111.

9. Josef Žalud, "Z minulosti a přítomnosti židů v Čechách," *KČŽ* 12 (1892–93): 67.

10. *Modlitby pro dcery israelské* (Prague, 1881).

11. *Haggadah pro první dva večery pasahu* (Prague, 1889).

12. *Žalmy a modlitby v den narozenin Jeho Veličenstva* (1886); *Patero modliteb pro sabat a svátky* (1886); *Pohřební Modlitba* (1887); and *České modlitby při veřejné bohoslužbě v synagoze spolku "Or-Tomid"* (1888).

13. *Maarche-lew. Modlitby Israelitův.*

14. August Stein, "Předmluva" (Foreword) to *Maarche-lew. Modlitby Israelitův,* pp. i–iii.

15. A. Kohn, *Výtah z mojžíšského náboženství* (1883); Lev Thorsch, *Nauka o náboženství mojžíšském pro střední a měšťanské školy* (1884); August Stein, *Děje israelitův,* 2 vols. (1885–86); Filip Bondy, *Torat Mosheh, Učení mojžíšského pro školní mládež* (1886); Hynek Baum,

Základy mojžísského náboženství (1890); Filip Bondy, *Počátky vyučování náboženství mojžíšského* (1891); L. Butter, *První čítánka jazyka hebrejského* (1892). For a complete description of the works published by Or-Tomid during its first decade, see Žalud, "Z minulosti a přítomnosti židů v Čechách," pp. 67–69.

Yet another textbook, not mentioned by Žalud but reviewed in *Jüdische Chronik* in 1895–96, was written by Samuel Königsberg of Benešov. Its title was *Emunath Jisroel. Věro a mravouka israélské* (The faith of Israel. Israelite belief and ethics), and it was intended for use in the fourth and fifth classes of the *Volksschule* and the three classes of the *Bürgerschule* (two types of primary school).

16. Karel Adámek, *Z naší doby* (Velké Meziříčí, 1887), 2: 60.

17. Pech, *The Czech Revolution of 1848*, pp. 31–32.

18. Prinz, "Das kulturelle Leben," 4: 160–61; Adámek, *Z naší doby, 2: 77.*

19. Garver, *The Young Czech Party*, pp. 41–42; Jaroslav Kopáč, *Dějiny české školy a pedagogiky v letech 1867–1914* (Brno, 1968), pp. 16–19; and Jan Šafránek, *Školy české: Obraz jejich vývoje a osudů* (Prague, 1918), 2: 226 ff. The Concordat between Vienna and the Vatican, signed on 4 August 1855, had awarded the church wide-ranging powers, particularly in education. All instruction given to Catholic children—whether in public or in private schools—had to be approved by the church. All teachers in Catholic schools were subject to church supervision, and the church could block the distribution of books that it considered to be morally objectionable (Macartney, *The Habsburg Empire*, p. 458).

20. As late as 1865, the Prague Jewish community maintained fifteen private elementary schools for Jewish children, ten for boys and five for girls. At the same time, the Catholic church ran twenty-four private schools, twenty-one for girls and only three for boys. By the late 1880s the Jewish community had relinquished control of all but two of its schools (Šafránek, *Školy české*, 2: 201; and Adámek, *Z naší doby*, 4: 80).

21. Kopáč, *Dějiny české školy*, pp. 18–19; Garver, *Young Czech Party*, pp. 10, 42. The first Czech-language polytechnic was established in Prague in 1869.

22. The figures come from Adámek, *Z naší doby,* 2: 10–11, which in turn were based on official census reports.

23. Ibid., 2: 77.

24. Ibid., 2: 12, 77.

25. Ibid., 2: 11–12.

26. Ibid., 2: 12.

27. Ibid., 2: 83.

28. K. K. Statistische Central-Commission, *Österreichisches Statistisches Handbuch* 10 (1892): 40–43. On the eve of the partition of the University of Prague (winter and summer semesters 1880–81), Czechs composed 66.2 percent and 67.3 percent of the total student body (*Österreichiches Statistisches Handbuch* 1 [1883]: 46–49).

29. Ibid., 56–59.

30. Ibid., 10 (1892): 48–51. For German nationalist fears concerning the deleterious effects of the Czech schools on the German-speaking population of Bohemia, see Hillel J. Kieval, "Education and National Conflict in Bohemia: Germans, Czechs, and Jews," in Ezra Mendelsohn, ed., *Studies in Contemporary Jewry*, vol. 3 (New York, 1987), pp. 49–51.

31. The figure for 1886 comes from Adámek, *Z naší doby*, vol. 2: 81.

32. On the German Schulverein in Bohemia, see Franz Perko, "Die Tätigkeit des deutschen Schulvereines in Böhmen," *Deutsche Arbeit* 3 (1903–4): 386–410. For the activities of the Schulverein in Prague before 1914, see Cohen, *The Politics of Ethnic Survival*, pp. 158–62.

33. Adámek, *Z naší doby*, 2: 14. The figure of 4,470 may have included non-Jewish students who for one reason or another attended German-Jewish schools. Adámek lists them as Jews, but Josef Kořán, writing in the *KČŽ* (1886–87), claims that 192 Catholics and 17 Protestants were enrolled in Jewish communal schools in the Czech countryside in 1885–86 (see n.37 below).

The total number of Jewish students enrolled in Volks- and Bürgerschulen (obecné and měšťanské školy), both public and private, in Bohemia in 1880 was 13,574—about 1.6 percent of the total primary school enrollment. See *Österreichisches Statistisches Handbuch* 1 (1883): 82–83. The Bureau für Statistik der Juden, *Die Juden in Österreich* (Berlin, 1908), gives the percentage of Jewish boys at public elementary schools in all of Austria as 2 percent in 1880, 2.35 percent in 1890, and 2.6 percent in 1900. The percentage of girls was 3.18 percent in 1880, 3.81 percent in 1890, and 4.31 percent in 1900 (*Die Juden in Österreich*, p. 87).

34. Adámek, *Z naší doby*, 2: 14.

35. See Kestenberg-Gladstein, "The Jews between Czechs and Germans," pp. 49–50.

36. Šafránek, *Školy české*, 2: 201.

37. Josef Kořán, "Židovské školy v Čechách," *KČŽ* 6 (1886–87), and "Židovské školy v Čechách roku 1894–95," *KČŽ* 16 (1896–97).

38. Cohen, "Ethnicity and Urban Population Growth," pp. 25–26; Cohen, *The Politics of Ethnic Survival*, pp. 224–25; and Cohen, "Jews in German Society," p. 38.

39. Bureau für Statistik der Juden, Berlin, *Die Juden in Österreich*, p. 92. *Österreichisches Statistisches Handbuch* 1 (1883) gives slightly different figures. For the academic year 1880–81: number of Jewish students at gymnasia and Realgymnasia in Bohemia—1,761 (11.1 percent of the total); at Realschulen/Reálky—544 (10.8 percent) (*Österreichisches Statistisches Handbuch* 1 (1883): 70–71).

40. Bureau für Statistik der Juden, Berlin, *Die Juden in Österreich*, p. 94. The tables compiled by Gustav Otruba in *Die Juden in den böhmischen Ländern* (Munich, 1983)—which are derived from *Österreichische Statistik*, Bd. 9, Heft 1—are largely in agreement ("Statistische Materialien zur Geschichte der Juden in den böhmischen Ländern"). One exception concerns Jewish attendance at Czech Reálky, which is given as 48 by *Die Juden in Österreich* but as 495 by Otruba! The latter is obviously in error. A perusal of figures for the two decades beginning in 1882 reveals that the number of Jewish studenst at Czech Reálky never exceeded 315. As late as 1890, the number was only 76.

41. G. Otruba, "Die Universitäten in der Hochschulorganisation der Donau-Monarchie," in M. Rassem, ed., *Student und Hochschule im 19. Jahrhundert* (Göttingen, 1975), pp. 75–155; *Österreichisches Statistisches Handbuch* 1 (1883): 46–49 and 56–59. I do not have at my disposal the precise number of Bohemian Jews who chose to attend the University of Vienna rather than Prague. Marsha Rozenblit's *The Jews of Vienna, 1867–1914* (Albany, N.Y., 1983), offers data on the place of birth of Jewish gymnasium students in Vienna but nothing concerning Jewish university students.

42. Bureau für Statistik der Juden, Berlin, *Die Juden in Österreich*, p. 102.

43. Adámek, *Z naší doby*, 2: 20.

44. On Havlíček's rejection of Kapper's pro-Czech writings, see Guido Kisch, *In Search of Freedom: A History of American Jews from Czechoslovakia* (London, 1949), pp. 26–44 and 213–14.

45. Adámek, *Z naší doby*, 2: 32–33.

46. Ibid., 2: 33. In the fourth and final volume of the work, published in 1890, Adámek indicated that the Schulverein subsidized 14 percent of the private Jewish elementary schools in Bohemia, certainly a low figure given the ardor of the Czech national grievance against the Jews (Adámek, *Z naší doby*, 4: 80).

47. Kořán, "Židovské školy v Čechách," pp. 97–102.

48. Ibid., p. 101.

49. J. S. Kraus, "Německo-židovské školy v Čechách," *KČŽ* 2 (1882–83): 117–25.

50. On Bondy, see *Ottův slovník naučný 4 (1891): 337*, and "Bohumil Bondy," *KČŽ* 4 (1884–85): 57–59. For Zucker, see Žalud, "Prof. Dr. Alois Zucker," *KČŽ* 6 (1886–87): 58–63. And for Žalud, Fischer, "J.U. Dr. Josef Žalud," *KČŽ* 8 (1888–89): 55–58.

51. The National Liberals emerged in 1874 as a break-away wing of the National party, which opposed the prevailing policy of "passive resistance," that is, nonparticipation in the Diet and

the Reichsrat. On the split between Old and Young Czechs, see Garver, *The Young Czech Party*, pp. 1–87.

52. The Central School Foundation had been created to counteract the influence of the Austrian-German Schulverein (which also was established in 1880) essentially by setting up and funding private Czech schools in areas that were predominantly German and that possessed less than the minimum number of children required by law to support a public Czech school (forty children divided among five grades). The Národní jednoty in turn provided peripheral support to the Central School Foundation, offered legal aid to Czechs in predominantly German districts who were involved in litigation with local or imperial authorities, and conducted private censuses in such districts—encouraging Czech residents to take the opportunity to declare their Czech nationality. The largest and most powerful of the "national unions" were the Národní jednota pošumavská (founded in 1884) and the Národní jednota severočeská (1885). See Garver, *The Young Czech Party*, pp. 112–15.

53. *Dějiny českožidovského hnutí*, p. 8.

54. "Náš úkol" (Our mission), *Českožidovské listy*, 15 September 1894. *Českožidovské listy* (1894–1907) began as a fortnightly publication but eventually appeared every week. Issued from Prague, it reflected the official views of both the SČAŽ and the Czech-Jewish National Union. It was also closly allied to the Young Czech party on national issues.

55. *Českožidovské listy*, 15 October 1894, pp. 1–2.

56. Ibid., 1 November 1894, p. 1.

57. Kořán, "Židosvké školy v Čechách roku 1894–95," pp.152–57.

58. Kořán, "Židosvké školy v Čechách roku 1894–95," pp. 155–56. Many of these Catholic and Protestant children actually attended Jewish-supported schools (180 Catholics and 17 Protestants in 1885; 163 and 13, respectively, in 1894).

59. Ibid., pp. 155–57. Kořán continued to demonstrate dissatisfaction with the overall educational situation of the Jews. In 1890 there were more children between the ages of six and fourteen in Jewish schools than the total number of registered Germans in those localities (a measurement which ordinarily would indicate the need for a minority school). In Nový Bydžov, for example, only 28 people in the entire town registered as Germans, yet there were 53 children in the German school; in Hořice the figures were 14 (Germans) and 28 (children); in Mělník, 18 and 40; in Kolín, 98 and 131. There were even instances of German-Jewish schools in areas where not a single person had registered as German. These statistics indicate a sociocultural phenomenon unique to Bohemian Jewry. Normally bilingual, and sensitive to the political climate, the Jews readily indicated their national standing as Czech, yet demonstrated unwavering loyalty to the ideal of a German education.

60. *Českožidovské listy*, 1 February 1898.

61. See ibid., 1 January 1898, p. 7.

62. Ibid., 15 March 1898, p. 3.

63. Ibid., pp. 3–4. Emphasis in the original.

64. "Národní Jednota Českožidovská," *KČŽ* 26 (1906–7): 181–82.

65. Compare the figures in the two articles by Kořán: "Židovské školy v Čechách," and "Židovksé školy v Čechách roku 1894–95." Even the attendance figure of 4,240 for 1885 represented a drop of over 600 from that of 1880 (*Die Juden in Österreich*, p. 82).

66. The population of the school dropped by about 23 percent (from 190 to 147) between 1885 and 1898. The 1885 figure is given in Kořán, "Židovské školy v Čechách."

67. The radicalization of Czech and German political life is examined in detail in Chapter 3.

68. Bohemia, Statistisches Landesamt, *Statistická příručka království českého*, p. 131; and Bureau für Statistik der Juden, Berlin, *Die Juden in Österreich*, p. 87.

69. *Die Juden in Österreich*, pp. 82–84.

70. *Die Juden in den böhmischen Ländern* (Munich and Vienna, 1983). Appendix V: "Der Anteil der Juden am höheren Schulwesen Böhmens, Mährens, und Schlesiens," pp. 348–49. The figures in this table accord in nearly all instances with the data provided by *Die Juden in Österreich* for the school years 1881–82 through 1903–4.

71. *Die Juden in den böhmischen Ländern*, pp. 348–49.

72. The total number of Jewish students registered at Bohemian middle schools rose in absolute terms only slightly between 1882 and 1912, from 3,129 to 3,441. As a percentage of the student body, the second figure represented a decline from 12.1 percent to 8.4 percent. According to *Die Juden in Österreich*, the Jewish population in Bohemian gymnasia and Realschulen may have reached its peak in absolute terms in 1903–4, when it reached 2,744. However, the relative weight of Jewish attendance was never greater than in 1888–89, when 2,528 Jewish students in gymnasia and Realschulen stood for 12 percent of the student body (*Die Juden in Österreich*, pp. 94–95, 97).

73. Figures derived from *Die Juden in den böhmischen Ländern*, pp. 348–49.

In the technical high schools (Reálky or Realschulen) Jewish attendance patterns took a different course. In 1882 the 495 Jews who went to Czech Reálky represented a healthy 11.3 percent of the student body. Thereafter the number dropped off precipitously (250, or 2.3 percent, by 1912), but the reasons for this are not apparent. On the German side, meanwhile, the number of Jews attending Realschulen nearly doubled between 1882 and 1912 (from 448 to 804), while their relative weight as a percentage of the whole declined slightly from 18.6 to 15.8 percent.

74. *Die Juden in den böhmischen Ländern*, p. 350; K. K. statistische Central-Commission, *Österreichisches Statistisches Handbuch* 1 (1883): 46–47. In contrast, Jews made up more than 25 percent of the student body at the University of Vienna in 1880–81, 11.7 percent of the University of Lemberg (Lwów), 8.9 percent of Krakow, and 27.7 percent of Czernowitz.

75. *Österreichisches Statistisches Handbuch* 10 (1892): 40–43.

76. Ibid. 20 (1902): 78–81; *Die Juden in den böhmischen Ländern*, p. 350. During the same winter semester 1899–1900, Jews composed 24.7 percent of the student body at the University of Vienna, 19.8 percent of the University of Lemberg, 15.8 percent of Krakow, and 44.4 percent of Czernowitz.

77. Figures derived from *Die Juden in Österreich*, p. 102.

78. Ibid., pp. 103–4.

79. Ratios derived from ibid., p. 103.

80. "Gesetz vom 21. März 1890, betreffend die Regelung der äusseren Rechtsverhältnisse der israelitischen Religionsgesellschaft," in *Jahrbuch für die israelitischen Cultusgemeinden Böhmens* (Prague, 1893), pp. 269–78.

81. "Statut der israelitischen Cultusgemeinde in Prag, welches der h.k.k. Statthalterei zur Genehmigung vorgelegt wurde," in ibid., pp. 136–49.

82. See in particular Jakub Scharf, *Národní jednota českožidovská ve světle české veřejnosti* (Prague, 1893), a compilation of two speeches by Scharf that had been delivered in Plzeň and Benešov.

83. Garver, *The Young Czech Party*, p. 110. Under Austrian law an organization chartered as a "patriotic and cultural society" could not engage directly in politics and could lose its charter if imperial authorities judged that it had done so.

84. *Dějiny českožidovského hnutí*, pp. 8–9. Sometime between the banning and the reinstatement of the Czech-Jewish National Union, the rarely mentioned Politická jednota českožidovská (Czech-Jewish Political Union) came into existence. This was to be the openly political arm of the Czech-Jewish movement, closely aligned with the Young Czech party, and charged with informing Czech Jews how to vote in upcoming elections. The Political Union appears to have been relegated to the shadows after 1895. It appeared again briefly in 1912 and was officially reactivated early in 1918 in anticipation of the resumption of political life in Bohemia. See *KČŽ* 32 (1912–13), and 38 (1918–19).

85. *Israelitische Gemeindezeitung. Central-Organ für die Gesammtinteressen des Judentums* (Prague, 1873–1901). The Central-Verein apparently assumed control of the paper shortly after the organization was established in 1885.

86. *Českožidovské listy*, 15 January 1898, p.5.

87. Ibid., 1 July 1899, pp. 3–4; 19 July 1899, p. 1.

88. Ibid., 16 October 1899, p. 2; 1 June 1900, p. 5.

89. According to František Friedmann, Czoernig's *Ethnographie der österreichischen Monarchie* (1849–57) included Jews in the section on "Small Races" (*die kleinen Völkerstämme*). Josef Hain's *Handbuch der Statistik des österreichischen Kaiserstaates* (1853) presented the Jews alternatively as a nation and as a religious group; figures for both categories were the same. And Czoernig's *Statistisches Handbuchlein für die österreichischen Monarchie* (1861), based on the census of 1857, once again described the Jews as a national group. See Friedmann, "Židé v Čechách," in Hugo Gold, ed., *Židé a židovské obce v Čechách v minulosti a v přítomnosti* (Brno and Prague, 1934), p. 733; Heinrich Rauchberg, *Der nationale Besitzstand in Böhmen* (Leipzig, 1905), 1: 8–11.

90. See the discussion in Rauchberg, *Der nationale Besitzstand,* 1: 10–14; also Emil Brix, *Die Umgangssprachen in Altösterreich zwischen Agitation und Assimilation* (Vienna, Cologne, and Graz, 1982). The president of the Central Statistical Commission explained that the term "Umgangssprache" was meant to indicate "that language, which the population of local towns and communities actually spoke" (quoted in Rauchberg, 1: 13–14). If this had really been the case, however, the government would have sent teams of observers throughout the monarchy who, on the basis of firsthand experience, would later map the country's linguistic divisions. In fact, individuals were allowed to declare their "everyday language" to census takers, with the restriction that only answers that corresponded to languages actually used in the region in question (hence, "landesüblich") would be counted.

91. Friedmann, "Židé v Čechách," p. 733; also Ezra Mendelsohn, "Jewish Assimilation in L'viv: The Case of Wilhelm Feldman," in Andrei S. Markovits and Frank E. Sysyn, eds., *Nationbuilding and the Politics of Nationalism: Essays on Austrian Galicia* (Cambridge, Mass., 1982), p. 94.

92. Cohen,, *The Politics of Ethnic Survival,* p. 101; Cohen, "Jews in German Society," p. 38. For the countrywide census, see *Österreichische Statistik,* vol. 32, pts. 1 and 3 (1895).

93. *Österreichische Statistik,* vol. 63, pt. 3 (1902), p. 178; *Die Juden in Österreich,* p. 109; Cohen, "Ethnicity and Urban Population Growth," p. 14. The breakdown for the 1900 census was as follows:

For Bohemia as a whole:	Czech	50,080
	German	40,521
	Other	177
For the city of Prague:	Czech	9,880
	German	8,230

94. *Dějiny česko židovského hnutí,* p. 19.

95. Gary Cohen appears to argue for this interpretation in "Jews in German Society": "The experience of the Jews who aspired to join Czech society awaits systematic treatment, but one suspects that their adoption of Czech allegiances represented more an act of necessity than a sign of any great mutual affection" (p. 36). And again, "The general weakening of the German Liberals in the 1890s, the increasing militancy of the Czech parties, and the shock of the Czech anti-Semitic violence in 1897 apparently persuaded many of the less prosperous Jews to hold out the olive branch to the Czechs and affirm Czech allegiances in the 1900 census" (pp. 37–38).

96. Cohen, *The Politics of Ethnic Survival,* p. 102.

97. Cohen, "Ethnicity and Urban Population Growth," p. 16; Cohen, *The Politics of Ethnic Survival,* pp. 101–7.

98. Cohen, "Ethnicity and Urban Population Growth," pp. 16–17.

Chapter 3

1. Historic "state right" refers to the doctrine, developed by conservative Czech nationalists in the 1850s, that that part of the Habsburg monarchy corresponding to the ancient borders of the Kingdom of Bohemia had a historic right to autonomous government. On the early history of the Young Czech party, see Garver, *The Young Czech Party,* pp. 61–69; Stanley B. Winters, "The Young Czech Party (1874–1914): An Appraisal," *Slavic Review* 28 (1969): 426–44; and (on the policy of passive resistance) Stanley Z. Pech, "Passive Resistance of the Czechs, 1863–

1879," *Slavonic and East European Review* 36 (1958): 434–52. Parts of this chapter have appeared in my article "Nationalism and Antisemitism: The Czech-Jewish Response," in Jehuda Reinharz, ed., *Living with Antisemitism: Modern Jewish Responses* (Hanover and London, 1987), pp. 210–33.

2. The Austrian bureaucracy distinguished between "external" and "internal" services. Customarily linguistic equality meant the right to employ one's own language in face-to-face relations with court officers and government officials. Such encounters fell under the category of "external" service. Increasingly, Czech nationalists sought to extend the areas in which Czech could or had to be employed. Above all, they wanted to include their language in the internal proceedings of governmental bodies (that is to say, in communications among government officials or court officers). These areas were referred to as "internal" services. See H. Gordon Skilling, "The Politics of the Czech Eighties," in Peter Brock and H. Gordon Skilling, eds., *The Czech Renascence of the Nineteenth Century* (Toronto, 1970), pp. 254–81; Friedrich Prinz, "Die böhmischen Länder von 1848 bis 1914," in Karl Bosl, ed., *Handbuch der Geschichte der böhmischen Länder* (Stuttgart, 1968), 3: 3–235; and Berthold Sutter, *Die Badenischen Sprachverordnungen von 1897: Ihre Genesis und ihre Auswirkungen vornehmlich auf die innerösterreichischen Alpenländer* (Graz and Cologne, 1960–65), vol. 1.

3. Skilling, "Politics of the Czech Eighties," p. 258; and H. Gordon Skilling, "The Partition of the University in Prague," *Slavonic and East European Review* 27 (1949): 430–49.

4. Skilling, "Politics of the Czech Eighties," p. 272; Garver, *The Young Czech Party,* pp. 146–53; and Stanley B. Winters, "Kramář, Kaizl, and the Hegemony of the Young Czech Party, 1891–1901," in Brock and Skilling, eds., *The Czech Renascence of the Nineteenth Century,* pp. 282–314. See also Tomáš Vojtěch, *Mladočeší a boj o politickou moc v Čechách* (Prague, 1980).

5. Garver, *The Young Czech Party,* pp. 108, 152–53.

6. Winters, "Kramář, Kaizl, and the Hegemony of the Young Czech Party, 1891–1901," pp. 282–314.

7. František Červinka, *Český nacionalismus v 19. století* (Prague, 1964); *Boje a směry českého studentstva na sklonku minulého a na počátku našeho století* (Prague, 1962). For a more charitable view of Young Czech attitudes, see Garver, *The Young Czech Party,* pp. 302–3.

8. Michael A. Riff, "Czech Antisemitism and the Jewish Response before 1914," *Wiener Library Bulletin* 29 (1976): 8–9. See J. Svozil, "Několik slov o hesle 'Svůj k svému,'" *Naše Doba* 8 (1900–1901): 641–46, for a moderate Czech view on the use of economic boycott as a weapon in the national controversy; and *Českožidovské listy,* 1 March 1898, pp. 1–2, for a Czech-Jewish view.

9. Riff, "Czech Antisemitism," pp. 9–10.

10. Both statements recorded in ibid., p. 10.

11. On the occasion of the Christian Socialists' first municipal victory, the emperor simply refused to seat Lueger. The next year he persuaded him to accept the position of vice-mayor instead. See C. A. Macartney, *The Habsburg Empire, 1790–1918* (New York, 1969), p. 672.

12. František Červinka, "The Hilsner Affair," *LBIYB* 13 (1968): 142–43.

13. On the elections of 1897 generally, see Garver, *The Young Czech Party,* pp. 234–37.

14. See the discussion in Christoph Stölzl, *Kafkas böses Böhmen,* pp. 61–62.

15. *Israelitische Gemeindezeitung,* 1897, p. 66; quoted in Stölzl, *Kafkas böses Böhmen,* p. 61.

16. Garver, *The Young Czech Party,* p. 236, p. 477, n. 77.

17. Reported in the *Israelitische Gemeindezeitung,* 1897, p. 77; quoted in Stölzl, *Kafkas böses Böhmen,* p. 62.

18. Rudolf Vrba, *Národní sebeochrana. Úvahy o hmotném a mravním úpadku národa českého* (Prague, 1898), p. 57.

19. Ibid., p. 322.

20. Ibid., pp. 396–98.

21. Garver, *The Young Czech Party,* p. 302; based on Jaromír Vana, ed., *Volby do říšské rady v Království českém roku 1897* (Prague, 1897).

22. Jaroslava Procházková, *Český lid a český žid: Časové úvahy* (Žižkov [Prague], 1897), pp. 17–18.

23. Ibid., pp. 7–9.

24. Ibid., p. 22.

25. Adámek, *Z naší doby,* 4: 80.

26. Adámek, *Slovo o židech,* esp. pp. 40–42.

27. Procházková, *Český lid,* p. 31:

Takový antisemitismus není pak protižidovskou agitace, nýbrž obsahlou společenskou reformaci, jež jest nanejvýš nutná, nemá-li lidstvo upadati dále a dále do kalu hmotné i duševní bídy.

Tento ethický antisemitismus, jenž nemá za poklad nesnášenlivost náboženskou ani nevraživost plemennou ani zášť třídní, jenž zamyšlí umravnění lidstva, hajení národních prav, ochranu slabších proti silnějším, vymanění ostátních tříd z podruží třídy jedině a zlepšení poměru všech tříd, tento antisemitismus jest oduvodněn se stanoviska náboženského, národnostního, svobodomyslného, národohospodařského i humanního.

(Such antisemitism, then, is not anti-Jewish agitation, but rather broad, social reform, which is most necessary if the people are not to sink further and further into the mud of material and spiritual poverty.

This ethical antisemitism, which does not value religious intolerance or racial malice or class hatred; which is preoccupied with the improvement of mankind, the defense of national rights, the shielding of the weaker from the stronger, the freeing of the other classes from the oppression of one class, and the improvement of the relations among all classes—this antisemitism is justified from the religious, the national, the liberal, the economic, and the humanitarian perspective.)

Elsewhere (p. 56) Procházková argues *against* what she refers to as "unenlightened" *(neuvědomelý)* antisemitism.

28. Adámek, *Slovo o židech,* pp. 45–47.

29. Winters, "Kramář, Kaizl, and the Hegemony of the Young Czech Party," p. 304; Sutter, *Die Badenischen Sprachverordnungen von 1897,* 1: 11.

30. Sutter, *Die Badenischen Sprachverordnungen,* 2: 231–32; Riff, "Czech Antisemitism," pp. 11–13.

31. Sutter, *Die Badenischen Sprachverordnungen,* 2: 231; Riff, "Czech Antisemitism," p. 12.

32. Riff, "Czech Antisemitism," p. 12.

33. "Bouřlivý den v Praze" *Národní listy,* 30 November 1897; and "Druhý den po německé provokáci," 1 December 1897. Cf. Michael Riff, "Czech antisemitism," pp. 11–12.

34. See later in this chapter for an analysis of Czech Jewish responses to the events of 1897–1900.

35. Červinka, "The Hilsner Affair," p. 145; Arthur Nussbaum, "The 'Ritual Murder' Trial of Polná," *Historia Judaica* 9 (1947): 57–58.

36. Červinka, "The Hilsner Affair," p. 147; Nussbaum, "Ritual Murder Trial," pp. 57–60.

37. T. G. Masaryk, *Nutnost revidovati proces polenský* (Prague, 1899). On Masaryk's role in the defense of Hilsner against the blood libel, see Ernst Rychnovsky, "Im Kampf gegen den Ritualmord-Aberglauben," in E. Rychnovsky, ed., *Masaryk und das Judentum* (Prague, 1931), pp. 166–273.

38. Červinka, "The Hilsner Affair," p. 149.

39. On the German national workers' associations in northern Bohemia, see Andrew G. Whiteside, *Austrian National Socialism before 1918* (The Hague, 1962), pp. 51–87.

40. On Lueger and the Christian Social movement as an antisemitic force, see Peter G. J. Pulzer, *The Rise of Political Anti-Semitism in Germany and Austria* (New York, 1964), pp. 127–88; and Carl E. Schorske, "Politics in a New Key: An Austrian Trio," in his *Fin-de-Siècle Vienna: Politics and Culture* (New York, 1980), pp. 116–80.

41. Cohen, *The Politics of Ethnic Survival,* pp. 59–60, 177–82, 260–61.

42. Friedrich Jodl to Karl von Amira, in Margarete Jodl, *Friedrich Jodl: Sein Leben und Werk* (Stuttgart, 1920), pp. 117–18. This letter is quoted in Kurt Krolop, "Zur Geschichte und Vorgeschichte der Prager deutschen Literatur," in *Weltfreunde: Konferenz über die Prager deutsche Literatur* (Prague, 1967), pp. 50–51; and also referred to in Cohen, *The Politics of Ethnic Survival,* p. 180.

43. Cohen, *The Politics of Ethnic Survival,* p. 136.

44. Ibid., Table 9, Appendix II, pp. 299–301; and, for membership figures, pp. 177, 260.

45. Ibid., pp. 160, 181–82.

46. Meir Färber, "Jewish Lodges and Fraternal Orders Prior to World War II," in *The Jews of Czechoslovakia* (Philadelphia, 1971), 2: 299–42. B'nai B'rith was founded in New York in 1843, but the first European chapter—The Lodge of the German Empire—was not established until 1882 (see *Encyclopaedia Judaica,* vol. 4, cols. 1143–49).

47. Borman, "The Prague Student Zionist Movement," pp. 7–8; Cohen, *Politics of Ethnic Survival,* pp. 210–12. On anti-Habsburg German sentiment see Macartney, *The Habsburg Empire,* pp. 654–55; and Robert A. Kann, *The Multinational Empire, 1848–1918* (New York, 1950), 1: 97–101.

48. Borman, "The Prague Student Zionist Movement," p. 8; Krolop, "Zur Geschichte und Vorgeschichte," p. 49; and Cohen, *Politics of Ethnic Survival,* p. 212.

49. Borman, "The Prague Student Zionist Movement," p. 8; Cohen, *Politics of Ethnic Survival,* p. 212. Cohen cites a report that listed the membership of the Lese- and Redehalle for 1891 at 635 and for 1892 at only 334. Ernst Pawel, in a recent biography of Franz Kafka, puts the membership of the association during Kafka's university years (1901–6) at approximately 450, but he does not cite a source for this figure. See Ernst Pawel, *The Nightmare of Reason: A Life of Franz Kafka* (New York, 1984), p. 106.

50. Pawel, *Nightmare of Reason,* p. 106.

51. Although he does not take as strong a view of the decline of German liberalism in Prague, see Cohen, *Politics of Ethnic Survival,* pp. 254–55, 260–61 and, generally, pp. 184–273. The Casino had 1,280 members in 1898–99, and this figure remained fairly constant until 1914.

52. See, for example, the report to *Českožidovské listy* from the town of Domažlice, which analyzed local antisemitic senitment this way: "This anti-Semitism of the more educated strata rests on national considerations. What compromises Jewry the most in the eyes of the local intelligentsia is the German confessional school, stubbornly maintained up to now in defiance of numerous reprimands and friendly suggestions" (*Českožidovské listy,* 1 April 1898, p. 5).

53. A number of articles appeared on this theme in the Czech-Jewish press between 1897 and 1900. In particular I would point to the lead article ("Svůj k svému") in *Českožidovské listy* on 1 March 1898. It appeared under the by-line "L.," indicating that the author may have been Eduard Lederer.

54. Eduard Lederer, "Lueger triumfans," *Českožidovské listy* 15 April 1897.

55. Eduard Lederer, "Politické strany české a hnutí českožidovské," *Českožidovské listy,* 15 September 1897. *Samostatnost* (Independence) was a "radical progressive" journal founded by Antonín Hajn in 1897. *Rozhledy* (Perspectives) was edited by progressive, reformist intellectuals from 1892 to 1901.

56. Eduard Lederer, "Pražská tragedie židovská," *Českožidovské listy,* 15 December 1897.

57. Maxim Reiner, "O nynějších poměrech hnutí cěskožidovského," speech delivered to the general meeting of the Czech-Jewish Political Union on 10 June 1899, published in *Českožidovské listy,* 15 June 1899.

58. Ibid., p. 4.

59. "Národní jednota českožidovská," *KČŽ* 21 (1901–2): 146.

60. Ibid., pp. 146–47.

61. *Českožidovské listy,* 15 June 1898. The paper's editors, aware of the volatile nature of the piece, placed the word "uvažuje" (contemplates) in front of the author's name rather than the usual "napsal" (written by).

62. Eduard Lederer, "Židé a sociální demokracie," *Českožidovské listy,* 15 June, 1898, p. 2.

63. Ibid., p. 3. In subsequent years both Lederer and Viktor Vohryzek advocated closer relations with Social Democracy and support for the legitimate causes of the party. In a *Rozvoj* article entitled "K prvému máji" (For the first of May), Vohryzek pointed out the identity of working-class and Jewish interests, arguing that Jews had to accept those movements which—unlike the National Liberal party—were truly progressive. What really attracted Vohryzek to the Social Democrats was their moral claim and the concomitant conviction that Jews had to work toward social justice. See "K prvému máji," *Rozvoj* (1904); reprinted in V. Vohryzek, *K židovské otázce: Vybrané úvahy a články* (Prague, 1923), pp. 90–98.

64. *Českožidovské listy,* 1 July 1898, p. 2.

65. Ibid., 15 July 1898, p. 4. The author was a Dr. Bergmann from Pardubice.

66. Ibid., 1 August 1898, pp. 3–4. Václav Klofáč, a former activist in the student progressive movement and editor of *Národní listy,* founded the overtly antisemitic Czech National Socialist party (Strana národně sociální) in 1898.

67. Viktor Vohryzek, "Epištoly k českým židům," *Českožidovské listy,* 15 March 1900; reprinted in *K židovské otázce,* pp. 15–16.

68. Vohryzek, "Epištoly," pp. 26–31, 35.

69. Ibid., pp. 26–31.

70. Ibid., p. 33.

71. Ibid., pp. 33–34.

72. Ibid., p. 34.

73. Ibid.

74. Although I have not been able to procure a copy of the text of the interview, it was reported and commented on by a number of observers, among them Otakar Guth ("Dr. Vohryzek," *KČŽ* 34 [1914–15]: 136–40); J. Rokycana ("Freunde in der Not," in Ernst Rychnovsky, ed., *Masaryk und das Judentum* [Prague, 1931], pp. 309–10); and Eduard Lederer ("Čeští židé a český nacionalism," *Čas,* 9 December 1901, pp. 1–2).

75. Eduard Lederer, "Čeští židé a český nacionalism," pp. 1–2.

76. Eduard Lederer, *Žid v dnešní společnosti* (Prague, 1902).

77. "Zpráva o činnosti spolku 'Rozvoj' v Pardubicích," *KČŽ* 25 (1905–6): 178–79.

78. Among them were Adolf Bergmann, who spoke twice—once on Judaism and once on Zionism; Vílem Steinschneider on assimilation; B. Thein on Jewish Reform; Lev Thein on medicine and science; Viktor Vohryzek on Spinoza and Tolstoy; and Lev Vohryzek on Czech-Jewish writers ("Zpráva o činnosti spolku 'Rozvoj' v Pardubicích," pp. 177–81).

79. Ibid., p. 180.

80. On Vohryzek's early life see Guth, "Dr. Vohryzek," pp. 136–40; also O. Guth, "Úvodem," in Vohryzek, *K židovské otázce,* pp. 3–13. The indication of Vohryzek's membership in the SČAŽ can be found in *Výroční Zpráva Spolek českých akademiků-židů* (1883–84), where he is listed under the Slavicized "Vítězslav."

81. Donath, *Židé a židovství v české literatuře 19. a 20. století,* 2: 186–94. The first number of the Prague-based *Rozvoj* was issued on 5 July 1907.

82. *Dějiny českožidovského hnutí,* pp. 10–11.

83. V. Vohryzek, "Kterák doplniti náš program,' *Rozvoj* (Pardubice, 1904); reprinted in *K židovské otázce,* p. 142.

84. Vohryzek, "Několik Slov úvodem," *Rozvoj* (Pardubice, 1904); reprinted in *K židovské otázce,* p. 42.

85. Ibid., p. 42.

86. Ibid., pp. 43–44.

87. Ibid., pp. 46–47.

88. This section is reprinted in part from Hillel J. Kieval, "In the Image of Hus: Refashioning Czech Judaism in Post-Emancipatory Prague," *Modern Judaism* 5 (1985): 141–57.

89. Vohryzek, "Několik slov úvodem," p. 43.

90. Vohryzek, "K myšlenkové krisi našich dnů," *Rozvoj* (1904); reprinted in *K židovské otázce,* pp. 103–18. As Vohryzek wrote, "What we long for is not the philosophical transformation of religion, but the religious transformation of philosophy; we do not want religion to become popular philosophy, but rather philosophy [i.e., moral philosophy] to be our faith" (p. 106).

91. See, among other works, T. G. Masaryk's *Česká otázka: Snahy a tužby národního obrození* (Prague, 1895); his *Naše nynější krise* (Prague, 1896); and his *Jan Hus* (Prague, 1896).

92. Vohryzek, "Několik slov úvodem," p. 43. In an apologetic tone, Lederer argued that the modern Jew, on the strength of Judaism's ethical teachings, could grow to the same moral and humanistic heights as his Christian neighbor. Moreover, the values of Judaism, as manifested in the ideals of the prophets, were worthy of serving as ethical models for all people the world over (*Žid v dnešní společnosti,* pp. 73–74).

93. Perhaps the clearest statement of Masaryk's views on Hus, the Czech Reformation, and contemporary Czech nationalism can be found in a speech that he delivered several years later, in 1910. Entitled "Master Jan Hus and the Czech Reformation," it has been reprinted as "Jan Hus and the Czech Reformation" in T. G. Masaryk, *The Meaning of Czech History,* ed. René Wellek, trans. Peter Kussi (Chapel Hill, N.C., 1974), pp. 3–14.

94. Lederer, *Žid v dnešní společnosti,* p. 152; Masaryk, *Česká otázka* and *Naše nynější krise.*

95. Masaryk, "Jan Hus and the Czech Reformation," p. 14.

96. Vohryzek, "Národohospodářské úvahy," *Rozvoj* (1904); reprinted in *K Židovské otázce,* p. 127.

97. Lederer, *Žid v dněsní společnosti,* p. 111.

98. Vohryzek,"Jakými cestami by se mělo bráti naše hnutí" *Rozvoj* (1904); reprinted in *K židovské otázce,* p. 78.

99. Lederer's views on the subject can be seen most plainly in *Žid v dnešní společnosti* (pp. 47–84). In his exposition on rabbinic Judaism, Lederer was able to quote from a wide variety of sources, including *Tanchuma Lech Lecha, Pesikta Rabbati, Exodus Rabba,* and *Sifra* (all Midrashic compilations), as well as from various tractates of the Talmud. It is not clear, however, whether he used the Hebrew and Aramaic originals or German translations.

100. Vohryzek, "Úvodem k třetímu ročníku *Rozvoje,*" *Rozvoj* (1906); reprinted in *K židovské otázce,* pp. 197–98.

101. Vohryzek, "Pryč od Haliče," *Rozvoj* (1904); in *K židovské otázce,* pp. 134, 135.

102. Vohryzek, "K myšlenkové krisi našich dnů," pp. 105–6.

103. When Masaryk urged his listeners at a gathering in 1910 to "break [their] ties with Rome," he meant at the same time that they must loosen their ties to the Catholic Habsburg dynasty and also overcome the "Rome" within themselves in order to bring about a moral rebirth of the nation (Masaryk, "Jan Hus and the Czech Reformation," pp. 13–14).

104. Moritz Lazarus, *The Ethics of Judaism,* trans. Henrietta Szold (Philadelphia, 1900–1901), 1: 113–14. On pp. 112–13, Lazarus writes: "The fundamental law, 'you shall be holy,' which sums up all morality in one comprehensive expression, does not continue with 'for I so will it,' nor with 'for I so command'; it reads, 'you shall be holy, for I am Holy,' and other moral laws close simply with the declaration, 'I am God.' "

105. Vohryzek, "Zápas o reformy," *Rozvoj* (1906); reprinted in *K židovské otázce,* pp. 207–8.

106. Ibid., p. 208.

107. Vohryzek, "K myšlenkové krisi našich dnů," p. 111. In a similar tone, Bohdan Klineberger proclaimed in a small work in 1911 that the password of the renewed Judaism would be "integrity toward everyone." By this he meant openness and honesty on the part of Jews toward all members of society. See Klineberger, *Naše budoucnost. Sociologická studie* (Prague, 1911), p. 40.

108. Ibid., p. 41.

109. See O. Kraus, "Počátky berlinské reformy," *KČŽ* 25 (1905–6): 119–25, in which he gives his full support to the German Reform movement led by Samuel Holdheim. The basis of religion, Kraus argues, is not ritual practice, but good behavior and thought. See also his contribution of the following year: "O vývoji židovského náboženství," *KČŽ* 26 (1906–7): 120–28. See also Bohdan Klineberger, *Náboženský cit: Rozbor hodnoty náboženství* (Prague, 1906), a lengthy philosophical-psychological study of the nature of religious sensibility.

Chapter 4

1. Dr. W., "Vor zwanzig Jahren," *Selbstwehr,* 8 May 1914, pp. 1–2.

2. Ibid., p. 2. See also Ruth Kestenberg-Gladstein, "Atḥalot Bar Kochba," in Felix Weltsch, ed., *Prag vi-Yerushalayim* (Jerusalem, 1954), p. 89.

3. Dr. W., "Vor zwanzig Jahren," p. 2; see Hugo Bermann, writing under the name dr. b., "Bar Kochba (Zum dreissigsemestrigen Stiftungsfest des Vereines 'Bar Kochba')," *Selbstwehr,* 17 January 1908. Aronowitsch emigrated to Palestine in 1901; taught in the Beẓalel Art School in Jerusalem, and went on to become a well-known zoologist (see *Encyclopaedia Judaica,* vol. 2, col. 451).

4. "Aufruf der Prager 'Makabäa' " (June 1894), reprinted in N. M. Gelber, "Kavim le-kidmat toldoteha shel ha-ẓiyyonut be-Vohemia u-Moravia," in Felix Weltsch, ed., *Prag vi-Yerushalayim,* pp. 48–49.

5. There are no archival collections that document the early history of Zionism in Prague; one is forced to rely on contemporary press accounts and reminiscences. One such reminiscence-cum-history was compiled by Viktor Freud (1884–1943) on behalf of Bar Kochba and presented to Hugo Bergmann on the occasion of his fiftieth birthday. It was reissued as the Chanuka (December) 1954 issue of *Zirkular,* published by the Association of Past Bar Kochba Members (Iggud Vatikei Bar Kochba) and hereafter referred to as *Bar Kochba Zirkular.*

6. dr. b., "Bar Kochba," *Selbstwehr,* 17 January 1908.

7. T. Herzl, "Die Jagd in Böhmen," *Die Welt,* 5 November 1897.

8. Karl Fischl, "Die Juden in Böhmen," *Die Welt,* 9 March 1900.

9. Ibid., p. 3.

10. On the early history of Jewish nationalism in Prague, see Arthur Bergmann, "Zikhronot mi-tekufat Bar Kochba," in F. Weltsch, ed., *Prag vi-Yerushalayim,* pp. 111—19; Gelber, "Kavim," pp. 36–51; and Kestenberg-Gladstein, "Atḥalot Bar Kochba," pp. 86–110.

11. Bergmann, "Zikhronot," p. 111; Borman, "The Prague Student Zionist Movement, 1896–1914," pp. 76–81; Kestenberg-Gladstein, "Atḥalot Bar Kochba," pp. 90–91; also V. Vohryzek, "Kterak doplniti náš program," *Rozvoj* (1904).

12. Löwy, who was to become the first president of Bar Kochba, grew up in Domažlice in the Šumava region of western Bohemia. He attended a Czech gymnasium and was graduated from the Czech Medical Faculty in Prague. Kohn was born and raised in Litomysl in eastern Bohemia. He also attended a Czech gymnasium, but, when his family moved to Prague in 1900, entered the German Medical Faculty. He joined Bar Kochba later that year. See *Bar Kochba Zirkular,* January 1967, and March 1962; and Bergmann, "Zikhronot," pp. 111–12.

13. Lebenhart to Herzl, 6 May 1901:

Ich habe mich bestrebt, ihn so ziemlich zu unterrichten, musste ihm versprechen, Behelfe zur Verfügung zu stellen, damit er imstande sei, sein Urteil abzugeben. Ich hoffe nämlich, dass er für unsere Sache von grösstem Vorteil wäre, wenn er für uns öffentlich wirken möchte. Die Unterhaltung, über die ich hier im Detail nicht berichten kann, drehte sich um die Möglichkeit der Assimilation. Sein bisheriger Umgang mit Juden beschränkte sich nur auf jene, welche im Verschwinden ihr Heil sehen. Nun er aber, nach meinen Aufklärungen so manches, was er bisher rätselhaft fand, sich zu erklären vermochte, so ist er über die Lösung der Judenfrage, wie sie die Zionisten anstreben, heute auf dem Weg, ihr selber das Wort zu reden" (quoted in *Bar Kochba Zirkular,* April 1967, p. 2).

14. "Zionismus na cestách," *Českožidovské listy,* 15 February 1900, pp. 1–2. See also Kestenberg-Gladstein, "Aṭhalot Bar Kochba," p. 91.

15. A prime example of early Czech-Jewish concern over Zionism can be found in the article "Budiž jasno mezi námi," which appeared in *Českožidovské listy* between January and March 1897. In it the paper argued that a nation could exist only where its members occupied a common territory, spoke the same language, and possessed a shared consciousness and a common history (one that continued to develop in the present and was not cut off at some point in the distant past). It appears that the editors of *Českožidovské listy* were responding to a recent piece in the Realist newspaper *Čas,* which had argued that the Jews did, in fact, possess many of the characteristics of a modern nation, including a shared language, Hebrew. The writer of the Czech-Jewish response asked rhetorically whether the ability to speak another language (read here German) detracted from the national integrity of the Czechs themselves.

16. Lev Vohryzek, "Dva přátelé," *Rozvoj,* 19 July 1919, p. 2.

17. Waldstein's affiliation with the SČAŽ can be found in the association's annual report *(Výroční zpráva)* for 1909–10. On his Zionist activities see A. M. Rabinowicz, "The Jewish Minority," in *The Jews of Czechoslovakia* (Philadelphia, 1968), 1: 157; and A. M. Rabinowicz, "The Jewish Party," in *The Jews of Czechoslovakia,* 2: 256.

18. See *Českožidovské listy* for 1 March and 15 March 1900. For a short biography of Singer, see F. Weltsch, "Dr. Ludwig Singer," in F. Weltsch, ed., *Prag vi-Yerushalayim,* pp. 73–74; and *Selbstwehr,* 12 February 1926, p. 2.

19. *Českožidvoské listy,* 15 February 1900, p. 5.

20. Encyclopaedia Judaica, vol. 14, col. 1613; *Selbstwehr,* 12 February and 19 February 1926.

21. On the existence of a "Prague stream," see: Yehoshua [Stuart] Borman, "Ha-zerem ha-pragi bi-tenuah ha-ẓiyonit ha-'olamit, 1904–1914," in *Yahadut Czechoslovakia* (Jerusalem, 1969), pp. 243–50; Kestenberg-Gladstein, "Aṭhalot Bar Kochba," pp. 86–110; and Gelber, "Kavim," pp. 36–51.

22. Hugo Bergmann, "Petaḥ davar," in *Yahadut Czechoslovakia,* pp. 7–9..

23. Ibid., pp. 7–8. Bergmann relates that his family even ate pork *(Schinken)* in the house from time to time. Nevertheless, holidays such as Passover, Simḥat Torah (Celebration of the Torah, at the conclusion of Sukkot), and the High Holidays, were observed in the home and at the synagogue. Bergmann's father also sent his two sons to the community religious school, Talmud Torah, in the afternoons where they were taught the Pentateuch and the books of the Prophets.

24. Ibid., p. 9.

25. Ibid.

26. Hans Tramer, "Prague—City of Three Peoples," *LBIYB* 9 (1964): 316.

27. Ibid.; and Miriam Samburski, "Zionist und Philosoph: Das Habilitierungsproblem des jungen Hugo Bergmann," *BLBI* 58 (1981): 17.

28. Written in 1905 and quoted in Kestenberg-Gladstein, "Aṭhalot Bar Kochba," p. 94.

29. R. Pacovský, "Zur Geschichte des 'Bar–Kochba,' " *Bar Kochba Zirkular,* April 1967, pp. 3–4. Copy in the Central Zionist Archives (CZA), Jerusalem, File A 317.

30. Quoted in Kestenberg-Gladstein, "Aṭhalot Bar Kochba," p. 98.

31. Quoted at least twice in the *Bar Kochba Zirkular,* December 1954 and April 1967.

32. "Der Zionismus ist die Heimkehr zum Judentum noch vor der Rückkehr ins Judenland." ("Eröffnungsrede zum ersten Kongress," repr. in Theodor Herzl, *Zionistische Schriften,* 3d ed. [Tel Aviv, 1934], p. 176).

33. On cultural Zionism in general, see Adolf Böhm, *Die zionistische Bewegung,* vol. 1 (Berlin, 1935); also Jehuda Reinharz, *Chaim Weizmann: The Making of a Zionist Leader* (New York, 1985), pp. 65–91.

34. *Encyclopaedia Judaica,* vol. 4, cols. 1040–42.

35. This work was Nathan Birnbaum, *Achad ha-am, Ein Denker und Kämpfer der jüdischen Renaissance* (Berlin: Jüdischer Verlag, 1903). On the overall question of the transmission of

Aḥad Ha'am's thought to German Zionism, see the thoughtful essay by Jehuda Reinharz, "Achad Haam und der deutsche Zionismus," *BLBI* 61 (1982): 3–27.

36. This, for example, is Kestenberg-Gladstein's opinion ("Atḥalot Bar Kochba," p. 94).

37. Richard Pacovský, "Zur Geschichte des 'Bar Kochba,' " *Bar Kochba Zirkular,* November 1966 (from Alfred Löwy's diary); on the Bergmann family see *Bar Kochba Zirkular,* 13 November 1958; finally, Oskar K. Rabinowicz, "Czechoslovak Zionism: Analecta to a History," in *The Jews of Czechoslovakia* (Philadelphia, 1971), 2: 23. Rabinowicz feels that Feiwel was encouraged to make his proposal as a result of the resolution on national autonomy put forward by the Austrian Social Democrats at their Brno conference in 1899. Karl Renner, the major force behind the Brno resolution, envisaged a cultural autonomy tied not to regions or territories but to individuals. This idea undoubtedly attracted Jewish student nationalists who sought a means of expressing their cultural independence within the context of the Habsburg monarchy. See also Ruth B. Roebke-Behrens, "The Austrian Social Democratic Party, Nationalism, and the Nationality Crisis of the Habsburg Empire, 1897–1914," *Canadian Review of Studies in Nationalism* 8 (1981): 343–63.

38. Reinharz, *Chaim Weizmann,* pp. 65–91; *Encyclopaedia Judaica,* vol. 6, cols. 1215–16, and vol. 5, cols, 1492–93.

39. Borman, "The Prague Student Zionist Movement," pp. 140–41.

40. See R. Pacovský, "Zur Geschichte des 'Bar Kochba,' " *Bar Kochba Zirkular,* April 1967, p. 11, and March 1968, p. 6. The Kharkov Conference of Russian Zionists, meeting in November 1903, resolved to demand of Herzl, among other things, the abandonment of the East Africa project and the inclusion of practical work in Palestine within the program of the World Zionist Organization. See Reinharz, *Chaim Weizmann,* pp. 176–78.

41. Grete Schaeder, *The Hebrew Humanism of Martin Buber,* trans. by Noah J. Jacobs (Detroit, 1973), pp. 30–53; and Hans Kohn, *Martin Buber, sein Werk und seine Zeit,* 2d enl. ed. (Cologne, 1961), pp. 19–27. See also Gershom Scholem, "Martin Buber's Conception of Judaism," in his *On Jews and Judaism in Crisis: Selected Essays* (New York, 1976), pp. 131–33.

42. Felix Weltsch, "Realism and Romanticism: Observations on the Jewish Intelligentsia of Bohemia and Moravia," in *The Jews of Czechoslovakia* (Philadelphia, 1971), 2: 440–54; Kohn, *Martin Buber,* pp. 59–61.

43. Kohn, *Martin Buber,* pp. 60–61.

44. Johann Gottlieb Fichte (1762–1814), German philosopher and nationalist educator. Hans Kohn, *Living in a World Revolution: My Encounters with History* (New York, 1964), p 64

45. *Bar Kochba Zirkular,* December 1963, p. 7.

46. Pacovský, "Zur Geschichte des 'Bar Kochba,' " *Bar Kochba Zirkular,* April 1967, p.3.

47. Part II of the essay was added in 1910, and the two sections together were included in the volume *Die Jüdische Bewegung: Gesammelte Aufsätze und Ansprachen* (Berlin, 1916). The complete essay has been reprinted in Martin Buber, *Der Jude und sein Judentum: Gesammelte Aufsätze und Reden* (Cologne, 1963). All references are to this edition.

48. Martin Buber, "Renaissance und Bewegung," in *Der Jude und sein Judentum,* p. 272.

49. Ibid., pp. 273–74.

50. Ibid., pp. 273.

51. Ibid., p. 275.

52. Ibid., p. 276.

53. Ibid., p. 277.

54. Scholem, "Martin Buber's Conception of Judaism," pp. 126–71.

55. Hugo Bergmann to Franz Kafka, 1901. This letter is quoted in a Hebrew translation by Kestenberg-Gladstein ("Atḥalot Bar Kochba," p. 92), but no indication is given concerning its present location.

56. Hugo Bergmann, *Die Judenfrage und ihre Lösungsversuche* (Prague, 1903), p. 10.

57. Kestenberg-Gladstein, "Atḥalot Bar Kochba," p. 99. See also the remarks of Felix Weltsch to the effect that Masaryk taught the Jews that nationalism was compatible with internationalism, that national independence was not a goal in itself, but the means to a higher

end—improving the lot of mankind. See Felix Weltsch, "Masaryk und der Zionismus," in E. Rychnovsky, ed., *Masaryk und das Judentum* (Prague, 1931), pp. 96–98.

58. Quoted in Felix Weltsch, "Masaryk und der Zionismus," pp. 68–69. The review appeared in *Sborník historický* (Historical miscellany), in 1883.

59. F.B., "Sionism," *Naše doba* 5 (1897–98): 439–43. The quotation is from p. 440.

60. Ibid., pp. 440–42.

61. Ibid., p. 443.

62. Quoted in Weltsch, "Masaryk und der Zionismus," p. 69.

63. Quoted in R. Pacovský, "Zur Geschichte des 'Bar-Kochba,' " *Bar Kochba Zirkular,* November 1966, p. 3.

64. Ibid.

65. Pacovský, "Zur Geschichte des 'Bar Kochba,' " *Bar Kochba Zirkular,* April 1967, p. 9.

66. T. G. Masaryk, "Život církevní a náboženský roku 1904," *Naše doba* 12 (1905): six parts.

67. Ibid., p. 522.

68. Ibid., pp. 522–23.

69. "Aḥad Ha'am fights against Nietzschean individualism; he demonstrates that the Old Testament in the end is social, demanding loyalty to the collectivity" (ibid., p. 523). It may be of interest to note that Hugo Bergmann at first sided with Berdyczewski over Aḥad Ha'am, finding the former's revolutionary position to be the more convincing. See Pacovský, "Zur Geschichte des 'Bar-Kochba,' " *Bar Kochba Zirkular* (April 1967), p. 3.

70. Masaryk, "Život církevní," p. 523.

71. Ibid.

72. Christoph Stölzl, "Die 'Burg' und die Juden. T. G. Masaryk und sein Kreis im Spannungsfeld der jüdischen Frage: Assimilation, Antisemitismus, und Zionismus," in Karl Bosl, ed., *Die 'Burg': Einflussreiche politische Kräfte um Masaryk und Beneš* (Munich and Vienna, 1974), 2: 102–3.

73. T. G. Masaryk, *Národnostní filosofie* (1905), p. 14; quoted in F. Weltsch, "Masaryk und der Zionismus," p. 102.

74. Viktor Vohryzek, "Náboženská společnost, či národnost?" *Rozvoj* (1906); reprinted in his *K židovské otázce,* pp. 218–28. Vohryzek acknowledged in his introductory remarks that this kind of attitude on the part of non-Jewish Czech intellectuals challenged all of the efforts and achievements of the Czech Jews.

75. Jan Herben, "Julius Taussig," *KČŽ* 32 (1912–13): 15–16.

76. Krejčí's remarks were published in *Selbstwehr,* 11 June 1909, under the title "Assimilation und Zionismus vom ethischen Standpunkt."

77. Krejčí, "Assimilation und Zionismus," p. 1.

78. Ibid.

79. Ibid., pp. 1–2.

80. Ibid., p. 2: "In demselben Sinne und demselben Vorbehalt, wie man sagen kann: Wo die tschechische Sprache tönt, dort ist das tschechische Volk—so kann man sagen: wo die jüdische Religion—dort ist das jüdische Volk."

81. *Selbstwehr,* 1910 and 1911.

82. *Selbstwehr,* 24 March 1911, pp. 1–2.

83. Hugo Bergmann, "Prager Brief," *Jüdische Volksstimme* (Brno), 15 January 1904, p. 4.

84. Ibid.

85. Ibid., pp. 4–5, emphasis mine.

86. Ibid., p. 5.

87. "Česko-židovství," *Selbstwehr,* 8 May 1908; Hugo Herrmann, "Zur čechisch-jüdischen Frage," *Selbstwehr,* 7 April 1911.

88. On this issue also, see "Česko-židovství," *Selbstwehr,* 8 May 1908:
Für uns Juden in der Diaspora bildet unsere jeweilige Umgangssprache kein Kriterium unserer Nationalität. Lernet drum Alle deutsch und tschechisch, um Euch und Euren Kindern eine Existenzmöglichkeit, welche ohnedies immer beschränkter wird, zu bieten

und überlasset die Austragung des Kampfes um die Vorherrschaft der einen oder andern Sprache . . . ihren berufenen Vertretern und Organen.

89. "Von den böhmischen Juden verlangen die Tschechen, welche uns als Konnationale nicht anerkennen, dass wir ihren nationalen und politischen Aspirationen nicht störend oder feindlich entgegentreten und diesem gerechten Verlangen können und sollen wir genügen . . ." (ibid., p. 2).

90. Dr. Kadisch, "Deutsche, Tschechen, Juden," *Selbstwehr,* 21 August 1908.

91. Kestenberg-Gladstein, "Aṭhalot Bar Kochba," pp. 98–99; Borman, "The Prague Student Zionist Movement," pp. 104–5.

92. Hugo Brauner, "Zur Geschichte der Verbindung," in *Fünfzig Semester "Barissia"* (Prague, 1928), pp. 86–87.

93. Ibid., pp. 88–89; Bergmann, "Zikhronot mi-tekufat Bar Kochba," p. 117.

94. Brauner, "Zur Geschichte der Verbindung," p. 89; Borman, "The Prague Student Zionist Movement," pp. 55–56; and Bergmann, "Zikhronot mi-tekufat Bar Kochba," p. 117.

95. Brauner, "Zur Geschichte der Verbindung," pp. 90–96.

96. Viktor Kellner, a leading member of Bar Kochba, later offered this interpretation: Barrisia fought its battle—through a conscious appropriation of foreign forms—*outwardly* against assimilation. It adopted these forms in the conviction that it would thus be easier to win over Jewish *society.* Bar Kochba pursued the path that led inward; it plunged into the Jewish problem and began to treat Hebrew seriously. There the struggle was for the Jewish *community,* which they wanted to win over to Zionism; here it was the struggle for Jewish spirituality, for Jewish values, which were more sensed than really understood and experienced" (quoted in *Bar Kochba Zirkular,* April 1967, pp. 4–5).

97. Kellner, again, on this point, ibid., p. 5.

98. Brauner, "Zur Geschichte der Verbingung," pp. 116–17.

99. Ibid., pp. 114–15.

100. Ibid., pp. 120–21.

101. Ibid., pp. 112–13.

102. Borman, "The Prague Student Zionist Movement," pp. 64–65; Brauner, "Zur Geschichte der Verbindung," pp. 115–16.

103. Borman, "The Prague Student Zionist Movement," pp. 73–75; Brauner, "Zur Geschichte der Verbindung," pp. 118–19. Total membership of the Lese- und Redehalle in 1908 was between 150 and 200 students; at the time there were approximately 700 Jewish students in Prague.

104. Brauner, "Zur Geschichte der Verbindung," pp. 121–22; Bergmann, "Zikhronot mitekufat Bar Kochba," p. 118. The handwriten protocol of the duel, which is located in the Leo Herrmann Collection of the CZA, indicates clearly that the incident took place in March 1909, and not, as Bergmann remembers, 1908 (CZA, A 145/160).

105. Tramer, "Prague—City of Three Peoples," pp. 305–6.

106. Pacovský, "Zur Geschichte des 'Bar-Kochba,' " *Bar Kochba Zirkular,* April 1967, p. 9.

107. Borman, "The Prague Student Zionist Movement," p. 99.

108. Ibid., pp. 86–91.

109. Ibid., pp. 91–94.

110. *Selbstwehr,* 1 March 1907, p. 1.

111. Ibid.

112. Ibid.

113. "Nur als sebstbewusste, willenskräftige, zielbewusste Juden können wir uns um wirkliche Freunde ansehen und erst wenn wir uns selbst achten, selbst rühren und zur Einheit zusammenschliessen ist die Vorbedingung für eine ernste, vollständige und endgültige Lösung der Judenfrage erfüllt" (ibid).

114. Niels [pseudonym], "Zur nationalen Emanzipation der österreichischen Juden," *Selbstwehr,* 1 March 1907, pp. 2–3.

115. See ibid., p. 3: "Es war eine Fiktion, die versagen und verblassen musste vor dem ersten Ansturm des wiedererwachten jüdischen Volksbewusstseins, eine Fiktion aber, die mit solcher Zähigkeit und solcher Applomb festgehalten wurde und wird, dass ihre Ausrottung eine wahre Herkulesarbeit ist."

116. Ibid.

117. "Die Wiedergeburt des deutschen Fortschritts im Kasino zu Prag," *Selbstwehr,* 27 May 1910, p. 1.

118. Ibid., p. 2.

119. *Selbstwehr,* March through May 1907.

120. *Selbstwehr,* 17 May 1907, p. 1.

121. The Prague Zionists pursued the same tactics during the 1911 elections, according to a report in the *Jüdische Rundschau* by Leo Herrmann. The Czech-Jewish Political Union, meanwhile, urged support of Baxa out of "party discipline"; see "Die politische Situation in Prag," pt. 1, *Jüdische Rundschau,* 26 May 1911.

122. Mendelsohn, *The Jews of East Central Europe Between the World Wars,* pp. 18–19.

123. Following the Galician electoral campaign, Jewish nationalists formed the Jüdische politische Verein in Prag (1908). The Verein does not appear to have made much of an impact on the political activity of most Czech Jews. In point of fact, even the gains that had been made in Galicia proved to be short lived; following a wave of intimidations and violence, the Jewish party lost its mandates during the elections of 1911.

124. Niels, "Zur nationalen Emanzipation der österreichischen Juden," p. 3.

125. The Habsburg monarchy continued to place formidable obstacles in the way of any real implementation of Jewish national politics down to the end of the First World War. As has already been noted, Yiddish was not recognized as a distinct language but rather as a form of German, and Yiddish-speaking Jews were lumped together with Germans in state censuses. As a result, even in those regions with heavy concentrations of Jews (Bukovina, 13 percent of the population in 1910; Galicia, 11 percent), they were not able to enjoy fully the constitutional guarantees for every ethnic group to "cultivate and preserve its nationality and language." By law the Jews of Bohemia and Moravia were not allowed to declare themselves as belonging to the Jewish nationality until 1921 under the First Czechoslovak Republic (see note 91, Chapter 2).

Chapter 5

1. For biographical sketches of Leo Herrmann, see Felix Weltsch, ed., *Prag vi-Yerushala-yim,* pp. 125–97; Hugo Bergmann, "Leo Herrmann zum Gedenken," *Mitteilungsblatt Irgun Olej Merkaz Europa* (hereafter *Mitteilungsblatt),* 21 September 1951; Hugo Bergmann, "Reshito shel Leo Herrmann," *Ha'arez,* 15 March 1938; Hugo Bergmann, "Leo Herrmann 50 Jahre," *Jüdische Rundschau,* 15 March 1938; and "Leo Herrmann," *Keren Hayesod Bullletin,* 7 October 1951.

2. Emmy Herrmann, "Meine Erinnerungen an Leo," Jerusalem, March 1952, Robert Weltsch Collection, Leo Baeck Institute Archives.

3. Leo Herrmann, "Erinnerungen eines Sudetendeutschen Zionisten," *Mitteilungsblatt,* April 1938, nos. 1 and 2. English translation: "Recollections of a Sudeten-German Zionist," CZA, Leo Herrmann Collection, A145/97.

4. Herrmann, "Recollections of a Sudeten-German Zionist," p. 2.

5. Herrmann, "Meine Erinnerungen an Leo," pp. 2–3.

6. Herrmann, "Recollections of a Sudeten-German Zionist," pp. 7–8.

7. See Robert Wistrich, *Socialism and the Jews: The Dilemmas of Assimilation in Germany and Austria-Hungary* (Rutherford, N.J., 1982), pp. 237–39, 300–01, and 343–48. The Austrian Social Democrats adopted a national program that called for the division of Austria-Hungary along federal lines at their party congress in Brno in 1899.

8. Herrmann, "Recollections of a Sudeten-German Zionist," p. 5.

9. Bergmann, "Leo Herrmann zum Gedenken." Bergmann quotes the following from the group's Semester Report of the winter term 1909–10 (the year following Herrmann's tenure as chairman): "We wish . . . to direct our energies not so much to propaganda but much more to what appears to us to be a more difficult and also more important task—the deepening of Zionism." The report went on to explain this to mean "taking possession of all that Jewish culture is today."

10. *Selbstwehr,* 6 January 1911, p. 1.

11. Ibid.

12. Ibid.

13. Leo Herrmann, "Reshimot 'al siḥot u-fegishot," in F. Weltsch, ed., *Prag vi-Yerushalyim,* pp. 77–85. See also his somewhat shorter "Aus Tagebuchblättern," *Der Jude, Sonderheft zu Martin Bubers 50. Geburtstag* (Berlin, 1928), pp. 159–64.

14. Leo Herrmann to Martin Buber, 14 November 1908 (Buber Archives, MS Var 350/281); published in Martin Buber, *Briefwechsel aus sieben Jahrzehnten* (Heidelberg, 1972), 1: 268–69.

15. Leo Herrmann to M. Buber, 14 November 1908, ibid.

16. Ibid.

17. Ibid.

18. Robert Weltsch elaborates on the theme of Buber's seclusion during this perriod in his "Einleitung" to Martin Buber, *Der Jude und sein Judentum;* see also Buber's own essay "My Way to Hasidism," in *Hasidism and Modern Man* (New York, 1958), pp. 47–69.

19. Buber's paternal grandfather, Solomon Buber (1827–1906), was a well-known scholar and authority on Midrashic literature.

20. On this point see Scholem, "Martin Buber's Conception of Judaism," p. 130. Buber commented on the linguistic complications of his adoptive city in his *Autobiographische Fragmente,* published in English under the title *Meetings* (La Salle, Ill., 1973):

The multiplicity of human languages, their wonderful variety in which the white light of human speech at once fragmented and preserved itself, was already at the time of my boyhood a problem that instructed me ever anew. I followed time after time an individual word or even structure of words from one language to another, found it there again and yet had time after time to give up something there as lost that apparently only existed in a single one of all the languages. That was not merely "nuances of meaning": I devised for myself two-language conversations between a German and a Frenchman, later between a Hebrew and an ancient Roman and came ever again, half in play and yet at times with beating heart, to feel the tension between what was heard by the one and what was heard by the other, from his thinking in another language. That had a deep influence on me and has issued in a long life into ever clearer insight (*Meetings,* p. 21).

21. Herrmann and Buber corresponded weekly between November 1908 and January 1909. Unfortunately only Herrmann's letters to Buber are still extant. Those of 22 November, 1 December, and 4 December 1908 can be found in the Martin Buber Archives, Jewish National and University Library, Jerusalem, MS Var 350/281. On 1 December 1908, Herrmann wrote: ". . . above all many thanks for the intense interest that you have shown for our [upcoming] event and for the unusually helpful suggestions that you have given us. If I have not been able to respond as quickly as I would have liked, it is only because I must first bring every step to my fellow members for advice and approval."

22. Buber's three addresses were published together in 1911 as *Drei Reden über das Judentum* (Frankfurt a.M.: Rütten & Lönig). A second printing appeared in 1916 and a third, representing a total sale of 17,000 copies, in 1920. An English translation can be found in his *On Judaism,* ed. Nahum Glatzer (New York, 1967), pp. 3–55. All references are to this edition.

23. L. Herrmann to Buber, 22 November 1908.

24. Buber, "Judaism and the Jews," in *On Judaism,* p.. 13.

25. Ibid., pp. 13–14.

26. Ibid., p. 14.

27. Ibid.

28. Ibid., p. 15.

29. Ibid., p. 16.

30. Ibid., p. 17.

31. Ibid., p. 18.

32. Ibid., p. 20.

33. Ibid., p. 21. The last phrase, "that he redeem himself," was for some reason omitted from this edition.

34. Martin Buber, "Judaism and Mankind," in *On Judaism*, pp. 22–33.

35. Ibid.

36. Ibid., p. 28.

37. Ibid., p. 32.

38. Ibid., p. 33.

39. Buber, "Renewal of Judaism," in *On Judaism*, pp. 34–55.

40. Ibid., p. 40.

41. Ibid., p. 42.

42. Ibid., p. 49.

43. Ibid., pp. 52–53.

44. Buber, "Judaism and the Jews," in *On Judaism*, p. 21.

45. Scholem, "Buber's Conception of Judaism," p. 138; originally published in *Eranos Jahrbuch* 25 (1967) as "Martin Bubers Auffassung des Judentums."

46. Scholem, "Buber's Conception of Judaism," p. 138.

47. Hugo Herrmann, "Martin Buber," *Selbstwehr,* 16 December 1910.

48. Herrmann, "Aus Tagebuchblättern," p. 158.

49. Ibid.

50. Robert Weltsch to Martin Buber, 22 March 1910 (Buber Archives, MS Var 350/880).

51. Herrmann, "Aus Tagebuchblättern," p. 160; see also Herrmann, "Reshimot 'al siḥot u-fegishot," pp. 84–85.

52. Herrmann, "Aus Tagebuchblättern," pp. 160–61.

53. See Max Brod, *Der Prager Kreis* (Stuttgart, 1966); also Brod's autobiography, *Streitbares Leben, 1884–1968* (Munich, 1969).

54. Martin Buber Archives, MS Var 350/80. Among other things, Baum hoped that Buber would help to publish his "jüdischer Kleinstadroman," *Die böse Unschuld* (Frankfurt a.M., 1913). See Baum to Buber, 20 November 1910 and 31 January 1913.

55. Herrmann's review had appeared in *Selbstwehr* in April 1909 and also in the Brno newspaper *Jüdische Volksstimme*.

56. Max Brod, *Ein tschechisches Dienstmädchen* (Stuttgart, 1909), pp. 117–19.

57. Brod, *Streitbares Leben,* pp. 220–21. Brod identifies his critic simply as "the Czech publicist Jesenská"; he is probably referring to the poet and playwright Růžena Jesenská (1863–1940).

58. *Jüdische Volksstimme,* 20 April 1909.

59. See Brod, *Streitbares Leben,* pp. 48–51.

60. Ibid., pp. 49–50.

61. Brod first enticed his friend to accompany him in May 1910. However, the visit did not elicit much enthusiasm from Kafka. A second troupe, presumably from Lwów, performed in Prague from the fall of 1911 to the spring of 1912. It was with this group, and its leader Yitshok Levi, that Kafka became involved. See the excellent summary in Pawel, *The Nightmare of Reason,* pp. 239–50; also the overstated case argued by Evelyn Beck, *Kafka and the Yiddish Theater: Its Impact on His Work* (Madison, Wis., 1971).

62. Franz Kafka, *Diaries, 1910–1913,* ed. Max Brod (New York, 1948), pp. 79–278. See also Pawel, *Nightmare of Reason,* p. 242; and Beck, *Kafka and the Yiddish Theater,* pp. 12–15. On

November 3, 1912, Kafka wrote the following to Felice Bauer: "I love the Yiddish theater; last year I may have gone to 20 of their performances, and possibly not once to the German theater." See Franz Kafka, *Letters to Felice*, ed. E. Heller and J. Born (New York, 1967), p. 26.

63. Kafka, *Diaries, 1910–1913*, pp. 223–35.

64. Franz Kafka, "An Introductory Talk on the Yiddish Language," in *Dearest Father: Stories and Other Writings* (New York, 1954), pp. 381–86; quoted in Pawel, *Nightmare of Reason*, p. 248.

65. Kafka, *Diaries, 1910–1913*, pp. 125, 223. The entry for 1 November 1911, is characteristic: Today, eagerly and happily began to read the *History of the Jews* by Graetz. Because my desire for it had far outrun the reading, it was at first stranger to me than I thought, and I had to stop here and there in order by resting to allow my Jewishness to collect itself. Toward the end, however, I was already gripped by the imperfection of the first settlements in the newly conquered Canaan and the faithful handing down of the imperfection of the popular heroes (Joshua, the Judges, Elijah).

On Kafka's relations with Bar Kochba and *Selbstwehr*, see Hartmut Binder, "Franz Kafka und die Wochenschrift 'Selbstwehr,' " *Deutsche Vierteljahrsschrift für Literaturwissenschaft und Geistesgeschichte* 41 (1967): 283–304.

66. Pawel, *Nightmare of Reason*, p. 240.

67. Kafka, *Diaries, 1910–1913*, p. 108 (21 October 1911). See also the entry for 6 January 1912:

When I saw the first plays it was possible for me to think that I had come upon a Judaism on which the beginnings of my own rested, a Judaism that was developing in my direction and so would enlighten and carry me farther along in my own clumsy Judaism; instead, it moves farther away from me the more I hear of it. The people remain, of course, and I hold fast to them (p. 215).

68. Kafka to F. Bauer, 16 January 1913, in *Letters to Felice*, p. 157.

69. Kafka to F. Bauer, 19 January 1913, ibid., p. 161.

70. Leo Herrmann to Martin Buber, 4 December 1908 (Buber Archives, MS Var 350/281).

71. Robert Weltsch to Martin Buber, 12 November 1911 (Buber Archives, MS Var 350/880). The person in question, a Professor Goldstein, galled Weltsch with the declaration, "Wir Juden sind Erhalter des Deutschtums, wir sind dem Wesen, dem Geiste, dem Schicksal nach—*Deutsche.*"

72. Herrmann to Buber, 4 December 1908.

73. Verein der jüdischen Hochschüler "Bar Kochba" in Prag. *Bericht über die Tätigkeit des Vereins*, winter semester 1909–10 (Prague, 1910), p. 19.

74. Lederer's talk, it was reported in *Selbstwehr*, occasioned a "von beiden Seiten sachlich geführten Auseinandersetzung über die Prinzipien der Judenfragelösung" (*Selbstwehr*, 15 March 1912).

75. The series began on 1 January 1912 with the speech "O významu židovství pro Židy" (On the meaning of Judaism for the Jews, the original title of "Das Judentum und die Juden"), translated by A. Kollmann. Later in 1912 the three speeches were published together as *Tři řeči o židovství*. The Zionist organization of Bohemia also issued, in 1908, a Czech translation of Hugo Bergmann's *Die Judenfrage und ihre Lösungsversuche* (*Židovská otázka a její řešení*), published originally in 1903.

76. Hugo Herrmann, "Zur čechisch-jüdischen Frage," *Selbstwehr*, 7 April 1911.

77. The review appeared on the front page of *Selbstwehr*, 22 September 1911. Robert Weltsch was the chairman of Bar Kochba during the year 1911–12, and Kohn succeeded him in that position in 1912–13. See Hans Kohn, "Rückblick auf eine gemeinsame Jugend," in Hans Tramer and Kurt Loewenstein, eds., *Robert Weltsch zum 70. Geburtstag* (Tel-Aviv, 1961), p. 115.

78. Selbstwehr, 22 September 1911, p. 1.

79. Kohn, *Martin Buber, sein Werk und seine Zeit*, p. 315.

80. *Selbstwehr,* 22 September 1911, p. 1.

81. *Ma'aseh ha-merkava:* Hebrew expression that refers to mystical secrets, to knowledge of God; based on the prophet Ezekiel's vision of the chariot of the Lord (Ezekiel 1 and 10). *Ma'aseh bereshit:* the creation of the world; also used figuratively to mean a powerful, fundamental act.

82. *Selbstwehr,* 22 September 1911, p. 2.

83. Hugo Bergmann, "Shalosh derashot 'al ha-yahadut," *Ha-shiloah* 26 (1912): 549.

84. Ibid.

85. Ibid., p. 550.

86. Ibid., p. 552.

87. Ibid.

88. Hans Kohn to Robert Weltsch [undated] summer 1911; Leo Baeck Institute, Robert Weltsch Collection. Emphasis in the original.

89. Ibid. The reader is also directed to the following pieces of correspondence: Buber to Hans Kohn, 19 November 1912, in Buber, *Briefwechsel* 1: 320; Max Brod to Martin Buber, 25 November 1913, and Buber to Brod, 5 December 1913, 1: 348–51.

90. Verein der jüdischen Hochschüler "Bar Kochba" in Prag. *Bericht über die Tätigkeit des Vereins,* summer semester 1912 (Prague, 1912), pp. 4–8.

91. S. Kaznelson to Robert Weltsch, 23 July 1911, CZA, Robert Weltsch Collection, A167/20.

92. Hans Kohn to Martin Buber, 10 November 1912, Buber Archives, MS Var 350/376.

93. Hans Kohn to Martin Buber, 2 July 1913, ibid. Emphasis in the original.

94. Oskar Epstein, "Erhaltung oder Erneuerung?" in *Vom Judentum* (Leipzig, 1914), pp. 173–78.

95. Ibid., pp. 173–74.

96. *Golusjude* literally meant "diaspora Jew," but it had specifically negative connotations. The Golusjude, because of continued spiritual enslavement to the old forms of Jewish culture, could exist in Palestine as well as outside of it. *Urjude,* or "primal Jew," was one whose actions revealed that Jewish essence or quality that was eternal, that existed outside of history. Alternatively the Urjude was the type of Jew characterized by the Maccabean revolt against the Greek Seleucid Kingdom, a type that could be purposefully recreated.

97. Epstein, "Erhaltung oder Erneuerung?" p. 177. Emphasis in the original.

98. Hugo Herrmann to Robert Weltsch, 5 December 1912, CZA, Robert Weltsch Collection, A167/10.

99. Hugo Herrmann to Robert Weltsch, 7 September 1911, ibid.

100. See Jehuda Reinharz, *Fatherland or Promised Land: the Dilemma of the German Jew 1893–1914* (Ann Arbor, Mich., 1975); and Stephen Poppel, *Zionism in Germany, 1897–1933* (Philadelphia, 1977).

101. See the extensive correspondence between Buber and the chairmen of Bar Kochba, Robert Weltsch and Hans Kohn, during 1912–13 in Buber, *Briefwechsel,* vol. 1. Kohn, who was named editor of the enterprise, besieged Buber with requests for his personal intervention with publishers as well as with writers who were reluctant to contribute to the volume. He kept Buber up to date on whom the group had asked to write, who had accepted, and who had not.

102. "Der Mythos der Juden," first published in Martin Buber, *Vom Geist des Judentums* (Leipzig, 1916), pp. 75–95; translated as "Myth in Judaism," in Martin Buber, *On Judaism,* pp. 95–107. For Buber's reluctant acceptance of Bar Kochba's invitation, see Martin Buber to Hans Kohn, 23 October 1912, in *Briefwechsel,* 1: 315: "Was Sie mir über meine Teilnahme am Festabend sagen, ist solcher Art, dass es mir unmöglich ist, darauf aus persönlichen Gründen (deren es schwerwiegende gibt) mit einem Nein zu antworten."

103. Hans Kohn to Martin Buber, 31 January 1913, Buber Archives, MS Var 350/376.

104. See Robert Weltsch to Martin Buber, 6 May 1912, *Briefwachsel,* 1: 304–5; and 21 May 1912, Buber Archives, MS Var 350/880. Buber eventually realized his project with the publica-

tion of *Der Jude,* the first volume of which appeared in 1916. Although *Vom Judentum* had no formal connection to *Der Jude,* Bar Kochba veterans occupied important positions on its editorial board, and Siegmund Kaznelson eventually succeeded Buber as its editor.

105. Hans Kohn to Martin Buber, 17 February 1913, Buber Archives, MS Var 350/376.
106. H. Kohn to Martin Buber, [May] 1913, ibid.
107. Kohn, "Geleitwort," to *Vom Judentum,* p. v. Emphasis in the original.
108. Ibid. Emphasis in the original.
109. Ibid., p. vii. Emphasis in the original.
110. In fairness to Kohn, it must be pointed out that he did express concern over how to achieve the right balance between complete freedom of expression on the part of the contributors and a coherent formulation of the Prague Zionist position. In late January 1913 he wrote to Buber:

> Vor allem ist das Wichtige, dass zwischen Ihrem und Landauers Beitrag und Kurt Singer und Susman eine gewisse Gemeinsamkeit der geistigen Atmosphäre bestehen wird und sich so—wenigstens eine Art einheitlichen Kernes herauskristalisiert, die das Buch vor dem Mangel der Zufälligkeit und innerer Zusammenlosigkeit, vor dem Gesamteindruck des Diletantismus bewahren soll (Kohn to Buber, 31 January 1913, Buber Archives, MS Var 350/376).

111. Kohn, "Geleitwort," p. viii.
112. J. Wassermann, "Der Jude als Orientale," in *Vom Judentum,* pp. 5–8.
113. Kurt Singer, "Von der Sendung des Judentums," in *Vom Judentum,* pp. 71–100.
114. Moses Calvary, "Das neue Judentum und die schöpferische Phantasie," in *Vom Judentum,* pp. 103—16.
115. Alfred Wolff, "Jüdische Romantik," in *Vom Judentum,* p. 124. Emphasis in the original.
116. H. Bergmann, "Die Heiligung des Namens," in *Vom Judentum,* pp. 32–43.
117. Ibid., p. 33.
118. Ibid., p. 36.
119. *Pesikta di R. Kahana,* 102b.
120. Bergmann, "Die Heiligung des Namens," p. 41.
121. Bergmann, "Shalosh derashot 'al ha-yahadut," p. 555.

Chapter 6

1. Viktor Teytz, "Národnostní boj a židé," *Rozvoj,* 12 January 1912.
2. See, for example, J. Kohn, "My a sionisté," speech delivered to the open meeting of the Jewish National Council, 10 November 1918, for the program "The Jews in the Czechoslovak State": "Our responsibility at this moment is to educate the nationally indifferent Jews to the rights and responsibilities of Czech citizenship." (Jindřich Kohn, *Asimilace a věky* [Prague, 1936]: 1: 41.)
3. Alfred Fuchs, *O židovské otázce* (Prague, 1911, rev. ed., 1919), p. 5.
4. Evžen Stern, "O současném českožidovství," *KČŽ* 35 (1915–16): 12–13.
5. Ibid., p. 13.
6. Ibid., pp. 13–15.
7. Jindřich Kohn, "Otázka židovská ve světle české otázky," *Rozvoj,* 3 May 1912; reprinted in his *Asimilace a věky,* 1: 14–18. Kohn, though only ten years younger than Vohryzek, did not achieve prominence in the Czech-Jewish movement until the eve of the First World War. For a brief biography see Tohn, "Dr. Jindřich Kohn," pp. 18–21.
8. Viktor Teytz, *Několik poznámek k otázce českožidovské* (Prague, 1913), pp. 15–16.
9. Kohn, "Otázka židovská," p.14.
10. Ibid. Kohn argues further for the confluence of Czech and Jewish interests in "Židovství, češství, lidství," *Směr,* 7 February 1914; reprinted in *Asimilace a věky,* 1: 28–34 (see in particular pp. 33–34).

11. "The Czech nation simply does not want to assimilate. . . . Likewise the Czech-Jewish movement works primarily against the unnatural assimilation of Jews to German culture" (Kohn, "Otázka židovská," p. 14).

12. Ibid., pp. 14–15.

13. Kohn, "Židovství, češství, lidství," pp. 32–33.

14. These speeches have been published as "My a sionisté" (*Asimilace a věky,* 1: 40–42); and "Otázka židovská a česká víra" (*Asimilace a věky,* 1: 43–45).

15. Kohn, "My a sionisté," p. 40.

16. Ibid., p. 41.

17. Kohn, "Otázka židovská a česká víra," p. 44.

18. *Rozvoj,* 27 September 1907. As for Buber's methodology, the reviewer added that it was impossible to verify what belonged to the original legends and what lay in the domain of their subsequent embellishment.

19. *Rozvoj,* 22 January 1909, p. 5.

20. Otakar Guth, "Sny mystikovy," *Rozvoj,* 3 November 1911. Otakar Březina (Václav Jebavý, 1868–1929), was a Czech writer greatly influenced by medieval Christian mysticism.

21. Donath, *Žide a židovství v české literatuře 19. a 20. století,* 2: 190.

22. Jaroslav Kunc, *Slovník soudobých českých spisovatelů, 1918–1945* (Prague, 1945), 1: 174–75; František Langer, "My Brother Jiří," Foreword to Jiří Langer, *Nine Gates to the Chassidic Mysteries,* trans. Stephen Jolly (New York, 1976), pp. vii–xxxi.

23. Martin Buber, *Tři řeči o židovství* (Prague, 1912).

24. Viktor Vohryzek, "Absurdnosti Buberovy," *Rozvoj,* 28 November, 5 December, and 12 December 1913.

25. Donath, *Židé a židovství,* 2: 190.

26. On political censorship during the war, see Macartney, *The Habsburg Empire,* pp. 818–19.

27. Stölzl, "Die 'Burg' und die Juden," pp. 88–89. Theobald von Bethmann-Holweg, the German chancellor, bluntly characterized the war as a struggle between the German world and the Slavic. See Kohn, *Living in a World Revolution,* p. 86.

28. Donath, *Židé a židovství,* 2: 190; Avigdor Dagan, "The Press," in *The Jews of Czechoslovakia: Historical Studies and Surveys* (Philadelphia, 1968), 1: 524. *Rozvoj* resumed publication in 1918 and continued as a weekly until Hitler's entry into Prague in March 1939.

29. Donath, *Židé a židovství,* 2: 202.

30. Ibid. Echoes of this incident can also be found in Bohdan Klineberger's postwar essay, "Episoda," *KČŽ* 44 (1924–25): 168–79.

31. Akademický spolek "Kapper," *Výroční zpráva akademického spolku "Kapper" za období od roku 1914 do roku 1921* (Prague, 1921), pp. 3–4.

32. See the detailed reports in "Z organisací českožidovských," *KČŽ* 38 (1918–19): 113–18.

33. Macartney, *Habsburg Empire,* p. 812.

34. Ibid.

35. Ibid., pp. 812–13.

36. See the discussion in Antony Polonsky and Michael Riff, "Poles, Czechoslovaks and the 'Jewish Question,' 1914–1921: A Comparative Study," in V. R. Berghahn and M. Kitchen, eds., *Germany in the Age of Total War* (London and Totowa, N.J., 1981), pp. 83–85.

37. "České veřejnosti!" *Rozvoj,* 27 November 1914: this was a front-page appeal, signed by forty-four Czech Jewish leaders, which renounced all "denunciations" against Czech nationals (reissued on 11 December 1914). See also the earlier editorial "Nepěkné zjevy" (Unseemly phenomena), *Rozvoj,* 23 October 1914.

38. Polonsky and Riff, "Poles, Czechoslovaks and the Jewish Question," p. 84. Brod relates the incident in his autobiography, *Streitbares Leben,* pp. 95–98.

39. "Světová válka a naše hnutí," *Rozvoj,* 30 October 1914, p. 2.

40. "Židovská otázka," *Národní listy,* 15 November 1914; reprinted and commented on in *Rozvoj,* 11 December 1914.

41. *Rozvoj,* 11 December 1914, p. 1.

42. Stern, "O současném českožidovství," pp. 15–22.

43. Ibid., pp. 19–22.

44. In 1913–14 Hans Kohn taught Jewish history, Robert Weltsch Zionism and a seminar on Martin Buber, and Hugo Bergmann Hebrew in Prague's Zionistische Mädchenklub. See the reminiscences of Frida Löwy in *Bar Kochba Zirkular,* December 1963, pp. 14—15. Kohn and Weltsch joined the same infantry regiment in August 1914 (Kohn, *Living in a World Revolution,* p. 86).

45. See Robert Weltsch's introduction ("Zur Einführung") to the recent republication of *Das jüdische Prag* (Jüdischer Verlag, Kronberg/Ts., 1978), p. viii. See also Siegmund Kaznelson, [Albrecht Hellmann], "Erinnerungen an gemeinsame Kampfjahre," in F. Weltsch, ed., *Dichter, Denker, Helfer: Max Brod zum 50. Geburtstag,* pp. 49–50.

46. Kaznelson, "Erinnerungen an gemeinsame Kampfjahre," pp. 49–50; Weltsch, "Zur Einführung," p. viii. Brod in fact had been mobilized in August 1914 and spent a brief time on the Galician front (Brod, *Streitbares Leben,* pp. 81–101). For Kafka's relationship to the editors of *Selbstwehr* and to Jewish nationalism in general, see Binder, "Franz Kafka und die Wochenschrift 'Selbstwehr,' " pp. 283–304.

47. Martin Buber to Hans Kohn, 30 September 1914, in Buber, *Briefwechsel,* 1: 370–71. The biblical verse alluded to is from Zechariah 4.6: "This is the word of the Lord unto Zerubbabel saying: Not by might, nor by power, but by My spirit, saith the Lord of hosts."

48. Buber to Kohn, 30 September 1914, in Buber, *Briefwechsel,* 1: 371. Buber's "Aktion" was to operate in conjunction with the Kommittee für den Osten, formerly the Kommittee zur Befreiung der russischen Juden, which had been formed in Berlin at the beginning of the war.

49. Buber to Kohn, 30 September 1914.

50. Martin Buber to Hugo Bergmann, 26 April 1915, in Buber, *Briefwechsel,* 1: 387.

51. Paul Mendes-Flohr comments that Buber's position on the war diverged somewhat from that of other European intellectuals because he tended to view it from the perspective of *Erlebnis* mysticism rather than pure patriotism. Erlebnis, affective experience, allowed one to overcome the divisions and contradictions of the phenomenal world and to achieve unity with the world spirit. See Paul R. Mendes-Flohr, "The Road to *I and Thou:* An Inquiry into Buber's Transition from Mysticism to Dialogue," in Michael A. Fishbane and Paul R. [Mendes-]Flohr, eds., *Texts and Responses: Studies Presented to Nahum N. Glatzer* (Leiden, 1975), pp. 201–10; also Paul R. Mendes-Flohr, *Von der Mystik zum Dialog: Martin Bubers geistige Entwicklung bis hin zu "Ich und Du"* (Königstein/Ts., 1978), ch. 5.

Buber nevertheless saw the war as a victory for *Gemeinschaft* over egotism and social alienation. He likened the war, in a 1914 speech to an audience of Zionists, to the Maccabean revolt against the Seleucids. Basing himself on a Hasidic interpretation of the term *malkhut yavan harasha*—the "evil Greek kingdom"—Buber concluded that the modern-day Jewish warrior, too, was leading his people to victory over "man's egotistical desire." The whole conflict was seen as a liberating "Geminschaftserlebnis." See Mendes-Flohr, "The Road to *I and Thou,*" pp. 209–10.

52. See in general the correspondence for the period 1914 through 1916 in Buber, *Briefwechsel,* vol. 1.

53. Martin Buber, "Die Losung," *Der Jude* 1 (1916–17): 1.

54. Ibid., p. 2. The historian of Jewish mysticism Gershom Scholem was in attendance at Buber's December 1914 speech and has reported that he was scandalized by it. Scholem's biographer, David Biale, suggests that it was this incident that began the split between the two men (David Biale, *Gershom Scholem: Kabbalah and Counter-History* [Cambridge, Mass., 1979], pp. 58–60).

55. Buber, "Die Losung," p. 2.

56. Hugo Bergmann to Martin Buber, 11 May 1915, in Buber, *Briefwechsel,* 1: 388.

57. Robert Weltsch to Hugo Bergmann, 11 May 1915, in *Robert Weltsch zum 60. Geburtstag. Ein Gedenkbuch gewidmet von Freunden* (Tel Aviv and Jerusalem, 1951), p. 5.

58. See Weltsch to Buber, 18 July 1915, 11 September 1915, and 23 November 1915, in Buber, *Briefwechsel,* 1: 392, 400, and 404–5.

59. Kohn devotes many pages of his autobiography *Living in a World Revolution* to his years of imprisonment. See in particular chapters 7–11; also Hans Kohn to Robert Weltsch, 26 August 1917 (Buber Archives, MS Var 350/376).

60. Kohn to Buber, 21 November 1917, in Buber, *Briefwechsel,* 1: 510. Kohn was placed in a liberal form of solitary confinement in 1916 for attempting to escape to Afghanistan (*Living in a World Revolution,* pp. 95–99).

61. Mendes-Flohr forcefully argues that it was Gustav Landauer who ultimately convinced Buber to reject not only his "aesthetic" appreciation of violence, but also mysticism in general. Indeed Landauer vented much anger and frustration at his friend between 1914 and 1916, and Buber appears to have modified his position by the summer of 1916 (Mendes-Flohr, "Buber's Road to *I and Thou,*" pp. 210–25). I would only add to this picture the fact that Buber received numerous calls throughout this period to renounce his earlier support for the war, not the least of which came from his protégés in the Prague Zionist circle.

62. Hugo Bergmann to Martin Buber, 11 May 1915, in Buber, *Briefwechsel,* 1: 388–89: "Dieser Krieg wird für den Menschen die ungeheuren Segen haben, dass er gezeigt hat, was wirklich ist, was an Realität da ist."

63. Ibid.

64. Ibid., p. 389.

65. Hans Kohn to Robert Weltsch, 19 August 1917 (Buber Archives, MS Var 350/376). See also Hans Kohn, "Rückblick auf eine gemeinsame Jugend," in Tramer and Loewenstein, eds., *Robert Weltsch zum 70. Geburtstag,* p.116:

Als ich im Früjahr 1920 nach Mitteleuropa zurückkehrte, war so manches anders geworden, in Mitteleuropa und in mir. Der Krieg, das Erlebnis Russlands, der Kontakt mit den zentralasiatischen mohammedanischen Kolonialvölkern, die Revolution, hatten mein Interesse für Geschichte und Politik geweckt und mein Verständnis des Nationalismus vertieft.

66. Hans Kohn to Martin Buber, 21 November 1917, in Buber, *Briefwechsel,* 1: 511. See also Grete Schaeder's Introduction to the *Briefwechsel,* 1: 46–47.

67. Kohn to Buber, 21 November 1917.

68. Martin Buber to Hans Kohn, 5 August 1917, in Buber, *Briefwechsel,* 1: 503–5.

69. See Hugo Bergmann to Martin Buber, 30 December 1918, and Buber to Bergmann, 21 January 1919, in ibid., 2: 20–21 and 27–28.

70. Brod, *Streitbares Leben,* pp. 230–33; Max Brod, "Erfahrungen im ostjüdischen Schulwerk," *Der Jude* 1 (1916–17): 32–36. On the establishment of the Jewish National Council, see A. M. Rabinowicz, "The Jewish Minority," pp. 155–264; and O. Rabinowicz, "Czechoslovak Zionism: Analecta to a History," pp. 19–136.

In the introduction to his selection of articles from *Der Jude,* Arthur A. Cohen has earmarked the prominent role of Prague Jews in both the publication of the journal and the determination of editorial policy. See his *The Jew: Essays from Martin Buber's Journal Der Jude, 1916–1928* (University, Ala., 1980), pp. 10–11.

71. *Encyclopaedia Judaica,* vol. 10, col. 860.

72. On Hugo Herrmann, see ibid., vol. 8, col. 393; and V. Kellner, "Ben dodo shel Leo," in F. Weltsch, ed., *Prag vi-Yerushalayim,* pp. 120–21.

73. *Encyclopaedia Judaica,* vol. 8, col. 365; also Robert Weltsch, "Leo Herrmann: Darko u-tekufato"; G. Herlitz, "Pe'ula ẓiyonit bereshit milḥemet ha-'olam ha-rishona"; and Ya'akov Hodes, "Ha-yamim ha-rishonim shel ha-keren ha-yesod," all in F. Weltsch, ed., *Prag vi-Yerushalayim,* pp. 125–42, 153–55, and 156–59.

74. Felix Weltsch, "Shnei ẓiyonim czechi'im," in F. Weltsch, ed., *Prag vi-Yerushalayim,* pp. 73–74; also *Selbstwehr,* 12 February 1926, p. 2.

75. Grete Schaeder, Introduction to Buber, *Briefwechsel,* 1: 46–47; also *Robert Weltsch zum*

60. Geburtstag; and Hans Tramer and Kurt Löwenstein, eds., *Robert Weltsch zum 70. Geburtstag.*

76. Kohn, *Living in a World Revolution,* pp. 47–155.

77. Buber, "Die Losung," p. 2.

78. Hugo Bergmann, "Der jüdische Nationalismus nach dem Krieg," *Der Jude* 1 (1916–17): 7–13.

79. Ibid., p. 7.

80. Ibid., pp. 7–8.

81. Ibid., p. 8.

82. Ibid., p. 9.

83. Ibid., p. 13. Bergman's call for an all-encompassing, yet practical, Zionism contained echoes of some of his earlier work and was inspired primarily by the writings of Micah Joseph Berdyczewski (later Micha Yosef bin Gorion, 1865–1921). In opposition to the prevailing opinion put forward by Aḥad Ha'am, Berdyczewski had argued that one is a Jew for no other reason than that one is a member of the Jewish people; furthermore, one's human qualities were equivalent to one's Judaism. Bergmann paraphrased Berdyczewski's position in an article that he published in 1914 in *Die Welt* ("Das zionistische Problem bei M. J. Berdyczewski," pp. 679–82, later included in Bergmann's *Jawne und Jerusalem* [Berlin, 1919] under the title that he chose for the book as a whole).

84. Reprinted in Bergmann, *Jawne und Jerusalem* under the title "Die zionistische Kulturarbeit im Westen," pp. 12–15.

85. Ibid., p. 13.

86. Ibid., pp. 14–15.

87. Oskar Epstein, "Grundsätzliches zur zionistischen Gegenwartsarbeit," *Der Jude* 1 (1916–17): 100–104.

88. Epstein, "Grundsätzliches," pp. 102–3.

89. Hans Kohn, "Aufgaben der Stunde," in his *Nationalismus: Über die Bedeutung des Nationalismus im Judentum und in der Gegenwart* (Vienna and Leipzig, 1922), p. 93.

90. Hugo Bergmann, "Das hebräische Buch und die deutschen Zionisten," *Der Jude* 4 (1919–20): 287–88. Martin Buber to Hugo Bergmann, 9 September 1919; and Hugo Bergmann to Martin Buber, 19 September 1919: in Buber, *Briefwechsel,* 2: 57–59.

91. Bergmann to Buber, 19 September 1919, pp. 58–59.

92. Martin Buber to Hugo Bergmann, 21 October 1919, in Buber, *Briefwechsel,* 2: 60–61. It should also be pointed out that there were other Zionists in Central Europe at the time who echoed Bergmann's concern for the Hebrew literacy of European Jewry, but not very many. Perhaps the most visible was Gershom Scholem (1897–1982), who caused much bad feeling in the Jüdisches Volksheim (Jewish community center) in Berlin when he suggested to Siegfried Lehmann, its director, that one could further Jewish education more by learning Hebrew and returning to the Jewish sources than by concerning oneself with the aesthetic problems of European literature. See Gershom Scholem, *From Berlin to Jerusalem: Memories of My Youth* (New York, 1980), pp. 76–80.

93. See Steven E. Aschheim, *Brothers and Strangers: The East European Jews in German and German Jewish Consciousness, 1800–1923* (Madison, Wis., 1982), esp. pp. 80–138. Also Jehuda Reinharz, "East European Jews in the Weltanschauung of German Zionists, 1882–1914," and Paul Mendes-Flohr, "Fin-de-Siècle Orientalism, the Ostjuden and the Aesthetics of Jewish Self-Affirmation," both in *Studies in Contemporary Jewry* 1 (1984): 55–95 and 96–139.

94. See discussion in Chapter 5.

95. Max Brod, who first introduced Kafka to Yiddish theater, recalls that he attended the Yiddish productions in the first place as a protest against the abstract intellectualism of the Prague Zionists. The other members of Bar Kochba rarely attended the group's performances, and when they did, they were unimpressed with what they saw. See Max Brod, *Franz Kafka: Eine Biographie* (Frankfurt a.M., 1974), pp. 98–102.

96. Quoted in Moses Wiesenfeld, "Begegnung mit Ostjuden," in F. Weltsch, ed., *Dichter, Denker, Helfer: Max Brod zum 50. Geburtstag*, pp. 54–55.

97. Quoted in ibid., p. 55.

98. Brod, "Erfahrungen im ostjüdischen Schulwerk," pp. 32–36.

99. Ibid., p. 35:

If I might draw from my modest experiences conclusions concerning the formation of a Jewish school system in occupied Russia, it would appear to me that it is essential, not only in the interests of Jewry, but also of the Austrian and German Empires—who need full, upstanding characters as citizens—to establish Jewish schools on the basis of a sound, Jewish-national consciousness, Jewish spirituality, and religion. In that way not only are the intellectual, educational successes guaranteed, but also the cultivation of unbroken men and women, conscious of their responsibilities.

100. Ibid., p. 34.

101. See the account by the playwright František Langer, "My Brother Jiří," pp. xii–xxxi.

102. Ibid., p. xv.

103. Ibid., p. xviii; See also Jiří Langer's Introduction to his *Nine Gates to the Chassidic Mysteries*, pp. 3–29.

104. František Langer, "My Brother Jiří," pp. xviii–xix.

105. Franz Kakfa, *Diaries, 1914–1923* (New York, 1949, 1965), pp. 128–29.

106. See Brod's note to Kafka's letter of mid-July 1916, in Franz Kafka, *Letters to Friends, Family, and Editors* (New York, 1977), p. 449.

107. Of the Belzer Rebbe himself Kafka wrote:

To escape the rain we are about to enter the hotel vestibule, when L. suddenly jumps back and to one side. The rabbi is coming. No one must ever stand in front of him; there must always be a free passage before him, which is not easy to provide, since he often suddenly turns around and in the throng it is not easy to take evasive action speedily. (It's supposed to be still worse in his room, where the crowding is so great as to endanger the rabbi himself. Recently he is said to have cried out: 'You are Hasidim? You are murderers.') And of his entourage:

There are four *gabim* (or something like that) who play a special role among the entourage—they are his 'intimates'—employees, secretaries. The highest of the four, according to Langer, is an exceptional rogue; his huge belly, his smugness, his shifty eyes seem to bear that out. However, one must not hold this against him, for all the *gabim* go bad; people cannot bear the continual presence of the rabbi without suffering damage. It is the contradiction between the deeper meaning and the unrelenting commonplaceness that an ordinary head cannot sustain" (*Letters to Friends, Family, and Editors*, pp. 121–22).

108. Robert Weltsch, "Ein Feldpostbrief aus dem Osten," *Der Jude* 1 (1916–17): 530. For comparable experiences among Jewish soldiers in the German army, see Aschheim, *Brothers and Strangers*, pp. 139–84.

109. Robert Weltsch to Hugo Bergmann, 15 November 1916, in *Robert Weltsch zum 60. Geburtstag*, p. 5: "So ist mitten in Prag, via facti und völlig anerkannt, eine richtige nationale Schule entstanden. Es sind unbegrenzte Möglichkeiten, wenn man das Schulwesen wennigstens zum Teil in die Hand bekommen könnte. Ich gestehe, dass ich für diese Sache stärkeres Interesse habe als für die meisten andern."

110. Ḥayyim Naḥman Bialik (1873–1934) was probably the greatest Hebrew poet of modern times; author of two stirring poems written in the wake of the Kishinev pogroms of 1903, " 'Al ha-sheḥita" (On the slaughter) and "Be-'ir ha-harega" (In the city of slaughter). David Frischmann (1859–1922) was a well-known Hebrew and Yiddish writer, master of short stories, poems, and literary criticism.

111. Robert Weltsch to Hugo Bergmann, 25 April 1916, reprinted in *Bar Kochba Zirkular*, December 1971. Steven Aschheim reports that the encounter between German-Jewish soldiers and Jews in Poland and Lithuania, though often disquieting, on the whole left the Jewish

soldiers with a heightened sense of their own Jewish identity (Aschheim, *Brothers and Strangers*, pp. 150–53).

112. Weltsch, "Feldpostbrief," p. 532.

113. Kaznelson, "Erinnerung an gemeinsame Kampfjahre," pp. 50–51.

114. Siegmund Kaznelson, "Vorrede," *Das jüdische Prag: Eine Sammelschrift* (Prague, 1917), p. 1.

115. Ibid.

116. Ibid.

117. Ibid.

118. Otakar Březina's "Die Erbauer des Tempels" was translated by the Jewish poet Otto Pick; Machar's "Ein Jude wandelt zwischen den Trümmern des Forum Romanum" by Pavel Eisner; Vrchlický's "Motive aus Jehuda Halevi" by "M.W."; and Mácha's "Ewige Wanderung" by O. Rosenfeld. *Das jüdische Prag* also included a piece by Jan Neruda ("Böhmische Verse"), translated by the poet Rudolf Fuchs, and Julius Zeyer's "Gerechtigkeit," translated by "M.W." Both Pick and Fuchs wrote original pieces for the collection as well.

119. Among the illustrations is a stunning reproduction of a very German, very bourgeois wedding invitation of 1849 as well as twentieth-century caricatures of German Jews.

120. Robert Weltsch, "Die Jugend des jüdischen Prag," in *Das jüdische Prag,"* p. 17.

121. Ibid., pp. 17–18.

122. Max Brod, "Zum Problem der Gemeinschaft," in *Das jüdische Prag,* pp. 8–10.

123. Ibid., p. 10:

Zwischen den Nullpunkt der Einsamkeit und den Unendlichkeitspunkt der Freundschaft liegt die liebevolle, alle Fehler verzeihende und alle Vorzüge fördende, ehrliche, doch niemals verletzende, den Nebenmenschen als mir fremden Komplex und doch als zutiefst mir verbundene Wesenheit erfassende Gemeinschaft, wie wir sie als Kern für unseren Zionismus ersehnen.

124. Felix Weltsch, "Die ersten Elemente der sittlichen Entscheidung und das Sch'ma Israel," in *Das jüdische Prag,* pp. 12–13.

125. Ibid., p. 12.

126. Ibid., p. 13.

Chapter 7

1. Akademický spolek "Kapper," *Výroční zpráva akademického spolku "Kapper,"* pp. 4–5; "Z organisací českožidovských," p. 113; and *Zprávy spolkové,"* KČŽ 39 (1919–20): 137–38. Fuchs was elected president of the SČAŽ in December 1918. His address to the General Assembly, "O židovské otázce" (On the Jewish question) was later widely circulated as a brochure.

2. On the collapse of the Habsburg monarchy and the formation of the First Czechoslovak Republic, see Z. A. B. Zeman, *The Break-up of the Habsburg Empire, 1914–1918* (London, 1961); and Victor S. Mamatey and Radomír Luža, eds., *A History of the Czechoslovak Republic 1918–1948* (Princeton, 1973).

3. "Z organisací českožidovských," pp. 115–17.

4. "Zprávy spolkové," KČŽ 40 (1920–21): 110–12; *Dějiny českožidovského hnutí,* pp. 16–17. One of the first efforts of the Svaz Čechů-židů was to push for the creation of a Jewish Theological Faculty at the Czech University, which would be used to train Jewish rabbinical students. This plan, however, never materialized.

5. Akademický spolek "Kapper," *Výroční zpráva akademického spolku "Kapper,"* pp. 5–6; "Zprávy spolkové," KČŽ 40 (1920–21): 107.

6. "Z organisací českožidovských," pp. 114–15.

7. "Zprávy spolkové," KČŽ 39 (1919–20): 140–41.

8. Ibid., p. 141.

9. "Přátelé!" *KČŽ* 38 (1918–19): 3–4. The appeal was signed by Eduard Lederer, Vojtěch Rakous, Stanislav Schulhof, Lev Vohryzek, Viktor Vohryzek, Max Hirsch, and Rudolf Neuwirth.

10. "Přátelé" pp. 3–4.

11. Vyskočil, "Die Tschechisch-jüdische Bewegung," p. 47; Hostovský, "The Czech-Jewish Movement," pp. 151–52.

12. Polonsky and Riff, "Poles, Czechoslovaks, and the 'Jewish Question,' 1914–1921," pp. 83–85. For a more negative view of the Czech ruling elite, see Christoph Stölzl, "Die 'Burg' und die Juden: T. G. Masaryk und sein kreis im Spannungsfeld der jüdischen Frage," pp. 94–98. The Czech-Jewish press was fond of quoting the wartime speech of Karel Kramář, in which he warned: "No one ought to be excluded from national activity *(národní práce)* but rather to the contrary. . . . Everyone is invited in the struggle for the solid future of the nation, but he must serve the nation, nothing else" (*Rozvoj,* 8 January 1915, p. 4).

13. Polonsky and Riff, "Poles, Czechoslovaks, and the 'Jewish Question,' 1914–1921," p. 88, 99; *Selbstwehr,* 6 December 1918.

14. Polonsky and Riff, "Poles, Czechoslovaks, and the 'Jewish Question,' 1914–1921," pp. 92–93. Ludvík Singer, Zionist member of the Prague City Council, movingly protested the attack on the Jewish Town Hall before the City Council. See *Jüdische Rundschau,* 26 November 1920; quoted in Rabinowicz, "The Jewish Minority," p. 247, but wrongly attributed to 1918.

15. *Neue Freie Presse,* 19 November 1920; referred to in Polonsky and Riff, "Poles, Czechoslovaks, and the 'Jewish Question,' 1914–1921," p. 93.

16. Franz Kafka, *Letters to Milena,* ed. Willi Haas (New York, 1953, 1962), p. 213.

17. See the front-page articles in *Selbstwehr,* 23 and 30 March, 12 and 27 April, and 4 May 1917.

18. Kaznelson, "Errinerungen an gemeinsame Kampfjahre," pp. 51–52.

19. Ibid., p. 52.

20. Ibid., pp. 52–53. See also Max Brod's "Prag—Wien—Errinerungen," in Josef Fränkel, ed., *The Jews of Austria* (London, 1967), pp. 241–42.

21. Ludvík Singer, "Naše cíle," *Židovské zprávy,* 5 April 1918, p. 1.

22. Ibid., p. 2.

23. Kaznelson, "Erinnerungen an gemeinsame Kampfjahre," p. 53; also Brod, "Prag— Wien—Errinerungen," p. 241: "Frieden zwischen den Nationalitäten des alten Österreich—das war unser Programm, daneben eine bescheidene Autonomie des jüdischen Volkes, das ja im Westen noch gar nicht als solches erkannt und anerkannt war, Autonomie des Erziehungswesens vor allem."

24. See Tomáš G. Masaryk, *The Making of a State: Memories and Observations, 1914–1918* (New York, 1927), pp. 236–37.

25. Quoted in Rabinowicz, "The Jewish Minority," p. 165. On the relationship between Masaryk's Realist party and the Prague Zionists see Rabinowicz, "Czechoslovak Zionism: Analecta to a History," pp. 64–69; and Felix Weltsch, "Masaryk und der Zionismus," in Ernst Rychnovsky, ed., *Masaryk und das Judentum* (Prague, 1931), pp. 67–116. Oskar K. Rabinowicz relates, inter alia, that the "realist" wing in the Zionist movement was patterned after Masaryk's party.

26. Brod, *Streitbares Leben,* p. 104.

27. As late as 25 October 1918, *Selbstwehr* published a front-page editorial calling for the recognition of the Jewish nationality in a federated Austria (österreichische Bundesstaat). See "Das Gebot der Stunde," *Selbstwehr,* 25 October 1918. In the aftermath of the Second World War, Brod allowed himself to muse on what the fate of Europe might have been had Masaryk and other nationalists been less successful in 1918:

Nachträglich sieht man, dass es den Tschechen und der ganzen Welt viel Unglück erpsarrt hätte, wenn Masaryks Plan der Verwirklichung des tschechischen 'Staatsrechts' weniger geglückt wäre, wenn es Lebensfähiges Österreich als ein Föderation freier Völker als eine Art 'Völkerbund im kleinen' den Krieg überdauert hätte (*Streitbares Leben*, pp. 98–99).

28. "Der jüdische Nationalrat beim *Národní výbor*," *Selbstwehr*, 1 November 1918. See also Brod, "Prag—Wien—Erinnerungen," pp. 241—42; Rabinowicz, "Czechoslovak Zionism: Analecta to a History," p. 31; Weltsch, "Masaryk und der Zionismus," pp. 79–86.

29. *Selbstwehr*, 8 November 1918, p. 2. Weltsch, "Masaryk und der Zionismus," pp. 79–86; Rabinowicz, "The Jewish Minority," pp. 159–61. Rabinowicz produces an English translation of the memorandum on pp. 218–21.

30. *Selbstwehr*, 8 November 1918, p. 2; Rabinowicz, "The Jewish Minority," pp. 218–19.

31. *Selbstwehr*, 8 November 1918, p. 2; Rabinowicz, "The Jewish Minority," pp. 219–20.

32. Weltsch, "Masaryk und der Zionismus," pp. 80–81; Rabinowicz, "The Jewish Minority," p. 167.

33. Weltsch, "Masaryk und der Zionismus," p. 85. Beneš is reported to have explained that his views on the Jewish question were identical to those of President Masaryk.

34. See the discussion in Mendelsohn, *The Jews of East Central Europe Between the World Wars*, pp. 148–49.

35. Report by Max Brod of a meeting between Masaryk and representatives of the Jewish National Council, held on 22 March 1919; portions quoted in Weltsch, "Masaryk und das Judentum," pp. 83–84.

36. Quoted in Weltsch, "Masaryk und der Zionismus," p. 84.

37. Edvard Beneš to Ludvík Singer, 25 August 1919 (CZA Z4/583). Full text of the letter quoted (in English translation) in Rabinowicz, "The Jewish Minority," pp. 172–173.

38. Report of N. Sokolow (CZA Z4/583); reproduced in Rabinowicz, "The Jewish Minority," pp. 174–77.

39. Sokolow report, in Rabinowicz, "The Jewish Minority," pp. 176–77.

40. Weltsch, "Masaryk und der Zionismus," pp. 88–89; Rabinowicz, "The Jewish Minority," pp. 186–87, 199.

41. Cf. Simon Dubnov, *Nationalism and History: Essays on Old and New Judaism* (New York, 1970), esp. pp. 100–115.

42. See, for example, Masaryk's remarks concerning assimilation and Zionism, made in 1919 in an interview with the German paper *Telegraf*:

Was die Juden in unserem Staate betrifft, so gibt es neben den Zionisten sogenannte Assimilanten. Es handelt sich da um zwei Programme: Einerseits, wenn ein Mensch mir sagt, er sei ein Deutscher, so habe ich das zu akzeptieren. Das geht schon aus dem Selbstbestimmungsrecht hervor, das auch auf die Juden seine Anwendung finden muss (quoted in Weltsch, "Masaryk und der Zionismus," p. 82).

43. "Falešná hra sionistů," *Rozvoj*, 28 June 1919.

44. Ibid.

45. See in particular 'K židovské otázce školské," *Rozvoj*, 31 May and 7 June 1919; and [Kamil] Kleiner, "Židovské národní školství," *Rozvoj*, 10 and 17 July 1920.

46. "K židovské otázce školské," *Rozvoj*, 31 May and 7 June 1919. Czech nationalist Jews were not the only party to accuse the Zionists of betrayal. The *Rozvoj* article makes reference to a rumor that appeared in the German-language press (untrue according to *Rozvoj*) which charged that the Jewish National Council and the Národní výbor in Prague were in the process of establishing a statewide system of Jewish national, Czech-language schools, which all Jewish children would have to attend.

47. On the opening of the Jewish national school in Prague, see Rabinowicz, "The Jewish Minority," pp. 215–16; and H. Binder, "Franz Kafka und die Wochenschrift 'Selbstwehr,' " pp. 294–95.

48. Binder, "Franz Kafka und die Wochenschrift 'Selbstwehr,' " pp. 294–95.

49. Rabinowicz, "The Jewish Minority," p. 216; see also Aryeh Sole, "Subcarpathian Ruthenia, 1918–1938" in *The Jews of Czechoslovakia*, 1: 125–54; and Aryeh Sole, "Modern Hebrew Education in Subcarpathian Ruthenia," in *The Jews of Czechoslovakia*, 2: 401–39.

50. The Brno gymnasium opened in 1920. It, too, began as a German institution, but switched to Czech. The Mukačevo gymnasium opened in 1925, Užhorod in 1935. See Rabinowicz, "The Jewish Minority," p. 216; Sole, "Modern Hebrew Education."

51. Jan Heřman, "The Development of Bohemian and Moravian Jewry, 1918–1938," in U. O. Schmelz, P. Glikson, and S. Della Pergola, eds., *Papers in Jewish Demography, 1969* (Jerusalem, 1973), pp. 191–206. Heřman's figures vary slightly from those in *Dějiny českožidovského hnutí*, p. 19, and Friedmann, *Židé v Čechách*, p. 733.

52. Heřman, "The Development of Bohemian and Moravian Jewry," p. 201; *Dějiny českožidovského hnutí*, p. 19.

53. For Slovakia and Subcarpathian Ruthenia, see Mendelsohn, *The Jews of East Central Europe Between the World Wars*, p. 146. For Bohemia and Moravia in 1930, see Heřman, "The Development of Bohemian and Moravian Jewry," p. 201.

54. Jan Heřman, "The Evolution of the Jewish Population in Prague, 1869–1939," in U. O. Schmelz, P. Glikson, and S. Della Pergola, eds., *Papers in Jewish Demography, 1977* (Jerusalem, 1980), pp. 60–61.

Conclusion

1. In addition to the Introduction of this book, see Kieval, "Caution's Progress: The Modernization of Jewish Life in Prague, 1780–1830"; and Kestenberg-Gladstein, *Neuere Geschichte der Juden in den böhmischen Ländern.*

2. *Encyclopaedia Judaica*, vol. 4, col. 1179; Heřman, "The Evolution of the Jewish Population in Prague, 1869–1939," p. 57; Heřman, "The Evolution of the Jewish Population in Bohemia and Moravia, 1754–1953," p. 259.

3. On assimilation and social mobility among the Jews of Hungary, see William O. McCagg, *Jewish Nobles and Geniuses in Modern Hungary* (Boulder, Colo., 1972); George Barany, " 'Magyar Jew or Jewish Magyar?' Reflections on the Question of Assimilation," in Bela Vago and George Mosse, eds., *Jews and Non-Jews in Eastern Europe* (New York, 1974), pp. 51–98; William McCagg, "Jewish Conversion in Hungary," in Todd M. Endelman, ed., *Christian Missionaries and Jewish Apostates* (New York, 1986); and Michael K. Silber, "Roots of the Schism in Hungarian Jewry: Cultural and Social Change from the Reign of Joseph II until the Eve of the 1848 Revolution" [Hebrew], Ph.D. Diss., Hebrew University, Jerusalem, 1985.

Bibliography

Primary Sources

Archival Collections

Archiv Statního Židovského Muzea (Archives of the State Jewish Museum), Prague: Archives of the Jewish Religious Community of Prague; Archives of the Jewish Religious Communities of Bohemia and Moravia.

Archiv Univerzity Karlovy (Charles University Archives), Prague: Archives of the Spolek českých akademiků-židů, 1878–1919; Archives of the Student Association "Kapper," 1914–38.

Archives of the Leo Baeck Institute, New York: Robert Weltsch, Fritz Mauthner, Urzidil-Thieberger, and Paul Amann Collections; Memoir Collection.

Hugo Bergmann [Shmuel Hugo Bergman] Archives, Jewish National and University Library, Jerusalem (Arc 4 1502).

Martin Buber Archives, Jewish National and University Library, Jerusalem (MS Var 350).

Central Zionist Archives, Jerusalem: Bar Kochba Collection; Prague Zionism; Zionism in Bohemia; Jewish National Council for the Czechoslovak Republic; Leo Herrmann, Robert Weltsch, and Richard Pacovský Collections.

Avigdor Dagan [Viktor Fischl] Archives, Jewish National and University Library, Jerusalem (MS Var 581).

Památník Národního Písemnictví (Memorial for National Literature), Literární Archiv, Prague: Otokar Fischer, Arné Laurin, Rudolf Fuchs, Franz Kafka, Viktor Vohryzek, Eduard Lederer, František Langer, Richard Weiner, Ignát Arnstein, and František Gottlieb Collections.

Newspapers and Periodicals

A. H. Blätter der jüd. nat. akad. tech. Verbindungen "Barissia" und "Jordania" [Barissen Blätter]. Prague, 1918–33.

B'nai B'rith, Monatsblätter der Grossloge für den Čechoslovakischen Staat. Prague, 1922–39.

Bohemia [Deutsche Zeitung Bohemia]. Prague, 1910–14.

Brandeis' illustrierter israelitischer Volkskalender. Prague, 1881–1929.

Čas, List věnovaný veřených otázkám. Prague, 1886–1923.

Centralverein zur Pflege jüdischer Angelegenheiten in Prag. *Berichte*. Prague, 1886–93.

Českožidovské listy. Prague, 1894–1904.

245

Deutsche Arbeit. Monatschrift für das geistige Leben der Deutschen in Böhmen. Prague, 1901–25.

Dr. Bloch's Österreichische Wochenschrift. Central-Organ für die gesamten Interessen des Judentums. Vienna, 1884–1920.

Herder-Blätter. Prague, 1911–12.

Iggud Vatikei Bar Kochba-Theodor Herzl, Prag. *Zirkular [Bar-Kochba Zirkular].* Hrsg. R. G. Pacovský. Tel-Aviv, 1954–72.

Israelitische Gemeindezeitung. Central-Organ für die Gesammtinteressen des Judentums. Prague, 1873–1901 (from 1873 to 1883: *Israelitische Lehrerbote*).

Israelitischer Landes-Lehrer-Verein in Böhmen. *Mitteilungen.* Prague, 1895–1917.

Jahrbuch für die israelitischen Cultusgemeinden Böhmens. Prague, 1893–95.

Der Jude. Eine Monatsschrift. Hrsg. Martin Buber. Berlin, 1916–28.

Jüdische Chronik. Hrsg. Adolf Kurrein, Simon Stern, und Ignaz Ziegler. Saaz, 1894–96.

Jüdische Rundschau. Berlin, 1895–1938.

Jüdische Volksstimme. Brno, 1900–1933.

Jüdischer Almanach. Hrsg. im Auftrage des Keren Kajemeth Lejisrael in Prag. Prague, 1924–31.

Jüdisches Gefühl. Jung Juda. Hrsg. Filip Lebenhart. Prague, 1900–14.

Kalendář česko-židovský. Spolek českých akademiků-židů v Praze. Prague, 1881–1939.

Mitteilungsblatt Irgun Olej Merkaz Europa (orginally: Irgun Olej Germania). Tel-Aviv, 1933–68.

Národní listy. Prague, 1897–1901.

Naše doba. Prague, 1893–1914.

Pascheles' illustrierter israelitischer Volkskalender. Prague, 1868–1910.

Prager Presse. Prague, 1921–38.

Prager Tagblatt. Prague, 1910–14.

Přehled. Týdenník věnovaný veřejným otázkám. Prague, 1902–14.

Rozhledy sociální, politické a literární. Chrudim, 1892–1909.

Rozvoj. Pardubice, 1904–07. Prague, 1907–39.

Selbstemanzipation. Vienna, 1885–94.

Selbstwehr. Prague, 1907–38.

Ha-Shiloaḥ. Berlin, Krakow, Odessa, Jerusalem, 1896–1926.

Talmud-Thora. Bericht. Prague, 1909–14.

Tribuna. Prague, 1919–21.

Všestudentský kalendář. Svaz českoslovanského studentsva v Praze. Prague, 1911–14.

Die Welt. Zentralorgan der zionistischen Bewegung. Vienna, 1897–1914.

Židovské listy pro Čechy, Moravu a Slezsko. Prague, 1913, 1915.

Židovské zprávy. Prague, 1918–39.

Židovský kalendář. Vydal Spolek žid. akademiků "Theodor Herzl," Židovské zprávy. Prague, 1920–39.

Židovský lidový list. Organ všesvětové židovské socialistické strany dělnické "Poale Zion" v Čechách. Prague, 1910–12.

Zionistische Briefe. Hrsg. Verein der jüdischen Hochschüler Bar Kochba in Prag. Prague, 1910–11.

Statistical Sources

Austria. Statistische Central-Commission. *Österreichische Statistik.* Vienna, 1882–1918.

———. *Österreichisches statistisches Handbuch.* Vienna, 1883–1917.

———. *Statistisches Jahrbuch.* Vienna, 1863–81.

Bohemia. Statistisches Landesamt. *Statistická příručka Království českého* (Statistical handbook of the Kingdom of Bohemia). 2d ed. Prague, 1913.

Bureau für Statistik der Juden, Berlin. *Die Juden in Österreich.* Berlin, 1908.

Czechoslovakia. Státní úřad statistický. *Manuel statistique de la République Tchécoslovaque.* Prague, 1920–25.

———. *Statistická ročenka Republiky československé* (Statistical yearbook of the Czechoslovak Republic). Prague, 1934–.

———. *Statistický lexikon obcí v zemí České* (Statistical lexicon of localities in the Czech lands). Prague, 1934.

Czoernig, Carl Frh. von. *Ethnographie der österreichischen Monarchie.* 3 vols. Vienna, 1849–57.

Kohn, Albert, ed. *Die Notablenversammlung der Israeliten Böhmens in Prag, ihre Berathungen und Beschlüsse. Mit statistischen Tabellen über die israelitischen Gemeinden, Synagogen, Schulen und Rabbinate in Böhmen.* Vienna, 1852.

Pliwa, Ernst. *Österreichs Universitäten 1863/4–1902/3: Statistisch-graphische Studie.* Vienna, 1908.

Prague. Statistická Kommisse. *Sčítání lidu v král. halvní městě Praze a obcech sousedních provedené 31. prosince 1900* (Census of the capital city of Prague and neighboring communities of 31 December 1900). Ed. Jan Srb. 3 vols. Prague, 1902–8.

———. *Statistická zpráva hlavního města Prahy/Annuaire statistique de la capitale de Prague.* Prague, 1881–1914.

Rauchberg, Heinrich. *Die Bevölkerung Österreichs auf Grund der Ergebnisse der Volkszählung vom 31. December 1890.* Vienna, 1895.

———. *Der nationale Besitzstand in Böhmen.* 3 vols. Leipzig, 1905.

———. "Der nationale Besitzstand in Böhmen und die Wanderbewegung." *Deutsche Arbeit* 2 (1902–3): 585–625.

———. "Das Zahlenverhältnis der Deutschen und der Tschechen in Böhmen." *Deutsche Arbeit* 2 (1902–3): 1–33.

Živanský, Theodor. "Náboženská a církevní statistika Rakousko-Uherska" (Religious and Church statistics of Austria-Hungary). In Z. Tolbolka, ed., *Česká Politika,* vol. 1. Prague, 1906, pp. 678–718.

Letters, Memoirs, and Diaries

Adámek, Karel. *Paměti z doby Badeniovy* (Reminiscences from the Badeni era). Prague, 1910.

Beneš, Edvard. *My War Memoirs.* Boston and New York, 1971.

Bergmann, Arthur. "Zikhronot mi-tekufat Bar Kochba" (Memories from the Bar Kochba period). In Felix Weltsch, ed., *Prag vi-Yerushalayim: Sefer le-zekher Leo Herrmann.* Jerusalem, 1954, pp. 111–19.

Bergmann, Else. "Familiengeschichte" (1962). MS, Leo Baeck Institute Archives, New York, Memoir Collection.

Bergmann, Hugo [Shmuel Hugo Bergman]. *Tagebücher und Briefe, 1901–1975.* Ed. Miriam Sambursky. 2 vols. Königstein/Ts., 1985.

Brod, Max. "Erfahrungen im ostjüdischen Schulwerk (Nach Tagebuchnotizen)." *Der Jude* 1 (1916–17): 32–36.

———. "Prag—Wien—Erinnerungen." In Josef Fränkel, ed., *The Jews of Austria.* London, 1967, pp. 241–42.

———. *Der Prager Kreis.* Stuttgart, 1966.

———. *Streitbares Leben, 1884–1968.* Munich, 1969.

Buber, Martin. *Briefwechsel aus sieben Jahrzehnten.* 2 vols. Heidelberg, 1972–73.

———. *Meetings.* La Salle, Ill., 1973.

———. "My Way to Hasidism." In Buber, *Hasidism and Modern Man.* New York, 1958, pp. 47–69.

Dr. W. "Vor zwanzig Jahren: Prager Erinnerungen." *Selbstwehr,* 8 May 1914.

Ehrmann, Salomon, "Böhmische Dorfjuden: Erinnerungen aus früher Jugend." *B'nai B'rith. Monatsblätter der Grossloge für den Čechoslovakischen Staat* 4 (1925): 217–23, 235–44, 261–68.

Feder, Richard. *Život a odkaz* (Life and legacy). Prague, 1973.

Fischer, Karel. "Po pětadvaceti letech: Vzpomínky z českožidovského hnutí" (After twenty-five years: Memoirs of the Czech-Jewish movement). *Českožidovské listy,* 15 March 1901–15 May 1901.

Fleischner, Jindřich. "Kámen" (The stone). *KČŽ* 38 (1918–19): 32–45.

Frankl, Ludwig August. *Erinnerungen.* Prague, 1910.

Frýd, Norbert. *Vzorek bez ceny a Pan Biskup, aneb začátek posledních sto let* (The free sample and the bishop: Or the start of the last one hundred years). Prague, 1966.

Fuchs, Alfred. *Oltář a rotačka* (The altar and the press). Prague, 1930.

Grégr, Edvard. *Denník* (Diary). 2 vols. Prague, 1908–14.

Guth, Otakar, ed. *1876–1926: Vzpominky a úvahy* (1876–1926: Memoirs and essays). Vydána k jubileu padesátiletého trvání Akademického spolku "Kapper" v Praze. Prague, 1926.

Haas, Willy. *Die literarische Welt: Erinnerungen.* Munich, 1960.

Herben, Jan. *Kniha vzpomínek* (Book of reminiscences). Prague, 1936.

Herrmann, Emmy. "Meine Erinnerungen an Leo [Herrmann]." Jerusalem, March 1952. Typescript. Leo Baeck Institute Archives, New York, Robert Weltsch Collection.

Herrmann, Leo. "Aus Tagebuchblättern." *Der Jude. Sonderheft zu M. Bubers 50. Geburtstag* (Berlin, 1928), pp. 159–64.

———. "Erinnerungen an Buber's Drei Reden." *Mitteilungsblatt Irgun Olej Merkaz Europa,* 26 October 1971.

———. "Erinnerungen eines Sudetendeutschen Zionisten." *Mitteilungsblatt der Hitachdut Olej Germania* (later: Irgun Olej Merkaz Europa), April 1938, nos. 1 and 2, pp. 7–9 and 8–10.

———. "Recollections of a Sudeten-German Zionist." Typescript. Central Zionist Archives, Jerusalem, Leo Herrmann Collection (A145/97).

———. "Reshimot 'al siḥot u-fegishot" (Notes on conversations and meetings). In Felix Weltsch, ed., *Prag vi-Yerushalayim: Sefer le-zekher Leo Herrmann.* Jerusalem, 1954, pp. 77–85.

Illový, Rudolf. "Z rodinné historie" (Family history). *KČŽ* 50 (1930–31): 18–37.

Janouch, Gustav. *Conversations with Kafka: Notes and Reminiscences.* New York, 1953.

———. *Prager Begegnungen.* Leipzig, 1959.

Kafka, Franz. *Briefe: 1902–1924.* Hrsg. Max Brod. New York, 1958. *Letters to Friends, Family, and Editors.* Trans. Richard Winston and Clara Winston. New York, 1977.

———. *The Diaries of Franz Kafka, 1910–1913.* Ed. Max Brod. New York, 1948.

———. *The Diaries of Franz Kafka, 1914–1923.* Ed. Max Brod. New York, 1949.

———. *Das Kafka-Buch: Eine innere Biographie in Selbstzeugnissen.* Hrsg. Heinz Politzer. Frankfurt a.M., 1965.

———. *Franz Kafka in Selbstzeugnissen und Bilddokumenten.* Dargestellt Klaus Wagenbach. Reinbeck bei Hamburg, 1964.

———. *I Am a Memory Come Alive: Autobiographical Writings.* Ed. Nahum N. Glatzer. New York, 1974.

———. *Letters to Felice.* Ed. Erich Heller and Jürgen Born. Trans. James Stern and Elisabeth Duckworth. New York. 1973.

———. *Letters to Milena.* Ed. Willi Haas. Trans. Tania Stern and James Stern. London, 1953, 1962.

———. *Letters to Ottla and the Family.* Ed. N. N. Glatzer. Trans. Richard Winston and Clara Winston. New York, 1982.

Kaznelson, Siegmund [Albrecht Hellmann]. "Erinnerungen an gemeinsame Kampfjahre." In F. Weltsch, ed., *Dichter, Denker, Helfer: Max Brod zum 50. Geburtstag.* Moravská-Ostrava, 1934, pp. 49–54.

Kisch, Egon Erwin. *Briefe an den Bruder Paul und an die Mutter, 1905–1936*. Ed. Josef Poláček. Berlin and Weimar, 1978.

———. *Erlebtes und Erstrebtes*. Stuttgart and Berlin, 1914.

Klineberger, Bohdan [Antonín Rataj]. "Episoda" (The incident). *KČŽ* 44 (1924–25): 168–79.

Kohn, Hans. *Living in a World Revolution: My Encounters with History*. New York, 1964.

———. "Rückblick auf eine gemeinsame Jugend." In Hans Tramer and Kurt Loewenstein, eds., *Robert Weltsch zum 70. Geburtstag*. Tel-Aviv, 1961, pp. 113–20.

———. "Zwanzig Jahre." *Selbstwehr*, 29 March 1926.

Kohn, Jindřich. "Okno s mechem" (The moss-covered window). *KČŽ* 41 (1921–22) and 42 (1922–23). Repr. in his *Asimilace a věky*, vol. 1. Prague, 1936, pp. 1–13.

Langer, František. *Byli a bylo* (They were and it was). Prague, 1963.

———. "My Brother Jiří." Foreword to Jiří Langer, *Nine Gates to the Chassidic Mysteries*. Trans. Stephen Jolly. New York, 1976, pp. vii–xxxi.

Masaryk, Tomáš G. *The Making of a State: Memoirs and Observations, 1914–1918*. New York, 1927, 1969.

Mauthner, Fritz. *Prager Jugendjahre: Erinnerungen*. Frankfurt a.M., 1969.

Pacovský, Richard. "Zur Geschichte des 'Bar-Kochba.' " *Bar Kochba Zirkular,* November 1966, January 1967, April 1967, June 1967, December 1967, March 1968, September 1968. (Incorporates diary entries from Alfred Löwy, notes of Josef Kohn, and an earlier "history" by Viktor Freud.)

Rakous, Vojtěch. "Drobné vzpomínky" (Minor reminiscences). *KČŽ* 38 (1918–19): 17–23.

———. "Hrst vzpomínek" (A fistfull of memories). *KČŽ* 25 (1905–6): 97–106.

———. "Ještě hrst vzpomínek" (Another fistful of memories). *KČŽ* 30 (1910–11): 94–99.

———. "Karel Fischer." *KČŽ* 26 (1906–7): 71–74.

Scharf, Jakub. "Deset let" (Ten years). *KČŽ* 6 (1886–87): 138–46.

———. "Po dvaceti letech" (After twenty years). *KČŽ* 16 (1896–97): 185–93.

Scholem, Gershom. *From Berlin to Jerusalem: Memories of My Youth*. Trans. Harry Zohn. New York, 1980.

Stein, August. "Ze začátku Spolku českých akademiků-židů" (The beginnings of the Association of Czech Academic Jews). In Otakar Guth, ed., *1876–1926: Vzpomínky a úvahy*. Prague, 1926.

Šubert, Fr. Ad. "Židovský element v mém mládí" (The Jewish element in my youth). *KČŽ* 25 (1905–06): 114–18.

Teweles, Heinrich. *Theater und Publikum. Erinnerungen und Erfahrungen*. Prague, 1927.

Teytz, Viktor. "Trochu retrospektivy a vzpomínek" (A little retrospect and some memories). *KČŽ* 28 (1908–9): 155–59.

Urzidil, Johannes. *Prager Triptychon*. Munich, 1960.

Vohryzek, Viktor. "Můj dědeček" (My grandfather). *KČŽ* 26 (1906–7): 129–37.

Wechsberg, Joseph. *The Vienna I Knew: Memories of a European Childhood*. Garden City, N.Y., 1979.

Wiener, Oskar. *Alt-Prager Guckkasten*. Prague, Vienna, and Leipzig, 1922.

Books, Pamphlets, and Articles

Adámek, Karel. *Slovo o židech* (A word about the Jews). Chrudim, 1899.

———. *Z naší doby* (Of our times). 4 vols. Velké Meziříčí, 1886–90.

Adler, Norbert. *Nová doba a židé* (The new age and the Jews). Prague, 1919.

Afike Jehuda. *Festschrift, 1869/70–1929/30*. Prague, 1930.

Aḥad Ha'am [Asher Ginzberg]. *'Al parashat derakhim* (At the crossroads). 3d ed. Berlin, 1920; Tel-Aviv, 1948.

Akademický spolek "Kapper." *Výroční zpráva akademického spolku "Kapper" za období od roku 1914 do roku 1921* (Annual report of the "Kapper" Academic Society from 1914 to 1921). Prague, 1921.

Arnstein Ignát. "Slovo o emancipaci a assimilace židů" (A word about Jewish emancipation and assimilation). *KČŽ* 12 (1892–93): 110–16.

Bachmann, Hermann, ed. *Deutsche Arbeit in Böhmen, Kulturbilder.* Berlin, 1900.

Bauer, Otto. *Die Nationalitätenfrage und die Sozialdemokratie* (1907). 2d ed. Vienna, 1924.

Baum, Oskar, *Die Böse Unschuld: Ein jüdischer Kleinstadtroman.* Frankfurt a.M., 1913.

———. *Ein Schicksal. Erzählungen.* Heidelberg, 1913.

———. *Die verwandelte Welt. Roman.* Vienna and Leipzig, 1919.

———. *Das Volk des harten Schlafes.* Vienna and Jerusalem, 1937.

Bergmann, Hugo [Shmuel Hugo Bergman]. "Achad Haam: Am Scheidewege, Bd. 1." *Archiv für Sozialwissenschaft und Sozialpolitik* 38 (1914): 554–56.

———. "Bar Kochba (Zum dreissigsemestrigen Stiftungsfest des Vereines 'Bar Kochba,' 18. Januar 1908)." *Selbstwehr,* 17 January 1908.

———. "Begriff und Wirklichkeit: Ein Beitrag zur Philosophie Martin Bubers und J. G. Fichtes." *Der Jude* 10 (1928): 89–101.

———. "Bermerkungen zur arabischen Frage." *Palästina* 8 (1911): 190–95. Repr. in his *Jawne und Jerusalem: Gesammelte Aufsätze.* Berlin, 1919.

———. "Das hebräische Buch und die deutschen Zionisten." *Der Jude* 4 (1919–20): 287 ff.

———. "Die Heiligung des Namens (Kiddusch Hashem)." In Verein der jüdischen Hochschüler "Bar Kochba" in Prag, *Vom Judentum: Ein Sammelbuch.* Leipzig, 1914, pp. 32–43.

———. *Jawne und Jerusalem: Gesammelte Aufsätze.* Berlin, 1919.

———. *Die Judenfrage und ihre Lösungsversuche: Zur Aufklärung der Studentenschaft.* Prague, 1903.

———. "Der jüdische Nationalismus nach dem Krieg." *Der Jude* 1 (1916–17): 7–13. In Czech: "Židovský nacionalism po válce." *Židovské zprávy,* 15 September 1918.

———. "Leo Herrmann 50 Jahre." *Jüdische Rundschau,* 15 March 1938.

———. "Leo Herrmann zum Gedenken." *Mitteilungsblatt Irgun Olej Merkaz Europa,* 21 September 1951.

———. "Die nationale Bedeutung Achad Haams." *Der Jude* 1 (1916–17): 358–61.

———. "Petah davar" (Foreword). In *Yahadut Czechoslovakia.* Jerusalem, 1969, pp. 7–10.

———. "Prag." In *Yahadut Czechoslovakia.* Jerusalem, 1969, pp. 83–91.

———. "Prager Brief." *Jüdische Volksstimme* (Brno), 15 January 1904.

———. "Reshito shel Leo Herrmann" (Leo Herrmann's early years). *Ha'arez,* 15 March 1938.

———. "Shalosh derashot 'al ha-yahadut" (Three Addresses on Judaism). *Ha-Shiloah* 26 (1912): 549–56.

———. "These pro program Národní Rady Židovské v otázce židovských obci" (Propositions for the program of the Jewish National Council on the question of the Jewish communities). *Židovské zprávy,* 31 December 1918. In German in *Selbstwehr,* 3 January 1919.

———. "Über die Bedeutung des Hebräischen für die jüdischen Studenten." *Unsere Hoffnung* 1, no. 3 (1904).

———. "Die wahre Autonomie." *Der Jude* 3 (1918–19): 368–73.

———. "Der Weg ins Freie." *Ost und West* 8 (1908): cols. 491–96.

———. "Židé a sociální převrat v novém státě" (The Jews and social revolution in the new state). *Židovské zprávy,* 25 November 1918.

———. "Die zionistische Kulturarbeit im Westen." In his *Jawne und Jerusalem: Gesammelte Aufsätze.* Berlin, 1919, pp. 12–15.

———. "Das zionistische Problem bei M. J. Berdyczewski." *Die Welt* (1914), pp. 679–82. Repr. as "Jawne und Jerusalem," in his *Jawne und Jerusalem: Gesammelte Aufsätze.* Berlin, 1919, pp. 34–42.

Birnbaum, Nathan. *Achad ha-am, ein Denker und Kämpfer der jüdischen Renaissance.* Berlin, 1903.

"Bohumil Bondý." *KČŽ* 4 (1884–85): 57–59.

"Bouřlivý den v Praze" (Stormy day in Prague). *Národní listy,* 30 November 1897.

Brod, Max. *Arnold Beer: Das Schicksal eines Juden.* Berlin, 1912.

———. *Die dritte Phase des Zionismus.* Berlin, 1917.

———. *Ein tschechisches Dienstmädchen. Kleiner Roman.* Stuttgart, 1909.

———. "Die Hochmütigen." *Selbstwehr,* 31 March 1916.

———. *Im Kampf um das Judentum.* Vienna and Berlin, 1920.

———. "Juden, Deutsche, Tschechen: Eine menschlich-politische Betrachtung." In his *Im Kampf um das Judentum.* Vienna and Berlin, 1920, pp. 7–36.

———. "Ein menschlich-politisches Bekenntnis." *Die neue Rundschau* 29 (1918): 1580 ff.

———. *Sozialismus im Zionismus.* Vienna, 1920.

———. "Die Tschechen und die jüdische Künstler." *Selbstwehr,* 12 November 1918.

———. *Tycho Brahes Weg zu Gott. Roman.* Leipzig, 1916.

———. "Zum Problem der Gemeinschaft." In *Das jüdische Prag: Eine Sammelschift.* Prague, 1917, pp. 8–10.

Brod, Max, and Felix Weltsch. *Anschauung und Begriff: Grundzüge eines Systems der Begriffsbildung.* Leipzig, 1913.

———. *Zionismus als Weltanschauung.* Moravská-Ostrava, 1925.

Buber, Martin. *Daniel: Dialogues on Realization.* Trans. with Introductory Essay by Maurice Friedman. New York, 1964.

———. *Drei Reden über das Judentum.* Frankfurt a.M., 1911 (1916, 1920). In Czech: *Tři řeči o židovství.* Prague, 1912.

———. *Der Jude und sein Judentum: Gesammelte Aufsätze und Reden.* Mit einer Einleitung von Robert Weltsch. Cologne, 1963.

———. *A Land of Two Peoples: Martin Buber on Jews and Arabs.* Ed. with Commentary by Paul R. Mendes-Flohr. New York, 1983.

———. *Die Legende des Baal-Schem* (1907). Frankfurt, 1916. *The Legend of the Baal-Shem.* Trans. Maurice Friedman. New York, 1955.

———. "Die Losung." *Der Jude* 1 (1916–17): 1–3.

———. *On Judaism.* Ed. Nahum N. Glatzer. New York, 1967.

———. "Rede auf dem XII. Zionistenkongress in Karlsbad (2 September 1921)." In his *Der Jude und sein Judentum: Gesammelte Aufsätze und Reden.* Cologne, 1963, pp. 468–75.

———. "Renaissance und Bewegung." In his *Der Jude und sein Judentum: Gesammelte Aufsätze und Reden.* Cologne, 1963, pp. 272–79.

———. *Völker, Staaten und Zion.* Vienna, 1917.

"Budiž jasno mezi námi" (Let it be clear between us). *Českožidovské listy,* 1 January 1897–1 March 1897.

Čapek, Karel. *President Masaryk Tells His Story.* (Trans. of *Hovory s Masarykem.*) New York, 1935, repr. 1971.

Das Centenarium S. J. L. Rapoports. Festgabe der "Österreichischen Wochenschrift." Vienna, 1890.

České modlitby při veřejné bohoslužbě v synagoze spolku "Or-Tomid" v Praze (Czech prayers for public worship at the synagogue of the Or-Tomid Society in Prague). Z německého a hebrejského přeložil Mořic Kraus, kantor spolku. Prague, 1888; 2d ed., 1889.

"Česko-židovství." *Selbstwehr,* 8 May 1908.

Chasanowitsch, Leon, and Leo Motzkin. *Die Judenfrage der Gegenwart.* Stockholm, 1919.

Cohen, Arthur A., ed. *The Jew: Essays from Martin Buber's Journal Der Jude, 1916–1928.* University, Ala., 1980.

Deutscher Volksrat für Böhmen. *Prag als deutsche Hochschulstadt.* Prague, 1911.

Dr. Kaddisch. "Deutsche, Tschechen, Juden." *Selbstwehr,* 21 August 1908.

"Dr. Ludwig Singer (Zu seinem 50. Geburtstage)." *Selbstwehr,* 12 February 1926 and 19 February 1926.

"Druhý den po německé provokáci" (The second day following German provocations). *Národní listy,* 1 December 1897.

"Dva Přední buditelé českožidovství" (Two early awakeners of Czech Jewry). *KČŽ* 16 (1896–97): 72–74.

"Das Ende der deutschen Liberalismus." *Selbstwehr,* 4 March 1910.

Epstein, Oskar, "Erhaltung oder Erneuerung?" In Verein der jüdischen Hochschüler "Bar Kochba" in Prag, *Vom Judentum: Ein Sammelbuch.* Leipzig, 1914, pp. 173–78.

———. "Grundsätzliches zur zionistischen Gegenwartsarbeit," *Der Jude* 1 (1916–17): 100–104.

"Falešná hra sionistů" (The false game of the Zionists). *Rozvoj,* 28 June 1919.

F.B. "Sionism." *Naše doba* 5 (1897–98): 439–43.

Feder, Richard, ed. *Židovské besídky (Pro zábavu a poučení mládeže židovské)* (Jewish stories: For the amusement and education of Jewish youth). 3 vols. Roudnice, 1912–24.

Festschrift anlässlich des 30-jährigen Bestandes der Loge "Bohemia" I.O.B.B. in Prag. Prague, 1923.

Fischer, Karel. "J.U.Dr. Josef Žalud," *KČŽ* 8 (1888–89): 55–58.

Fischl, Karl. "Die Juden in Böhmen." *Die Welt,* 9 March 1900.

Friedmann, František. *Mravnost či oportunita? Několik poznámek k anketě akad. spolku "Kapper" v Brně* (Morality or opportunism? Some thoughts on the public inquiry of the "Kapper" Academic Society in Brno). Prague, 1927.

Fuchs, Alfred. "Můj názor na boj se sionismem" (My opinion on the struggle with Zionism). *Rozvoj,* 25 October 1919.

———. "Několik poznámek k Rakousovým 'Vojkovickým a přespolním' " (Some thoughts on Rakous's *Vojkovičtí a přespolní*). *KČŽ* 32 (1912–13): 52–54.

———. *O židovské otázce* (On the Jewish question). Prague, 1911; rev. ed. 1919.

Fuchs, Rudolf. *České a německé básnictví v Československu* (Czech and German poetry in Czechoslovakia). Prague, 1937.

Fünfzig Semester "Barissia." Festschrift. Hrsg. anlässlich des 50.-semestrigen Stiftungsfestes der jüdisch-akademischen Verbindung "Barissia." Prague, 1928.

Gellner, František, *Cesta do hor a jiné povídky* (Path to the mountains and other stories). Prague, 1914; reissued as his *Spisy,* vol. 2. Prague, 1927.

———. *Spisy* (Works). 3 vols. Prague, 1926–28.

———. "Vliv a zvyklosti středoevropských židu" (The influence and customs of Central European Jews). In his *Spisy,* vol. 3. Prague, 1928, pp. 274–81.

———. "Židovská otázka" (The Jewish question). In his *Spisy,* vol. 3. Prague, 1928, pp. 271–73.

Goldstein, Angelo. "Právní doklady židovské politiky v Československu" (The legal foundations of Jewish politics in Czechoslovakia). In Czechoslovak Jewish Representative Committee, *Czechoslovak Jewry: Past and Future.* New York, 1943.

Gottlieb, František. *Cesta do Kanaán. Verše* (The road to Canaan. Verses). Prague, 1924.

Guth, Otakar. "Dr. Bohdan Klineberger." *KČŽ* 36 (1916–17): 3–11.

———. "Dr. Viktor Vohryzek k 50. narozeninám" (Dr. Viktor Vohryzek on the occasion of his fiftieth birthday), *KČŽ* 34 (1914–15): 136–40.

———. "K 50. narozeninám Dra. Eduarda Lederera" (On the fiftieth birthday of Dr. Eduard Lederer). *KČŽ* 29 (1909–10): 70–72.

———. "O dru Viktoru Vohryzkovi" (On Viktor Vohryzek). *KČŽ* 41 (1921–22): 62–72.

———. "Po XI. sjezdu sionistickém" (After the Eleventh Zionist Congress). *Rozvoj,* 18 October 1913–5 December 1913.

———. *Podstata židovství a jiné úvahy* (The essence of Judaism and other essays). Prague, 1925.

———. "Salten a Buber." *Rozvoj,* 22 January 1909.

———. "Sny mystikovy: Marginalie ke knize Martina Bubra: *Drei Reden über das Judentum*" (The dreams of a mystic: Marginal comments on Martin Buber's *Drei Reden über das Judentum*). *Rozvoj,* 3 November 1911.

———. "Vojtěch Rakous. Poznámky nad knihou V. Rakouse, *Vojkovičtí a přespolní*" (Vojtech Rakous. Thoughts on Rakous's book *Vojkovičtí a přespolní*). *Rozvoj*, 16 December 1910.

———. "Za Dr. Bohdanem Klinebergrem" (Necrology for Dr. Bohdan Klineberger). *KČŽ* 48 (1928–29): vii–xii.

Henner, Kamíl. "Poměr mezi státem a církví v Rakousku" (The relationship between church and state in Austria). In Z. Tobolka, ed., *Česká politika*, vol. 1. Prague, 1906, pp. 719–809.

Herben, Jan. "Julius Taussig." *KČŽ* 32 (1912–13): 15–16.

Herrmann, Hugo. "Martin Buber." *Selbstwehr*, 16 December 1910.

———. "Zur čechisch-jüdischen Frage." *Selbstwehr*, 7 April 1911.

Herrmann, Leo. *Treue: Eine jüdische Sammelschrift*. Berin, 1916.

Herzl, Theodor. "Die Jagd in Böhmen." *Die Welt*, 5 November 1897.

———. *Zionistische Schriften*. 3d ed. Tel-Aviv, 1934.

Hulík, V. "Česká politika středoškolská" (Czech middle-school politics). In Z. Tobolka, ed., *Česká politika*, vol. 5. Prague, 1913, pp. 434–606.

Iggers, Wilma, ed. *Die Juden in Böhmen und Mähren: Ein historisches Lesebuch*. Munich, 1986.

Illový, Rudolf. *Kročeje. Verše* (Footsteps. Verses). Prague, 1908.

Der isr. Humanitätsverein "Bohemia." *Festschrift*. Hrsg. Ernst Rychnovsky. Prague, 1913.

"Jak dál?" (How much longer?). *Českožidovské listy*, 1 January 1898.

"Jaroslava Vrchlického Bar-Kochba" (Jaroslav Vrchlický's "Bar-Kochba"). *Českožidovské listy*, 1 April 1897–1 June 1897.

Die Juden und die Nationalen: Ein Gegenstück zur Broschüre: "Die Juden in Böhmen." Von einem Juden. Prague, 1863.

Die jüdische Aktion. Programmschrift des Herdervereines in Prag. Prague, 1919.

"Der jüdische Nationalrat beim Národní výbor." *Selbstwehr*, 1 November 1918.

Das jüdische Prag: Eine Sammelschrift. Prague, 1917; Kronberg/Ts., 1978.

"K židovské otázce školské" (On the Jewish school question), *Rozvoj*, 31 May 1919–7 June 1919.

Kádner, Otakar. "Politika českého školství vysokého" (The politics of Czech higher education). In Z. Tobolka, ed., *Česká politika*, vol. 5. Prague, 1913, pp. 932–63.

Kaznelson, Siegmund [Albrecht Hellmann]. "Die Juden in der Weltpolitik." *Der Jude* 3 (1918–19): 7–15.

———. "Nationale Minderheitsrechte der Juden." *Der Jude* 4 (1919–20): 481–88.

———. "Verzweiflung und Besinnung." *Der Jude* 4 (1919–20): 289–96.

———. "Vorrede." In *Das jüdische Prag: Eine Sammelschrift*. Prague, 1917, p. 1.

Kisch, Egon Erwin. "Deutsche und Tschechen." In his *Marktplatz der Sensationen*. Mexico City, 1942; Vienna, 1948.

———. *Marktplatz der Sensationen*. Mexico City, 1942; Vienna, 1948.

Kleiner, Kamil. "Židovské národní školství" (The Jewish national school system). *Rozvoj*, 10 July 1920–17 July 1920.

Klineberger, Bohdan [Antonín Rataj]. "Assimilace" (Assimilation). *Rozvoj*, 27 July 1909–3 August 1909.

———. "Cizinec" (The foreigner). *KČŽ* 25 (1905–6): 154–58.

———. *Náboženský cit: Rozbor hodnoty náboženství* (Religious feeling: Analysis of the value of religion). Prague, 1906.

———. *Národ a národnost* (Nation and nationality). Prague, 1919.

———. *Naše budoucnost. Sociologická studie* (Our future: A sociological study). Prague, 1911.

Koerner, E. "Národnostní a jazyková otázka v Předlitavsku" (The nationality and language question in Cisleithania). In Z. Tobolka, ed., *Česká politika*, vol. 1. Prague, 1906, pp. 340–469.

Kohn, Hans. "Asia ha-ḥadasha" (The new Asia). *Ha-Shiloaḥ* 45 (1926): 519 ff.

———. "Aufgaben der Stunde." In his *Nationalismus*. Vienna, 1922, pp. 87–100.

———. "Briefe an Freunde." In his *Nationalismus*. Vienna, 1922, pp. 32–52.

———. *The Idea of Nationalism.* New York, 1944.

———. Introduction to *Nationalism and the Jewish Ethic: Basic Writings of Achad Ha'am.* New York, 1962.

———. *Nationalismus: Über die Bedeutung des nationalismus im Judentum und in der Gegenwart.* Vienna and Leipzig, 1922.

———. "Perspektiven." *Der Jude* 4 (1919–20): 488–92.

———. *Die politische Idee des Judentums.* Munich, 1924.

———. "Stimmen." *Der Jude* 6 (1923): 552–56.

———. "Zur Araberfrage." *Der Jude* 4 (1919–20): 567–69. Repr. in his *Nationalismus.* Vienna, 1922, pp. 61–71.

Kohn, Jindřich. *Asimilace a věky* (Assimilation and the ages). 2 vols. Prague, 1936.

———. *Co jest a co není národní právo sebeurčení* (What is and what is not the national right to self-determination). Prague, 1919.

———. "Kulturní konfese a program kulturní (Navrh Čechům-židům)" (Cultural confession and cultural program—proposal to Czech Jews). In his *Asimilace a věky,* vol. 1. Prague, 1936, pp. 97–102.

———. "My a sionisté" (We and the Zionists). In his *Asimilace a věky,* vol. 1. Prague, 1936, pp. 40–42.

———. "Otázka židovská a česká víra" (The Jewish question and Czech faith). In his *Asimilace a věky,* vol. 1. Prague, 1936, pp. 43–45.

———. "Otázka židovská ve světle české otázky" (The Jewish question in light of the Czech question), *Rozvoj,* 3 May 1912. Reprinted in his *Asimilace a věky,* vol. 1. Prague, 1936, pp. 14–18.

———. "Sociologische Einführungsskizze in die Geschichtsschreibung des Judentums in der tschechoslowakischen Republik." *JGGJČR* 2 (1930): 1–16.

———. "Židovství a teorie malého národa" (Judaism and the theory of the small nation). *Rozvoj,* 8 May 1914–5 June 1914.

———. "Židovství, češství a lidství" (Jewry, the Czech people, and humanity). In his *Asimilace a věky,* vol. 1. Prague, 1936, pp. 28–34.

Kořán, Josef J. "Židovské školy v Čechách" (Jewish schools in Bohemia). *KČŽ* 6 (1886–87): 97–102.

———. "Židovské školy v Čechách roku 1894–95" (Jewish schools in Bohemia in 1894–95). *KČŽ* 16 (1896–97): 152–57.

Kraus, J. S. "Německo-židovské školy v Čechách" (German-Jewish schools in Bohemia). *KČŽ* 2 (1882–83): 117–25.

———. "Or-Tomid: Spolek českých židů pro pěstování bohoslužby jazykem českým a hebrejským" (Or-Tomid: Association of Czech Jews for Worship in Czech and in Hebrew). *KČŽ* 4 (1884–85): 109–12, and 5 (1885–86): 111–13.

Kraus, Otakar. "Masarykovo náboženství a ethika" (Masaryk's religion and ethics). *KČŽ* 30 (1910–11): 9–14.

———. "O vývoji židovského náboženství" (On the evolution of the Jewish religion). *KČŽ* 26 (1906–7): 120–28.

———. "Počátky berlínské reformy" (The beginnings of the Berlin reform). *KČŽ* 25 (1905–6): 119–25.

Kraus, Vlastimil. "K naši otázce náboženské" (On our religious question). *KČŽ* 17 (1897–98): 156–64.

———. "Ku dnešní otázce náboženské" (On the contemporary religious question). *KČŽ* 18 (1898–99): 129–33.

Krejčí, František. "Assimilation und Zionismus vom ethischen Standpunkt." *Selbstwehr,* 11 June 1909.

Landauer, Gustav. "Sind das Ketzergedanken?" In Verein der jüdischen Hochschüler "Bar Kochba" in Prag, *Vom Judentum: Ein Sammelbuch.* Leipzig, 1914, pp. 250–57.

Langer, Jiří [Mordechai Georg Langer]. *Devět bran. Chasidů tajemství.* Prague, 1937. *Nine Gates to the Chassidic Mysteries.* Trans. Stephen Jolly. New York, 1976.
———. *Die Erotik der Kabbala.* Prague, 1923.
———. *Piyyutim ve-shirei yedidut* (Poems and songs of friendship). Prague, 1929.
Lazarus, Moritz. *The Ethics of Judaism.* Trans. Henrietta Szold. 2 vols. Philadelphia, 1900–1901.
Lederer, Eduard [Leda]. "Archiv a museum židovské" (The Jewish Archive and Museum). *KČŽ* 18 (1898–99): 59–65.
———. *Českožidovská otázka* (The Czech-Jewish question). Smíchov, 1899.
———. "Čeští židé a český nacionalism" (Czech Jews and Czech nationalism). *Čas,* 9 December 1901.
———. *Kapitoly o židovství a židovstvu* (Chapters on Judaism and Jewry). 2 vols. Prague, 1925.
———. "Lueger triumfans." *Českožidovské listy,* 15 April 1897.
———. "O češství a židovství" (On Czech culture and Judaism). *Rozvoj,* 29 May 1914–26 June 1914.
———. "Patologické zjevy v české inteligenci" (Pathological manifestations in the Czech intelligentsia). *Českožidovské listy,* 1 February 1899.
———. "Politické strany české a hnutí českožidovské" (Czech political parties and the Czech-Jewish movement). *Českožidovské listy,* 15 September 1897.
———. "Pražská tragedie židovská" (The Prague Jewish tragedy). *Českožidovské listy,* 15 December 1897.
———. "Rása, národnost a stát" (Race, nationality, and the state). In his *Kapitoly o židovství a židovstvu,* vol. 1. Prague, 1925, pp. 123–66.
———. "Svůj k svému" (Each to his own). *Českožidovské listy,* 1 March 1898.
———. *Žid v dnešní společnosti* (The Jew in contemporary society). Prague, 1902.
———. "Židé a sociální demokracie" (The Jews and social democracy). *Českožidovské listy,* 15 June 1898.
Lederer, Max. *Českožidovská otázka* (The Czech-Jewish question). Prague, 1909.
———. "Deset let zionismu" (Ten years of Zionism). *Rozvoj,* 19 July 1907–16 August 1907.
"Leo Herrmann." *Keren Hayesod Bulletin,* 7 October 1951.
Levi, Yitshok. "Tsvey Prager Dikhter." *Literarishe Bletter* (1934): 557–58.
Lichtwitz, Hans. "Dem Zionisten." In F. Weltsch, ed., *Dichter, Denker, Helfer: Max Brod zum 50. Geburtstag.* Moravská-Ostrava, 1934, pp. 44–49.
Maarche-lew. Modlitby Israelitův pro dny všední, pro sabáty i svátky (Extensions of the heart: Jewish prayers for every day, the Sabbath, and holidays). Czech trans. Dr. August Stein. Prague, 1884.
Masaryk, T. G. *Die Bedeutung des Polnäer Verbrechens für den Ritualglauben.* Berlin, 1900.
———. *Česká otázka: Snahy a tužby národního obrození* (The Czech question: Efforts and aspirations of the national revival). Prague, 1895.
———. *Jan Hus.* Prague, 1896.
———. *The Meaning of Czech History.* Ed. with Introduction by René Wellek. Trans Peter Kussi. Chapel Hill, N.C., 1974.
———. *Naše nynější krise* (Our contemporary crisis). Prague, 1895.
———. *Nutnost revidovati proces polenský* (The necessity of revising the Polná trial). Prague, 1899.
———. *Otázka sociální: základy marxismu filosofické a sociologické* (The social question: Philosophical and sociological foundations of Marxism). Prague, 1898.
———. "Život církevní a náboženský roku 1904" (Church and religious life in 1904). *Naše doba* 12 (1905): six parts.
"Das Memorandum des Jüdischen Nationalrats an den Národní výbor," *Selbstwehr,* 8 November 1918.

Meyrink, Gustav. *Der Golem. Ein Roman.* Leipzig, 1915.

M.L. "František Gellner." *KČŽ* 38 (1918–19): 30–31.

Moravec, F. V. "Česká politika obecnoškolská" (Czech primary-school politics). In Z. Tobolka, ed., *Česká politika*, vol. 5. Prague, 1913, pp. 195–334.

Musil, Alois. "Židé v Palestině" (The Jews in Palestine). *Česká Revue* 14 (1921): 4–15.

"Náš úkol" (Our mission). *Českožidovksé listy*, 15 September 1894.

"Několik slov o antisemitismus" (A few words on antisemitism). *KČŽ* 2 (1882–83): 72–77.

Neruda, Jan. *Pro strach židovský* (On the Jewish fear). Prague, [1869] 1942.

Niels [pseudonym]. "Zur nationalen Emanzipation der österreichsichen Juden." *Selbstwehr*, 1 March 1907.

Padesát let ústřední matice školské, 1880–1930 (Fifty years of the Central School Foundation). Prague, 1931.

Perko, Franz. "Die Tätigkeit des deutschen Schulvereines in Böhmen." *Deutsche Arbeit* 3 (1903–4): 386–410.

Pick, Otto. "Neue tschechische Literatur." *Herder-Blätter*, October 1912, pp. 47 ff.

Poláček, Karel. *Židovské anekdoty* (Jewish jokes). 3d ed. Hradec Králové, 1967.

Posnanski, Adolf. "Die Cultusgemeinden Böhmens und deren religiöse Institutionen." *Jüdische Chronik* 1 (1894–95): 14–17, 48–53, 83–85, 113–15, 144–46, 183–84, 209–12, 270–73, 371–72.

"Přátelé!" *KČŽ* 38 (1918–19): 3–4.

Příbram, A. F., ed. *Urkunden und Akten zur Geschichte der Juden in Wien*, vol. 1. Vienna and Leipzig, 1918.

Procházková, Jaroslava. *Český lid a český žid. Časové úvahy* (The Czech people and the Czech Jew: Timely essays). Žižkov (Prague), 1897.

Rádl, Emanuel. *La question religieuse en Tchécoslovaquie.* Prague, 1922.

———. *Rassová teorie a národ* (Racial theory and the nation). Prague, 1918.

Rakous, Vojtěch [Adalbert Österreicher]. *Modche a Rezi (výbor)* (Modche and Rezi [selection]). Prague, 1968.

———. "Rozbitá okna" (Broken windows). *Českožidovské listy*, 2 November 1899. Repr. in his *Vojkovičtí a přespolní.* Prague, 1910, pp. 153–56.

———. "Strýc Václav" (Uncle Václav). *KČŽ* 26 (1906–7): 81–93.

———. *Vojkovičtí a přespolní* (The people of Vojkovice and environs). Introduction by Leda [Eduard Lederer]. Prague, 1910.

———. "Židovské dítě v české škole" (Jewish children in Czech schools). *Rozvoj*, 19 July 1907.

Reiner, Maxim. "Dr. Jakub Scharf." *Rozvoj*, 18 September 1922.

———. "O nynějších poměrech hnutí českožidovského" (On the current relations of the Czech-Jewish movement). *Českožidovské listy*, 15 June 1899.

Renner, Karl [Rudolf Springer]. *Der Kampf der österreichischen Nation um den Staat.* Leipzig and Vienna, 1902.

Rokycana, Jaroslav. "JUDr. Augustin Stein." *Rozvoj*, 13 October 1922.

———. "Na kořeny českožidovského hnutí" (On the roots of the Czech-Jewish movement). *Rozvoj*, 18 February 1927–4 March 1927.

Rosenfeld, Max. "Für eine nationale Autonomie der Juden in Österreich." *Der Jude* 1 (1916–17): 290–97.

———. "Die jüdischen Gemeinden in Österreich." *Der Jude* 2 (1917–18): 152–62.

Rüst, Anselm. "Der Max Brod Abend." *Die Aktion* 1 (1911). Repr. in Paul Raabe, ed., *Ich schneide die Zeit aus: Expressionismus und Politik in Franz Pfemferts "Aktion."* Munich, 1964, pp. 43–45.

Scharf, Jakub. *Národní jednota českožidovská ve světle české veřejnosti* (The National Union of Czech Jews in the light of the Czech public). Prague, 1893.

Scheinpflug, Karel. *Otázka židovská* (The Jewish question). Prague, 1910.

Schulhof, Stanislav. "Bez půdy: Črta z našich dob" (Without ground: Sketch of our times). *KČŽ* 32 (1912–13): 149–61.

———. *Jsou židé semity a národem?* (Are the Jews Semites and a nation?) Proslovil ve "Spolku českých adademiků-židů. Prague, n.d.

Singer, Ludvík. "Asimilace či fluktuace?" (Assimilation or fluctuation?). *Židovské zprávy*, 7 November 1918.

———. "Naše cíle" (Our goals). *Židovské zprávy*, 5 April 1918.

"Slavnost čtvrtstoletého trvání spolku českých akademiků-židů" (Celebration of the first quarter-century of the Association of Czech Academic Jews). *KČŽ* 21 (1901–2): 125–41.

Soudek, Gabriel. "Konec pohádky" (The end of the story). *KČŽ* 23 (1903–4): 97–110.

Společnost pro dějiny židů v československé republice/Gesellschaft für Geschichte der Juden in der Čechoslowakischen Republik. *Zprávy/Mitteilungen*. Prague, 1928.

Spolek českých akademiků-židů v Praze. *Stanovy Spolku* (Bylaws of the Association). Prague, 1891.

———. *Výroční zpráva* (Annual report). Prague, 1876–1912.

Stein, August. "Židé v Čechách" (The Jews in Bohemia). *KČŽ* 1 (1881–82): 83–107.

Stenographisches Protokoll der Verhandlungen des XII. Zionisten-Kongresses in Karlsbad (vom 1. bis 14. September 1921). Berlin, 1922.

Stern, Evžen. "O současném českožidovství" (On contemporary Czech Jewry). *KČŽ* 35 (1915–16): 12–22.

Stránský, Jaroslav. "O židovské otázce v českém životě" (The Jewish question in Czech life). *Rozvoj*, 19 March 1926.

Svaz Čechů-židů v Československé Republice. *Kritika sionismu*. Prague, n.d.

Svaz českých pokrokových židů v Praze. *Škola matkou a škola macechou* (Mother school and step-mother school). Prague, 1908.

"Světová válka a naše hnutí" (The world war and our movement). *Rozvoj*, 30 October 1914.

Svozil, J. "Několik slov o hesle 'Svůj k svému' " (A few words on the slogan "Svůj k svemu"). *Naše doba* 8 (1900–1901): 641–46.

"La Tchéco-Slovaquie reconnaît la nationalité juive." *Bulletin du Comité des Délégations Juives auprés de la Conférence de la Paix*, 30 March 1920.

Teweles, Heinrich, ed. *Prager Dichterbuch*. Prague, 1894.

Teytz, Viktor. "Čech-Žid" (Czech-Jew). *Rozvoj*, 3 January 1913–10 January 1913.

———. "Národnostní boj a židé" (The nationality struggle and the Jews). *Rozvoj*, 12 January 1912.

———. *Několik poznámek k otázce českožidovské* (A few thoughts on the Czech-Jewish question). Prague, 1913.

———. "Židovské motivy v poesii Jaroslava Vrchlického" (Jewish motifs in the poetry of Jaroslav Vrchlický). *KČŽ* 23 (1903–4): 111–18.

———. "Židovský Tolstoj" (The Jewish Tolstoj). *KČŽ* 25 (1905–6): 107–13.

Tobolka, Zdeněk V., ed. *Česká politika* (Czech politics). 5 vols. Prague, 1906–13.

Tohn, Zdeněk. "Dr. Jindřich Kohn (7.III.1874–12.III.1935)." *KČŽ* 55 (1935–36): 14–32.

Tokstein, Antonín F. *Židé v Čechách* (The Jews in Bohemia). 2d ed. Prague, 1939.

Träger, Josef. "Osobnost Františka Gellnera" (The personality of František Gellner). *KČŽ* 49 (1929–30): 12–16.

"Über die wahre Stellung des Judentums zur Nationalen Bewegung. Von einem Juden." *Politik*, 14 October 1865–26 October 1865.

Vana, Jaromír, ed. *Volby do říšské rady v Království českém roku 1897* (The 1897 Reichsrat elections in the Kingdom of Bohemia). Prague, 1897.

Verein der jüdischen Hochschüler "Bar Kochba" in Prag. *Bericht über die Tätigkeit des Vereins*. Prague, 1908–12.

———. *Neue Wege*. Prague, 1903.

———. *Vom Judentum: Ein Sammelbuch*. Leipzig, 1914.

Vohryzek, Lev. "Dr. V. Vohryzek a rakouská válečná persekuce" (Dr. V. Vohryzek and wartime persecution in Austria). *Rozvoj*, 13 April 1923.

———. "Dva přátelé" (Two friends). *Rozvoj*, 19 July 1919.

Vohryzek, Viktor. "Absurdnosti Buberovy" (Buber's absurdities). *Rozvoj,* 28 November 1913–
12 December 1913.
———. "Episody." *KČŽ* 32 (1912–13): 161–76.
———. "Epištoly k českým židům" (Letters to Czech Jews). *Českožidovské listy* (1900). Repr.
in his *K židovské otázce.* Prague, 1923, pp. 15–19.
———. "Jak rozumíme assimilaci" (How we understand assimilation). *Rozvoj* (1904). Repr. in
his *K židovské otázce.* Prague, 1923, pp. 71–77.
———. "Jakými cestami by se mělo bráti naše hnutí!" (What paths ought our movement to
have taken!). *Rozvoj* (1904). Repr. in his *K židovské otázce.* Prague, 1923, pp. 77–84.
———. "K myšlenkové krisi našich dnů" (On the intellecutual crisis of our day). *Rozvoj* (1904).
Repr. in his *K židovské otázce.* Prague, 1923, pp. 118–23.
———. "K prvému máji" (On the first of May). *Rozvoj* (1904). Repr. in his *K židovské otázce.*
Prague, 1923, pp. 90–98.
———. *K židovské otázce: Výbrané úvahy a články* (On the Jewish question: Selected essays
and articles). Prague, 1923.
———. "Kterák doplniti náš program" (How to fulfill our program). *Rozvoj* (1904). Repr. in
his *K židovské otázce.* Prague, 1923, pp. 142–47.
———. "Mosaism v praxi" (Mosaism in practice). *Rozvoj,* 22 August 1913.
———. "Myšlenková osnova mosaismu: Myšlenky o myšlenkách a myslitelích" (The intellec-
tual renewal of Mosaism: Thoughts on thoughts and thinkers). *KČŽ* 34 (1914–15): 97–107.
———. "Náboženská společnost, či národnost?" (Religious society or nationality?). *Rozvoj*
(1906). Repr. in his *K židovské otázce.* Prague, 1923, pp. 218–28.
———. "Několik slov úvodem" (A few words of introduction). *Rozvoj* (1904). Repr. in his *K
židovské otázce.* Prague, 1923, pp. 41–47.
———. "Pod praporem Rozvoje" (Under the banner of "Rozvoj"). *Rozvoj,* 12 October 1918.
———. "Pryč od Haliče" (Away from Galicia). *Rozvoj* (1904). Repr. in his *K židovské otázce.*
Prague, 1923, pp. 130–35.
———. "T. G. Masaryk." *Rozvoj,* 19 November 1909–31 December 1909.
———. "Zápas o reformy" (Struggle for reform), *Rozvoj* (1906). Repr. in his *K židovské
otázce.* Prague, 1923, pp. 204–8.
Vrba, Rudolf. *Národní sebeochrana. Úvahy o hmotném a mravním úpadku národa českého*
(National self-preservation: On the material and moral decline of the Czech nation). Prague,
1898.
Vrchlický, Jaroslav. *Bar Kochba. Báseň* (Bar Kochba: A poem). Prague, 1897.
———. *Rabínská moudrost. Veselohra o tři jednáních* (Rabbinical wisdom: Comedy in three
acts). Prague, 1886.
Weltsch Felix. "Bohemian Jewry in Transition (Prague)." *Menorah Journal* 9 (1923): 332–37.
———. "Die ersten Elemente der sittlichen Entscheidung und das Sch'ma Israel." In *Das
jüdische Prag: Eine Sammelschrift.* Prague, 1917, pp. 12–13.
———. *Gnade und Freiheit: Untersuchungen zum Problem des schöpferischen Willens in Reli-
gion und Ethik.* Munich, 1920.
———. *Nationalismus und Judentum.* Berlin, 1920.
———. "Organische Demokratie." *Die neue Rundschau* 4 (1918): 433–54.
———. "Philosophie eines Dichters." In F. Weltsch, ed., *Dichter, Denker, Helfer: Max Brod
zum 50. Geburtstag.* Moravská-Ostrava, 1934, pp. 8–26.
Weltsch, Robert. "Ein Feldpostbrief aus dem Osten." *Der Jude* 1 (1916–17): 529–34.
———. "Die Jugend des jüdischen Prag." In *Das jüdische Prag: Eine Sammelschrift.* Prague,
1917, p. 17–18.
———. "Leo Herrmann: Darko u-tekufato" (Leo Herrmann: His work and his age). In F.
Weltsch, ed., *Prag vi-Yerushalayim.* Jerusalem, 1954, pp. 125–42.
———. "Theodor Herzl und Wir." In Verein der jüdischen Hochschüler "Bar Kochba" in Prag,
Vom Judentum: Ein Sammelbuch. Leipzig, 1914, pp. 155–65.

Weltsch, Theodor. "Dreissig Jahre 'Centralverein.' " In *Das jüdische Prag: Ein Sammelschrift.* Prague, 1917, p. 52.

Wertheimer, Josef von. *Die Juden in Österreich. Vom Standpunkte der Geschichte, des Rechts und des Staatsvortheils.* 2 vols. Leipzig, 1842.

Wiener, Oskar, ed. *Deutsche Dichter aus Prag.* Vienna, 1919.

Wiesenfeld, Moses. "Begegnung mit Ostjuden." In F. Weltsch, ed., *Dichter, Denker, Helfer: Max Brod zum 50, Geburtstag.* Moravská-Ostrava, 1934, pp. 54–57.

Wodak, Ernst. *Prag von Gestern und Vorgestern.* Tel-aviv, 1948.

Wolf, Richard. *České studentstvo v době prvního třicetiletí české univerzity (1882–1912)* (Czech student life during the first thirty years of the Czech University). Prague, 1912.

"Z organisací českožidovských" (Czech-Jewish organizations). *KČŽ* 38 (1918–1919): 113–18.

Žalud, Josef. "Náš Kalendář" (Our almanac). *KČŽ* 10 (1890–91): 121–27.

———. "Prof. Dr. Alois Zucker," *KČŽ* 6 (1886–87): 58–63.

———. "Z minulostí a přítomností židů v Čechách" (From the past and the present of the Jews in Bohemia). *KČŽ* 12 (1892–93): 55–70.

"Židovská otázka" (The Jewish question). *Národní listy,* 15 November 1914. Repr. with Commentary in *Rozvoj,* 11 December 1914.

Ziegler, J. *Laikovy myšlenky o židovství* (Lay thoughts on Judaism). Přeložil Dr. O. Kraus, rabín v Benešově. Benešov, 1910.

"Zionismus na cestách" (Zionism on the road). *Českožidovské listy,* 15 February 1900.

"Zpráva o činnosti spolku 'Rozvoj' v Pardubicích, v obdobích r. 1903–1905" (Report on the activity of the "Rozvoj" Association in Pardubice for the period 1903–1905). *KČŽ* 25 (1905–6): 177–81.

"Zprávy spolkové" (Reports on organizations). *KČŽ* 39 (1919–20): 137–38.

"Zprávy spolkové" (Reports on organizations). *KČŽ* 40 (1920–21): 110–12.

Secondary Works

Adler, Friedrich. "Zur Geschichte der Lese- und Redehall der deutschen Studenten in Prag." *Deutsche Arbeit* 9 (1910): 545 ff.

Aschheim, Steven E. *Brothers and Strangers: The East European Jew in German and German Jewish Consciousness, 1800–1923.* Madison, Wis., 1982.

Band, Arnold J. "Kafka and the Beiliss Affair." *Comparative Literature* 32 (1980): 168–83.

Barany, George. " 'Magyar Jew or Jewish Magyar?' Reflections on the Question of Assimilation." In Bela Vago and George Mosse, eds., *Jews and Non-Jews in Eastern Europe.* New York, 1974, pp. 51–98.

Batowski, Henryk. "Die Polen." In Adam Wandruszka and Peter Urbanitsch, eds., *Die Habsburgermonarchie, 1848–1918,* vol. 3. Vienna, 1980, pp. 522–54.

Beck, Evelyn Torton. *Kafka and the Yiddish Theater: Its Impact on His Work.* Madison, Wis., 1971.

Bergl, Josef. "Judaica v archivu ministerstva vnitra v Praze" (Judaica in the Archives of the Ministry of the Interior in Prague). *Sborník Archivu Ministerstva Vnitra Republiky Československé* 6 (1933): 5–64.

Bergmann, Hugo [Shmuel Hugo Bergman] "Emil Utitz: Darko ha-tragit shel melumad yehudi" (Emil Utitz: the tragic course of a Jewish intellectual). *Molad* 15 (1957): 625–29.

Bernard, Paul P. "Joseph II and the Jews: The Origins of the Toleration Patent of 1782." *Austrian History Yearbook* 4/5 (1968–69): 101–19.

Biale, David. *Gershom Scholem: Kabbalah and Counter-History.* Cambridge, Mass., 1979.

Bihl, Wolfdieter. *Bibliographie der Dissertationen über Judentum und jüdische Persönlichkeiten, die 1872–1962 an österreichischen Hochschulen (Wien, Graz, Innsbruck) approbiert wurden.* Vienna, 1965.

————. "Die Juden." In Adam Wandruszka and Peter Urbanitsch, eds., *Die Habsburger monarchie, 1848–1918*, vol. 3. Vienna, 1980, pp. 880–948.

Binder, Hartmut. "Franz Kafka und die Wochenscrift 'Selbstwehr.' " *Deutsche Vierteljahrsschrift für Literaturwissenschaft und Geistesgeschichte* 41 (1967): 283–304. (Abridged English trans. in *LBIYB* 12 (1967): 135–48.)

Blau, Bruno. "Statistika židovské Prahy" (Statistics of Jewish Prague). *Židovský Kalendář na rok 5699 (1938–39): 134–45.*

Bock, Eve. "The German-Jewish Writers of Prague: Interpreters of Czech Literature." *LBIYB* 23 (1978): 239–46.

Böhm, Adolf. *Die zionistische Bewegung.* 2 vols. Berlin, 1935–37.

Borman, Stuart [Yehoshua]. "The Prague Student Zionist Movement, 1896–1914." Ph.D. Diss. Univ. of Chicago, 1972.

————. "Ha-zerem ha-pragi be-tenua ha-ẓiyonit ha-'olamit, 1904–1914" (The Prague stream in the world Zionist movement, 1904–1914). In *Yahadut Czechoslovakia.* Jerusalem, 1969, pp. 243–50.

Born, Jürgen. "Vom 'Urteil' zum *Prozess:* Zu Kafkas Leben und Schaffen in den Jahren 1912–1914." *Zeitschrift für deutsche Philologie* 86 (1967): 186–96.

Born, Jürgen, et al., eds. *Kafka-Symposion.* Berlin, 1965.

Bosl, Karl. "Kultur und Gesellschaft in der ersten Tschechoslowakischen Republik." *Bohemia* 21 (1980): 145–54.

Bosl, Karl, ed. *Die 'Burg': Einflussreiche politische Kräfte um Masaryk und Beneš.* 2 vols. Munich, 1973–74.

————. *Handbuch der Geschichte der böhmischen Länder.* 4 vols. Stuttgart, 1968.

Boyer, John W. *Political Radicalism in Late Imperial Vienna: Origins of the Christian Social Movement 1848–1897.* Chicago, 1981.

Brauner, Hugo. "Zur Geschichte der Verbindung." In *Fünfzig Semester "Barissia." Festschrift.* Prague, 1928.

Brilling, Bernhard. "Neures Schrifttum zur Geschichte der Juden in der Tschechoslowakei." *Zeitschrift für Ostforschung* 6 (1957): 572 ff.

Brix, Emil. *Die Umgangssprachen in Altösterreich zwischen Agitation und Assimilation: Die Sprachenstatistik in den zisleithanischen Volkszählungen 1880 bis 1910.* Vienna, Cologne, and Graz, 1982.

Brod, Max. *Franz Kafka: Eine Biographie.* Frankfurt a.M., 1974.

Brosche, Wilfried. "Das Ghetto von Prag." In *Die Juden in den böhmischen Ländern.* Vorträge der Tagung des Collegium Carolinum in Bad Wiesse vom 27. bis 29. November 1981. Munich, 1983, pp. 87–122.

Brügel, J. W. *Czechoslovakia before Munich.* Cambridge, 1973.

Buriánek, František. *Česká literatura XX. století: Od české moderny do roku 1945* (Twentieth-century Czech literature: From Czech modernism to 1945). Prague, 1966.

Butvín, Jozef, and Jan Havránek. *Dějiny Československa od roku 1781 do roku 1918* (History of Czechoslovakia from 1781 to 1918). Prague, 1968.

Cahnmann, W. J. "Village and Small Town Jews—A Typological Study." *LBIYB* 19 (1974): 107–33.

Červinka, František. *Boje a směry českého studentstva na sklonku minulého a na počátku našeho století* (Struggles and currents of the Czech student movement at the end of the last century and the beginning of our century). Prague, 1962.

————. *Český nacionalismus v 19. století* (Czech nationalism in the nineteenth century). Prague, 1964.

————. "The Hilsner Affair." *LBIYB* 13 (1968): 142 57.

————. *Přehled dějin Československa v epoše kapitalismu* (Survey of the history of Czechoslovakia under capitalism). 2 vols. Prague, 1959.

Cohen, Gary B. "Ethnicity and Urban Population Growth: The Decline of the Prague Germans, 1880–1910." In Keith Hitchins, ed., *Studies in East European Social History*, vol. 2. Leiden, 1981, pp. 3–26.

———. "Jews in German Society: Prague, 1860–1914." *Central European History* 10 (1977): 28–54.

———. *The Politics of Ethnic Survival: Germans in Prague, 1861–1914*. Princeton, 1981.

———. "Recent Research on Czech Nation-Building." *Journal of Modern History* 51 (1979): 760–72.

Dagan, Avigdor. "Ha-'itonut ha-yehudit be-Czechoslovakia" (Jewish journalism in Czechoslovakia). In *Yahadut Czechoslovakia*. Jerusalem, 1969, pp. 219–26.

———. "Nos'im yehudi'im be-sifrut ha-tshekhit be-me'ah ha-tesha-'esrei veha-'esrim" (Jewish themes in Czech literature of the nineteenth and twentieth centuries). In *Yahadut Czechoslovakia*. Jerusalem 1969, pp. 227–34.

"David Kuh." In *Pascheles' Illustrierter Israelitischer Volkskalender, 5640*. Prague, 1879–80, pp. 87–90.

Dějiny českožidovského hnutí (History of the Czech-Jewish movement). Svaz Čechů-Židů v Československé republice. Prague, 1932.

Demetz, Peter. "The Czech Themes of R. M. Rilke." *German Life and Letters* 6 (1952–53): 35–49.

Denis, Ernest. *La Bohème dupuis la Montagne-Blanche*. 2 vols. Paris, 1903.

Deutsch, A. "60 Jahre Verein 'Afike Jehuda' in Prag." *Zeitschrift für Geschichte der Juden in der Tschechoslowakei* 1 (1930–31): 174–79.

Dolenský, Antonín. *Kulturní adresář ČSR. Bibliografický slovník žijících kulturních pracovníků a pracovnic* (Cultural directory of the Czechoslovak Republic. Bibliographical dictionary of living artists). Prague, 1936.

Donath, Oskar. "Jüdisches in der neuen tschechischen Literatur." *JGGJČR* 3 (1931): 1–144.

———. "Jüdisch-tschechische Schriftsteller." *B'nai B'rith: Monatsblätter der Grossloge für den ČSR* 7 (1928): 15–20.

———. "Siegfried Kapper." *JGGJČR* 6 (1934): 323–442.

———. *Židé a židovství v české literatuře 19. a 20. stoleti* (Jews and Judaism in nineteenth- and twentieth-century Czech literature). 2 vols. Brno, 1923–30.

Dubnov, Simon. *Nationalism and History: Essays on Old and New Judaism*. New York, 1970.

Eisner, Paul. "Německá literatura na půdě ČSR od roku 1848 do našich dnů" (German literature in the territory of Czechoslovakia from 1848 to our days). In *Československá vlastivěda*, vol 7. Prague, 1933, pp. 325–37.

———. *Tschechische Schriftsteller in Prag*. Prague, 1937.

———. "Yehudim kotvei germanit be-sifrut ha-tshekhoslovakit" (Jewish writers of German in Czechoslovak literature). In *Yahadut Czechoslovakia*. Jerusalem, 1969, pp. 213–18.

Färber, Meir. "Jewish Lodges and Fraternal Orders Prior to World War II." In *The Jews of Czechoslovakia*, vol. 2. Philadelphia, 1971, pp. 229–42.

Fink, Carole. "Franz Kafka and the Dilemma of Ethnic Nationalism." *Canadian Review of Studies in Nationalism* (Spring 1981): 17–36.

Fleischmann, Gustav. "The Religious Congregation, 1918–1938." In *The Jews of Czechoslovakia*, vol 1. Philadelphia, 1968, pp. 267–329.

Fränkel, Josef, ed. *The Jews of Austria: Essays on their Life, History, and Destruction*. 2d ed. London, 1970.

Franková, Anita. "Erfassung der jüdischen Bevölkerung in Böhmen im 18. und in der ersten Hälfte des 19. Jh. und die Bestrebungen, den Anteil der jüdischen Bevölkerung einzuschränken, im Lichte einige historischer Quellen." *Judaica Bohemiae* 6 (1970): 55–69.

Freeze, Karen Johnson. "The Young Progressives: The Czech Student Movement, 1887–1897." Ph.D. Diss., Columbia Univ., 1974.

Friedmann, František. *Einige Zahlen über die tschechoslowakischen Juden*. Prague, 1933.

————. "Židé v Čechách." In Hugo Gold, ed., *Židé a židovské obce v Čechách v minulosti a v přítomnosti*. Brno and Prague, 1934, pp. 729–35.

Fuchs, Albert. *Geistige Strömungen in Österreich 1867–1918*. Vienna, 1949.

Garver, Bruce M. *The Young Czech Party, 1874–1901, and the Emergence of a Multi-Party System*. New Haven, Conn., 1978.

Gelber, Nathan M. "Kavim le-kidmat toldoteha shel ha-ziyyonut be-Vohemia u-Moravia" (On the origins of the Zionist movement in Bohemia and Moravia). In F. Weltsch, ed., *Prag vi-Yerushalayim*. Jerusalem, 1954, pp. 36–51.

Gold, Hugo, comp. *Österreichische Juden in der Welt: Ein Bio-Bibliographisches Lexikon*. Tel-Aviv, 1971.

Gold, Hugo, ed. *Židé a židovské obce v Čechách v minulosti a v přítomnosti* (Jews and Jewish communities of Bohemia in the past and in the present). Brno and Prague, 1934. In German: *Die Juden und Judengemeinden Böhmens in Vergangenheit und Gegenwart*. Brno, 1934.

Goldstücker, Eduard. *The Czech National Revival, the Germans and the Jews*. Los Angeles, 1973.

————. "Die Prager deutsche Literatur als historisches Phänomen." In *Weltfreunde: Konferenz über die Prager deutsche Literatur*. Prague, 1967, pp. 21–45.

————. "Zum Profil der Prager deutschen Dichtung um 1900." *Philologica Pragensia* 5 (1962).

Goldstücker, Eduard, et al., eds. *Franz Kafka aus Prager Sicht*. Prague, 1965.

Goll, Jaroslav. *Rozdělení pražské university Karlo-Ferdinandovy roku 1882* (The division of Prague's Karl Ferdinand University in 1882). Prague, 1908.

Graus, František. "Prologomena zu einer Geschichte der Juden in den böhmischen Ländern." *Judaica Bohemiae* 3 (1967).

Grosman, Ladislav. "Harhek me-erez avot: Hirhurim 'al sifrut le-regel me-le'at elef shanah le-kiyyum hayyim yehudi'im be-Czechoslovakia" (Far from the land of the fathers: Thoughts on literature on the occasion of the one-thousandth anniversary of Jewish life in Czechoslovakia). In *Yahadut Czechoslovakia*. Jerusalem, 1969, pp. 104–24.

Haas, Willy. "Der junge Max Brod." *Tribüne* 3 (1964).

Hamáčková, Vlastimila. "Débuts du mouvement assimilateur tchéco-juif." *Judaica Bohemiae* 14 (1978): 15–23.

Hanák, Peter, ed. *Die nationale Frage in der österreichisch-ungarischen Monarchie, 1900–1918*. Budapest, 1966.

Hassenpflug-Elzholz, Elia. "Toleranzedikt und Emanzipation." In *Die Juden in den böhmischen Ländern*. Vorträge der Tagung des Collegium Carolinum in Bad Wiesse vom 27. bis 29. November 1981. Munich, 1983, pp. 145–59.

Haumann, Heiko. "Das jüdische Prag (1850 bis 1914)." In Bernd Martin and Ernst Schulin, eds., *Die Juden als Minderheit in der Geschichte*. Munich, 1981, pp. 209–30.

Häusler, Wolfgang. "Toleranz, Emanzipation und Antisemitismus: Das österreichische Judentum des bürgerlichen Zeitalters (1782–1918)." In Nikolaus Vielmetti, ed., *Das österreichische Judentum: Voraussetzungen und Geschichte*. Vienna and Munich, 1974.

Havránek, Jan. "Demografický vývoj Prahy v druhé polovině 19. století" (The demographic evolution of Prague during the second half of the nineteenth century). *Pražský Sborník Historický* (1969–70): 70–103.

————. "The Development of Czech Nationalism." *Austrian History Yearbook* 3, pt. 2 (1967): 223–60.

————. "Počátky a kořeny pokrokového hnutí studentského na počátu devadesatých let 19. století" (Origins and sources of the progressive student movement at the beginning of the 1890s"). *Acta Universitatis Carolinae—Historia Universitatis Carolinae Pragensis* 2 (1961): fasc. 1, pp. 5–33.

————. "Social Classes, Nationality Ratios, and Demographic Trends in Prague 1880–1900." *Historica* 13 (1966): 171–208.

———. "Soziale Struktur und politisches Verhalten der grossstädtischen Wählerschaft im Mai 1907—Wien und Prag im Vergleich." In Isabella Ackerl et al., eds., *Politik und Gesellschaft im alten und neuen Österreich,* vol. 1. Munich, 1981, pp. 150–66.

———. "Studenten an der Schwelle des modernen tschechischen politischen Lebens." *Acta Universitatis Carolinae—Philosophica et Historica,* (1969: no. 4), pp. 29–52.

Hayman, Ronald. "In Search of Kafka: Berlin, Prague, Vienna, London, Tel Aviv." *Encounter* 56 (1981): 52–59.

Heilig, B. "Ziele und Wege einer Wirtschaftsgeschichte der Juden in der tschechoslowakischen Republik." *JGGJČR 4 (1932): 7–62.*

Heller, Erich. "The World of Franz Kafka." In his *The Disinherited Mind: Essays in Modern German Literature and Thought.* New York, 1975, pp. 199–231.

Herlitz, G. "Pe'ula ẓiyonit bereshit milḥemet ha-'olam ha-rishona" (Zionist activity at the beginning of the First World War). In F. Weltsch, ed., *Prag vi-Yerushalayim.* Jerusalem, 1954, pp. 153–55.

Heřman, Jan. "The Conflict between Jewish and Non-Jewish Population in Bohemia before the 1541 Banishment." *Judaica Bohemiae* 6 (1970): 39–54.

———. "The Development of Bohemian and Moravian Jewry, 1918–1938." In U. O. Schmelz, P. Glikson, and S. Della Pergola, eds., *Papers in Jewish Demography, 1969.* Jerusalem, 1973, pp. 191–206.

———. "The Evolution of the Jewish Population in Bohemia and Moravia, 1754–1953." In U. O. Schmelz, P. Glikson, and S. Della Pergola, eds., *Papers in Jewish Demography, 1973.* Jerusalem, 1977, pp. 255–65.

———. "The Evolution of the Jewish Population in Prague, 1869–1939." In U. O. Schmelz, P. Glikson, and S. Della Pergola, eds., *Papers in Jewish Demography, 1977.* Jerusalem, 1980, pp. 53–67.

———. "Jewish Community Archives from Bohemia and Moravia." *Judaica Bohemiae* 7 (1971): 3–44.

Heřman, Jan, and Misha Louvish. "Bohemia." In *Encyclopaedia Judaica,* vol. 4. Jerusalem, 1972, cols. 1173–81.

Herrmann, Ignát, Josef Teig, and Zikmund Winter. *Pražské Ghetto* (The Prague ghetto). Prague, 1902.

Hlaváčová, Jiřina. "Franz Kafkas Beziehungen zu Jicchak Löwy." *Judaica Bohemiae* 1 (1965): 75–78.

Hodes, Yaakov. "Ha-yamim ha-rishonim shel ha-keren ha-yesod" (The first days of the Keren ha-Yesod). In F. Weltsch, ed., *Prag vi-Yerushalayim.* Jerusalem, 1954, pp. 156–59.

Hoch, Karel. "Dějiny novinářství od r. 1860" (The history of journalism since 1860). In *Československá vlastivěda,* vol. 3. Prague, 1933, pp. 437–514.

Hostovský, Egon. "The Czech-Jewish Movement." In *The Jews of Czechoslovakia,* vol. 2. Philadelphia, 1971, pp. 148–54.

Hroch, Miroslav. *Social Preconditions of National Revival in Europe.* Cambridge, 1985.

Hugelmann, Karl Gottfried, ed. *Das Nationalitätenrecht des alten Österreich.* Vienna and Leipzig, 1934.

Hus, Václav. *Dějiny Československa* (History of Czechoslovakia). Prague, 1962.

Iggers, Wilma A. "The Flexible National Identities of Bohemian Jewry." *East Central Europe* 7 (1980): 39–48.

———. "Leopold Kompert, Romancier of the Bohemian Ghetto." *Modern Austrian Literature* 6 (1973): 117–38.

———. "Vojtěch Rakous: A Forgotten Czech Storyteller." In Miloslav Rechcigl, ed., *Czechoslovakia Past and Present,* vol. 2. The Hague, 1968, pp. 940–50.

Israel, Jonathan I. *European Jewry in the Age of Mercantilism 1550–1750.* Oxford, 1985.

Jakobovits, Tobiáš. *Dějiny vzníku knihovny isr. náboženské obce v Praze* (The origins of the library of the Jewish religious community of Prague). Prague, 1927.

————. "Das Prager und Böhmische Landesrabbinat Ende des siebzehnten und Anfang des achtzehnten Jahrhunderts." *JGGJČR* 5 (1933): 79–136.

Janowsky, Oscar. *The Jews and Minority Rights, 1898–1919.* New York, 1933.

Jenks, William A. "The Jews in the Habsburg Empire, 1879–1918." *LBIYB* 16 (1971): 155–62.

The Jews of Czechoslovakia: Historical Studies and Surveys. 3 vols. Philadelphia, 1968–84.

Jirát, Vojtěch, A. M. Píša et al., *Otokar Fischer: Kniha o jeho díle* (Otokar Fischer: A volume on his work). Prague, 1933.

Johnston, William M. *The Austrian Mind: An Intellectual and Social History, 1848–1938.* Berkeley and Los Angeles, 1972.

Die Juden in den böhmischen Ländern. Vorträge der Tagung des Collegium Carolinum in Bad Wiesse vom 27. bis 29. November 1981. Munich and Vienna, 1983.

Die Juden in Prag: Bilder aus ihrer tausendjährigen Geschichte. Festgabe der Loge Praga des Ordens B'nai B'rith zum Gedenken ihres 25-jährigen Bestandes. Prague, 1927.

Kamper, Jaroslav. "Siegfried Kapper: Literární siloueta" (Siegfried Kapper: A literary outline). *KČŽ* 24 (1904–5): 59–76.

Kann, Robert A. "Die Habsburgermonarchie und das Problem des übernationalen Staates." In Adam Wandruszka and Peter Urbanitsch, eds., *Die Habsburgermonarchie, 1848–1918,* vol. 2. Vienna, 1975, pp. 1–56.

————. *A History of the Habsburg Empire, 1526–1918.* Berkeley and Los Angeles, 1974.

————. *The Multinational Empire, 1848–1918.* 2 vols. New York, 1950, 1977.

————. *A Study in Austrian Intellectual History.* New York, 1960.

Kann, Robert A., Bela K. Kiraly, and Paula S. Fichtner, eds. *The Habsburg Empire in World War I.* Boulder, Colo., 1977.

Karady, Victor. "Jewish Enrollment Patterns in Classical Secondary Education in Old Regime and Interwar Hungary." In Jonathan Frankel, ed., *Studies in Contemporary Jewry,* vol. 1. Bloomington, Ind., 1984, pp. 225–52.

Karady, Victor, and Istvan Kemeny. "Les Juifs dans la structure des classes en Hongrie," *Actes de la Recherche en Sciences Sociales* 22 (1978): 25–60.

Karníková, Ludmila. *Vývoj obyvatelstva českých zemích 1754–1914* (The evolution of the population of the Czech lands, 1754–1914). Prague, 1965.

Katz, Jacob. *Out of the Ghetto: The Social Background of Jewish Emancipation, 1770–1870.* Cambridge, Mass., 1973.

Kayser, Werner, and Horst Gronemeyer. *Max Brod.* Hamburg, 1972.

Kazbunda, Karel. *České hnutí roku 1848* (The Czech movement of 1848). Prague, 1929.

————. *Stolice dějin na pražské universitě: Od obnovení stolice dějin do rozdělení university (1746–1882)* (The history chair at the University of Prague: From the renewal of the chair until the division of the university). 2 vols. Prague, 1965.

Kestenberg-Gladstein, Ruth. "Aṭhalot Bar Kochba" (The origins of Bar Kochba). In F. Weltsch, ed., *Prag vi-Yerushalayim.* Jerusalem, 1954, pp. 86–110.

————. "Identifikation der Prager Juden vor und während der Assimilation." In *Die Juden in den böhmischen Ländern.* Vorträge der Tagung des Collegium Carolinum in Bad Wiesse vom 27. bis 29. November 1981. Munich, 1983, pp. 161–200.

————. "The Jews between Czechs and Germans in the Historic Lands, 1848–1918." In *The Jews of Czechoslovakia,* vol. 1. Philadelphia, 1968, pp. 21–71.

————. "Mifkad yehudei Beim she-miḥuẓ le-Prag bi-shnat 1724" (Census of 1724 of nonmetropolitan Jews in Bohemia). *Ẓion* 9 (1944): 1–26.

————. "Ha-nedida ha-penimit shel yehudei Beim be-me'ah ha-19 u-mashma'uteha" (The internal migration of Bohemian Jewry in the nineteenth century and its implications). In *Proceedings of the Fourth World Congress of Jewish Studies,* vol. 2. Jerusalem, 1969.

————. *Neuere Geschichte der Juden in den böhmischen Ländern. Erster Teil: Das Zeitalter der Aufklärung, 1780–1830.* Tübingen, 1969.

————. "Ofiyah ha-leumi shel haskalat Prag" (The national character of the Prague Haskalah). *Molad* 23 (1965): 221–33.

————. "Perakim le-toldot ha-yehudim be-arẓot ha-Tshekhot" (Chapters in the history of the Jews in the Czech lands). In *Yahadut Czechoslovakia*. Jerusalem, 1969, pp. 11–82.

————. "Toldot ha-kalkala shel yehudei Beim she-miḥuẓ le-Prag be-me'ah ha-17 veha-18" (Economic history of the Jews of non-metropolitan Bohemia in the seventeenth and eighteenth centuries). *Ẓion* 12 (1947): 49–65, 160–88.

Kieval, Hillel J. "Autonomy and Interdependence: The Historical Legacy of Czech Jewry." In David Altshuler, ed., *The Precious Legacy: Judaic Treasures from the Czechoslovak State Collections*. New York, 1983, pp. 46–109.

————. "Caution's Progress: The Modernization of Jewish Life in Prague, 1780–1830." In Jacob Katz, ed., *Toward Modernity: The European Jewish Model*. New Brunswick, N.J., 1987, pp. 71–105.

————. "Education and National Conflict in Bohemia: Germans, Czechs, and Jews." In Ezra Mendelsohn, ed., *Studies in Contemporary Jewry*, vol 3. Bloomington, Ind., 1987, pp. 49–71.

————. "Gary B. Cohen, *The Politics of Ethnic Survival: Germans in Prague, 1861–1914*." In Jonathan Frankel, ed., *Studies in Contemporary Jewry*, vol. 1. Bloomington, Ind., 1984, pp. 424–27.

————. "In the Image of Hus: Refashioning Czech Judaism in Post-Emancipatory Prague." *Modern Judaism* 5 (1985): 141–57.

————. "Nationalism and Antisemitism: The Czech-Jewish Response." In Jehuda Reinharz, ed., *Living With Antisemitism: Modern Jewish Responses*. Hanover and London, 1987, pp. 210–33.

Kimball, Stanley B. *Czech Nationalism: A Study of the National Theatre Movement, 1845–83*. Urbana, Il., 1964.

Kisch, Guido. *Alexander Kisch, 1848–1917. Eine Skizze seines Lebens und Wirkens Zugleich ein Beitrag zur Geschichte der Juden in Prag*. Halle, 1934.

————. *In Search Freedom: A History of American Jews from Czechoslovakia*. London, 1949.

————. "Jewish Historiography in Bohemia, Moravia, Silesia." In *The Jews of Czechoslovakia*, vol. 1. Philadelphia, 1968, pp. 1–11.

————. "Das jüdische Prag vor zwei Generationen: Zur fünfzigsten Wiederkehr des Todestages von Rabbiner Alexander Kisch." *Judaica Bohemiae* 3 (1967): 87–100.

————. "Linguistic Conditions among Czechoslovak Jewry." *Historia Judaica* 8 (1946): 19–32.

Klausner, Israel. *Mi-Kattowitz ad Basel* (From Kattowice to Basel). 2 vols. Jerusalem, 1965.

————. *Oppozizyah le-Herzl* (The opposition to Herzl). Jerusalem, 1960.

Klemperer, Gutmann. "The Rabbis of Prague: A History of the Rabbinate of Prague." *Historia Judaica* 13 (1951): 55–82.

Klíma, Arnošt. *Revoluce 1848 v českých zemích* (The revolution of 1848 in the Czech lands). Prague, 1974.

Knobloch, Erhard J. *Kleines Handlexikon deutsche Literatur in Böhmen, Mähren, Schlesien von den Anfängen bis heute*. 2d enl. ed. Munich, 1976.

Kohn, Hans, *Martin Buber, sein Werk und seine Zeit: Ein Beitrag zur Geistesgeschichte Mitteleuropas 1880–1930*. 2d enl. ed. Cologne, 1961.

Kohn, Jindřich. "Masaryks Schule der Weisheit und das Judentum." In Ernst Rychnovsky, ed., *Masaryk und das Judentum*. Prague, 1931, pp. 7–33.

Komlos, John, ed. *Economic Development in the Habsburg Monarchy in the Nineteenth Century*. Boulder, Colo., 1983.

Kopáč, Jaroslav. *Dějiny české školy a pedagogiky v letech 1867–1914* (History of Czech education and pedagogy from 1867 to 1914). Brno, 1968.

Kořálka, Jiří. "K některým problémům národní a národnostní otázky v českých zemích v období kapitalismu" (Some national problems and nationality questions in the Czech lands during the age of capitalism). *Československý časopis historický* 3 (1962): 376–91.

————. "Das Nationalitätenproblem in den böhmischen Ländern 1848–1918." *Österreichsche Osthefte* 5 (1963): 1–12.

Kořálka, Jiří, and R. J. Crampton. "Die Tschechen." In Adam Wandruszka and Peter Urbanitsch, eds., *Die Habsburgermonarchie, 1848–1918,* vol. 3. Vienna, 1980, pp. 489–521.

Kosta, Oskar. "Wege Prager deutsche Dichter zum tschechischen Volk." *Aufbau* 14 (1958): 566 ff.

Krejčí, Jan. *Siegfried Kapper.* Prague, 1919.

Křížek, Juríj. *T. G. Masaryk a česká politika. Politické výstoupení českých 'realistů' v letech 1887–1893* (T. G. Masaryk and Czech politics: The emergence of the Czech "Realists," 1887–1893). Prague, 1959.

Krofta, Kamíl. *Národnostní vývoj zemí československých* (The development of nationalities in the Czechoslovak lands). Prague, 1938.

Krolop, Kurt. "Zur Geschichte und Vorgeschichte der Prager deutschen Literatur des 'expressionistishcen Jahrzehnts.' " In *Weltfreunde: Konferenz über die Prager deutsche Literatur.* Prague, 1967, pp. 47–96.

Kultur und Gesellschaft in der Ersten Tschechoslowakischen Republik. Munich and Vienna, 1982.

Kunc, Jaroslav. *Slovník soudobých českých spisovatelů, 1918–1945* (Dictionary of contemporary Czech writers). 2 vols. Prague, 1945–46.

Kurz, Gerhard. "Kafka zwischen Juden, Deutschen und Tschechen." In *Kultur und Gesellschaft in der Ersten Tschechoslowakischen Republik.* Munich and Vienna, 1982, pp. 37–50.

Lador-Lederer, J. J. "Jews in Austrian Law." *East European Quarterly* 12 (1978): 27–41, 129–42.

Lamed, Meir. "Gesetz und Wirklichkeit. Zur Lage der Juden in Böhmen und Mähren in der Zeit des Vormärz." *BLBI* 8, no. 32 (1965): 302–14.

Landes, Zdeněk. "Künder tschechischer Kunst." In F. Weltsch, ed., *Dichter, Denker, Helfer: Max Brod zum 50. Geburtstag.* Moravská-Ostrava, 1934, pp. 89–92.

Laqueur, Walter. *A History of Zionism.* New York, 1972.

Laube, Gustav C. "Die Entstehung der farbentragenden Verbindungen an den Prager Hochschulen." *Deutsche Arbeit* 1 (1902): 519–34.

Lemberg, Eugen. "Der Staat im Denken des tschechischen Volkes." *Jahrbücher für Geschichte Osteuropas* 3 (1938): 357–94.

———. "Volksbegriff und Staatsideologie der Tschechen." In Ernst Birke and Kurt Oberdorfer, eds., *Das böhmische Staatsrecht.* Marburg, 1960.

———. "Zum Selbstverstandnis und Rollenbewusstsein der Tschechen: Nationale Ideologien zwischen Ost und West." *Bohemia* 15 (1974): 51–60.

Lipscher, Ladislav. "Die soziale und politische Stellung der Juden in der Ersten Republik." In *Die Juden in den böhmischen Ländern.* Vorträge der Tagung des Collegium Carolinum in Bad Wiesse vom 27. bis 29. November 1981. Munich, 1983, pp. 269–80.

———. *Verfassung und politische Verwaltung in der Tschechoslowakei, 1918–1939.* Munich, 1979.

Lube, Manfred. "Zur Entstehungsgeschichte von Gustav Meyrinks Roman 'Der Golem.' " *Österreich in Geschichte und Literatur* 15 (1971): 521–41.

Macartney, C. A. *The Habsburg Empire, 1790–1918.* New York, 1969.

McCagg, William O. "Jewish Conversion in Hungary." In Todd M. Endelman, ed., *Christian Missionaries and Jewish Apostates.* New York, 1986.

———. *Jewish Nobles and Geniuses in Modern Hungary.* Boulder, Colo., 1972.

McGrath, William J. "Student Radicalism in Vienna." *Journal of Contemporary History* 2 (1967): 183–95.

März, David. P. "Terumat yehudei Czechoslovakia le-vinyan ha-areẓ" (The contribution of the Jews of Czechoslovakia to the building of Eretz Yisrael). In *Yahadut Czechoslovakia.* Jerusalem, 1969, pp. 251–59.

Magocsi, Paul R. *Galicia: An Historical Survey and Bibliographic Guide.* Toronto and Buffalo, 1982.

Mamatey, Victor S., and Radomír Luža, eds. *A History of the Czechoslovak Republic 1918–1948.* Princeton, 1973.

Markovits, Andrei S., and Frank E. Sysyn, eds. *Nationbuilding and the Politics of Nationalism: Essays on Austrian Galicia.* Cambridge, Mass., 1982.

Marzik, Thomas D. "Masaryk's National Background." In Peter Brock and H. Gordon Skilling, eds., *The Czech Renascence of the Nineteenth Century.* Toronto, 1970, pp. 239–53.

Meissner, Frank. "German Jews of Prague: A Quest for Self-Realization." *Publications of the American Jewish Historical Society* 50 (1960–61): 98–120.

Mendelsohn, Ezra. "From Assimilation to Zionism: The Case of Alfred Nossig." *Slavonic and East European Review* 49 (1971): 521–534.

———. "Jewish Assimilation in Lvov: The Case of Wilhelm Feldman." *Slavic Review* 28 (1969): 577–90. Repr. as "Jewish Assimilation in L'viv: The Case of Wilhelm Feldman," in Andrei S. Markovits and Frank E. Sysyn, eds., *Nationbuilding and the Politics of Nationalism: Essays on Austrian Galicia.* Cambridge, Mass., 1982, pp. 94–110.

———. *The Jews of East Central Europe Between the World Wars.* Bloomington, Ind., 1983.

Mendes-Flohr, Paul R. "Fin-de-Siècle Orientalism, the Ostjuden and the Aesthetics of Jewish Self-Affirmation." In Jonathan Frankel, ed., *Studies in Contemporary Jewry,* vol. 1. Bloomington, Ind., 1984, pp. 96–139.

———. "The Road to *I and Thou:* An Inquiry into Buber's Transition from Mysticism to Dialogue." In Michael A. Fishbone and Paul R. [Mendes-] Flohr, eds., *Texts and Responses: Studies Presented to Nahum N. Glatzer.* Leiden, 1975, pp. 201–25.

———. *Von der Mystik zum Dialog: Martin Bubers geistige Entwicklung bis hin zu "Ich und Du."* Königstein/Ts., 1978.

Mischler, E., and J. Ulbrich. *Österreichisches Staatswörterbuch.* 4 vols. 2d ed. Vienna, 1905–9.

Molisch, Paul. *Politische Geschichte der deutschen Hochschulen in Österreich von 1848 bis 1918.* Vienna, 1939.

Mommsen, Hans. *Die Sozialdemokratie und die Nationalitätenfrage im habsburgischen Vielvölkerstaat.* Vienna, 1963.

Mühlberger, Josef. *Geschichte der deutschen Literatur in Böhmen, 1900–1939.* Munich and Vienna, 1981.

———. *Zwei Völker in Böhmen: Beitrag zu einer nationalen, historischen und geistesgeschichtlichen Strukturanalyse.* Munich, 1973.

Muneles, Otto. *Bibliographical Survey of Jewish Prague.* Prague, 1952.

———. "Die hebräische Literatur auf dem Boden der ČSSR." *Judaica Bohemiae* 5(1969): 108–39.

Novák, Arné. *Czech Literature.* Trans. Peter Kussi. Ed. with Supplement by William E. Harkins. Ann Arbor, Mich., 1976.

Nussbaum Arthur. "The 'Ritual Murder' Trial of Polná." *Historia Judaica* 9 (1947): 57–74.

Otruba, Gustav. "Der Anteil der Juden am Wirtschaftsleben der bömischen Länder seit dem Beginn der Industrialisierung." In *Die Juden in den böhmischen Ländern.* Vorträge der Tagung des Collegium Carolinum in Bad Wiesse vom 27. bis 29. November 1981. Munich, 1983, pp. 209–68.

———. "Statistische Materialien zur Geschichte der Juden in den böhmischen Ländern seit dem Ausgung des 18. Jahrhunderts." In *Die Juden in den böhmischen Ländern.* Vorträge der Tagung des Collegium Carolinum in Bad Wiesse vom 27. bis 29. November 1981. Munich, 1983, pp. 323–51.

———. "Die Universitäten in der Hochschulorganisation der Donau-Monarchie." In M. Rassen, ed., *Student und Hochschule im 19. Jahrhundert.* Göttingen, 1975, pp. 75–155.

Ottův slovník naučný (Otta's encyclopaedia). Prague, 1888–1907. Supplement: *Ottův slovník naučný. Nové doby.* Prague, 1930–33.

Pass, Harriet Z. "Kadimah: Jewish Nationalism in Vienna before Herzl." In *Columbia University Essays on International Affairs,* vol. 5. New York, 1970, pp. 119–36.

Pawel, Ernst, *The Nightmare of Reason: A Life of Franz Kafka*. New York, 1984.

Pazi, Margarita. *Fünf Autoren des Prager Kreises*. Frankfurt a.M., 1978.

Pech, Stanley Z. *The Czech Revolution of 1848*. Chapel Hill, N.C., 1969.

———. "F. L. Rieger: The Road from Liberalism to Conservatism." *Journal of Central European Affairs* 17 (1957): 3–23.

———. "František Ladislav Rieger: Some Critical Observations." *Canadian Slavonic Papers* 2 (1957): 57–67.

———. "The Nationalist Movements of the Austrian Slavs in 1848: A Comparative Sociological Profile." *Histoire Sociale/Social History* 9 (1976): 336–56.

———. "Passive Resistance of the Czechs, 1863–1879." *Slavonic and East European Review* 36 (1958): 434–52.

Peška, Zdeněk. *Kulturní samospráva národnich menšin* (The cultural autonomy of national minorities). Prague, 1938.

Pick, F. K. "30 Jahre Bohemia." In *Festschrift anlässlich des 30.-jährigen Bestandes der Loge "Bohemia" in Prag*. Prague, 1923, pp. 165–91.

Pirchegger, H., J. Mayer, and F. Kaindl. *Geshichte und Kulturleben Österreichs*. 5th ed. 3 vols. Vienna and Stuttgart, 1960.

Plaschka, Richard Georg. "Prag September 1914. Nationale Impulse unter dem Eindruck der ersten Kriegswochen." In Isabella Ackerl et al., eds., *Politik und Gesellschaft im alten und neuen Österreich*, vol. 1. Munich, 1981, pp. 356–64.

Polišenský, Josef V. *Revoluce a kontrarevoluce v Rakousku 1848* (Revolution and counterrevolution in Austria in 1848). Prague, 1975.

Politzer, Heinz. "Prague and the Origins of Rainer Maria Rilke, Franz Kafka, and Franz Werfel." *Modern Language Quarterly* 16 (1955): 49–63.

Polonsky, Antony, and Michael Riff. "Poles, Czechoslovaks and the 'Jewish Question,' 1914–1921: A Comparative Study." In V. R. Berghahn and M. Kitchen, eds., *Germany in the Age of Total War. Essays in Honor of Francis Carsten*. London and Totawa, N.J., 1981, pp. 63–101.

Poppel, Stephen M. *Zionism in Germany, 1897–1933: The Shaping of a Jewish Identity*. Philadelphia, 1977.

Přehled československých dějin (Survey of Czechoslovak history). 3 vols. Ceskoslovenská Akademie Věd. Prague, 1960.

Prinz, Friedrich. "Die böhmischen Länder von 1848 bis 1914." In Karl Bosl, ed., *Handbuch der Geschichte der böhmischen Länder*, vol. 3. Stuttgart, 1968, pp. 3–235.

———. "Das kulturelle Leben (1867–1939): Vom österreichischen Ausgleich bis zum Ende der Ersten Tschechoslowakischen Republik." In Karl Bosl, ed., *Handbuch der Geschichte der böhmischen Länder*, vol 4. Stuttgart, 1969–70, pp. 151–299.

———. "Nation und Gesellschaft in den bömischen Ländern im 19. und 20. Jahrhundert." In F. Prinz, F.-J. Schmale, and F. Seibt, eds., *Geschichte in der Gesellschaft: Festschrift für Karl Bosl zum 65. Geburtstag*. Stuttgart, 1974, pp. 333–49.

———. *Prag und Wien 1848*. Munich, 1968.

Pulzer, Peter G. J. *The Rise of Political Anti-Semitism in Germany and Austria*. New York, 1964.

Purš, Jaroslav. "The Industrial Revolution in the Czech Lands." *Historica* 2 (1960): 183–272.

Rabinowicz, Aharon Moshe. "The Jewish Minority." In *The Jews of Czechoslovakia*, vol. 1. Philadelphia, 1968, pp. 155–265.

———. "The Jewish Party." In *The Jews of Czechoslovakia*, vol. 2. Philadelphia, 1971, pp. 253–346.

Rabinowicz, Oskar K. "Czechoslovak Zionism: Analecta to a History." In *The Jews of Czechoslovakia*, vol. 2. Philadelphia, 1971, pp. 19–136.

Rachmuth, Michael. "Zur Wirtschaftsgeschichte der Prager Juden." *JGGJČR* 5 (1933): 9–78.

Rádl, Emanuel. *Der Kampf zwischen Tschechen und Deutschen*. Liberec [Reichenberg], 1928.

Rechcigl, Miloslav, ed., *Czechoslovakia Past and Present*. 2 vols. The Hague, 1968.

Reinharz, Jehuda. "Achad Haam und der deutsche Zionismus." *BLBI* 61 (1982): 3–27.

———. *Chaim Weizmann: The Making of a Zionist Leader.* New York, 1985.

———. "East European Jews in the Weltanschauung of German Zionists, 1882–1914." In Jonathan Frankel, ed., *Studies in Contemporary Jewry*, vol. 1. Bloomington, Ind., 1984, pp. 55–95.

———. *Fatherland or Promised Land: The Dilemma of the German Jew, 1893–1914.* Ann Arbor, Mich., 1975.

Riff, Michael. "Assimilation and Conversion in Bohemia: Secession from the Jewish Community in Prague, 1868–1917." *LBIYB* 26 (1981): 73–88.

———. "The Assimilation of the Jews of Bohemia and the Rise of Political Anti-Semitism, 1848–1918." Ph.D. Diss., Univ. of London, 1974.

———. "Czech Antisemitism and the Jewish Response before 1914." *Wiener Library Bulletin* 29, nos. 39/40 (1976): 8–20.

———. "Jüdische Schriftsteller und das Dilemma der Assimilation im böhmischen Vormärz." In Walter Grab and Julius Schoeps, eds., *Juden im Vormärz und in der Revolution von 1848.* Stuttgart and Bonn, 1983, pp. 58–82.

Robert Weltsch zum 60. Geburtstag. Ein Gedenkbuch gewidmet von Freunden. Tel-Aviv and Jerusalem, 1951.

Robinson, Jacob. *Das Minoritätenproblem und seine Literatur.* Berlin, 1926.

Roebke-Berens, Ruth. "The Austrian Social Democratic Party, Nationalism, and the Nationality Crisis of the Habsburg Empire, 1897–1914." *Canadian Review of Studies in Nationalism* 8 (1981): 343–63.

Rokycana, Jaroslav. "Freunde in der Not." In Ernst Rychnovsky, ed., *Masaryk und das Judentum.* Prague, 1931, pp. 300–15.

———. "Fünfzig Jahre des 'Českožidovský Kalendář.' " *JGGJČR* 2 (1930): 501–32.

———. "Seznam prací otištěných v *Českožidovském kalendáři* od I. roč. (r. 1881) do roč. XLIX (r. 1929/30)" (List of works published in the *Kalendář česko–židovský* from 1881 to 1929/30). *KČZ* 50 (1930–31): 247–63.

Roubík, František. *Bibliographie časopisectva v Čechách z let 1863–1895* (Bibliography of periodicals in Bohemia from 1863 to 1895). Prague, 1936.

———. *Český rok 1848* (The Czech year, 1848). Prague, 1931, 1948.

———. "Drei Beiträge zur Entwicklung der Judenemanzipation in Böhmen." *JGGJČR* 5 (1933): 313–428.

———. "Von den Anfängen des Vereines für Verbesserung des israelitischen Kultus in Böhmen." *JGGJČR* 9 (1938): 411–47.

———. "Zur Geschichte der Juden in Böhmen im neunzehnten Jahrhundert." *JGGJČR* 7 (1935): 305–85.

———. "Zur Geschichte der Juden in Böhmen in der ersten Hälfte des neunzehnten Jahrhunderts." *JGGJČR* 6 (1934): 285–322.

Rozenblit, Marsha L. "The Assertion of Identity: Jewish Student Nationalism at the University of Vienna before the First World War." *LBIYB* 27 (1982): 171–86.

———. *The Jews of Vienna, 1867–1914: Assimilation and Identity.* Albany, N.Y., 1983.

Rudolph, Richard. *Banking and Industrialization in Austria-Hungary.* Cambridge, 1976.

———. "The Pattern of Austrian Industrial Growth from the Eighteenth to the Early Twentieth Century." *Austrian History Yearbook* 2 (1975): 3–25.

Rychnovsky, Ernst. "Im Kampf gegen den Ritualmord-Aberglauben." In Ernst Rychnovsky, ed., *Masaryk und das Judentum.* Prague, 1931, pp. 166–273.

———. *Masaryk.* 2d ed. Prague, 1930.

———. "Werden und Wachsen der 'Bohemia.' " In *Festschrift, Isr. Humanitätsverein "Bohemia."* Prague, 1913, pp. 7–63.

Rychnovsky, Ernst, ed. *Masaryk und das Judentum.* Prague, 1931. *Thomas G. Masaryk and the Jews.* Trans. Benjamin R. Epstein. New York, 1941.

Sadek, Vladimír. "Dr. Otto Muneles und sein wissenschaftliches Werk." *Judaica Bohemiae* 3 (1967): 73–78.

———. "La Synagogue Réformée de Prague (La 'Vieille École') et les Études juives au cours du 19è siècle." *Judaica Bohemiae* 16 (1980): 119–23.

Šafránek, Jan. *Školy české: Obraz jejích vývoje a osudů* (The Czech schools: Portrait of their development and fortunes), vol. 2, 1848–1913. Prague, 1918.

Sambursky, Miriam. "Zionist und Philosoph: Das Habilitierungsproblem des jungen Hugo Bergmann." *BLBI* 58 (1981): 17–40.

Schaeder, Grete. *The Hebrew Humanism of Martin Buber.* Trans. Noah J. Jacobs. Detroit, 1973.

———. "Martin Buber: Ein biographischer Abriss." In Martin Buber, *Briefwechsel aus sieben Jahrzehnten,* vol. 1. Heidelberg, 1972, pp. 19–141.

Schoeps, Julius H. "Modern Heirs of the Maccabees—the Beginnings of the Vienna Kadimah." *LBIYB* 27 (1982): 155–70.

Scholem Gershom. "Martin Bubers Auffassung des Judentums." *Eranos Jahrbuch* 25 (1967): 9–55.

———. "Martin Buber's Conception of Judaism." In his *On Jews and Judaism in Crisis.* New York, 1976, pp. 126–71.

———. "Martin Buber's Interpretation of Hasidism." In his *The Messianic Idea in Judaism and Other Essays on Jewish Spirituality.* New York, 1971, pp. 227–51.

Schorske, Carl E. "Politics in a New Key: An Austrian Trio." In his *Fin-de-Siècle Vienna: Politics and Culture.* New York, 1980, pp. 116–80.

Schubert, Kurt. "Der Einfluss des Josefinismus auf das Judentum in Österreich." *Kairos* 14 (1972): 81–97.

Shatzky, Jacob. "Jewish Ideologies in Austria During the Revolution of 1848." In Salo W. Baron et al., eds., *Freedom and Reason: Studies in Philosophy and Jewish Culture in Memory of Morris Raphael Cohen.* Glencoe, Ill., 1951, pp. 413–37.

Shohetman, Barukh, and Shlomo Shunami, eds. *Kitvei Shmuel Hugo Bergman: Bibliografiya 1903–1967* (The writings of Hugo Bergmann: A Bibliography, 1903–1967). Jerusalem, 1968.

Silber, Michael K. "Roots of the Schism in Hungarian Jewry: Cultural and Social Change from the Reign of Joseph II until the Eve of the 1848 Revolution" [Hebrew]. Ph.D. Diss., Hebrew University, Jerusalem, 1985.

Simon, Ernst. "Martin Buber und das deutsche Judentum." In Robert Weltsch, ed., *Deutsches Judentum, Aufstieg und Krise.* Stuttgart, 1963.

Simon, Walter. "The Jewish Vote in Austria." *LBIYB* 16 (1971): 97–121.

Singer, Ludvík. "Die Entstehung des Juden-Systemalpatentes von 1797." *JGGJČR* 7 (1935): 199–263.

———. "Zur Geschichte der Juden in Böhmen in den letzten Jahren Josefs II. und unter Leopold II." *JGGJČR* 6 (1934): 193–284.

———. "Zur Geschichte der Toleranzpatente in den Sudetenländern." *JGGJČR* 5 (1933): 231–311.

Skilling, H. Gordon. "The Partition of the University of Prague." *Slavonic and East European Review* 27 (1949): 430–49.

———. "The Politics of the Czech Eighties." In Peter Brock and H. Gordon Skilling, eds., *The Czech Renascence of the Nineteenth Century.* Toronto, 1970, pp. 254–81.

Slovník českých spisovatelů (Dictionary of Czech writers). Prague, 1964.

Sole, Aryeh. "Modern Hebrew Education in Subcarpathian Ruthenia." In *The Jews of Czechoslovakia,* vol. 2. Philadelphia, 1971, pp. 401–39.

———. "Subcarpathian Ruthenia, 1918–1938." In *The Jews of Czechoslovakia,* vol. 1. Philadelphia, 1968, pp. 125–54.

Šolle, Z. "Die Sozialdemokratie in der Habsburger Monarchie und die tschechische Frage." *Archiv für Sozialgesschichte* 6/7 (1966–67): 315–90.

Srb, Adolf. *Politické dějiny národa českého od roku 1861* (Political history of the Czech nation since 1861). 2 vols. Prague, 1899–1901.

Srb, Vladimír, and Milan Kučera. "Vývoj obyvatelstva českých zemí v 19. století" (Population development in the Czech lands in the nineteenth century). *Statistika a demografie* 1 (1959): 109–52.

Stein, Adolf. *Die Geschichte der Juden in Böhmen. Nach amtlichen gedruckten und ungedruckten Quellen.* Brno, 1904.

Stein-Taborský, Vojta. *Žid v českém dramatě* (The Jew in Czech drama). Prague, 1910.

Steinherz, Samuel. "Gerush ha-yehudim mi-Beim bi-shnat 1541" (The expulsion of the Jews from Bohemia in 1541). *Zion* 15 (1950): 70–92.

Stillschweig, Kurt. *Die Juden Osteuropas in den Minderheitenverträgen.* Berlin 1936.

Stölzl, Christoph. *Die Ära Bach in Böhmen: Sozialgeschichtliche Studien zum Neoabsolutismus, 1849–1859.* Munich and Vienna, 1971.

———. "Die 'Burg' und die Juden: T. G. Masaryk und sein Kreis im Spannungsfeld der jüdischen Frage: Assimilation, Antisemitismus und Zionismus." In Karl Bosl, ed., *Die 'Burg': Einflussreiche politische Kräfte um Masaryk und Beneš,* vol 2. Munich, 1974, pp. 79–110.

———. *Kafkas böses Böhmen: Zur Sozialgeschichte eines Prager Juden.* Munich, 1975.

———. "Zur Geschichte der böhmischen Juden in der Epoche des modernen Nationalismus." Pt. I, *Bohemia* 14 (1973): 179–221; Pt. II, *Bohemia* 15 (1974): 129–57.

Stručné dějiny University Karlovy (A brief history of Charles University). Prague, 1964.

Sturm, Heribert, ed. *Biographisches Lexikon zur Geschichte der böhmischen Länder.* Munich, 1974–.

———. *Ortslexikon der böhmischen Länder, 1910–1965.* Munich and Vienna, 1977–83.

Sutter, Berthold. *Die Badenischen Sprachverordnungen von 1897: Ihre Genesis und ihre Auswirkungen vornehmlich auf die innerösterreichischen Alpenländer.* 2 vols. Graz and Cologne, 1960–65.

Szporluk, Roman. *The Political Thought of Thomas G. Masaryk.* Boulder, Colo., 1981.

Thieberger, Friedrich. "Masaryks Credo und die jüdische Religion." In Ernst Rychnovsky, ed., *Masaryk und das Judentum.* Prague, 1931, pp. 34–66.

Thomson, S. Harrison. "The Czechs as Integrating and Disintegrating Factors in the Habsburg Empire." *Austrian History Yearbook* 3 (1967): 203–22.

Tramer, Hans. "Prague—City of Three Peoples." *LBIYB* 9 (1964): 305–39.

Tramer, Hans, and Kurt Loewenstein, eds. *Robert Weltsch zum 70. Geburtstag von seinen Freunden.* Tel-Aviv, 1961.

Urzidil, Johannes. *There Goes Kafka* (trans. of *Da geht Kafka*) Detroit, 1968.

Utitz, Emil. *Egon Erwin Kisch: Der klassische Journalist.* Berlin, 1956.

Vago, Bela, and George L. Mosse, eds. *Jews and Non-Jews in Eastern Europe 1918–1945.* New York and Jerusalem, 1974.

Vielmetti, Nikolaus, ed. *Das österreichische Judentum: Voraussetzungen und Geschichte.* Vienna and Munich, 1974.

Vital, David. *The Origins of Zionism.* Oxford, 1975.

Vojtěch, Tomáš. *Mladočeší a boj o politickou moc v Čechách* (The young Czechs and the struggle for political power in Bohemia). Prague, 1980.

Volávková, Hana. *Schicksal des jüdischen Museums in Prag.* Prague, 1966.

Všný, P. *Neo-Slavism and the Czechs 1898–1914.* New York, 1976.

Vyskočil, Josef. "Die tschechisch-jüdische Bewegung." *Judaica Bohemiae* 3 (1967): 36–55.

Waber, Leopold. "Die zahlenmässige Entwicklung der Völker Österreichs 1846–1910." *Statistische Monatschrift* n.s. 20 (Brno, 1915): 593–721.

Wagenbach, Klaus. *Franz Kafka: Eine Biographie seiner Jugend, 1883–1912.* Bern, 1958.

Wallace, William V. *Czechoslovakia.* Boulder, Colo., 1976.

Wandruszka, Adam, and Peter Urbanitsch, eds. *Die Habsburgermonarchie, 1848–1918.* 3 vols. Vienna, 1975–80.

Wechsberg, Joseph. *Prague the Mystical City.* New York, 1971.

Weltsch, Felix. "Demut deyoknam shel yehudei Beimen u-Meiren" (Profile of Bohemian and Moravian Jewry). In F. Weltsch, ed., *Prag vi-Yerushalayim.* Jerusalem, 1954, pp. 23–35. Repr. in *Yahadut Czechoslovakia* (Jerusalem, 1969), pp. 207–12.

―――. "Franz Kafkas Geschichtsbewusstsein." In Robert Weltsch, ed., *Deutsches Judentum: Aufsteig und Krise*. Stuttgart, 1963, pp. 271–88.

―――. "Masaryk und der Zionismus." In Ersnt Rychnovsky, ed., *Masaryk und das Judentum*. Prague, 1931, pp. 67–116.

―――. "Realism and Romanticism: Observations on the Jewish Intelligentsia of Bohemia and Moravia." In *The Jews of Czechoslovakia*, vol. 2. Philadelphia, 1971, pp. 440–54.

―――. *Religion und Humor im Leben und Werk Franz Kafkas*. Berlin, 1957.

Weltsch, Felix, ed. *Dichter, Denker, Helfer: Max Brod zum 50. Geburtstag*. Moravská-Ostrava, 1934.

―――, ed. *Prag vi-Yerushalayim: Sefer le-zekher Leo Herrmann* (Prague and Jerusalem: Memorial volume for Leo Herrmann). Jerusalem, 1954.

Weltsch, Robert. "Max Brod and His Age." *The Leo Baeck Memorial Lecture*, no. 13. New York, 1970.

Whiteside, Andrew G. *Austrian National Socialism before 1918*. The Hague, 1962.

Wininger, Salomon. *Grosse jüdische National-Biographie*. 7 vols. Czernowitz, 1925–36.

Winter, Eduard. "Early Liberalism in the Habsburg Monarchy: Religious and National Thought, particularly of the Austrian Slavs, 1792–1868." *East Central Europe/L'Europe du Centre-Est* 1 (1974): 1–11.

―――. *Frühliberalismus in der Donaumonarchie: Nationales und religiöses Denken von 1790 bis 1868*. Berlin, 1968.

Winters, Stanley B. "Kramář, Kaizl, and the Hegemony of the Young Czech Party, 1891–1901." In Peter Brock and H. Gordon Skilling, eds., *The Czech Renascence of the Nineteenth Century*. Toronto, 1970, pp. 282–314.

―――. "The Young Czech Party (1874–1914): An Appraisal." *Slavic Review* 28 (1969): 426–44.

Winters, Stanley B., and Joseph Held, eds. *Intellectual and Social Developments in the Habsburg Empire from Maria Theresa to the First World War*. Essays dedicated to Robert A. Kann. New York, 1976.

Wiskemann, Elizabeth. *Czechs and Germans: A Study of the Struggle in the Historic Provinces of Bohemia and Moravia*. 2d ed. London and New York, 1967.

Wistrich, Robert. "Georg von Schönerer and the Genesis of Modern Austrian Antisemitism." *Wiener Library Bulletin* 29 (1976): 20–29.

―――. "Socialism and Antisemitism in Austria before 1914." *Jewish Social Studies* 37 (1975): 323–32.

―――. *Socialism and the Jews: The Dilemmas of Assimilation in Germany and Austria-Hungary*. Rutherford, N.J., 1982.

Wurzbach, C. von, ed. *Biographisches Lexikon des Kaiserthums Österreich*. 60 vols. Vienna, 1856–91.

Yahadut Czechoslovakia (Czechoslovak Jewry). Special issue of *Gesher* 15 (Jerusalem, 1969).

Yahil, Chaim. " 'Al ha-ẓiyonut be-Czechoslovakia" (On Zionism in Czechoslovakia). In *Yahadut Czechoslovakia*. Jerusalem, 1969, pp. 125–40.

Žáček, V. "Eine Studie zur Entwicklung der jüdischen Personennamen in neuerer Zeit." *JGGJČR* 7 (1935): 310–34.

―――. "Zwei Beiträge zur Geschichte des Frankismus in den böhmischen Ländern." *JGGJČR* 9 (1938): 343–410.

Zechlin, E. *Die deutsche Politik und die Juden im Ersten Weltkrieg*. Göttingen, 1969.

Zeman, Z. A. B. *The Break-up of the Habsburg Empire, 1914–1918*. London, 1961.

Zöllner, Erich. *Geschichte Österreichs*. Vienna, 1961.

Zwergbaum, Aharon. "Yahadut Czechoslovakia bein shtei milḥamot ha-'olam" (The Jews of Czechoslovakia between the two world wars). In *Yahadut Czechoslovakia*. Jerusalem, 1969, pp. 182–91.

Zwitter, Fran. *Les problèmes nationaux dans la monarchie des Habsbourg*. Belgrade, 1960.

Index